D0984065

SAUDI ARABIA IN THE BALANCE

PAUL AARTS
GERD NONNEMAN
editors

Saudi Arabia in the Balance

Political Economy, Society, Foreign Affairs

NEW YORK UNIVERSITY PRESS
Washington Square, New York

First published in the USA by
New York University Press
Washington Square, New York
www.nyupress.org

Printed in India

A Cataloging-in-Publication Data record for this book
is available from the Library of Congress.

ISBN-10: 0-8147-0717-3 cloth
ISBN-13: 978-0-8147-0717-3 cloth

CONTENTS

THE EDITORS

Paul Aarts is Senior Lecturer in International Relations at the Department of Political Science, University of Amsterdam. He has published widely on Middle East politics and economics, including seven edited volumes in Dutch and numerous contributions to scholarly journals and books. He has undertaken consultancy work on the Middle East for the Dutch Ministry of Foreign Affairs, the European Commission and other institutions. For many years he served as a member of the board of the Dutch Association for Middle Eastern and Islamic Studies (MOI) and was co-editor of its journal *Shaqiyyât*. Recently he became co-editor of *ZemZem*, a journal on the Middle East, North Africa and Islam.

Among his publications are: 'Lions of Tawhid in the Polder', *Middle East Report*, Summer 2005, No. 235 (with Fadi Hirzalla); 'The Internal and the External: The House of Saud's Resilience Explained' (European University Institute, EUI Working Papers No. 2004/33). 'Shades of Opinion: The Oil-Exporting Countries and International Climate Politics', in *The Review of International Affairs* (Winter 2003/2004) (with Dennis Janssen); *The Oil Weapon: a One-Shot Edition?* (Abu Dhabi: ECSSR, 1999); 'The Middle East: Eternally out of Step with History?', in K. Thomas & M. Tétreault (eds.), *Racing to Regionalize. Democracy, Capitalism, and Regional Political Economy* (Lynne Rienner, 1999); 'The Middle East: A Region without Regionalism or the End of Exceptionalism?', *Third World Quarterly*, Vol. 20, No. 5; 'The New Oil Order: Built on Sand?' *Arab Studies Quarterly*, Vol. 16, No. 2; 'Les limites du "tribalisme politique". Le Koweit d'aprèsguerre et le processus de démocratisation', *Monde arabe, Maghreb-Machrek*, No. 142, October–December 1993.

Gerd Nonneman is Reader in International Relations and Middle East Politics at Lancaster University, having previously taught Middle East politics and political economy at Manchester and Exeter

Universities, and as Visiting Professor at the International University of Japan. He was a member of the UK's 2001 national Research Assessment Exercise (RAE) panel on Middle Eastern Studies, and served as Executive Director of the British Society for Middle Eastern Studies (BRISMES), 1998–2002. He has done extensive Middle East consultancy work for a range of government and non-government bodies, including the European Commission. In 2004 he worked for the Omani Ministry of Foreign Affairs, developing the blueprint and curriculum for a Diplomatic College. In 2005 he was the Sir William Luce Fellow at Durham University's School of Government & International Affairs.

Among his publications are: *Analyzing Middle Eastern Foreign Policies, and the relationship with Europe* (Routledge, Summer 2005); 'The Gulf States and the Iran-Iraq War: Pattern Shifts and Continuities', in L. Potter and G. Sick (eds.), *Iran, Iraq and the Legacies of War* (New York: Palgrave, 2004); *Terrorism, Gulf Security and Palestine: Issues for an EU-GCC Dialogue* (Florence: European University Institute, 2002); *Governance, Human Rights & the Case for Political Adaptation in the Gulf* (European University Institute, 2001); 'Rentiers and Autocrats, Monarchs and Democrats, State and Society,' *International Affairs,* Vol. 77, No. 1 (January 2001); 'Saudi-European Relations, 1902–2001,' *International Affairs,* Vol. 77, no. 3 (July 2001); *Muslim Communities in the New Europe*, (Reading: Ithaca Press, 1996); *Political and Economic Liberalization* (Boulder, CO: Lynne Rienner, 1996); and *The Middle East and Europe: The Search for Stability and Integration* (London: Federal Trust, 1993).

THE CONTRIBUTORS

Madawi Al-Rasheed is Professor of Anthropology of Religion at King's College London. Her research focuses mainly on Saudi Arabia's history, society and politics. She has written several books and articles in academic journals on nineteenth-century history in the Arabian Peninsula and contemporary issues related to the formation of the modern state, social and economic development, and the engagement with modernity. She has also conducted research on Arab migration with special focus on the Iraqi community in London; and on Gulf transnationalism and heritage in the context of globalisation and the region's incorporation in global flows. Her books include: *Politics in an Arabian Oasis* (I.B. Tauris 1991), *Iraqi Assyrian Christians in London* (The Edwin Mellen Press 1998), *A History of Saudi Arabia* (Cambridge University Press 2002), *Counter Narratives: History, Contemporary Society and Politics in Saudi Arabia and Yemen* (Palgrave 2004), and *Transnational Connections and the Arab Gulf* (Routledge 2005).

Rachel Bronson is a Senior Fellow and Director of Middle East Studies at the Council on Foreign Relations (CFR), where she is currently finishing her forthcoming book *Thicker than Oil: The United States and Saudi Arabia, a History*, under contract with Oxford University Press. She co-directed the January 2003 report 'Guiding Principles for US Post-Conflict Policy in Iraq,' co-sponsored by CFR and the James A. Baker III Institute for Public Policy at Rice University. She has testified before Congress's Joint Economic Committee on the topic of Iraq's reconstruction, and the President's 9/11 Commission on whether the US is involved in a 'Clash of Civilizations.' Dr Bronson is the recipient of the Carnegie Corporation's 2003 Carnegie Scholars award. She has served as a senior fellow at the Center for Strategic and Inernational Studies (CSIS) and as a fellow at Harvard's Belfer Center for Science and International

Affairs. Her writings have appeared in publications such as *Foreign Affairs, Survival, The National Interest, The New York Times* and *The International Herald Tribune.*

Iris Glosemeyer specialises in the analysis of political developments in the states of the Arabian peninsula, in particular Yemen and Saudi Arabia where she has undertaken frequent fieldwork since 1992. In 2001 her doctoral dissertation on elections, parties and parliaments in the Republic of Yemen was published (in German) by the German Orient Institute in Hamburg. Between 2001 and 2005 she was research associate at the German Institute for International Security Studies (Stiftung Wissenschaft und Politik, SWP). Recent publications include 'Saudi Arabia: Dynamism Uncovered' (in Volker Perthes (ed.), *Arab Elites. Negotiating the Politics of Change*) and 'Jemen: Staatsbildung mit Hindernissen' (in Ulrich Schneckener (ed.), *States at Risk, Fragile Staaten als Sicherheitsproblem*). She has acted as consultant for a number of German and international institutions and organizations and took up a teaching position at the Otto-Suhr Institute of the Free University of Berlin in 2005.

Steffen Hertog has worked as a technical adviser in a Saudi government organisation for the past two years, and is completing his doctoral thesis on the politics of Saudi economic reform, at St Antony's College, Oxford. He has an MA in politics, economics and public law from the University of Bonn and an MSc in Theory and Method in the Study of Politics from SOAS (London). He is publishing a paper on 'Corporatism in Saudi Arabia' in *Chroniques Yemenites* (2005), and has a chapter appearing on 'Building the Body Politic: Emerging Corporatism in Saudi Arabia', in the forthcoming book by Giacomo Luciani & Abdulhadi Khalaf (eds), *Constitutional Reform in the GCC States* (2006).

Joseph Kostiner is Professor at the Dept. of Middle-Eastern and African History at Tel Aviv University, and a senior research fellow at the Moshe Dayan Center for Middle Eastern and African Studies there. He was head of Tel Aviv University's Graduate School of History (2000–2004) and held visiting professorships and fellowships at Harvard, Georgetown, Johns Hopkins (SAIS), London,

Munich and Hagen Universities. Among his recent books are: *Tribes and State Formation in the Middle East* (ed. with P.S. Khoury, University of California Press, 1991); *The Making of Saudi Arabia, from Chieftaincy to Monarchical State, 1916–1936* (Oxford University Press, 1993); and *Middle East Monarchies. the Challenge of Modernity* (ed., Lynne Rienner, 2000).

Stéphane Lacroix is completing a PhD on intellectual and political movements in Saudi Arabia, for which he has done extensive fieldwork in the kingdom. He teaches at the Institute of Political Studies (Sciences-Po) in Paris. His most recent publication is an article entitled 'Between Islamists and Liberals: Saudi Arabia's New Islamo-Liberal Reformists' in the *Middle East Journal* (Summer 2004).

Giacomo Luciani is Professor of Political Economy and co-director of the Mediterranean Programme of the Robert Schuman Centre for Advanced Studies at the European University Institute (since 2000), and Professorial Lecturer in Middle Eastern Studies at the Bologna Center of SAIS (Johns Hopkins University). His career has been marked by repeated 'trespassing' between academia, industry and government, and he has consulted for various international organisations and Gulf governments. His research interests include the political economy of the Middle East and North Africa and the geopolitics of energy. His main line of research has been on the rentier state and democratisation. Publications include *The Rentier State* (co-editor and co-author); *The Politics of Arab Integration* (co-editor; *The Arab State* (editor and co-author); and chapters in such books as *Democracy without Democrats?* (ed. G. Salamé); *Political Liberalization and Democratization in the Arab World* (ed. R. Brynen, B. Khorany and P. Noble); and *Modernization, Democracy and Islam* (ed. S. Hunter and H. Malik). Most recently, he has worked on EU-GCC relations, contributing to the Bertelsmann Foundation's report on 'The EU and the GCC. A New Partnership' (2005), co-authoring (with Tobias Schumacher) *Relations Between the European Union and the Gulf Cooperation Council* (2004), and co-editing and co-authoring *Regime Change in Iraq* (2004). In 2005 he co-directed (with Abdelhadi Khalaf) a workshop on "Constitutional Reform and Political Participation in the Gulf", out of which a book will be published in English and Arabic.

Monica Malik obtained her PhD from the University of Durham with a thesis on private sector development in Saudi Arabia. Since 2001, she has been Senior Economist for the Middle East and North Africa (MENA) at Country Risk Services (CRS), Dun & Bradstreet. The MENA team produces analysis on key economic, commercial and political developments and risk in the region. Dr Malik is responsible for ratings, reports and forecasts for the MENA region, and covers nine of the MENA states including the main oil and gas exporters (determining CRS's oil price forecast), as well as key emerging market countries such as Turkey, Israel and Egypt.

Roel Meijer is a historian, teaching at Radboud University in Nijmegen. His publications include *The Quest for Modernity. Secular Liberal and Left-Wing Political Thought in Egypt, 1945–1958* (RoutledgeCurzon, 2002). He currently has a grant from the International Institute for the Study of Islam in the Modern World (ISIM) in Leiden, to conduct research on the debate on violence within the Islamist movement in Egypt, Saudi Arabia, Iraq and Syria.

Tim Niblock is Director of the Institute of Arab and Islamic Studies at the University of Exeter, and Professor of Arab Gulf Studies. He began his academic career at the University of Khartoum in Sudan (1969–77), moving to Exeter in 1978 as Research Fellow in Arab Gulf Studies. In that position he helped to establish the Centre for Arab Gulf Studies, of which he became deputy director. Transferring to the Department of Politics in 1982, he became Director of the newly-established Middle East Politics Programme there. In 1993 he was appointed to the Chair in Middle Eastern Politics at the University of Durham, becoming Director of the Centre for Middle Eastern and Islamic Studies. He returned to Exeter in 1999 to take up his current position. Among his books related to the Gulf region are: *'Pariah States' and Sanctions in the Middle East: Iraq, Libya and Sudan* (Lynne Rienner, 2001), *Economic and Political Liberalisation in the Middle East* (ed., with Emma Murphy, British Academic Press, 1993), *Iraq: the Contemporary State* (ed., Croom Helm, 1982), *State, Society and Economy in Saudi Arabia* (ed., Croom Helm, 1981), and *Social and Economic Development in the Arab Gulf* (ed., Croom Helm, 1980).

Michaela Prokop works at the Asian Development Bank, where she is currently the country economist for Afghanistan. She obtained her PhD from the Institute for Middle Eastern and Islamic Studies at the University of Durham, with a thesis on the political economy implications of the fiscal crisis in the 1980s and 1990s in Saudi Arabia. She has worked as a researcher in the Middle East Programme at the International Secretariat of Amnesty International and as Gulf analyst for the International Crisis Group. Her publications include a general book on Saudi Arabia (*Saudi-Arabien*, Hugendubel Verlag, Munich, 2005) and several articles on the Saudi education system (including 'The Politics of Education in Saudi Arabia,' *International Affairs*, Vol. 79, no.1, January 2003; and 'Education in Saudi Arabia—the Challenge of Reforming the System and Adapting the Message,' *Orient*, December 2002).

Abdulaziz O. Sager is Chairman of the Gulf Research Center (GRC), which he established in Dubai in July 2000. He is also Chairman of the Sager Group Holding founded in 1980 in Saudi Arabia which is active in the fields of information technology, aviation services and investments. In November 2003, he was appointed as a member of the Mecca Province Council. He has a special research interest in Gulf political and strategic issues and is a regular contributor to many Gulf newspapers including *Khaleej*, *Al Sharq Al Awsat* and *Arab News*. He is a frequent participant in regional and international forums and conferences on Gulf issues, and through GRC has organised joint events with NATO, IISS, Carnegie, the Bertelsmann Foundation and many others. He holds an M.A. degree in International Relations from the University of Kent at Canterbury, and is currently working on a research program entitled 'Gulf Security: Political Interactions and Perceptions (1971–2003)—A Comparative Study of the GCC States.'

Guido Steinberg is an Islamicist and Middle East historian. He currently works as an advisor on international terrorism in the German Federal Chancellery and teaches at the Otto Suhr Institute for Political Science, Free University of Berlin. His publications on Saudi Arabian history and politics, the Wahhabiya, Islamism and terrorism include: *Der nahe und der ferne Feind. Die Netzwerke des islam-*

istischen Terrorismus (Munich, 2005); *Religion und Staat in Saudi-Arabien. Die wahhabitischen Gelehrten (1902–1953)* (Würzburg, 2002); 'The Shiites in the Eastern Province of Saudi Arabia (al-Ahsa') 1913–1953,' in Werner Ende & Rainer Brunner (eds), *The Twelver Shia in Modern Times. Religious Culture & Political History* (Leiden, 2001), pp. 236–54.

TRANSLITERATION

There is a huge variety of ways in which Arabic names and terms can be, and have been, rendered—ranging from a number of scholarly philological conventions to a range of Anglicised forms. In this volume we wanted to combine accuracy with accessibility, while remaining consistent. Rendition of these terms and names has been made uniform, reflecting as closely as possible the Arabic pronunciation while remaining accessible to non-Arabists. The exceptions are: (1) citations and bibliographical references (e.g. authors' names in published pieces), where the form used in the source is maintained; and (2) transliterations of Arabic-language phrases or references in the footnotes, *as* Arabic, where linguistic accuracy is observed, albeit without indicating long vowels—hence *Al-Qa'ida* rather than *Al-Qā'ida*, and *Sa'ud* rather than *Sa'ūd*—and without other diacritical marks indicating the different *h*, *d*, *s*, or *z* sounds.

Thus, for Arabic bibliographical references or rendition of Arabic phrases (*as* Arabic), we have used the diacritical marks (' for *'ayn*, ' for *'alif*) throughout, while in normal (English) text we have dropped such marks if they occur at the beginning of the word or name (thus, *Umar* rather than *'Umar*, and *al-Awda* rather than *al-'Awda*).

Where, in the main text, the intention is to show the original Arabic in transliteration, this is indicated also by placing the word or phrase in italics. Otherwise, the rendition is simplified by using well-established English-language versions where these exist, or at least by dropping the 'ayn or 'alif signs at the beginning of the word or name in question.

We distinguish between the article (al-), which is written in lower case and joined to the word it determines; and the word *Al* for 'family' (pronounced with a long 'aa'), as in 'the Sa'ud family' or *Al Sa'ud*. The one exception is in our spelling of *Al-Qa'ida* where the article is capitalised as that has become part of the commonly used name of the organisation in English.

Names are spelled following the same principle: thus, *Abd al-Aziz* (rather than *Abdulaziz* or *'Abd al-'Aziz*), and *Muhammad ibn Abd al-Wahhab* (rather than *Mohammed ibn Abdelwahhab*), reflecting the Arabic structure (the one exception comes in our spelling of the name Abdullah—as for the former Saudi Crown Prince, now King—as it was felt the latter version is the generally recognised one, while the form *Abd Allah* would throw many readers).

The word signifying 'son of' in Arabic names, is given as *ibn* (if in middle of name) or *Ibn* (if at the beginning) rather than *bin*, except for the now familiar *Usama bin Ladin*. Hence *Ibn Sa'ud*, but *Abd al-Aziz ibn Sa'ud*.

INTRODUCTION

Paul Aarts
Gerd Nonneman

In the aftermath of 'September 11' much comment was directed at the alleged clash between Islam and the West. As a long-time ally of the United States and a figurehead of Islamic politics, Saudi Arabia was caught in the middle. Because fifteen of the nineteen hijackers were of Saudi origin, and with accusations about Saudi co-responsibility for the direction which radicalised Islam had taken, the royal family was placed in the awkward situation of being called to account for the behaviour of a few Saudi citizens who were in fact simultaneously taking aim at the Al Sa'ud themselves. Indeed, after 9/11 Saudi Arabia became seen in some quarters not so much as a *victim* but as a *cause* of the problem. This was reflected also in the campaign rhetoric of the Democratic candidate in the 2004 US presidential election, John Kerry. At the same time pre-existing issues of concern, relating to Saudi Arabia's economy, its 'social contract', and its place in the region and the world, were highlighted further.

Combining the roles of the world's 'swing' oil producer, the guardian of the holiest places of Islam, and a crucial ally of the West in the Gulf, Saudi Arabia has acquired a high international profile which inevitably involves tensions. The spate of terrorist attacks within the Kingdom in 2003/4 brought acute uncertainty to the world oil market.

Yet to most outside observers the country's internal affairs remain opaque. Moreover, the tensions between the kingdom's roles regionally and globally in a changing international system intertwine with the dilemmas being faced at the domestic level. There is a need, therefore, to address these interlocking issues systematically by drawing on the insights of a variety of Saudi as well as specialist outside observers. This book attempts to do just that. The exercise is particularly timely when Saudis themselves, both among the leadership and elsewhere, are increasingly debating and acting on these questions.

The book is the outcome of an international project centred around a three-day workshop organised by the editors at the International Institute for the Study of Islam in the Modern World (ISIM) in Leiden in February 2004, and sponsored by ISIM, the Dutch Foreign Ministry, the European University Institute and Lancaster University in England. The workshop brought together a wide range of expertise and views on Saudi Arabia: from the United States, Europe and the Middle East, including the Kingdom itself. All contributors worked throughout according to clear specifications as part of a tightly organised project, and benefited from wide-ranging discussion with a highly specialist group of participants from academic, business and government backgrounds. While this formed the basis for the book's design, the final selection of chapters was fine-tuned to achieve the greatest possible coverage and balance: not all the workshop papers became chapters, and additional contributions were invited from Tim Niblock, Monica Malik and Roel Meijer.

The aim was to elicit a conversation and 'cross-fertilisation' between empirically and theoretically innovative work, bringing together a variety of perspectives to examine contemporary trends in Saudi Arabia's politics, society, economy and international relations, exploring their roots as well as possible future development. The focus is at once domestic and international: regional and global developments are seen through the Saudi lens, while Saudi developments are examined in the light of '9/11,' the Iraq crisis, and changing global politics.

This work is emphatically *not* an exercise in either accusation or justification; rather, the multiplicity of perspectives and areas of expertise brought to bear on these questions should allow a balanced understanding to emerge of Saudi Arabia's dynamics, challenges and responses. It is hoped that the book does so in a way that speaks both to specialist students of the country and the region, and to policy-makers and the wider public.

Yet the book's investigation of the Saudi case also illuminates a number of wider questions in political science, international relations, international political economy, political anthropology, and 'Third World' politics. Indeed it is through an awareness of the wider disciplinary questions that the case of Saudi Arabia itself can be examined most fruitfully: too often, area- and country-specialist work tends to eschew wider conceptual issues, while theoretical/conceptual work often suffers from the opposite affliction. The wider questions include the following:

- Where are the limits of the 'rentier state' model of political and economic organisation?
- What is the capacity of rentier economies to transform? Can they evolve into sustainable economies producing added value?
- How viable is 'monarchy' in the twenty-first century, and in the Middle East in particular?
- To what extent and under what conditions can autocratic systems transform themselves?
- What are the chances for democratisation in the Middle East?
- How, if at all, can 'civil society' develop and impact on social and political organisation in an autocratic system?
- What is the relationship between 'Islam'—in its various forms—and forms of political organisation?
- How do different Muslim societies view/respond to terror tactics?
- How do less-developed states of the 'periphery' relate to the 'core' in the international system?
- In explaining the foreign policies of developing states, what is the relative importance of the international system and region-specific dynamics? How much room for manoeuvre do these states have?

Consequently, questions directed specifically to the Saudi case include:

- How viable is the House of Sa'ud?
- Can the House of Sa'ud transform itself and if so, how?
- What is the nature of opposition, and what are its prospects?
- How should the nature of violent extremism and terrorism in Saudi Arabia, and its prospects, be assessed?
- What are the prospects for political reform?
- What are the key trends in the Saudi economy? To what extent has it been able, and is now likely, to transcend the limitations of

the rent-economy? Can a viable private sector producing added value emerge? Indeed, has it done so already?
- How are economic and political trends linked, and with what effect?
- How is the relationship between religion and politics evolving?
- What is the nature of 'Wahhabism,' and how is it evolving?
- What is the role of education in Saudi society and the economy, and what are the principal trends?
- What trends, if any, are observable in civil society and among the intelligentsia, that might be relevant to possible transformation in the social, economic and political domains?
- What are the determinants of Saudi foreign policy? What is the relative importance in this of domestic, regional and international factors? How much autonomy does the Saudi regime have at these three levels in fashioning its regional and global policies?
- What are the dynamics of Saudi Arabia's relations with the United States, what are the key patterns, and what is likely to happen in the future? Do current difficulties indicate a major shift or only a temporary blip?

It is hoped that the chapters that follow may help others to fine-tune their own answers, and pick up where we leave off.

The analysis is divided into four main parts—although it will be readily apparent that this division does not obscure the manifold linkages between their central subject matter: indeed, one of the main insights must be that none of them can be fully understood without the others. Grouped under the heading 'Ideology and Change' come three chapters that look at 'Wahhabism' and Saudi Arabia's Islamic ideology, since this is so often assumed to be at the root of a range of problems. That the usual assumptions are by no means a straightforward reflection of reality, as these chapters show, does not imply that it is not desirable to start the book with an in-depth look at the nature of Wahhabism, what its influence has been, how it and its variants have interacted with the state, and how it has itself been evolving and continues to do so. Guido Steinberg provides a historically-grounded survey on 'Wahhabism and the Saudi Ulama'; Stéphane Lacroix delves into the emergence of an 'Islamo-liberal trend' and its fortunes thus far; and Michaela Prokop addresses the ideological controversies surrounding the education system.

The book turns in Part II to what can be seen as the other essential determinant of the Saudi system: its political economy. It is no longer necessary to dwell for long on the now well-established dynamics of an ideal-type 'rentier state,' and in particular the case of the oil-surplus economies of the Gulf, as represented in the classic analyses by authors such as Beblawi and Luciani.[1] Rather, the three chapters grouped together here explore the extent to which Saudi Arabia's political economy may be moving beyond the limitations long assumed to be inherent to such rentier or 'allocation' states (in terms of the taxation-representation question, and of the presumed unproductive nature of much of the economy); and the extent to which limits on economic reform may be rooted in other characteristics of the socio-political system. Tim Niblock and Monica Malik set out the key challenges for the economy;[2] Steffen Hertog provides an innovative explanation for the nature and limitations of Saudi economic reform efforts, using the concept of 'segmented clientelism' to complement rentier state theory; and Giacomo Luciani examines to what extent the Saudi private sector may be turning into a genuine 'national bourgeoisie'—escaping the presumed constraints of rentierism with all the longer-term political as well as economic implications that such a development may have.

The third part of the book addresses the characteristics of regime and opposition politics head-on. Madawi Al-Rasheed uses the tools of anthropology to analyse royal family dynamics—a system she describes as one where five circles compete and collaborate within an 'acephalous tribal group'; she throws a highly critical light on the Al Sa'ud's relationship with Saudi society, pointing at faltering legitimacy and the use of repression. Iris Glosemeyer, working from a different angle, investigates the formal and informal checks and balances in the Saudi political system and suggests that the system is in fact slowly modernising in adaptation to a gradual redistribution of sources of power, both domestic and external. While opposition to the

1 Most readily accessible in Hazem Beblawi, 'The Rentier State in the Arab World', in Giacomo Luciani (ed.), *The Arab State*, London: Routledge, 1988, pp. 85–98; and Giacomo Luciani, 'Allocation versus Production States', in ibid., pp. 65–84.

2 Some of the material in this chapter is drawn from a book-length study by one of the authors, which will appear as: Tim Niblock, *Saudi Arabia: Power, Legitimacy and Survival*, London: Routledge, 2006.

regime is touched on in several preceding chapters, the following two deal with it directly. Abdulaziz Sager surveys the various strands of such opposition, indicating both its division and lack of effectiveness, and surveying the regime's responses. Roel Meijer focuses in particular on the most violent opposition, namely 'Al-Qa'ida in the Arabian Peninsula.' Using the concept of 'cycles of contention' from Social Movement Theory, he argues that, despite a string of violent attacks, there may be inherent limitations on the sustained effectiveness of this type of opposition activity in Saudi society.

In much of the foregoing the 'external' factor is a prominent feature, either as a resource or a constraint for the regime, as a resource or perceived target for domestic audiences, or as the wider context within which the Saudi political economy functions. In the fourth part of the book, the country's external relations become themselves the main focus, although it will immediately be clear that explanation here must very much bring the domestic back in. Gerd Nonneman outlines the determinants and patterns of Saudi foreign policy, arguing that what the regime has been doing for many decades, on the whole successfully, is 'omnibalancing' between different (and fluctuating) threats and needs located in its multiple environments (starting from the domestic), while attempting pragmatically to carve out a measure of autonomy from domestic, regional and international structures and actors simultaneously. This, he argues, is what explains the instances of apparent 'polygamy' in its external relations, both today and during much of the twentieth century. In that light neither the cautious and pragmatic regional policy nor the apparent cooling in relations with the United States should be particularly surprising. The latter two examples are dealt with in detail in the following two chapters. Yossi Kostiner examines the record of the Al Sa'ud in Arab peace initiatives *vis-à-vis* Israel, and argues that such involvement may at times have been less about a genuine practical push for peace than about diplomatic image-making. (Of course, one does not exclude the other, and indeed the previous chapter suggests that the continued festering of the Arab-Israeli dispute is an unwanted source of stress for the Al Sa'ud). Rachel Bronson discusses the recent evolution and underpinnings of the US–Saudi relationship, arguing that a significant deterioration has indeed taken place and that, in contrast to previous moments of friction, the 'glue' of the Cold War that gave the US and Saudi Arabia an overarching set of compatible interests is no longer present. Even so, Paul Aarts argues in the final chapter of Part IV, the most likely scenario is that rather than heading for separation the United States and Saudi Arabia are entering a more 'normal' relationship, which is nonetheless still very much dictated by the logic of energy and security.

The editors conclude by attempting to sum up the evidence presented, and to relate this back to the research questions that drove the project.

Part I. IDEOLOGY AND CHANGE

THE WAHHABI ULAMA AND THE SAUDI STATE: 1745 TO THE PRESENT

Guido Steinberg

In the course of over more than 250 years of Saudi history the Wahhabi ulama have developed a noteworthy political pragmatism. To preserve their alliance with the rulers, they supported Saudi policy even when it conflicted with their religiously based convictions. This pragmatism has repeatedly led 'radical' Wahhabis, who demanded an uncompromising implementation of Wahhabi tenets, to oppose the religious establishment.[1] The *Wahhabiyya* thus gave rise to opposition groups from within its own ranks in 1929, 1979, 1990–4, 2001 and 2003. Although the Muslim Brotherhood's and Sayyid Qutb's revolutionary thinking played a role in the formation of the Saudi Islamist opposition from the 1970s, the decisive impetus came from within the Najdi reform movement. The Saudi militant Islamists who have joined Usama bin Ladin's Al-Qa'ida are the descendants of these radical wings of the Wahhabiyya.[2] Contrary to the

[1] The term 'radical' will be used in this text for those Wahhabis who demanded an uncompromising implementation of Wahhabi tenets, regardless of the political consequences and who thereby stood in opposition to the Wahhabi religious establishment.

[2] It has been suggested to skip the term Wahhabiyya with regard to the transnational network of Al-Qa'ida. In fact, the term has been used as a delegitimising tool in the Indian, Caucasian and Central Asian contexts and should therefore not be used for movements outside of Saudi Arabia. However, it does not make sense to rename the Wahhabi movement in Saudi Arabia, due to the differences between it and other movements claiming an orientation towards the pious forefathers (*as-salaf as-salih*). For a more detailed discussion of the terms 'Wahhabiyya' and 'Salafiya', see Guido Steinberg, *Religion und Staat in Saudi-Arabien. Die wahhabitischen Gelehrten (1902–1953)*, Würzburg: Ergon, 2002, pp. 28–32.

widespread assumption that the 'new' terrorism is a transnational phenomenon, its groupings remain largely bound to certain home countries; it therefore remains a valid option to analyse parts of the Islamist networks from their national ('tellurian', as Carl Schmitt would have it) perspective, i.e. the Saudis of Al-Qa'ida as the militant wing of the Saudi Arabian opposition. Indeed, most of them have remained staunch Wahhabis, with the sole difference between them and the Wahhabi religious establishment being that they regard the rule of the Al Sa'ud as illegitimate.

The Wahhabiyya between Activism and Political Pragmatism

The history of Saudi Arabia is closely intertwined with the development of an eighteenth-century religious reform movement, the Wahhabiyya, who, from the 1740s entered into a symbiotic relationship with the Sa'ud family in which the Saudi state has relied on the religious legitimacy provided by the Wahhabi religious scholars, the ulama. Consequently, the Saudi rulers have posed as defenders of the true faith and thereby established three consecutive states: the first between 1744/5 and 1818, the second from 1824 to 1891, and the third, which was founded in 1902. In turn, the Wahhabiyya and its religious representatives, the Wahhabi scholars, profited greatly from their alliance with an emerging state, giving them the opportunity to enforce their vision of an Islamic society with all the coercive mechanisms this state was able to provide. This alliance proved to be so essential for the political survival and re-emergence—after the destruction of the first two Saudi states in 1818 and 1891—of the two partners on the Arabian scene, that they preserved it to this day.[3]

However, the relationship between state and religion changed with the course of time, the ulama losing the dominant position they enjoyed when the original founder of the Wahhabiyya, Muhammad ibn Abd al-Wahhab (d. 1792), reigned supreme during the founding era of the Saudi state. Indeed, reading between the lines of Wahhabi chronicles, it sometimes seems as if he—and not the rulers Muhammad ibn Sa'ud (d. 1765) and his son Abd al-Aziz (ruled 1765–1803)—

[3] If not otherwise stated, the historical material for this article has been drawn from *ibid., passim*.

dominated political decision-making until his death in 1792. As a result, Wahhabi principles were rigorously applied both in the newly founded state and in its foreign policy. Internally, Saudi society showed a marked purism, with all subjects being bound by a Wahhabi code of conduct that was rigorously enforced by the ruler, the ulama and their disciples. Externally, as all non-Wahhabi neighbours were considered infidels, the Wahhabis embarked upon a campaign of expansion, which they considered a holy war (*jihad*).

However, by 1792 the rulers of the Al Sa'ud had started to dominate politics while the scholars—most notably the descendants of Muhammad ibn Abd al-Wahhab, the so-called 'family of the Shaikh' (*Al ash-Shaikh*)—remained an important pressure group that dominated the realms of religion, education and the administration of justice. Having become the junior partner in the coalition, the ulama were no longer able to insist on the implementation of strict Wahhabi doctrine, especially where foreign policy was concerned. The result was an uneasy balance between Muhammad ibn Abd al-Wahhab's activist message and the necessities of political life, which was by and large dominated by the rulers' pragmatism. By legitimising controversial steps taken by the government, the Wahhabi scholars left a wide discursive space for radical Wahhabis opposing their pragmatic attitudes. As a result, the history of the Wahhabiyya has been marked by a continuous struggle between radical religious elements demanding an uncompromising enforcement of the original Wahhabi code of conduct as established during the eighteenth century, and the 'official' ulama, i.e. scholars with political functions or other influential positions close to the government, who acted according to the wishes of the ruling family.[4] And the deeper the cleavage between the leading ulama's political pragmatism and the teachings of the original Wahhabiyya, the more violent the conflict became. Indeed, reports about radical Wahhabi ulama supporting Al-Qa'ida's jihad against the United States and the West might be seen as just a manifestation of an inherent conflict between the pragmatism of the

[4] For this differentiation between 'official' and 'peripheral' scholars, see Malika Zeghal, *Gardiens de l'Islam: Les oulémas d'al-Azhar dans l'Egypte contemporaine'*, Paris: Presses de Sciences Po, 1996, pp. 31 and p. 47 ff. It has also been used in Annabelle Böttcher, *Syrische Religionspolitik unter Asad*, Freiburg: Arnold Bergstraesser Institut, 1998.

mainstream Wahhabiyya and the activism of some radical Wahhabi preachers.

The First Saudi State (1744–1818) and its Demise

Wahhabi-Saudi history began with the conclusion of an agreement between a religious scholar and a ruler in 1744/5. Muhammad ibn Sa'ud was the ruler of a small town in Central Arabia (Najd), ad-Dir'iyya, on the outskirts of today's Riyadh. His rule barely extended beyond the date gardens situated in the vicinity of the town. He seems to have recognised that a powerful expansive ideology might provide his little chiefdom with the legitimacy his neighbours lacked. Muhammad ibn Abd al-Wahhab, for his part, needed political support if he wanted to apply his purist ideology, whose propagation had already caused him much trouble in other towns in Najd and Iraq. The Najdi chronicles describe the pact as one in which the ruler protected Muhammad ibn Abd al-Wahhab and his family and enforced the reformer's interpretation of divine law, not only within the community, but also in a jihad against non-Wahhabi Muslims in surrounding territories. For his part, the scholar committed himself to joining his fate to the ruler's by permanently staying in Dir'iyya.[5]

In political reality, the agreement between ruler and religious scholar provided the emerging Saudi state with an expansive ideology based on the excommunication (*takfir*) of all non-Wahhabi Muslims as unbelievers. As such, true Muslims were obliged to wage a continuous jihad against neighbouring territories, resulting in the Saudi-Wahhabi alliance conquering Najd, the Eastern parts of the peninsula on the Persian Gulf shore and, finally, in 1803/4, the Hijaz with the Holy sites of Mecca and Medina.

However, this success already represented the beginning of the end of the first Saudi state. Conquering the Hijaz not only meant directly attacking the Ottoman Empire, but also one of the roots of its legitimacy as the protector of the Holy sites. Adding insult to injury, the Wahhabis even kept several pilgrimage caravans from performing the *hajj*, thereby forcing the Ottoman government's hand.

[5] Esther Peskes, *Muhammad b. Abdul-Wahhab (1703–92) im Widerstreit. Untersuchungen zur Rekonstruktion der Frühgeschichte der Wahhabiyya*, Beirut: Steiner, 1993, p. 284 ff and p. 243 ff.

The Sultan consequently ordered his governor in Egypt, Muhammad Ali Pasha, to retake the Hijaz and destroy the Saudi emirate in Najd. Muhammad Ali's troops invaded the Hijaz in 1811. After seven years of wars they took Dir'iyya and destroyed the Saudi capital. Most members of the ruling family were deported to Egypt and the ruler, Abdullah ibn Sa'ud, was sent to Istanbul where in 1819 he was decapitated. Recognising the important role of the Wahhabi ulama and their ideology for the aggressive expansion of the Saudi state, Muhammad Ali treated them extremely harshly. His troops killed several of them in what seems to have been a campaign of eradicating the Wahhabiyya in Najd. One of the Wahhabiyya's most radical and prominent proponents, Sulaiman ibn Abdullah Al ash-Shaikh (1785/6–1818), the leading scholar of the third generation of Muhammad ibn Abd al-Wahhab's family, was executed, having apparently first been tortured by the Egyptian troops under the command of Muhammad Ali's son Ibrahim.[6] The Saudi state's triumphant rise to hegemony on the peninsula had ended in total destruction. It took the Saudis and the Wahhabiyya alike a whole century to rebuild what they had lost in 1818.

In a book written more than a century later, Hafiz Wahba described the debates among the Wahhabi scholars following the defeat of 1818.[7] Some ulama in Qasim, i.e. the central region of Najd around the main trading cities of Unaiza and Buraida, accused the scholars of the Al ash-Shaikh of having caused the defeat of 1818 because they had been responsible for the uncompromising policy of expansion. The Al ash-Shaikh, according to Wahba, replied by accusing the inhabitants of Qasim of having collaborated with the Ottomans, claiming that they had called for the troops of Muhammad Ali and lead them to Dir'iyya, and as a consequence, the ulama of Qasim had no right to criticise the Al ash-Shaikh's attitude. However, the deeper reason for the downfall of the Saudi state had been its inhabitants' sins, which had provoked God to chastise them, and in order to prevent a similar catastrophe in the future, the Al ash-Shaikh concluded, God's commandments had to be applied even more rigorously than during the years before 1818.

[6] Elizabeth M. Sirriyeh, 'Wahhabis, Unbelievers and the Problems of Exclusivism', *British Society for Middle Eastern Studies Bulletin*, 16 (1989), pp. 123–32 (p. 124).

[7] Sheikh Hafiz Wahba, *Arabian Days*, London: Arthur Barker, 1964, pp. 98–100 and p. 112.

Although Hafiz Wahba's presentation is clearly biased, it is the only account of this debate to have come down to us, and furthermore reflects a discussion which has dominated Wahhabi history ever since, and which Sulaiman ibn Abdullah Al ash-Shaikh mentioned in some of his writings during the war. It is therefore quite likely that Wahba's description was close to what actually happened. The debate revolved around the question of how pragmatic Wahhabi scholars should be in order to support and preserve the state without giving up the original tenets of the Wahhabiyya.

During the eighteenth century the discrepancy between political needs and ideological tenets does not seem to have been an important factor, whether because Muhammad ibn Abd al-Wahhab dominated political decision-making or because he and Muhammad ibn Sa'ud agreed on the outlines of policy. But ever since the defeat of 1818 the question has been raised. In time the Wahhabi ulama drew the conclusion that they had to preserve the Saudi-Wahhabi state at all costs. It had become clear to them that, just as the state depended on the mobilising and legitimising force of the Wahhabi interpretation of the faith, they needed a strong state that secured their survival as the influential guardians of faith. Their political behaviour was from now on influenced by a strong pragmatism and their desire to strengthen the Saudi state and the ruling family. As a consequence, the ulama became ever more quietist in a state largely controlled by the rulers of the Sa'ud family.

Political Theory and Societal Practice in Central Arabia in the Eighteenth and Nineteenth Centuries

To this day the Wahhabi ulama have not developed a comprehensive political theory. In fact nearly 200 years passed before the Wahhabiyya developed a standard set of mainly theoretical rules for the most important political issues, like the succession of a ruler and the roles of the elites of an Islamic state. However, these have never been more than very general outlines quite unlike constitutional rules. Indeed, developing a political theory had apparently not been a necessity for Muhammad ibn Abd al-Wahhab. The lack of organisational complexity of the first Saudi state did not require any elaborate rules, probably because the Shaikh himself had enforced a quite clear-cut but informal differentiation of the functions of ruler and scholars. Ibn Abd al-Wahhab only adopted some rather general and vague thoughts of Ibn Taimiyya (d. 1328), the influential fourteenth-century Hanbali scholar and shining example for many Islamic reformers and Islamists to this day.[8]

In Ibn Abd al-Wahhab's vision of an Islamic state, the ruler had an extremely powerful position. His most important task was to implement the divine law as interpreted by the Wahhabi ulama. In practice Ibn Abd al-Wahhab demanded a radical implementation of all Wahhabi tenets, including more controversial political aspects like the excommunication (*takfir*) of non-Wahhabi Muslims and issues of minor importance like the prohibition of smoking, singing and laughing.

For a society to thrive, rulers and scholars had to cooperate intensively. Therefore, the ulama's position in the state remained central. They controlled the administration of justice and the educational system and gave the ruler 'good advice' (*nasiha*) in every question they deemed necessary. However, their competences were limited by their duty of obedience towards the ruler, which of course applied to ordinary citizens as well. The ulama themselves stressed this duty whenever addressing political questions. Even if the ruler had usurped his position by violent means, Muhammad ibn Abd al-Wahhab and his successors regarded him as legitimate. One of the most-quoted sentences in Wahhabi political treatises became Ibn Taimiyya's famous saying in his *As-Siyasa ash-shar'iya*: 'Sixty years with a tyrannical *imam* are better than one night without him.'[9] There was only one legitimate reason not to obey the ruler and that was if he tried to force his subjects to contravene the *shari'a*.[10]

While during the first Saudi state the ruler's succession seems to have been settled according to the principle of primogeniture, con-

[8] The best account of his life and teachings remains Henri Laoust, *Essai sur les doctrines sociales et politiques de Taki-d-Din Ahmad B. Taimiya*, Cairo: Institut Français d'Archéologie Orientale, 1939.

[9] In Wahhabi terminology, the ruler was named imam as well.

[10] Compare, for instance, Sulaiman ibn Suhman, *Al-Hadiya as-saniya wa-t-tuhfa al-wahbiya annajdiya li-jami' ikhwanina al-muwahhidin min ahl al-milla al-hanifiya wa-t-tariqa al-muhammadiya*, Cairo: al-Manar, 1344, 2nd edn, p. 109. For Ibn Taimiya's argumentation, see Laoust, *Essai sur les doctrines sociales et politiques de Taki-d-Din Ahmad B. Taimiya*, p. 527.

cepts of seniority and the pretendant's personal capabilities for office gained importance during the nineteenth century. Therefore, Wahhabi political concepts were to be tested more than once as soon as the new state lost its cohesion after the death of Imam Faisal ibn Turki in 1865, when his two sons began competing for the throne. The older one, Abdullah ibn Faisal, seems to have been the designated heir to the throne, while his brother Sa'ud had been appointed governor of the strategically important province of Southern Najd, providing him with an important base among the staunchest supporters of the house of Sa'ud and the Wahhabiyya. The ensuing civil war ended only with the destruction of the Saudi state in 1891. The rulers of the Rashid family from Ha'il in Northern Najd gained control over the whole of Najd.[11]

During most of the nineteenth century, the Wahhabi ulama had struggled—with only partial success—to put Ibn Abd al-Wahhab's political theory into practice. With the outbreak of the civil war, these efforts were nullified. Besides absolute obedience towards the ruler, the reformer's teachings had included an emphasis on what Henri Laoust called 'communal solidarity', i.e. the solidarity of the true Muslims in a strong community, which the ulama used to call *jama'a*. When confronted with the conflict between the royal brothers, the leading Wahhabi scholars took the side of Abdullah and reproached Sa'ud for leaving the Wahhabi community. In their writings of these years, the concept of *jama'a* became the dominant notion in Wahhabi political thought. Now the scholars realised how powerless they were when they did not have a strong ruler on their side. Diametrically opposed to the concept of *jama'a* was that of *fitna* (lit. temptation, sedition) describing every aspect threatening the unity of the true believers, be it an uncontrolled spread of sins, a lack of unity of purpose among Muslims in general and among the ruler and the scholars in particular, or indeed civil war. From now on, whenever a conflict between the ulama and the ruler emerged, they shrank back from open confrontation, because it might lead to *fitna* and the subsequent downfall of the Saudi state and the Wahhabiyya.

[11] The rulers of the Al Rashid had once been governors of the Northern Province of Jabal Shammar for the Saudis. They soon gained factual independence and eventually took Riyadh. See Madawi Al-Rasheed, *Politics in an Arabian Oasis: The Rashidi Tribal Dynasty*, London: I. B. Tauris, 1991.

Consequently, the civil war was one of the main reasons for a growing tendency towards quietism among the Wahhabi ulama.

In 1871 the conflict within the Wahhabiyya gained additional momentum. In a phase when Sa'ud seriously threatened his position, Abdullah approached the Ottoman governor of Baghdad, demanding military assistance. Thereby, the lawful ruler had asked the unbelievers for help. Among the ulama of Southern Najd a heated debate was ignited. Some scholars supported the call for help, most notably Muhammad ibn Ibrahim ibn Ajlan of Hariq.[12] But even those ulama who supported Abdullah ibn Faisal contradicted Ibn Ajlan. The then leading scholar of the Wahhabiyya, Abd al-Latif ibn Abdurrahman Al ash-Shaikh (d. 1876), warned all true believers that the text in which Ibn Ajlan had presented this argumentation constituted a 'devil's snare' (*hibalat ash-shaitan*). Hamad ibn Atiq (d. circa 1882/3), another leading Wahhabi scholar, even called Ibn Ajlan an apostate. Thereby, for the first time since the rise of the Wahhabiyya, scholars in Southern Najd excommunicated each other and, as a consequence, the Wahhabiyya as a religious movement seemed to be on the verge of collapse. Conflicts between the ulama of different regions, e.g. between those of Southern Najd and Qasim, further aggravated the crisis.[13] As a result, when Ibn Sa'ud founded the third Saudi state in 1902, the scholars' political thinking was dominated by the notions of community (*jama'a*) and obedience (*ta'a*). They thought a repetition of the events of the civil war (or *fitna*, as they would have it) could only be avoided by close to total obedience towards the ruler and the leading ulama in Riyadh. While these thoughts had not been alien to Ibn Taimiyya or Ibn Abd al-Wahhab themselves, this emphasis constituted a new phenomenon in Wahhabi political thought.[14]

[12] Abdullah ibn Abd al-Rahman al-Bassam, *'Ulama Najd khilal thamaniyat qurun*, 6 vols, Riyadh: Dar al-Asima, 1419/1998, 2nd edn, vol. V, pp. 469–71.

[13] For a detailed analysis of these conflicts, see Steinberg, *Religion und Staat in Saudi-Arabien*, pp. 168–203.

[14] A related detail of Ibn Abd al-Wahhab's political teachings became important during the civil wars. The reformer had written that even a ruler who had reached power by violent means had to be accepted as legitimate. So when Abdullah ibn Faisal had fled Riyadh in 1871 and his brother Sa'ud occupied the city, the judge Abd al-Latif ibn Abd al-Rahman Al ash-Shaikh pledged loyalty to the new ruler. Since Abd al-Latif had defended the legitimacy of Abdullah's

As a consequence of the ulama's defensive approach to politics, a strong ruler like Ibn Sa'ud proved able to consolidate his position. Whenever he made clear that he regarded a political decision as crucial and that he would not cede to the wishes of the ulama, they backed down. They sometimes even legitimised his policies by issuing supporting religious rulings (*fatwa*, pl. *fatawa*), even though they clearly rejected the measures in question. The scholars thus assisted Ibn Sa'ud in centralising his emerging state and in modernising key sectors of government activity. Hence, Ibn Sa'ud could make use of a powerful legitimising ideology without the ulama being able to limit his freedom of decision-making.

The Ikhwan Movement and the Ulama

Until 1929/30 the ulama had preserved their once dominant roles in Saudi society. They were still dominating the administration of justice and education and they were firmly entrenched as the interpreters of the divine law in a deeply religious society. Furthermore, their leader, Abdullah ibn Abd al-Latif Al ash-Shaikh (d. 1920), had been one of the early teachers of the new ruler and a guarantee of continuity between the second and the third Saudi states. His biographers describe him as a very strong personality, who had gained in status during the war years.[15] As a consequence, after 1902 the ulama were a force to be reckoned with.

With the emergence of the *Ikhwan* movement after about 1912 the ulama gained a new source of influence.[16] The *Ikhwan* (lit. bre-

---

imamate the years before, this step has to be understood as an implementation of the aforementioned principle. Again in 1902, when Ibn Sa'ud took Riyadh from the Al Rashid, the then leading scholar, Abdullah ibn Abd al-Latif Al ash-Shaikh (d. 1920) actively supported the Rashidi governor by taking refuge with his troops in the citadel. Only when Ibn Sa'ud had finally conquered the city did Abdullah pledge loyalty to the new ruler. He became one of Ibn Sa'ud's most loyal supporters and his most distinguished political counsellor until his death. See Abd al-Rahman ibn Abd al-Latif Al ash-Shaykh, *Mashahir 'ulama Najd wa-ghairihim*, Riyadh: Dar al-Yamama, 1974, 2nd edn, p. 131.

15 The most detailed biography is Al-Bassam, *'Ulama Najd khilal thamaniyat qurun*, vol. I, pp. 215–30.

16 John S Habib, *Ibn Sauds Warriors of Islam: The Ikhwan of Najd and Their Role in the Creation of the Saudi Kingdom, 1910–1930*, Leiden: Brill, 1978. For a critical dis-

thren) were former bedouin, who settled in agricultural settlements, so-called *hujar* or *hijar* (sing. *Hujra* or *hijra*). The term *hijra* alluded to the Prophet Muhammad's flight (*hijra*) from Mecca to Medina in 622, indicating that the Bedouin had left the realm of unbelief and joined the true Muslims. How the movement emerged has not yet been established, because the standard Saudi-Wahhabi narrative of a founder-hero Ibn Sa'ud, who had the brilliant idea of settling the bedouin and canalising their military energies is too perfect to be true. On the contrary, there is scattered evidence that many bedouin settled voluntarily because ecological and economic crises in the first two decades of the century threatened their way of living. Be that as it may, Ibn Sa'ud and the Wahhabi ulama quickly realised that by settling the bedouin and making use of their military prowess in a way that benefited the emerging central state could serve their interests. As a result, from about 1911/12 Ibn Sa'ud fostered the establishment of settlements by employing a subtle combination of coercion, financial incentives and religious indoctrination. Preachers were sent to the tribes and the *hujar* and taught the bedouin how to follow the Wahhabi path. They were taught that those of them who died in the jihad would immediately enter paradise. As a consequence, these once unreliable bedouin were transformed into a highly motivated fighting force. Ideologically, they joined forces with the ulama, who tried to use them as a means to enforce their notion of an expansive Islamic society, based on the doctrines of *hijra, takfir* and jihad. Many of them lived as preachers, judges and students among the *Ikhwan* and entered into an almost symbiotic relationship with the former bedouin. Until he conquered the Hijaz with the holy cities of Mecca and Medina in 1924/5 the movement

cussion of the standard Saudi narrative, see Abdullah S. Zaid, *The Ikhwan Movement of Najd, Saudi Arabia 1908–1930*, PhD dissertation, University of Chicago, 1989, pp. 31–7; Steinberg, *Religion und Staat in Saudi-Arabien*, pp. 433–7. Abdulaziz Al-Fahad has recently presented a similarly critical account, focusing on the continuity between Saudi policies of the second and the third Saudi states concerning the bedouins. He stresses the role of continuous proselytisation by urban Wahhabi preachers among the bedouins. See Abdulaziz H. Al-Fahad, 'The *'Imama* vs. the *'Iqal: Hadari*-Bedouin Conflict and the Formation of the Saudi State' in Madawi Al-Rasheed and Robert Vitalis (eds), *Counter Narratives: History, Contemporary Society, and Politics in Saudi Arabia and Yemen*, New York: Palgrave, 2004, pp. 35–75.

greatly aided Ibn Sa'ud's military campaigns. That year proved to be a turning point for his relations with the *Ikhwan*.

The *Ikhwan* had been a useful tool during the expansive period of the third Saudi state. However, following the conquest of the Hijaz, Ibn Sa'ud had to consolidate his realm, centralise power and modernise at least parts of Saudi society. Because he depended on the income of the yearly pilgrimage, he had to avoid unrest in the Hijaz, and the *Ikhwan* had already made clear that they were not willing to accept any moderate religious policy in the newly conquered provinces. When Ibn Sa'ud recalled them from the Hijaz and sent them back to Najd, conflict already loomed on the horizon. After some uneasy years of low-intensity conflict between the two sides, the *Ikhwan* rebelled and Ibn Sa'ud subdued their uprising in 1929/30. Although the *Ikhwan* more than anyone else in Arabia embodied the original Wahhabi ideals, a large majority of the ulama sided with Ibn Sa'ud, giving up their former allies.

The leading ulama in Riyadh desperately tried to avoid the decision over which side they should take in this conflict. At first they mediated between Ibn Sa'ud and the *Ikhwan*. Several high-ranking ulama visited their leaders after 1925 and attempted to convince them to back down. But they could not prevent the conflict from breaking out. The *Ikhwan* were defeated and the ulama lost an important source of political influence. After 1930 the ulama's political position was finally reduced to one of a junior partner.

Concerning the *Ikhwan*, the ulama's stance had been highly ambivalent. They knew that the settled bedouin were supporting their quest for an ideal purist state. So by fighting them they knowingly reduced their own influence. However, the leading ulama all supported Ibn Sa'ud. Still, some less important clerics sided with the *Ikhwan*. As one Saudi author wrote, some 'ulama of the bedouin' (*'ulama' al-badiya*) showed a remarkable tilt towards *takfir* and they were responsible for the bedouins' 'fanaticism'.[17]

Since most of the ulama who sided with the *Ikhwan* are no longer known, it might be conjectured that they were of a relatively humble social background. It seems logical that those ulama who formed a part of the urban upper classes had a special interest in the stability of

[17] Muhammad ibn Nasir ash-Shithri, *Ad-Da'wa fi 'ahd al-Malik 'Abd al-'Aziz*, 2 vols, n.p., 1417/1997, vol. I, pp. 149–51.

Ibn Sa'ud's rule. The lower-ranking ulama and students had less to lose and were therefore more prone to a radical interpretation of Wahhabi tenets. And in fact, all those scholars who *are* known to have sided with the *Ikhwan* did not belong to any of the famous notable families, although they all were of urban origin. Several ulama who sided with the *Ikhwan* had studied in Buraida, to this day a centre of Wahhabi radicals.[18] The most important among them was Abdur-Rahman ibn Abdullah ibn Uqla (1881–1933/4) from Hilaliya in Qasim, a village in the vicinity of Buraida.[19] After early studies in Buraida he had moved to Riyadh in order to study there, a necessity in the curriculum of successful students in Buraida. He then returned and developed a deep intellectual relationship with his teacher Umar ibn Muhammad ibn Salim (1880/81–1943). When he began working as a preacher among the *Ikhwan* of different *hijar*, Ibn Uqla preserved his relations to Umar and became well known as one of the most radical supporters of the revolt of the *Ikhwan*. He harshly criticised all scholars siding with Ibn Sa'ud. After the defeat he was shortly interned in Riyadh and was then allowed to return to his hometown.

Most interestingly, other ulama who supported the *Ikhwan* were students in the Buraida school headed by Umar ibn Salim. Their teacher, however, took the side of Ibn Sa'ud. The Salim family had gained prominence because Muhammad ibn Abdullah ibn Salim (1824/5–1905) had been an ardent supporter of the Wahhabiyya and Saudi rule during the last decade of the nineteenth century, when the Al Rashid ruled over Najd. As a consequence, his family began to dominate religious policy in Buraida and the Qasim province after Ibn Sa'ud had conquered it in 1906. Umar ibn Salim proved to be as uncompromising as his uncle and frequently posed problems for the ruler. In 1918/19 as the judge in the *hijra* of Artawiya he had stirred up the *Ikhwan*'s fanaticism so much that he had

[18] Many radical Wahhabi scholars come from this town, among them Salman al-Auda and Humud ash-Shu'aibi (d. 2002). There seems to have been a large proportion of dropouts of the Qasim branch of the Imam Muhammad ibn Sa'ud Islamic University who have joined Al-Qa'ida, most prominent among them Abd al-Aziz al-Umari, the 'Imam' of the hijackers of 9/11. For a different perspective, see 'Buraidah: A Misunderstood Saudi City', *Arab News*, 2 December 2002.

[19] Bassam, *'Ulama Najd khilal thamaniyat qurun*, vol. III, p. 106.

to be recalled.[20] His career is the best example of the ambivalence in the ulama's attitude towards the state. The Salim family headed a school of the Wahhabiyya in Buraida, which can best be described as an outpost of the Al ash-Shaikh (who remained in Riyadh) in the Qasim province. Although Ibn Salim was absolutely loyal to Ibn Sa'ud and the ulama of Riyadh, he propagated radical Wahhabi views which were more compatible with the *Ikhwan* ideology than with Ibn Sa'ud's state-building efforts. His students acted according to his teachings about *takfir, hijra* and jihad, but—contrary to his conviction—concluded that Ibn Sa'ud's rule was illegitimate. The *Ikhwan* reprimanded Ibn Salim in strong words; in fact they complained that the government bought him off.[21] One can assume that it was no easy choice for him, nor for some of his colleagues from Riyadh who had served as judges in the *hijar.* But they supported the Saudi-Wahhabi state in implementation of their political theory as it had developed during the years of civil wars.

Religion and State after 1930

1930 proved to be a turning point in the history of the Wahhabiyya and the Saudi state. The scholars were no longer able to shape important policy decisions. In less important instances, Ibn Sa'ud granted them a say concerning whether or not certain measures were implemented according to the *shari'a.* But regardless of their opposition in single cases as, for instance, over the introduction of technical innovations like the telegraph, radio and air traffic, Ibn Sa'ud embarked upon a modernising campaign without taking the ulama's positions into account. This not only affected the political system of the Saudi state, where one hitherto important actor was reduced to one among several, but the nature of the Wahhabi movement as well. There was a growing gap between the ruling family and the scholars as the guardians of the true faith.

Sometimes their relationship was tested. For example, the ulama opposed the presence of US personnel in Saudi Arabia in the early

[20] Steinberg, *Religion und Staat in Saudi-Arabien*, p. 449.

[21] Ibrahim ibn Ubayd Al Abd al-Muhsin, *Tadhkirat uli n-nuha wa-l-'irfan bi-ayyam Allah al-wahid wa-d-dayyan wa-dhikr hawadith az-zaman*, vols 1–4, Riyadh: An-Nur, n.d.; vol. 5, Buraida: as-Salman, 1406, vol 3, pp. 148 ff. and p. 203.

1940s. They had always rejected the presence of non-Muslims in the country and had resisted the treaty with Great Britain in 1915.[22] However, from 1930 a steadily growing number of foreigners entered the country with the permission of Ibn Sa'ud. For many inhabitants and the ulama this represented a cultural shock. When Americans took up the production of oil in the Eastern province in 1938 and an even greater number of foreigners began to enter the country, the ulama protested.

One especially courageous scholar opposed the influx of Americans in the town of Kharj in Southern Najd, about 60 miles south of Riyadh. This was one of the most conservative regions of Saudi Arabia, where the Wahhabiyya had always recruited its staunchest supporters. Egyptian agricultural experts had established a model farm in order to exploit the groundwater reservoirs in the region. Food supply was precarious during the war years, so the success of the project was of vital importance to Ibn Sa'ud. In 1941 American experts took over the farm with the assistance of the oil company CASOC and the Saudi Arabian Mining Syndicate.[23] However, the young local judge, Abd al-Aziz ibn Baz (1912–99), rejected the presence of Americans and started agitating against their activities. He criticised the King for giving the Americans land, which they used 'as if it was not the Muslims' territory'.[24] Ibn Sa'ud reacted swiftly and ordered Ibn Baz to his court in Riyadh, where he and other members of the Sa'ud family, counsellors and the leading ulama of Riyadh received the young scholar. Ibn Sa'ud asked him whether he had any complaint concerning his policy and reminded him that according to Islamic law accusations had to be brought forward while the accused was present and not behind his back. Ibn Baz repeated his complaint that the King had sold land to the infidels, in contradiction of his duties as a Muslim ruler. Ibn Sa'ud posted himself beside Ibn Baz and demanded a judgement by the ulama. Was it not true, he asked, that the Prophet had employed

[22] Harry St John Philby, *The Heart of Arabia*, 2 vols, London: Constable Co., 1922, vol. I, p. 360 and pp. 370 ff.

[23] United States National Archives 890F, *US Agricultural Mission to Saudi Arabia to Secretary of State*, report no. 1, 1 June 1942.

[24] Abd al-Aziz ibn Nasir al-Barrak (ed.), *Ibn Baz fi d-Dilam qadiyan wa-mu'alliman: jawanib min hayat Samahat ash-Shaikh 'Abd al-'Aziz b. Baz fatrata qada'ihi fi d-Dilam 'al-Kharj' 1357–1371*, Riyadh: Dar Tayyiba, 1416H, p. 30.

non-Muslims? When the ulama unanimously answered in the affirmative, Ibn Sa'ud continued by asking whether it contradicted the *shari'a* that he employed foreign experts in order to work on his behalf. He stressed that the foreigners in al-Kharj worked for him and under his control in order to produce oil, metals and water. After the ulama once again declared that Ibn Sa'ud's activities were strictly legal, the King asked Ibn Baz whether he was satisfied with the judgement. The latter answered that he had heard the decision and that he submitted to it, but that he was far from being convinced. Infuriated, Ibn Sa'ud jailed the scholar and threatened to have him executed if he did not repent. After he had calmed down, he invited Ibn Baz to a private audience and explained that his insubordination had threatened to damage public order. After Ibn Baz had accepted this argumentation, he was sent back home.[25]

Because of his courage, Ibn Baz earned himself a reputation of being a steadfast supporter of the original tenets of the Wahhabiyya even in the face of the ruler. This is how the later Grand Mufti of Saudi Arabia became a prominent scholar already in the 1950s. Even more important, the anecdote shows how far the 'official' ulama were ready to submit to the wishes of the king whenever an important political issue was at stake. It was well known at that time that many of the ulama rejected the presence of an ever-growing number of foreigners in the country. Many must have seen their stay in Southern Najd as a provocation. However, they decided according to the wishes of the ruler. Hence, in the early 1940s their political role was already severely limited.

However, Ibn Baz did not represent any opposition. His was rather a loyal voice calling for a more radical implementation of the original Wahhabi tenets than was reasonably possible for a state in the age of oil production. However, the example makes clear that even loyal ulama showed a marked ambivalence towards political necessities. The situation changed in the 1960s and 1970s. The state went through a period of profound social change, which was accelerated by the oil boom after 1973. Events in 1979 proved that the

[25] 'Complaints by Arab Fanatics against King Ibn Saud', Despatch of US Minister, Jedda, 4 December 1944, in Ibrahim al-Rashid (ed.), *Saudi Arabia Enters the Modern World: Secret US Documents on the Emergence of the Kingdom of Saudi Arabia as a World Power, 1936–1949*, part I, Documents on the History of Saudi Arabia, vol. IV, Salisbury, NC: Documentary Publications, 1980, pp. 201–3.

basic conflict between the leading ulama's submission to the state and the proponents of a return to the original tenets of the Wahhabiyya had not been solved. Rather, the ulama's pragmatism again opened the necessary discursive space for a new religious opposition.

On 20 November 1979, the first day of the Muslim fifteenth century, a group of young Saudi Islamists seized the Grand Mosque of Mecca and took several hundred pilgrims as their hostages.[26] The rebels were lead by a certain Juhaiman al-Utaibi, a Wahhabi zealot, who had elaborated the ideology of the group in a collection of letters.[27] He claimed that one of his companions, Muhammad ibn Abdullah al-Qahtani, was the expected *Mahdi*, or 'the one who is rightly guided'. The Muslim Mahdi closely resembles the Messiah in Christian and Jewish traditions and, while he does not play a prominent role in Wahhabi teachings, Wahhabis do believe in the concept. Among Sunnis, the Mahdi is widely believed to be one of the phenomena announcing the approach of the day of judgement.[28] Al-Utaibi and Qahtani demanded a return to the Islamic society of their pious forefathers (*as-salaf as-salih*) and harshly criticised the Sa'ud family for their corruption, the oppression of the population and their alliance with infidel powers, especially the United States. Between 500 to 1000 rebels held out for about two weeks against Saudi forces. They could only be overwhelmed with the help of French anti-terrorism units.[29] While Qahtani was killed during the fighting, al-Utaibi and sixty-three of his followers were executed in January 1980.

On the one hand, this revolt was a continuation of a tribal rebellion of parts of the Utaiba and Qahtan tribes as a result of government high-handedness. These tribes had already rebelled in

[26] James Buchan, 'The Return of the Ikhwan, 1979' in David Holden, and Richard Johns (eds), *The House of Saud: The Rise and Rule of the Most Powerful Dynasty in the Arab World*, London: Sidgwick Jackson, 1981, pp. 511–26; Johannes Reissner, 'Die Besetzung der Großen Moschee in Mekka', *Orient*, 21 (1980), pp. 193–203.

[27] Rif'at Sayyid Ahmad, *Rasa'il Juhaiman al-'Utaibi: qa'id al-muqtahimin li-l-Masjid al-Haram bi-Makka*, Cairo: Madbuli, 1988.

[28] For a Wahhabi viewpoint, see at-Tuwaijiri, Humud ibn Abdullah at-Tuwaijiri, *Ithaf al-jama'a bi-ma ja'a fi l-fitan wa-l-malahim wa-ashrat as-sa'a*, 2 vols, Riyadh: Medina, 1396/1976, especially vol. I, pp. 291–8.

[29] See 'Un précédent: les gendarmes français à La Mecque', *Le Monde*, 29 October 2002.

1929. The former *Ikhwan* had not been fully integrated into the Saudi state and suffered from socio-economic discrimination by the state, which had always drawn its support from the urban populations of Najd. Equally important though, Juhaiman and other rebels had studied under Ibn Baz, the former judge in al-Kharj and in 1979 the leading Wahhabi scholar and head of the Council of Senior Ulama (*Hay'at Kibar al-'Ulama'*).[30] His influence on the rebels was clearly discernible and his relationship with them closely resembled the one between Umar ibn Salim and his rebel students in 1929/30. In fact, Juhaiman al-Utaibi's thinking was firmly based on the teachings of the Wahhabiyya. Some observers called the group the 'Neo-*Ikhwan*' and they surely were a continuation of former radical trends among the Wahhabiyya. Al-Utaibi only differed from his former teacher in that he not only blamed the Sa'ud family for the Westernisation of the country and their alliance with the infidels, but demanded its downfall. As a consequence of these similarities, Ibn Baz and his colleagues of the Council of Senior Scholars only condemned the rebellion as such, but stopped short of denying the Muslim faith of the rebels. They clearly showed an ambivalence similar to that of their forefathers in 1929 when dealing with the *Ikhwan* rebellion. On the one hand, they sympathised with the rebels' aims and their worldview, but, on the other, could not accept their rebellion against the Saudi-Wahhabi state which, according to the ulama's political theory, was seen as the basis of the Wahhabiyya's very existence.

The Second Gulf War (1990–1) and the Emergence of an Islamist Opposition

After the rebellion was crushed, the Wahhabi ulama under the leadership of Ibn Baz reaped the fruits of their loyal performance during the critical phase of 1979/80. Driven also by the ideological challenge from the Islamic revolution in Iran, the Saudi government tried to enhance its religious legitimacy by enforcing a stricter Wahhabi code of conduct, authorising Ibn Baz and his colleagues to fight

[30] Joseph A. Kechichian, 'The Role of the Ulama in the Politics of an Islamic State: The Case of Saudi Arabia', *International Journal of Middle East Studies*, 18 (1986), pp. 53–71.

non-Wahhabi phenomena in religious and social life all over the Kingdom. The religious universities of Riyadh, Medina and Mecca, which were controlled by the ulama, were generously funded by the government. As a consequence, the number of religious students rose significantly and, in the early 1990s, about one quarter of all students in the Kingdom studied in one of the religious colleges.[31] The religious police, the so-called 'Committees of enjoining good and forbidding evil' (*Hay'at al-'amr bi-l-ma'ruf wa-n-nahy 'an al-munkar*), equally under the control of the ulama, was granted a substantial rise in its budget and what amounted to freedom of action in most Saudi Arabian cities. Their members (the so-called *mutawwa'in*) took the opportunity to violently try to establish their vision of a purist state in Saudi society. However, despite all these measures to co-opt the Wahhabi ulama and the radical Wahhabi elements, the government did not succeed in alleviating the Islamist threat. On the contrary, Islamism was on the rise and socio-economic problems in the wake of the oil crisis after 1985 threatened to broaden its base in society.

In 1990 a worst-case scenario became reality for the Sa'ud family. After Iraqi troops had entered Kuwait on 2 August, the Saudi government decided to call in American troops in order to defend the Kingdom from a further advance of the Iraqi army to the Eastern province. Considering the widespread anti-Americanism among the Saudi populace and the xenophobic attitudes of the Wahhabi scholars, this was a revolutionary step. Until then, the Saudi government had relied on a tacit alliance with the United States, but—because of internal considerations—always insisted on American military presence being 'over the horizon'. However, confronted with the threat of an Iraqi invasion, this policy had to be revised. The Council of Senior Scholars, still under the leadership of Ibn Baz, was asked to endorse the government's decision by a fatwa. Again, the scholars eventually complied with the rulers' wishes, although it was obvious that they disagreed with the presence of foreign troops on Saudi soil. At first, the ulama are said to have categorically refused to issue a fatwa endorsing the government decision. But after long discussions between the royal family and Ibn Baz, they convinced him of the

[31] Gwenn Okruhlik, 'Islamism and Reform in Saudi Arabia', *Current History*, January 2002, pp. 22–8 (p. 23).

imminent danger posed by the Iraqi troops, who were dislocated close to the Saudi border.[32]

Calling on the infidels for military help must have reminded the ulama of the crucial events after Abdullah ibn Faisal had called for Ottoman troops to assist him in his fight against his brother Sa'ud in 1871. Then the result had been the loss of the Eastern province to the Ottomans, a split between the Wahhabi ulama about the legal aspects of Abdullah's move and a weakening of the movement which contributed to the downfall of the Saudi state in 1891. This had been the most severe crisis the Wahhabiyya had experienced after 1818 and only Ibn Sa'ud had saved it from its total demise. The events of the civil war had marked Wahhabi political thought for decades and its lessons were not forgotten by the ulama. The parallels between 1990 and 1871 were too obvious to be ignored.

Furthermore, the ulama had always been among the first to reject the influx of foreigners into the Arabian Peninsula, which according to their worldview had to be free from non-Muslim interference. This, together with the fear that the American troops, once there, would not withdraw, must have prompted the ulama to consider the military build-up unlawful. However, in their fatwa of 13 August 1990 they explicitly endorsed the King's decision.[33] Thereby, the Wahhabi ulama's evolution from guardians of an activist ideology to state servants was completed. They had endorsed a decision which they thought was unlawful only because the government had demanded exactly that step. Furthermore, this decision also triggered the (re-)formation of the religious opposition. Its hitherto rather theoretical rejection of the pro-Western foreign policy of the regime became concrete. Its supporters protested the American presence on Saudi soil and the ulama's subservience to a state that had invited the unbelievers.

Among the Islamists opposing the policies of the Al Sa'ud were several younger scholars, most notably Salman al-Awda and Safar al-Hawali, who quickly gained prominence. They were middle-ranking Wahhabi scholars and had started protesting the decision to call

[32] Nawaf E. Obaid, 'The Power of Saudi Arabia's Islamic Leaders', *Middle East Forum*, http://www.meforum.org/meq/sept99/saudipower.shtml.

[33] Henner Fürtig, *Demokratie in Saudi-Arabien? Die Al Saud und die Folgen des Zweiten Golfkriegs*, Berlin: Das Arabische Buch, 1995, p. 20 ff.

American troops into the Kingdom from August 1990. When their agitation threatened to provoke serious security problems in Buraida and the south-western parts of the country, they were arrested in autumn 1994.[34] The governmental crackdown on the Islamist opposition calmed domestic discussions, although at a high price: It might be conjectured that the arrests led to a further radicalisation of militant elements, among them Usama bin Ladin, and therefore to the subsequent terrorist attack in Riyadh in 1995. The treatment of radical Wahhabi scholars and preachers by the Saudi government, most notably the arrests of al-Hawali and al-Awda, became an important aspect in militant publications in the following years. Both were released in 1999 when the internal situation had normalised.

At first it seemed as if al-Hawali (b. 1954) would become the leading figure among the Islamist opposition within Saudi Arabia. He is not only a Wahhabi preacher, but an internationally renowned Islamist intellectual. In 1988 he had already been appointed dean of the faculty for theology (*'aqida*)—the core discipline of the Wahhabi curriculum—at *Umm al-Qura* Islamic University in Mecca. His Master's thesis, titled 'Secularism' (*al-'Ilmaniya*), in which he interpreted this phenomenon as a Western concept whose aim was to undermine Islam from within, became known in Islamist circles across the region.[35] His writings show a peculiar combination of Saudi opposition themes—like the 'occupation' of the country by US forces—with a transnational Islamist argumentation focusing on Palestine and Iraq.[36] In his writings he develops a coherent anti-Western ideology, based on the assumption that the West, i.e. primarily the United States and Israel, aims at controlling and later destroying Islam.[37] The Gulf War in 1991 had been orchestrated by the United States as a first step in this direction with the aim of securing a permanent military basis in the Gulf region.[38] After his

[34] Joshua Teitelbaum, *Holier than Thou: Saudi Arabia's Islamic Opposition*, Washington, DC: Washington Institute for Near East Policy, 2000, p. 57.

[35] Mamoun Fandy, *Saudi Arabia and the Politics of Dissent*, New York: St Martin's Press, 1999, p. 63.

[36] For example, see Safar Ibn Abd Al-Rahman Al-Hawali, *The Day of Wrath: Is the Intifadha of Rajab only the Beginning?*, http://www.islaam.com/books/intifadha.htm. Al-Hawali's homepage is: www.alhawali.com.

[37] Fandy, *Saudi Arabia and the Politics of Dissent*, p. 61.

[38] *Ibid.*, p. 67–9.

release he moderated his views considerably and stopped agitating against the Saudi government. However, he was not prohibited from publishing anti-Jewish and anti-American texts. After 1999 he increasingly relied on these subjects, especially on Israeli and American policies in Palestine and Iraq, to garner support without addressing Saudi government policy directly.

His intellectual development closely resembles that of Usama bin Ladin: from a Saudi oppositionist (which he by and large remained until 1996) to the leader of a transnational Islamist network consisting of citizens from several Arab countries. Both careers mirror a tendency towards transnationalisation among Saudi Islamists. However, the development of Saudi religious policy remained similar to former crises, as the events after 1999 showed. Al-Hawali never openly admitted contacts to the militant scene and he cannot be considered part of terrorist circles. However, his and Salman al-Awda's moderation after their release from prison paved the way for a new group of radical Wahhabis appearing on the Saudi scene, who now openly supported Al-Qa'ida and the Taliban.

Shortly after 9/11 Humud ibn Uqla al-Shu'aibi gained prominence because of his support for the Taliban. He published a fatwa in which he argued that all Muslims had to join the Taliban in their fight against the US forces. This provoked a heated debate in Saudi Arabia, which ended with a decision by the government-controlled Council of Senior Scholars that only 'official' Muftis were supposed to issue fatawa. However, it soon became obvious that Shu'aibi represented a broader trend among Saudi scholars. The government's prompt reaction might be seen as evidence for this hypothesis.[39] After his death in early 2002, Shu'aibi's critique of the Saudi state and its support of US policies in the region was continued by some younger scholars, namely Ali al-Khudair, Ahmad al-Khalidi and Nasir al-Fahd.[40]

The situation escalated when Saudi militants—possibly in reaction to the US-led Coalition's campaign in Iraq—attacked foreigners' housing compounds in Riyadh on 12 May 2003. In early

[39] The fatwa was widely distributed on the internet. On the debate, see B. Trautner, 'Der Fatwa-Krieg im Cyberspace', http://www.bernhard-trautner.de/fatwakrieg.html.

[40] See also the chapter by Stéphane Lacroix in this volume.

May security forces had stormed a safe house of Al-Qa'ida close to one of the compounds and had subsequently published a list of nineteen suspects, when the aforementioned scholars demanded the government refrain from persecuting the '*mujahidin*'. During the crackdown on militants in the Kingdom after the bombings, all three of them were arrested, remaining in jail at the time of writing.[41]

A Pattern of Pragmatism Challenged

Political pragmatism, bordering on quietism, is clearly an important aspect of Wahhabi political thought and the Wahhabi ulama have acted accordingly—when important political decisions were at stake—ever since the establishment of the third Saudi state in 1902. Their deference to the rulers has developed as a reaction to political crises affecting the Saudi state and the Wahhabiyya alike; yet Wahhabi ideology continues to contain a significant activist element. In times of crisis these two trends in Wahhabi thought have provoked conflicting answers. Generally, the official ulama who supported the government's position—in 1929, 1979, 1990–4, 2001 and 2003—were confronted by a minority of often younger and lower-ranking ulama together with students, who adopted radical, activist interpretations of the early Wahhabiyya. Co-optation of radical elements promptly caused the emergence of new radical groups.

Furthermore, because of the conflicting trends inherent in Wahhabi tradition, many ulama could not hide their ambivalence towards the religious opposition. While they supported the government, they often sympathised with the radicalism of the younger rebels.

The ulama's political pragmatism was one of the reasons why the Saudi rulers did not have to fight their influence, as was the case in other states of the Islamic world. In fact, the Wahhabi scholars today exert more influence than any of their (Sunni) colleagues in the Muslim world.[42] Since they endorsed government policy, even when they were ambivalent about, or rejected, the lawful decision, there

[41] 'Clerics among Latest Arrests in Suicide Bombings', *Los Angeles Times*, 29 May 2003.

[42] The scholars' political positions are strong in Iran and Pakistan. For the Pakistani case, see S. V. R. Nasr, 'The Rise of Sunni Militancy in Pakistan: The Changing Role of Islamism and the Ulama in Society and Politics', *Modern Asian Studies*, 34, 1 (2000), pp. 139–80.

was until 9/11 no reason for the government to reduce their societal influence. Furthermore, the ulama proved to be useful because they exerted considerable influence among the deeply religious population of central Arabia. Therefore, support through a fatwa gave government measures a high degree of legitimacy. Indeed, the Al Sa'ud need the legitimacy bestowed upon them by the religious establishment, especially because the ruling family has not been able to distribute the country's oil income equitably, and has been unable to prevent the development of social problems.

However, this strategy might prove to be dangerous. Because of the official ulama's proximity to the rulers and their seemingly uncritical support of government policy they have damaged their own reputation. Many conservative Wahhabi Saudis consider the ulama corrupt and subservient to the political rulers, and this has stimulated the growth of the Islamist opposition. Since 1990 the widespread disappointment with the 'official' ulama appears to be on the rise. The appointment of a relatively weak Grand Mufti, Abd al-Aziz ibn Abdullah Al ash-Shaikh, after the death of Ibn Baz in 1999, may have damaged the collective standing of the leading ulama even further.

There are several indications that the government may have decided to address this problem by co-opting prominent Islamist scholars into leading positions in the religious hierarchy. It would thereby be able to replace at least parts of an elite which has lost its credibility in recent years. Especially Salman al-Awda seems to be working hard to consolidate his position by strengthening his ties with the liberal camp. His participation in the 'National Dialogue' in 2003, initiated by the Crown Prince in order to ease tensions between the different confessions and regional groupings in the country, might be a first indicator that the government tries to make use of his still immense popularity. However, this policy did not keep the radical Wahhabi camp from looking for a new spokesmen. After al-Awda and al-Hawali propagated moderation from 1999, other, more radical scholars gained publicity. The Wahhabiyya's struggle between loyalty and revolution has not yet come to an end.

ISLAMO-LIBERAL POLITICS IN SAUDI ARABIA

Stéphane Lacroix

The late 1990s have witnessed the simultaneous emergence on the Saudi Islamist scene of two new trends, each of them willing to challenge the long-time supremacy of *al Sahwa al-Islamiyya* (the Islamic Awakening), the main and most popular movement of the Islamic opposition of the early 1990s, which had, since the liberation of its leaders from 1997 onwards, once more come to occupy the centre of the stage.

On the ideological right of the *Sahwa*, a group of radical shaikhs rose to prominence, constituting what came to be known as the 'jihadi-salafi' trend. On social issues, they preached an extremely austere form of Islam, close to the views of the most uncompromising nineteenth-century Wahhabi *ulama*. On political issues they supported Usama bin Ladin and the global jihad and strongly criticised the Sahwa's new conciliatory approach towards the West. Later on they would provide many of the ideological justifications for the radical militants who launched a large-scale terrorist campaign on the Kingdom in May 2003.

At the same time a group of individuals, some of whom had been part of the Sahwist opposition, and some of whom had belonged to more radical groups that evolved on its margins, emerged on the left of the Sahwa and started to express views very critical of both traditional Wahhabi religious thought and the modern Sahwist political discourse. Simultaneously, most of them called for democratic change within an Islamic framework, therefore insisting on the necessity to combine political reform with religious reform. This new approach allowed them to forge alliances with individuals belonging to most of the remaining (non-Sunni Islamist) components of the Saudi political intellectual field, in particular liberals and Shi'ites. Through their efforts they managed to create together a common democratic, nationalist and anti-Wahhabi political platform, giving birth to a new 'centrist' trend within the Saudi political-intellectual field, which will be referred to here as the 'Islamo-liberal trend'.

There is no doubt that the tragic events of 11 September 2001 served as something of a catalyst for this Islamo-liberal reformism. Prior to that date, these intellectuals expressed their views informally in private salons, internet forums and articles in the press. But in the wake of the attacks, the more politicised fringe of the Islamo-liberals took advantage of the new political climate prevalent in the Kingdom to formalise its aspirations into political manifestos and petitions—the January 2003 one entitled 'Vision for the present and the future of the homeland' being the most elaborate—and attempted to create a wider consensus on its ideas. The movement's last political petition, in December 2003, represented a significant step in that direction with the inclusion of a number of prominent Sahwists among the signatories. The arrest to which a number of these Islamo-liberals were subject in March 2004 has, however, at least temporarily, put an end to the development of the movement.

In order to illuminate the significance of Saudi Islamo-liberal reformism, this chapter begins by elaborating a brief history of Saudi intellectual trends, thereby describing the various stages of the constitution of the Saudi political-intellectual field. A brief presentation of the movement through its various components will be followed by an examination of the conditions of its emergence in the late 1990s and, more important, the dynamics of its development after September 11th and its insertion into a Saudi political-intellectual field going through a process of complete recomposition.

The Constitution of the Saudi Political-Intellectual Field

Wahhabism and the Saudi religious establishment

Although one has to be very careful when employing the word 'Wahhabism', which in the last decades has become more of a political anathema than a suitable concept for the social scientist, this term can nevertheless be used as an operational tool on the condition of it being given a proper definition. Thus 'Wahhabism' is defined here as the religious tradition[1] developed over the centuries by the ulama of the official Saudi religious establishment founded by the heirs of Muhammad Abd al-Wahhab, an establishment which in return considers itself the legitimate guardian of this tradition.[2] 'Wahhabism' and the Saudi religious establishment historically constitute the core of the Saudi intellectual field. However, the Wahhabis never refer to themselves as such and always use the terms *Salafis*[3] or *Ahl al-Tawhid*.

The origins of Saudi liberalism

The first ideologies that developed in Saudi Arabia were Pan-Arabism and Marxism, which led to social movements and strikes in the Eastern province in the 1950s, and Western liberalism, which penetrated the country with the return of the first Saudis to have studied in the West. A number of groups supporting these ideologies were created inside the country throughout the 1950s and the 1960s and have, at times, constituted a threat to the regime. However, by the early 1970s, none of these were significantly active anymore and all that remained was their intellectual legacy.

The 1980s saw the emergence of a cultural and literary movement advocating modernism (*al-hadatha*), whose main figures were intellectuals such as literary critics Abdullah al-Ghaddhami and Abid Khazindar, poet Ali al-Dumaini and female novelist Raja' Alim. Among these, many had been part of the broader leftist political trend, represented by the movements mentioned earlier. Al-Ghaddhami's *al-Khati'a wa-l-Takfir* ('Sin and Excommunication'), published in 1985, has come to be considered the founding manifesto of

1 Tradition here means 'an argument extended through time in which certain fundamental agreements are defined and redefined in terms of two kinds of conflicts: those with critics and enemies external to the tradition who reject all or at least key parts of those fundamental agreements, and those internal interpretative debates through which the meaning and rationale of the fundamental agreements come to be expressed and by whose progress a tradition is constituted' (as defined by the moral philosopher Alasdair MacIntyre, quoted in Muhammad Qasim Zaman, *The Ulama in Contemporary Islam: Custodians of Change*, Princeton University Press, 2002).

2 See also Abdulaziz Al-Fahad, 'From Exclusivism to Accommodation: Doctrinal and Legal Evolution of Wahhabism', *New York University Law Review*, 2004, available on-line at http://www.saudi-us-relations.org/history/saudi-history.html.

3 Not only the Wahhabis *stricto sensu* (i.e. the 'ulama' of the official religious establishment) call themselves Salafis in Saudi Arabia, but also most of the Islamists.

the movement, not so much for its content, which is rather technical, but for the aggressive reactions it provoked in conservative circles. The principal aim of the movement was, in its early days, to criticise the fossilisation of Islamic literary tradition and to call for its renewal. Soon, however, this criticism no longer limited itself to literary issues but started to concern social issues as well.[4]

The birth of Saudi Islamism

Saudi Islamism can be described as historically twofold. The first main current in Saudi Islamism is *Sahwism*, which first appeared in the 1970s in Saudi universities. Its ideological content is a mix between traditional Wahhabi thought and the modern ideas of the Muslim Brotherhood. It must indeed be noted that the Egyptian and Syrian Muslim Brothers who found refuge in the Kingdom in the 1960s played a central role in the modernisation of the state, especially of its educational system. Many of them contributed to the elaboration of the curricula and subsequently became teachers and university professors. The most prominent among them was probably Muhammad Qutb, the brother of Sayyid Qutb, who fled from Egypt in the early 1970s. Under their influence, Saudi universities became an ideological melting-pot, from which the Sahwist hybrid emerged.

After the events of 1979, when Juhayman al-Utaibi and his group of *neo-ikhwan* attacked the sanctuary of Mecca, the Saudi government decided to reinforce the powers of the official Wahhabi religious establishment in order to prevent such unrest from happening again. But since *al-Sahwa al-Islamiyya* was not at that time considered an autonomous movement and was largely assimilated into the margins of the official establishment, it too benefited from this new governmental policy. The differences between the traditional ulama and the young Sahwists, however, were becoming significant: as opposed to the Wahhabi ulama, the Sahwists were taking stances on social and cultural issues and were willing to develop an Islamic discourse on modernity. They also appropriated modern technology—which the religious establishment regarded with suspicion—and no longer limited themselves to conferences and lessons in mosques, but started to

[4] Author's interviews with Abdullah al-Ghaddhami, Riyadh, June 2003. See also Mamoun Fandy, *Saudi Arabia and the Politics of Dissent*, Basingstoke: Macmillan, 1999.

record and distribute tapes of their sermons. *Al-sharit al-islami* (the Islamic tape) thus became the trademark of *al-Sahwa al-Islamiyya*.[5] The main figures of the Sahwa were A'idh al-Qarni, Salman al-Awda, Nasir al-Umar, and Safar al-Hawali, while intellectuals such as Abd al-Aziz al-Qasim or Abdullah al-Hamid played a minor—but already increasingly important—role. The latter two would later become the main ideologues of the Islamo-liberal trend.

Ideologically as well as sociologically distinct from Sahwism, the second main current in Saudi Islamism is *Neo-Salafism*,[6] which first appeared in the 1970s on the margins of the Sahwa. While Sahwists accepted the legitimacy of the state as a political structure and would only demand, after 1990, a reform of its policies, neo-salafis straightforwardly rejected its legitimacy. Therefore, while Sahwists were mostly found working in the State's administrations and universities, neo-salafis considered it sinful to be employed by public institutions and were generally found in the informal private sector. In extreme cases, they would choose to withdraw from day-to-day society and live in separate neighbourhoods. However, neo-salafis were not in general politicised and had no interest whatsoever in the social and cultural debates the Sahwists were eager to take part in. What mattered for them were questions of individual faith, and they could spend hours and days debating on apparently small details of the ritual. Their ideological references were mostly Wahhabi ulama from the nineteenth and early twentieth centuries, as well as Nasir al-Din al-Albani (1909–99), a Syrian scholar known for his opposition to all forms of *taqlid* (imitation) and the emphasis he put on the reliance on *hadith* (prophetic traditions) for religious rulings.

However, there have been at least two occurrences in which neo-salafism gave birth to violent and politicised movements: the first was in the mid-1970s when a group of young neo-salafis including Juhaiman al-Utaibi founded a movement known as *al-Jama'a al-Salafiyya al-Muhtasiba*. It is this same group which, a few years and a number of scissions later, would in 1979 attack the sanctuary of Mecca. Years after the failure of the insurrection 'the Seven Letters of Juhayman',

5 Author's interview with Ali al-Umaim and Mishari al-Zayidi, Riyadh, Jeddah, June 2003. See also Fandy, *Saudi Arabia and the Politics of Dissent*.

6 As Mansur al-Nuqaidan, a former *neo-salafi* himself, refers to it.

which had provided the ideological justifications for the attack, were republished in Kuwait and became a source of inspiration for a younger generation of neo-salafi ideologues, among whom Abu Muhammad al-Maqdisi, whose first book, *Millat Ibrahim* ('the Community of Abraham'), mainly draws on Juhayman's writings.

This leads to the second upsurge of neo-salafi violence: in the early 1990s, immediately following the second Gulf War, groups of young neo-salafis started to consider themselves the heirs of Juhayman and found inspiration in al-Maqdisi's books. After numerous discussions and scissions within these groups, some of these youngsters, having come into closer contact with the *jihadi* activists returning from Afghanistan, would take part in the 1995 Riyadh bombings. Others would quit, either because they were jailed or because they had fled the country. Among the latter were Mansur al-Nuqaidan, Mishari al-Zayidi and Abdullah bin Bejad al-Utaibi who would, a few years and a number of intellectual transformations later, become important figures in the critical wing of the growing Islamo-liberal trend.[7]

The Struggle between the Islamists and the Secular Intellectuals

The clash between the Islamists and the secular intelligentsia, which had been latent in Saudi Arabia since the 1970s, finally occurred at the end of the 1980s. Indeed, the emergence of Modernism acted as a trigger, since this new criticism was interpreted by the growing Sahwist movement as a secularist conspiracy willing to undermine the fundamental values of Saudi society. The Sahwist preachers, among them prominent figures such as Awadh al-Qarni and Sa'id al-Ghamidi, thus used all the means at their disposal—sermons in mosques, conferences, books and tapes—to lead a fierce charge against the tenants of Modernism, especially Abdullah al-Ghaddhami whom they nicknamed 'Abd al-Shaytan al-Ghaddhami'.[8] The debate between the Islamist Sahwists and the secular modernists became extremely virulent and each current radicalised its positions.

[7] Author's interviews with Mansur al-Nuqaidan, Mishari al-Zayidi and Abdullah al-Utaibi, Riyadh, Jeddah, June 2003. On the distinction between these two main currents of Saudi Islamism, see also 'Saudi Arabia Backgrounder: Who are the Islamists?', *ICG Middle East Report*, 31, 21 September 2004.

[8] Thus turning his name from 'the servant of God' into 'the servant of Satan'. Author's interview with Abdullah al-Ghaddhami, Riyadh, June 2003.

The Gulf War and the Politicisation of the Trends

Thus when the Gulf War broke out the Saudi intellectual field was already strongly polarised. However, in this new context the debates, most of which had focused on social and cultural issues, would now include a new element: politics.

Following the entry of Western troops to Saudi Arabia the first group to take action was the 'liberal trend', the term that was by then being used to designate the heterogeneous conglomeration of modernists, Pan-Arabists, leftists and Occidentalised intellectuals who were united in their opposition to the Islamists and to the religious establishment as a whole.[9] The women's driving protest that took place in Riyadh on 6 November 1990, in which forty-seven business women and female university professors took part, can be considered the first public move of the liberal trend. A petition asking for social and political reforms was subsequently signed by forty-three prominent 'liberal' intellectuals[10]—mainly from Jeddah and the Eastern Province—before being presented to King Fahd. However, not only were these liberal moves ignored by the government, they were also considered by the Sahwists as another 'secularist' provocation, triggering a shower of attacks on the liberal intellectuals.

A group of prominent Sahwist preachers, led by Salman al-Awda and Safar al-Hawali, became famous at this time for their virulent sermons against both the American presence in Saudi Arabia and the so-called 'secularist conspiracy'. The universities, where Sahwism had traditionally been very strong, became political bases of the movement. The Sahwists subsequently decided to formalise their demands and aspirations into a petition. In 1991 fifty-two prominent religious figures, mostly Sahwists, presented to King Fahd, with the support of the head of the official religious establishment, Shaikh Ibn Baz, a petition entitled *Khitab al-Matalib* ('The Letter of Demands'). It was followed in 1992 by another petition named *Mudhakkarat al-Nasiha* ('The Memorandum of Advice'), which develops

[9] As defined by Turki al-Hamad (author's interview with Turki al-Hamad, Riyadh, June 2003).

[10] While all researchers have presented this text as a 'liberal petition', there are signs that a small number of moderate Islamists from Jeddah—some of them close to the Muslim Brotherhood—took part in this move. This petition could therefore be considered as the first Islamo-liberal move in contemporary Saudi Arabia.

the same themes that were addressed in the Letter of Demands. This second one was signed by 107 Islamist intellectuals and ulama. It combined reformist demands (the creation of a consultative council, the respect of human rights and freedom of speech as defined by the *shari'a* etc.) with purely corporatist demands (the reinforcement of the power of the religious institutions and their control on Saudi society etc.). This corporatist dimension probably explains why the petition received support from high-ranking members of the official religious establishment. But the real strength of the Sahwist shaikhs was that they managed to gather the whole Saudi Islamic field under a single banner: indeed, even the neo-salafis, who disagreed with the Sahwa on numerous theological matters and still looked at politics with distrust, followed their leadership.

Presented with the 'Memorandum of Advice', the government was shocked by the boldness of the Sahwists and by the (though ultimately limited) rebellion that had taken place in the official religious establishment. But the royal family did not take significant measures against the Sahwists until 1993, when six of them (including Abdullah ibn Jibrin, Abdullah al-Hamid, Sulaiman al-Rashudi and Hamad al-Sulaifih) created the 'Committee for the Defence of Legitimate Rights' (CDLR) (*Lajnat al-Difa' 'an al-Huquq al-Shar'iyya*), which was considered an unforgivable crossing of the line. Subsequently mass arrests took place in the Sahwist circles and many preachers, among them al-Awda and al-Hawali, were sent to jail. Gradually, from 1997 onwards, they would be freed.

Islamo-Liberal Reformism

The emergence of Islamo-liberal reformism

According to Mansur al-Nuqaidan, the origins of Islamo-liberal reformism date back to 1998. At that time the historical figures of the Saudi Islamic opposition—al-Awda, al-Hawali and al-Umar—were still imprisoned, their absence leaving the field open for new ideas to emerge. In this context a group of minor Sahwists who had already been freed by the authorities, along with a number of former radical salafis, started to voice opinions that, while reflecting different approaches, tended to fall into a single intellectual 'Islamo-liberal' framework, thereby giving birth to a new kind of cultural, religious and political discourse. Indeed, these activists and thinkers were all expressing unprecedented criticism of the Wahhabi religious orthodoxy, while calling for democratic reform within an Islamic framework. As time passed their sympathisers became more numerous, notably among former liberals and Shi'ites, some of whom had previously expressed similar views. This improbable convergence at the centre of the Saudi political-intellectual field founded what is designated here as the 'Islamo-liberal trend'. This trend stands out within the field both because of the novelty of its religio-political discourse and because of the extreme diversity of its proponents, who come from very different generational, regional and intellectual backgrounds, reflecting in a way the Kingdom's own diversity.

By drawing a quick intellectual portrait of prominent figures representing the Islamo-liberal trend each key component will be introduced, also providing an overview of the Islamo-liberals' religio-political discourse. Within the Islamo-liberal trend will be distinguished a critical wing, which mainly sticks to social and religious criticism but doesn't become directly involved in politics, and a political wing, which translates its criticism into political moves, such as the drafting and signing of political manifestos and petitions. This is not to say there exists any such 'organisational' link between these groups, though they certainly constitute the two sides of what is here considered to be a single phenomenon. Indeed, there is no doubt that the critical intellectuals have played a major role in preparing the field for the demands of the political ones.

Key components of the Islamo-liberal trend[11]

The critical wing: Former radical salafis: Hasan al-Maliki, Mansur al-Nuqaidan and the 'Nuqaidan' phenomenon. Hasan al-Maliki and Mansur al-Nuqaidan were both born in 1970 and belong to what may be called the '*neo-salafi*' generation. Teenagers during the 1980s, at a time

[11] This section and parts of the following draw on a previous article written by the author, where more detailed biographies may be found: Stéphane Lacroix, 'Between Islamists and Liberals: Saudi Arabia's New Islamo-liberal Reformists', *Middle East Journal*, 58, 3 (summer 2004), pp. 345–64. However, the focus here is different: while the article concentrates on an analysis of the Islamo-liberals' political discourse, here the analysis is of the dynamics of their insertion and their rise to prominence in a Saudi political field in which they have to compete with other actors, in a process referred to here as 'Islamo-liberal politics'.

when Saudi society was undergoing a strong wave of Wahhabisation, they themselves became hard-core salafis. But since the middle of the 1990s they have both gone through a radical transformation and have begun expressing iconoclastic views. Hasan al-Maliki first concentrated his criticism on the teaching of Islamic history in Saudi Arabia and on the Saudi school curricula, but has more recently become much more polemical, leading frontal charges against Wahhabism, either through a critique of its main sources of inspiration, Ibn Taymiyya and Ibn Abd al-Wahhab, or through a denunciation of its tendency to imitate, rather than to innovate; Al-Maliki believes no social progress can be achieved without a comprehensive revision of Wahhabism. Mansur al-Nuqaidan's point is quite similar, but he goes further than al-Maliki in his criticism, for he rejects any kind of salafism—which he describes as 'containing by nature an inclination to *takfir* (excommunication of fellow Muslims) and exclusivism'—and calls for a revival of *Irja'*, an early Islamic school of thought renowned for its tolerance. Al-Nuqaidan, who works as a freelance journalist, has taken very strong stances in the wake of the Riyadh bombings, drawing an explicit link between jihadi violence and the Wahhabi dogma.[12] Until 2003 considered a liberal Islamist, al-Nuqaidan—who proudly calls himself a 'changing individual' and explains that he intends to follow his intellectual evolution to wherever it will lead him—has recently become more radically liberal in his declarations. Though he undoubtedly is one of the 'founders' of the Islamo-liberal trend, he can no longer be considered as part of it.

This 'Nuqaidan' phenomenon, as some name it in Saudi Arabia, is not isolated: there now exists a whole group of critical intellectuals belonging to the same generation as al-Nuqaidan and al-Maliki, former '*neo-salafis*' who became Islamo-liberals, for instance, Mishari al-Zayidi and Abdullah al-Utaibi, who both work as journalists in local and Pan-Arab newspapers.

The political wing: Former Sahwists: Abd al-Aziz al-Qasim and Abdullah al-Hamid. Abd al-Aziz al-Qasim and Abdullah al-Hamid are both aged 40–50 and belong to a different generation than al-Nuqaidan and al-Maliki, what we may call the 'Sahwa' generation. They have

[12] Author's interviews with Mansur al-Nuqaidan and Mishari al-Zayidi, Riyadh, Jeddah, June 2003.

in the last few years become the two main ideologues of the Islamo-liberal trend.

In the early 1990s, the jurist Abd al-Aziz al-Qasim was a young, but already quite prominent, figure of *al-Sahwa al-Islamiyya*. He is known to have signed the Letter of Demands and to have been one of the activists behind the CDLR. Since being freed in 1997 he has become a key member of the emerging Islamo-liberal trend and has continuously called for a rapprochement between the Islamists and the liberals. In his writings he has concentrated on the issues of democracy, civil society and Saudi nationalism, arguing that these concepts are perfectly compatible with Islam. In the December 2003 National Dialogue conference he strongly criticised the religious school curricula and elements of the Wahhabi dogma which inspired them, provoking a scandal in conservative circles.

Abdullah al-Hamid, a religious thinker and a literature professor, was also active in the Islamist opposition of the early 1990s. In 1993 he was one of the six founding members of the CDLR. He has become, in the last few years, together with al-Maliki, one of the prominent critics of the Wahhabi doctrine—'a caricature of salafism' as he names it—and has been calling for a revival of true salafism, in a sense close to that of Muhammad Abduh's Muslim reformism. For al-Hamid only religious reform can create the conditions for political reform and allow for the emergence of a true civil society and a pluralist system where human rights are respected.[13] These ideas have had a very strong impact on the Islamo-liberal trend, of which al-Hamid must be considered one of the key thinkers.

Liberals: Muhammad Sa'id Tayyib as an example. Muhammad Sa'id Ṭayyib, a former Arab nationalist, belongs to a third generation, what we may call the 'Gamal Abd al-Nasser' generation (he was born in 1939). He was one of the prominent figures of the 'liberal trend' in the wake of the Gulf war. However, since the end of the 1990s he has started to reformulate his political ideas in a new language, insisting on the centrality of Islam, and has, together with other liberals aware of their group's utter lack of popular support in Saudi Arabia, made pressing calls for a rapprochement with the Islamists: 'Making peace,

[13] Author's interview with Abdullah al-Hamid, Riyadh, June 2003.

getting together, coming to an agreement—call it as you like—is nowadays an urgent and pressing necessity, that can't be postponed... in this sense, it is exactly like the question of reform itself—and has no less importance.'[14]

Shi'ites: Muhammad al-Mahfuz, Zaki al-Milad and Ja'far al-Shayeb

Muhammad al-Mahfuz, Zaki al-Milad and Ja'far al-Shayeb are Shi'ite activists from the Eastern province who fled the country in the 1980s and came back after an agreement signed in 1993 with the Saudi government. In the late 1980s, as Mamoun Fandy argues, they abandoned their Khomeinist rhetoric for calls for democratic pluralism.[15] However, they had at that time no partner in the Sunni Islamist opposition, whose intransigence on the Shi'ite question was renowned. The emergence of the Islamo-liberal trend in the late 1990s gave them an opportunity to reintegrate themselves into the local Saudi political field. Al-Mahfuz and Al-Shayeb have since developed a political discourse similar to that of the remaining Islamo-liberals, while insisting on their absolute loyalty to their Saudi homeland, even going as far as championing Saudi nationalism.[16]

The development of the Islamo-liberal trend

The media *infitah* (opening), which began in 1999, clearly had a very positive effect on the development of the Islamo-liberal trend by creating more auspicious conditions for its promoters to express publicly their opinions and to interact with each other. The Saudi daily *al-Watan*, founded in May 1998, played a key role in this process, for it allowed genuine political debates to take place in its opinion pages. The Islamo-liberal intellectuals also became very active on internet forums (*muntadayat*), which they used to discuss and spread their theses. Two of these forums played a central role in the promulgation of this trend: the first, named *Muntada al-Wasatiyya*, was founded in the year 2000 by Muhsin al-Awaji, a former

14 Dialogue between Muhammad Sa'id Tayyib and Tuwa, www.tuwaa.com, 6 June 2003, http://bb.tuwaa.com/showthread.php?s=c07110b4f71da52c9d23d11bb-403b536&threadid=15856.

15 See Fandy, *Saudi Arabia and the Politics of Dissent*, p. 198.

16 Author's interview with Muhammad al-Mahfuz, Ja'far al-Shayeb and Zaki al-Milad, Qatif, June 2003.

Sahwist, as a platform for moderate Islamism and therefore attracted a number of Islamo-liberals.[17] The second, *Tuwaa*, was created at the beginning of 2002.[18] It defines itself as an 'area for free-thinkers who respect free-thinking'. Its users fall along a large ideological spectrum, from the anti-religious liberal intellectual to the Islamo-liberal one.

Since 9/11 the Western—and especially US—media have been replete with articles extremely critical of Saudi Arabia, its government and society alike, while US officials have made very harsh statements on the country from which fifteen out of the nineteen perpetrators of the terrorist attacks on New York and Washington had come. This violent anti-Saudi campaign has caused great trauma inside the country. In this sense, as J. E. Peterson argues, 'it may not be exaggerated to say that, after the United States, Saudi Arabia is one of the countries that have been most directly affected by the tragic events of 9/11.'[19] This context has largely contributed to the birth of a nationalist atmosphere of unity in the face of adversity. Since then the Islamo-liberal intellectuals have striven to take advantage of this situation, to carry out their project of creating a political platform aimed at unifying the whole of the Saudi intellectual field and, beyond the elite, the entire Saudi society itself. In this context, their first move was an attempt to gain the support of the senior shaikhs of the Sahwa, whose strong popularity would have greatly benefited the movement.

The Politics of Islamo-Liberal Reformism

The Islamo-liberals vs the Jihadi-Salafis: The battle for the Sahwa's soul

The senior shaikhs of the Sahwa had indeed, since their liberation in 1999, considerably modified their views, especially towards the West. Salman al-Awda and Safar al-Hawali had both unequivocally condemned the 9/11 bombings, and al-Hawali, considered the most

[17] The forum's address is www.wasatyah.com; However, since 2003 this forum has become more radical and most of its 'Islamo-liberal' figures have deserted it.

[18] www.tuwaa.com or http://bb.tuwaa.com.

[19] J. E. Peterson, *Saudi Arabia and the Illusion of Security*, New York: Oxford University Press, 2002, p. 59.

radical of the two, had even issued a 'statement to the Umma' in late 2001, in which he criticised the jihadis' strategy, followed by an open letter to president Bush, in which he expressed his readiness to live in peace with the West, if it would only 'stop its attacks on the Muslim World'. These new signs of moderation had made some of the Islamo-liberals, especially Abd al-Aziz al-Qasim, consider the possibility of gaining these shaikhs' support for their project.

Indeed, in April 2002 al-Qasim managed to get Salman al-Awda, Safar al-Hawali and Nasir al-Umar to join the signatories of a statement entitled 'How we can coexist'.[20] The text came as a response to an open letter signed by sixty American intellectuals—among them Samuel Huntington and Francis Fukuyama—which sought to provide moral justifications to the Bush Administration's 'War on Terror'. In their manifesto the 150 Saudi signatories called for peaceful coexistence with the West and expressed their readiness to pursue dialogue with their American counterparts, while strongly reasserting their attachment to their Saudi and Islamic specificity, in a tone that is unequivocally Saudi nationalistic. Moreover, the composition of the list of signatories aimed at reinforcing the nationalistic nature of the message. Al-Qasim and some of his fellow Islamo-liberals had indeed managed to gather support from almost all socio-political groups—Islamists and liberals, men and women. The inclusion of al-Awda, al-Hawali and al-Umar in such a project was unprecedented, and therefore almost all political trends seemed to be represented. The only significant absence was that of the Shi'ites, who probably resented the presence of ulama such as Shaikh Abdullah Bin Jibrin, notorious for having taken radical anti-Shi'ite stances in the past.[21]

Through the gathering of this wide coalition, al-Qasim and his companions' first objective was to make the exterior part of the Islamo-liberals' political programme—and, beyond this, the whole Islamo-liberal reformist project itself—appear as if it were the fruit of a consensus within Saudi society. On 5 May 2002 Islamo-liberal

[20] "Ala 'ayy 'asas Nata'ayish' ('How We Can Coexist'), posted at http://www.islamtoday.net/bayan/bayanm.cfm on 29 April 2002. The English translation is available at http://www.americanvalues.org/html/saudi_statement.html.

[21] In 1991 Ibn Jibrin issued a *fatwa* declaring the Shi'ite infidels and authorising their murder. (See Fandy, *Saudi Arabia and the Politics of Dissent*, p. 206).

columnist Yusuf al-Dayni, believing that the game had already been won, rejoiced in *al-Watan*:

'This manifesto inaugurates a new era of intellectual harmony that really represents our national unity (...). It has mostly succeeded in shaping a new, unitary intellectual vision capable of destroying the imaginary barriers of ice that have been raised through a long history of struggle between the supposed dualities of modernisation and authenticity, tradition and reason, nationalism and Islam, democracy and shura.'[22]

More important, the drafters' aim was indeed to durably gain the support of the senior Sahwist shaikhs and to have their legitimacy put at the service of the Islamo-liberal project.

However, the Islamo-liberals were not the only ones to struggle for the soul of the Sahwa. Presenting themselves as the 'real guardians' of the Wahhabi orthodoxy and of the sacrosanct principle of '*al-wala' wa-l-bara*'' (loyalty to fellow Muslims and rejection of the infidels), the shaikhs of the growing jihadi-salafi trend stepped into the debate and violently criticised the content of the manifesto, attacking al-Awda and al-Hawali for supporting it. A number of statements and books were written for that purpose, starting with Ali al-Khudair's 'Reviving the community of Abraham: an answer to the defeatist traitors'[23] and ending with Nasir al-Fahd's 'Condemnation of the errors contained in the intellectuals' manifesto',[24] in which he claimed to make an inventory of all the 'doctrinal mistakes' present in the text. The salafi forums on the internet soon abounded in denunciations of al-Awda and al-Hawali's 'defeatism' (*inhizamiyya*). As an example, al-Awda's website *al-Islam al-Yawm* ('Islam Today') quickly became known as *al-Istislam al-Yawm* ('Capitulation Today').[25]

The pressure on the two shaikhs became so strong that they were forced into signing an 'explanatory manifesto' in which they purely

[22] Yusuf al-Dayni, 'Bayan al-Muthaqqafin al-Sa'udiyyin Najah Dakhili wa Ikhfaq Khariji' (The Saudi Intellectuals' Manifesto: A Success at Home and a Failure Abroad), *al-Watan*, 5 May 2002.

[23] 'Ihya' Millat Ibrahim wa-l-Radd 'ala al-Mukhadhdhilin al-Munhazimin' (Reviving the Community of Abraham and Responding to the Defeatist Traitors), www.alsalafyoon.com/ArabicPosts/IslamTodayNetRad.htm.

[24] 'Al-Tankil bima fi Bayan al-Muthaqqafin min Abatil' (Castigating the Errors Contained in the Intellectuals' Manifesto), http://www.al-fhd.com/kutob.htm.

[25] Seen on 'al-Saha al-Islamiyya', www.alsaha.com.

and simply contradicted every single argument and principle they had stood for in the first text.[26] Similarly, many of the Sahwist signatories published separate statements in which they announced their withdrawal from the list. These moves triggered a shower of criticism in the Saudi press and on the internet, mainly directed against the Sahwist signatories for their opportunism. After two months of a genuine 'media-frenzy' surrounding the issue, nothing remained of the manifesto.

The 'manifesto affair' therefore represented the first clash between the two new rising trends of Saudi Islamism, struggling for the support of the only historically legitimate Islamist movement in Saudi Arabia, the Sahwa. The Sahwist shaikhs' withdrawal clearly represented a victory for the jihadi-salafis and a defeat for the Islamo-liberals, who had not been able to mobilise Saudi society as the jihadi-salafis had. However, the Islamo-liberal reformists undoubtedly ended up benefiting from this episode, as the long debate that followed gave them and their ideas, an unprecedented visibility on the political-intellectual Saudi scene, of which they would take advantage to carry on with their socio-political project. After the politically 'safer' issue of relations with the West, the next move—this time coming from the other main pole in the Islamo-liberal trend, centred around Abdullah al-Hamid and Muhammad Sa'id Tayyib—would deal with the domestic situation.

'Vision for the Present and the Future of the Homeland': The official birth of Islamo-liberal reformism[27]

In August 2002 a group of Islamo-liberal intellectuals, Shi'ites and Sunnis, embarked on the drafting of a new manifesto dealing in a direct and uncompromising way with the internal problems faced by the country and requesting the implementation of political, economic and social reforms. But it was only at the end of January 2003, after five months of debate, drafting and gathering signatures that a charter entitled 'Vision for the Present and the Future of the Homeland' was finally sent to Crown Prince Abdullah and a dozen other prominent members of the royal family.

[26] 'al-Bayan al-Tawdihi' (The Explanatory Manifesto), posted on 19 May 2002 on www.islamtoday.net and removed a few days later.

[27] 'Ru'ya li-hadhir al-watan wa mustaqbalihi' (Vision for the Present and the Future of the Homeland), *al-Quds al-'Arabi*, 30 January 2003.

The charter contains demands for significant political, economic and social reform, such as the creation of elected regional and national parliaments, measures against corruption and waste and an end to all forms of regional and confessional discrimination. As for the language of the text, although it may not sound as religious as, say, that of the 1992 'Memorandum of Advice', the signatories are careful enough to state several times in the document that the *shari'a* is the appropriate framework for all the reforms they demand. Moreover, although it is evident that the signatories endorse such concepts between the lines, the words 'democracy' and 'parliament' are absent and all that can be found within the text is a reference to the Islamic institution of *shura*. As al-Hamid—who is one of the authors of the text and whose influence is evident on this choice of terminology—argues, the aim is 'to root reformist discourse in Islam'.[28] This ambiguity of an Islamic discourse with a liberal flavour, or a liberal discourse with an Islamic flavour, explains why most Western—and even Arab—media misunderstood the initiative. Indeed, after many articles described the document as 'a liberal petition', some newspapers, such as the *Washington Post*,[29] preferred to warn their readers against a text written by dangerous fundamentalists opposed to the United States.

The drafters of the petition[30] succeeded in gathering a wide coalition of signatories belonging to distinct political trends, thereby giving reality to the growing Islamo-liberal impulse and producing a document that can indeed—after the failure of Al-Qasim's April 2002 initiative—be considered as the real birth certificate of the Islamo-liberal trend. Though the 104 signatories include a majority of figures generally considered as liberals, the Islamists' minority status is compensated for by the key role they have played in the project. As for the Shi'ites, they number around twenty.[31] As expected, 'critical Islamo-liberals', such as Mansur al-Nuqaidan and Hasan al-Maliki, have not signed the document, but have expressed

28 Author's interview with Abdullah al-Hamid, Riyadh, June 2003.

29 'Reform with an Islamic Slant', *Washington Post*, 9 March 2003.

30 Abdullah al-Hamid and Matruk al-Falih are said to have played a key role in drafting the text.

31 For more on the signatories, see Lacroix, 'Between Islamists and Liberals: Saudi Arabia's New Islamo-Liberal Reformists'.

support for it.[32] As they argue, they simply preferred not to get directly involved in politics, considering that their role lies elsewhere. Missing, however, are the 'big names' of the Sahwa who either simply preferred to keep away from the domestic political issues that had led them to jail in the early 1990s, disagreed with the demands (notably on the Shi'ite question), or feared another backlash. The inclusion of the Sahwa was, however, to remain an important objective for the Islamo-liberals, which would in part be achieved with the Islamo-liberals' December 2003 petition.

The Islamicisation of the Islamo-liberal trend

In the months that followed the 'vision', the Saudi government, and especially Crown Prince Abdullah, took a number of preliminary measures towards reform: a relative liberalisation of the media, the organisation of the first National Dialogue conference—which would end with the drafting of, and the Crown Prince's approval for, a charter calling for political and religious reform—and the announcement of partial municipal elections to be held within a year.

However, despite these important steps, the Islamo-liberals, who first gave these measures a warm reception, started to express criticism, considering the pace of reform was still too slow. As a result, in December 2003 they decided to send a new petition to Crown Prince Abdullah entitled 'A national call to both the government and the people: constitutional reform first',[33] in which they reiterated most of their previous requests and demanded the establishment of a constitutional monarchy within three years. Its timing is pretty significant: it came only ten days before the beginning of the second National Dialogue conference, as if the signatories wanted to make clear that they didn't expect the results of the session to fulfil their expectations.

As a collective move, this December petition corresponds to a significant internal evolution within the Islamo-liberal constituency. It indeed represents—after the April 2002 failure—a successful attempt from the Islamo-liberals to include prominent figures of the Sahwa in their movement. The text's explicit 'call to all classes and groups

[32] Author's interview with Mansur al-Nuqaidan, Riyadh, June 2003.

[33] 'Nida' watani: ila al-qiyada wa-l-sha'b ma'an—al-islah al-dusturi awwalan', www.elaph.com, 20 December 2003.

of people, especially the ulama, the jurists and the religious scholars to support the demands for constitutional reform' can be seen as illustrating this position. Therefore, the proportion of Islamist-oriented figures in the list of signatories is greater in this petition than in the January one. The Islamist wing here includes, in addition to all the individuals mentioned previously, such prominent Sahwist figures as: Muhsin al-Awaji, a former CDLR activist who was once Safar al-Hawali's right hand man in the 'Global Campaign against Aggression',[34] Muhammad al-Hudaif, Khalid al-Ujaimi, Sa'ud al-Funaisan and others, most of them signatories of the 'Memorandum of Advice' in 1992 and prominent figures of the CDLR. It is also worth noting that the petition appeared on Salman al-Awda's website, which had not been the case in January, meaning that the signatories could have received the shaikh's implicit support.

In attracting the Sahwa, the Islamo-liberals were helped by the disappearance of their main rival, the jihadi-salafi trend, so that no longer could anyone accuse the Sahwists of collusion with 'secularists'. Indeed, the May 2003 bombings had led to its main figures, Nasir al-Fahd, Ali al-Khudair and Ahmad al-Khalidi, being accused of involvement in the attacks and to their subsequent arrest in June 2003. Not that Saudi jihadi-salafi thought had itself disappeared—on the contrary, it had become one of the principal ideological resources of the radical militants—but it was no longer part of the intellectual debate as there were no more prominent ideologues to side with it on the Saudi public scene.

However, this time opposition came from the other side: many liberal-oriented Sunni or Shi'ite intellectuals who had signed the January petition either refused to sign the new one (Khalid al-Dakhil for example) or asked for their names to be removed from the list of signatories, arguing that they did not agree with some of the ideas formulated in the text (Abd al-Karim al-Juhaiman, Ali al-Dumaini, Najib al-Khunaizi, among at least ten others).[35] Apart from the strong Sahwist presence within the list of signatories, an attentive reading of

[34] 'al-Hamla al-'Alamiyya li-muqawamat al-'udwan' (The Global Campaign Against Aggression) was founded in Mecca in April 2003 by Safar al-Hawali, and Muhsin al-Awaji subsequently became its official spokesman. For more on this organisation, see www.maac.ws.

[35] www.elaph.com, 22 December 2003.

the text can provide an explanation for these reactions. First, its language is definitely more religious than that used in the January petition. Second, the text draws a direct parallel between the terrorist violence the country had been experiencing since May 2003 and, on the one hand the US foreign policy, and on the other the absence of political participation. Many liberals consider these parallels controversial and even see them as a way of justifying, or at least excusing, terrorism. However, such logic is central to Sahwists such as al-Awda and al-Hawali's rhetoric.[36]

Therefore, although the reformists' demands have globally remained the same, the December petition corresponds to an 'Islamicisation' of the Islamo-liberals' political discourse, mainly aimed at attracting Sahwist Islamists to its ranks and forming the widest consensus possible. However, such a move has prompted the withdrawal of the most liberal-minded signatories, thus also leading to a *de facto* 'Islamicisation' of the constituency.

An end to the story?

In contrast to what had happened in January 2003, this new petition received a cold reception from the government, to say the least. Crown Prince Abdullah, to whom the text was addressed, ignored it, while twenty of the signatories were summoned to Interior Minister Prince Nayif's office to give an explanation. Crown Prince Abdullah's speech on 14 January 2004 was indeed an indirect response to the Islamo-liberals' eagerness: 'The state is, with God's help, following its own gradual and well thought-out reformist path, and will not allow anyone to block reform, either by advocating immobilism and inaction, or by calling for the country to jump into the unknown and to embark on foolhardy ventures.'[37]

The creation by the Saudi government of a national human rights organisation described by the authorities as independent, while all of its members would be nominated, prompted the Islamo-liberals to announce the creation of their own independent human rights organisation. Such a move, which bore obvious resemblance to the

[36] The statement they issued to condemn the Riyadh bombings in May 2003 is a perfect example of this rhetoric.

[37] 'bima yatawafiq ma'a al-shari'a al-islamiyya: wali al-'ahd al-sa'udi yu'ayyad 'amaliyya islahat tadrijiyya wa mu'tadila', www.elaph.com, 14 January 2004.

creation of the CDLR in 1993, was too much of a provocation for the authorities. The next day twelve prominent Islamo-liberals were arrested, among them 'Islamists' Abdullah al-Hamid, Tawfiq al-Qusayyir and Sulayman al-Rashudi and 'liberals' Ali al-Dumaini, Abd al-Khaliq Al Abd al-Hayy and Matruk al-Falih.[38] At the beginning of 2005 Al-Hamid, al-Dumaini and al-Falih were still detained. Their public trial started on 9 August 2004.

This tragic turn of events for a movement that had, a year before, received the support of Crown Prince Abdullah needs to be accounted for. First, the form of the demands contained in the December petition was unprecedented: for the first time the drafters gave the regime an explicit timetable for its constitutionalisation—an unbearable provocation. However, contrary to what many observers have assumed, this wave of arrest was not just a late reaction to the content of the December 2003 text. Indeed, Ali al-Dumaini, who had played no role in the conception of the December 2003 petition and had even withdrawn his signature a day after its publication, arguing that he disagreed with some of its content, had, however, played a key role in the January 2003 petition, and had also participated in the drafting of two other liberal petitions in September 2003 and February 2004. It is therefore the 'petition phenomenon' itself that seems to be have been targeted by the authorities: faced with the multiplication of political manifestos, the regime wanted to send a strong signal to all potential drafters that it had had enough. Finally, the growing success of the Islamo-liberals in forming a wide coalition and, more important, in rallying prominent Sahwists to their cause (leading some to speculate that Salman al-Awda, who remains one the most popular Islamists in the country, might join[39]) may have been the main reason for these arrests. The Islamo-liberals would therefore have been the victims of their own success.

Conclusion: the Limitations of Post-Islamism

As argued elsewhere[40], the emergence of Saudi Islamo-liberal reformism as a unitary movement seeking a compromise between demo-

[38] www.elaph.com, 16 March 2004.

[39] See for example 'Saudi Arabia Backgrounder: Who are the Islamists?', *ICG Middle East Report*, 31, 21 September 2004.

[40] Lacroix, 'Between Islamists and Liberals'.

cracy and Islam is typical of a 'post-Islamist' evolution, similar to what has happened in Egypt with the foundation of the *Wasat* party aimed at unifying Islamists and Christians on an Islamo-democratic platform.

However, defining a 'post-Islamist' platform is one thing; gathering effective support for it is quite another. In strongly polarised political fields such as those of the Middle East, this can be particularly tricky. In the case of the Egyptian *Wasat*, the party was rapidly caught between liberal distrust, Islamist (mainly Muslim Brothers') accusations of opportunism, and finally the regime's fear of a new and potentially successful concept.[41] The *Wasat* therefore did not manage to become the powerful centrist pole it had envisioned to be, even being denied official recognition by the authorities.[42]

For the Saudi Islamo-liberals, it has not been too different: while they had at first managed to gather an even wider consensus than their Egyptian counterparts, the December 2003 inclusion of prominent Sahwists and the subsequent Islamicisation of their political discourse prompted severe criticism from liberal figures once close to the movement. This has put its very 'post-Islamist' nature into question. Wanting to become more popular by including more Islamists, the movement arguably ended up losing its liberal caution.

As in Egypt, the last word—at least thus far—appears to have been the regime's, which, worried by the momentum gained by the Islamo-liberals, decided to try and crush the development of the movement. The rise and seeming fall of the Islamo-liberal trend, caught between the rock of the traditional distrust and rivalry between Islamists and liberals and the hard place of the regime, therefore illustrates the difficulty for post-Islamist movements to impose themselves on Middle Eastern political scenes.

[41] Author's interviews, especially with Abu al-Ala Madi, Cairo, May 2004. See also Joshua A. Stacher, 'Post-Islamist Rumblings in Egypt: The Emergence of the Wasat Party', *Middle East Journal*, 56, 3 (summer 2002), pp. 414–32.

[42] On 2 October 2004 the Egyptian governmental commission in charge of political parties refused for the third time the party's chairman Abu al-Ala Madi's demand for official recognition (See 'rafd ta'sis hizbayn jadidayn fi masr', www.islamonline.net, 2 October 2004).

THE WAR OF IDEAS: EDUCATION IN SAUDI ARABIA

Michaela Prokop[1]

Have we helped create these monsters? Our education system, which does not stress tolerance of other faiths—let alone tolerance of followers of other Islamic schools of thoughts—is one thing that needs to be re-evaluated from top to bottom.[2]

Raid Qusti, *Arab News*, May 2004

Since 9/11 the Saudi education system has been accused of contributing to anti-Western sentiments and of providing fertile ground for extremism. Thomas Friedman, for instance, suggested, 'where would the terrorists have learned such intolerance and discrimination? Answer: in the Saudi public school system and religious curriculum.'[3] Claims of direct links between educational curricula and terrorism, while reductionist and ignoring the political, socio-economic and emotional dynamics at play, resonate well in a world of 'with us or against us'. Initially, Saudi media and officials portrayed the criticisms as a conspiracy and an attack against Islam. The Saudi Minister of Education declared: '[w]e do not claim that we are living on an isolated island, as the whole world has become a small global village. However, our national educational curricula never urged

[1] This chapter reflects solely the opinion of the author and should not be taken to represent the views of the Asian Development Bank.

[2] 'How Long before the First Step?', *Arab News*, 5 May 2004.

[3] 'The ABCs of Hatred', *New York Times*, 3 June 2004. See also 'A Nation Challenged: Education; Anti-Western and Extremist Views Pervade Saudi Schools', *New York Times*, 19 October 2001, or *The Boston Globe*, 13 January 2002.

extreme thinking,'[4] while Shaikh Sa'ud al-Shuraimi, Imam at the Haram of Mecca, declared that changing the content of religious education would be tantamount to 'high treason'.[5]

Over the last few years there has been a gradual evolution from outright rejection of any link between the education system and extremism, to a tacit and hesitant acknowledgement that the Saudi school curriculum has 'several defects' and that there is a need for a total re-evaluation of the education system.[6] In October 2002 the Saudi Foreign Minister indicated that the government is working to remove parts considered as 'objectionable', which he claimed constitute approximately 5 per cent of the curriculum.[7] The more open recognition may have been accelerated by recent events, in particular the 12 May and 8 November 2003 bombings. Shortly after the May 2003 attacks Mansour al-Nuqaidan, a Saudi newspaper columnist, wrote: 'The main problem is that these radical groups draw their justification from Wahhabi thoughts...It's a huge problem. It's an octopus with its arms everywhere, building these thoughts in everyone's mind.'[8] Following the November attacks Prince Turki al-Faisal conceded that Saudi Arabia was not only trying to hunt down members of the Al-Qa'ida network, but was also 'combating the ideas that made them terrorists [...] by educating youth and stressing the moderate nature of Muslims who reject extremism and violence and also by providing jobs and addressing economic difficulties to deny terrorism its tools for attracting citizens.'[9]

Acknowledgement that the education system has to be adapted to meet the changing economic and demographic circumstances is shared by many Saudis, including many conservative forces, and predates the events of 9/11. Despite huge investments in education, Saudi youth find themselves ill equipped for today's challenges and

[4] 'Saudis Will Not Allow Changes Imposed on National Curricula', *Gulf News* (Dubai), 7 March 2002.

[5] Hamza Olayen in the Daily Star, *Mideast Mirror*, 5 February 2002.

[6] *Arab News*, 7 January 2003.

[7] John Duke Anthony, 'The American-Saudi Relationship: A Briefing by HRH Prince Saud Al Faisal, Minister of Foreign Affairs', *Gulfwire Newsletter*, 13 October 2002.

[8] 'Saudis Re-examine an Islamic Doctrine Cited by Militants', *New York Times*, 25 May 2003.

[9] *Arab News*, 13 December 2003.

increasingly face the prospect of unemployment and poverty. Economic and demographic pressures currently also provide the main impetus for reform. The Saudi business community, for instance, has long been advocating educational reform. A 1990 petition signed by prominent businessmen demanded a review of the country's educational policy:

> we believe that our country's educational system is in need of comprehensive and fundamental reform to enable it to graduate faithful generations that are qualified to contribute positively and effectively in building the present and the future of the country, and to face the challenges of age, enabling us to catch up with the caravan of nations that have vastly surpassed us in every field.[10]

A statement by the Foreign Minister made in August 2004 indicated that the country is now seriously engaged in bridging this gap. He emphasised the need to acknowledge global developments and sources of knowledge and stressed that Saudi Arabia now has modern educational systems, curricula and teaching methods including IT training.[11]

While these are promising statements, the 'war of ideas', or the 'battle' over the revision of curricula, highlight how divergent and polarised opinions are between conservative religious forces and more liberal voices over the pace, extent and shape of reform.[12] The debate mirrors the divisions unleashed or exacerbated by 9/11 over national identity, the public role of women, the Kingdom's relations with the West and the relationship between the *ulama*, the royal family and the people. This chapter will look at how the concern for Islamic legitimacy has determined educational policies, shaped the evolution and expansion of the education system, its institutional structure and message, and how it circumscribes the margins of reform. Concessions to conservative religious forces in the field of education, particularly in politically sensitive periods, forfeited the creation of a knowledge society and ultimately the future of the

10 As translated by Human Rights Watch, 'Empty Reforms: Saudi Arabia's New Basic Laws', May 1992.

11 See *Al-Riyadh*, 27 August 2004, http://www.alriyadh-np.com/Contents/27-08-2004/Mainpage/LOCAL1_20613.php.

12 Yasser Al Zaatera, 'The War of Ideas', *Al Hayat*, 11 January 2004; Abdulaziz Qassem, 'The Battle of Educational Curricula', *Al Hayat*, 24 January 2004.

young generation, a trade-off that increasingly undermines the Kingdom's stability. The chapter will also briefly discuss the content of the teachings, but, more important, the impact of the underlying tone of the message, the efforts to instil fear of the 'other' and to enforce obedience towards those in authority, further reinforced by the teaching methods.

While the message propagated in schoolbooks does not directly encourage violent *jihad* (holy struggle) against the 'infidels' or rebellion against corrupt authorities, the indoctrination with parochial modes of thinking may pave the way for more radical inclinations, obstruct reform initiatives and lock the country in stagnation and retreat. It is the context, the socio-economic frustrations, the political siege mentality and social and cultural schizophrenia that the message engenders, which affects the students' perception and attitudes. In this sense, equally important is what schools, until recent hesitant changes, did not teach: tolerance and understanding about other cultures, religions or other interpretations of Islam. This applies equally to Saudi missionary activities abroad. The Wahhabi-inspired worldview, combined with the proselytising fervour of its messengers, often proved to be a destabilising element when exported to a context of conflict between Muslims and 'unbelievers' or to regions where the majority of the population did not follow the same strict version of Islam.[13] This chapter will then briefly touch upon the main economic and social 'side-effects' of the current system and the economic and demographic factors pressing for reform before discussing some of the obstacles to reforming the system and adapting the message.

[13] 'Wahhabis' are the followers of the teachings of Muhammad ibn Abd al-Wahhab (1703–92), who preached a return to the fundamentals of Islam, the Qur'an and the *Sunna*. The term Wahhabism is primarily used in the West. Initially it was mostly used by the movement's opponents, while adherents of Ibn Abd al-Wahhab's message prefer to be called *muwahhidun* (unitarians) since the fundamental principle of Islam, as emphasised by Ibn Abd al-Wahhab, is the oneness of God. See the in-depth survey of the evolution of Wahhabism, in Abdulaziz Al-Fahad, 'From Exclusivism to Accommodation: Doctrinal and Legal Evolution of Wahhabism', *New York University Law Review*, 2004, also available on-line at http://www.saudi-us-relations.org/history/saudi-history.html. See also Guido Steinberg's chapter in this volume.

Fateful Concessions

A Saudi observer noted that the government's reaction to the events in 1979 was an indication that the Islamists had started to dictate the rules of the game: 'it created a generation of angry, confused young people, many of whom have become fanatics, including those fifteen Saudis among the nineteen suspects in the September 11 terrorist attacks and the Saudi prisoners in Guantanamo.'[14] The government reacted to the 1979 Mecca uprising, the Shi'a demonstrations in the Eastern Province and to the Islamic revolution in Iran by reinforcing its Islamic credentials; schools ran summer centres to further religious education, the number of religious television and radio programmes rose, King Fahd opened the Islamic University of Umm al-Qura and funding for religious institutions increased. Missionary activities abroad accelerated in response to the Soviet invasion of Afghanistan in the same year.

In contrast, the educated that reached adulthood before 1979, many of whom received generous government scholarships to study in the United States or Europe, often showed great appreciation and gratitude for America, its scientific and cultural achievements. Many of their generation assumed important positions in the government upon their return. This lead to an interesting paradox, a younger generation that to some extent is much more conservative, religious and inward oriented than the older generation.

Particularly during the 1960s, 1970s and early 1980s many Saudis went abroad to study, first to other Arab countries such as Egypt and Lebanon and then increasingly to the United States and Europe. The number peaked in 1984/85 with more than 2,800 graduates (300 female), but dropped to 950 (150 female) in 1989/90.[15] With the expansion of Saudi universities and a wider subject variety, the number of students going abroad, particularly for undergraduate courses, gradually declined and fell further following the repercussions of 9/11.

Conceding decisions to conservative religious forces over the evolution of education, cultural expression and the public role of women, serves the regime to preserve its image of guardian of valued

[14] 'Saudi Government Urged to Update Education System', *Arab News*, 20 May 2002.

[15] Fouad al-Farsy, *Modernity and Tradition*, Channel Islands: Knight Communications, 2000.

traditions and the sanctity of women's morality.[16] However, while the ruling elite continues to stress that economic modernisation can be reconciled with the traditional cultural, religious and political values of Saudi Arabia, the resort to tradition and religious symbols and piety is often selective: a practice with contemporary objectives in mind, based on political expediency and the need for legitimation, particularly obvious when the Islamic legitimacy of the House of Sa'ud is challenged. In the past it has also often served as a convenient veneer to avoid political reforms that would touch upon the prerogatives of the Al Sa'ud.

The guiding principle of education is 'the duty of acquainting the individual with his God and religion and adjusting his conduct in accordance with the teaching of religion, in fulfilment of the needs of society and in achievement of the nation's objectives.'[17] Religious education is emphasised at all levels. The main religious subjects taught in Saudi schools and university are: *Qur'an, Tawhid, Tajwid* (recitation), *Tafsir* (interpretation, commentary of the Qur'an), *Hadith* (record of the sayings and doings of the Prophet Muhammad and his companions) and *Fiqh* (Islamic jurisprudence). Approximately 30 per cent of weekly hours in elementary school are dedicated to religious subjects, 24 per cent in intermediate school and in secondary school around 35 per cent for students in the *shari'a* and Arabic branch and approximately 14 per cent for those in the technical and natural science branch. Failure in any one of the religious subjects requires repeating the whole academic year. History classes such as history of Islamic civilisation, history of the life of the Prophet and his companions, or history of Saudi Arabia and Arabic literature classes are also heavily influenced by Islamic teachings. In non-religious universities, the amount of religious teachings varies. In humanities and social sciences approximately 40 to 45 per cent are dedicated to religious teachings and Arabic classes, while students at the King Fahd University of Petroleum and Minerals, for example, are required to

[16] On the role of women see Eleanor Doumato, 'Gender, Monarchy, and National Identity in Saudi Arabia', *British Journal of Middle Eastern Studies*, 19, 1 (1992).

[17] Saudi Arabian Cultural Mission in the United States of America, *Education in Saudi Arabia*, Washington, DC: Saudi Arabian Cultural Mission, first edn, 1991, p. 9.

take 14 semester credit hours in Islamic and Arab Studies equivalent to 10 to 15 per cent of the curriculum.[18]

The Other Half

The influence of religious forces is particularly felt in the field of female education. After violent protests erupted among the most conservative religious forces against the establishment of girls' schools in the 1960s, King Faisal, as a compromise, placed female education under the supervision of the ulama.[19] To date there is strict gender segregation in schools; curricula for girls and boys differ, reflecting the different societal roles and expectations. According to the Kingdom's educational policy, education should provide a woman with the skills 'to fulfil her role in society as a wife and a mother' and prepare her for 'other activities that are compatible with her nature, such as teaching girls, nursing, and other activities needed by society.'[20] This policy and the strict enforcement of gender segregation translate into limited choices of subjects at university, vocational training courses and occupational opportunities for women. Nevertheless, female education and enrolment ratios at all levels expanded rapidly during the oil boom and women now represent more that 50 per cent of university students. While higher enrolment ratios and educational attainment among women normally lead to greater participation in the employment market, only approximately 6 per cent of economically active women are currently employed in the formal labour market, mostly as teachers, nurses, doctors or administrative staff. The abundance of oil wealth allowed for the import of expatriate workers and the 'luxury' of excluding half of the population from full participation in the labour market.

Girls' education remained under the supervision of the ulama until an incident in a girls' school in Mecca in March 2002 that caused the death of at least fifteen students. The Saudi press reported that several members of the Committee for the Promotion of Virtue

[18] Interviews with Saudi students, London, 12 February 2002.

[19] Yahya S. al-Hegdhy, 'The Role of the Ulama (Islamic scholars) in Establishing an Islamic Education System for Women in Saudi Arabia', PhD thesis, Florida State University, 1994, p. 69.

[20] Saudi Ministry of Education, *The Educational Policy in the Saudi Arabian Kingdom*, Riyadh: Ministry of Education, 1974, pp. 28–9.

and the Prevention of Vice (religious police) interfered with rescue efforts because the girls were not wearing the obligatory *abaya* (black cloak and scarf) and it would have been 'sinful to approach them'.[21] The religious police was blamed for intentionally obstructing the evacuation efforts resulting in an increased number of casualties.[22] The ensuing public criticism of the role of the religious police was unprecedented, yet calls for further investigation and prosecution were not pursued. The inquiry into the incident concluded that the education authorities had neglected safety measures that could have prevented the death of the girls. More significant, the Head of the General Presidency for Girls Education, Ali ibn Murshid Al Murshid, was dismissed and the Presidency merged with the Ministry of Education.

To what extent the merger will reduce the leverage of the ulama and give women greater freedom in educational choice remains to be seen. Women have become increasingly vocal, demanding greater occupational opportunities, and with deteriorating economic fortunes, often need to complement household incomes. The third National Dialogue Forum in June 2004 outlined steps to increase job and business opportunities for women[23] and in the same year more job categories were opened for women. However, in light of the criticism of the ulama, the regime often backtracks. Even issues such as physical education for girls remain a hotly debated issue. In January 2004 Grand Mufti Shaikh Abd al-Aziz Al ash-Shaikh reiterated that the 'mixing between men and women is totally forbidden under *shari'a* and highly punishable. It is [...] the root of every evil and catastrophe.'[24] While the economic and demographic pressures will continue to drive the educational reform agenda, the regime's hesitant reforms suggest that more freedom and participation for women in public life and employment may continue to be 'traded off' as a concession to the religious establishment.

[21] See Human Rights Watch, 'Saudi Arabia: Religious Police Role in School Fire Criticised', 15 March 2002. The Saudi paper *Okaz* ran a story entitled 'Preventing Life and Propagating Death', May 2002; Alain Gresh, 'Death in a Girls' School Changes National Tone', *Le Monde Diplomatique*, May 2002.

[22] *Arab News*, 14 March 2002.

[23] Fawziah Al Bakr, 'Woman and Education in Saudi Arabia: Struggle for a Change', paper presented at the School of Oriental and African Studies, University of London, 25 June 2004.

[24] 'Saudi Arabia Clerics Set Boundaries on Reforms', Reuters, 28 January 2004.

The Message

The content of the teachings remains heavily influenced by the Wahhabi worldview and the centrality of *tawhid* (declaration of the oneness of God). While there have been efforts to tone down the message and to include teachings about tolerance, previous generations have already been indoctrinated by the message propagated over the last decades. Teachers have gone through similar indoctrination and will need to be retrained. The following section will therefore briefly look at the content and tone of the message prior to the recent revisions.

Teachings about the 'others', other cultures, ideologies and religions, or about adherents of other Muslim schools of jurisprudence or sects, reflect the Wahhabi worldview: a world divided into believers and preservers of the true faith and the infidels. A defensive tone underlies the messages about the 'others', which projects itself in the demonisation of everything different: other Islamic schools of thought, religious or cultural practices. The defence of the purity of the Wahhabi message against the onslaught of foreign ideas and the slow encroachment of Westernisation is also one of the guiding principles. Education should: 'Promote a spirit of loyalty to Islamic law by denouncing any system or theory that conflicts with it and by behaving with honesty and in conformity with Islamic tenets', it should 'awaken the spirit of Islamic struggle, fight our enemies, restore our rights, resume our glory and fulfil the mission of Islam' and 'project the unity of the Muslim nation.'[25] As a Saudi woman observed, 'the mind of each of us has been programmed since school age [...] that values and good deeds are ours only and that others lack them. They taught us that every non-Muslim is an enemy of ours, and that the West is equivalent to decadence.'[26] The defensive tone and projections of fear are reinforced by the various punishments for deviancy spelled out in great detail in the textbooks. Particularly the *tawhid* textbooks, denounce practices such as worshipping graves, witchcraft, fortune telling, seeking treatment through

[25] Saudi Ministry of Education, *Educational Policy in the Kingdom of Saudi Arabia*, Riyadh: Ministry of Education, 1978, pp. 5–9.

[26] Sahr Muhammad Hatem, letters to the editor, 'Our Culture of Demagogy/Mob Engendered bin Laden, Zawahiri and their Likes', *Sharq al-Awsat*, 21 December 2001.

witchcraft, sorcery etc., and classify them into small sins and big sins. For instance, crying and raising the voice after someone's death and repeating good attributes of the deceased, a practice typical of the Hijaz, is considered one of the big sins.

It is not only the content of the message that impacts upon the students' mindset, but also what is missing in the teachings in terms of objective treatment of alternative ideas and ideologies, the lack of historical context or consideration for the diversity of religious interpretations prevalent in the Kingdom and the Islamic world. A study of grades 4 to 12 history textbooks revealed that 68.5 per cent of subjects covered Islamic themes, 30 per cent Saudi history and only 1.5 per cent global developments.[27] Contemporary events, key developments in the Arab world such as the rise of pan-Arabism, revolutions in neighbouring countries and their origins and ideologies, as well as the Iraqi invasion of Kuwait are either denounced or not discussed. Arab nationalism, for instance, is denounced as an atheist idea and, as Madawi Al-Rasheed observed, 'a conspiracy promoted by the West and Zionism to undermine the unity of Muslims. The use of the rhetoric of atheism undermines the legitimacy of a number of neighbouring Arab states.'[28]

History is taught with the intention to Saudise the population. Thus history books ignore the rich history and contributions of non-Najdi Saudi Arabia, especially the history and cultural achievements of the Hijaz, Asir and the Shi'a. Ibn Sa'ud's role in unifying the tribes and regions, in establishing order and security and, most important, in giving the conquered tribes the 'opportunity' to return to the right path of Islam is glorified while the bloody conflicts that accompanied the conquest of the Arabian peninsula are omitted. Similarly, the campaigns of Ibn Sa'ud are described as unification, not as conquest.[29] Denying and denouncing the diversity of religious and historical traditions may, however, have the opposite effect and exacerbate or perpetuate sectarian consciousness.

The lack of a proper discussion of the historical context tends to distort the message and cuts students off from the ability to critically

27 'Saudi Textbooks Lack Global Dimension', *Arab News*, 23 May 2003.

28 Madawi Al-Rasheed, *A History of Saudi Arabia*, Cambridge University Press, 2002, p. 191.

29 *Ta'rikh al-mamlaka al-'arabiyya al-sa'udiyya*, 6th grade, elementary, boys, 1999, p. 11; and Al-Rasheed, *A History of Saudi Arabia*, p. 193.

interpret the socio-political and economic interdependencies shaping current events. It also alienates them from the rich non-Wahhabi Islamic historical experience, in particular that of other schools of jurisprudence that prevailed in the Hijaz and other parts of the Arab and Islamic world, such as the more tolerant Shafi'i and Maliki schools. For instance, the concept of *al-walaa'* and *al-baraa'*[30] is often cited in relation to specific events during the Meccan wars, without providing proper reference to the historical context, 'so as to prove the disassociation between Muslims and non-Muslims is a universal and eternal condition set forth by God.'[31] Demonising the 'other' and different religious practices and behaviour creates

> social dynamics that desensitise and deconstruct society's sense of moral virtue and ethics. Especially, as far as theological constructs are concerned, the commission and social responses to acts of cruelty typically undergo long processes of indoctrination, acculturation, and socialisation that both facilitate the commission of such acts and mute or mitigate the sense of social outrage upon the commission of offensive behaviour.[32]

The demonisation of the 'other' also bears similarities with the practice of *takfir* (accusing fellow Muslims of being infidels), a practice that has been widely used by groups and individuals associated with Al-Qa'ida. Following the May and November 2003 bombings King Fahd warned that the practice of *takfir* causes inter-Islamic strife and division and called upon the scholars to 'tackle the strife caused by "takfir" that is rearing its head in some Islamic societies [...] there is nothing more dangerous than the "takfir".'[33]

30 *Al-walaa'* and *al-baraa'* refers to two opposing concepts which need to be understood in their historical and cultural specificity. These are 'loyal' or 'true' with the community versus 'disloyal' or 'untrue' to the community's objectives, but not necessarily in opposition to the objective. However, depending on the circumstances, *al-baraa'* can also refer to not taking sides or impartiality rather than opposition. In classic Arabic, *al-walaa'* commonly occurs in combination with *al-taa'ah*, obedience or compliance with command. Breaching this command results in severe consequences to the person.

31 Eleanor Doumato, 'Manning the Barricades: Islam According to Saudi Arabia's School Texts', *Middle East Journal*, 57, 2 (spring 2003), p. 239, from *Tawhid*, 10th grade, General Presidency.

32 Khaled Abou El Fadl, 'The Culture of Ugliness in Modern Islam and Re-engaging Morality', *UCLA Journal of Islamic and Near Eastern Law*, 33 (2002/03), p. 54.

33 'King Fahd Calls for Streamlining Fatwas', *Arab News*, 14 December.

Until 1993 Saudi schoolbooks referred to the Shi'a as *rafida* or rejectionists, a very derogatory term.[34] Reflecting mainstream Wahhabi ideology, Shi'a are blamed for believing in innovations (*bida*), forbidden by Islam, and are often referred to as '*mushrikeen*' (polytheists) or unbelievers, against whom it is a duty to lead jihad. One should not mix with the innovators, unless to advise them, as mixing with them could have a dangerous influence. A *tawhid* book of 1992 also mentioned that the ulama extend great efforts and use various means such as newspapers, magazines, radio broadcasts and Friday sermons to denounce the practice of *bida*, in order to raise awareness among Muslims of the importance of getting rid of the innovations and to suppress or destroy the innovators.[35] The same book also blamed countries of unbelievers for encouraging the innovators and for assisting them in tarnishing the image of religion.[36] These accusations were addressed towards the Islamic Republic of Iran, which until a thaw in relations between Iran and Saudi Arabia, was accused of fomenting unrest among the Saudi Shi'a population. While the term *rafida* was dropped from official schoolbooks it continues to be widely used in books distributed elsewhere.[37] Schoolbooks no longer attribute 'repugnant' or 'deviating' religious opinions to a particular sect or individual. Instead books refer to religious practices such as hitting of cheeks or any part of the body, a Shi'a practice during Ashura, as sinful and forbidden[38] and saint worship and grave cults as *shirk* (polytheism). Shi'a or other members from religious minorities are not allowed to teach religion in Saudi schools, and are thus forced to teach in private homes and using smuggled books. These private classes are often interrupted and dissolved by the authorities.[39]

Schoolbooks do not condone violence, the concept of jihad appears mainly in a defensive context.[40] They distinguish between three aspects of jihad: the spiritual or personal struggle, the striving against

[34] See, for instance, *Al-tawhid*, 3rd grade, secondary, Riyadh: Ministry of Education, 1992, pp. 79, 87, 93, 107.

[35] See, for instance, *ibid.*, p. 102.

[36] *Ibid.*, p. 107.

[37] Interview with Ali Al Ahmed, Director of Saudi Institute, McLean, United States, March 2002.

[38] Intermediate, 2nd grade (14 years).

[39] Interview with Ali Al Ahmed, March 2002.

[40] Doumato, 'Manning the Barricades', p. 235.

sin and sinful inclinations; the struggle against the enemy to be fought with weapons; and the struggle with the tongue (through speeches etc.). In one of the textbooks the description of jihad was followed by discussions of Islam as a religion of love and peace, highlighting the often contradictory messages of Saudi schoolbooks.[41] While some passages denounced Christians and Jews clearly as unbelievers, whom one should not greet with salutations of peace, not take as friends or against whom jihad should be waged, other passages stressed the peaceful nature of Islam.[42] Jews or a Jewish conspiracy were blamed for many historical events: they 'used the French revolution to attack religions' and are responsible for Marxism.[43] A Yemenite Jew, Abdullah bin Sabaa, was blamed for the split of the Muslim community into Shi'a and Sunni.[44] The close relationship between Jews and Americans was also highlighted in history books: 'Their [the Palestinians'] jihad would have succeeded if it had not been for the assistance of the American government at the side of the Jews, which demanded the British to allow the entry of more than 100,000 Jews to Palestine in one year.'[45] Combined with the current situation in Israel/Palestine, featuring prominently in the Saudi and Arab media, these historical distortions can easily fuel anti-Western sentiments and influence perceptions and attitudes towards foreigners residing in the Kingdom.

Another central element of the educational policy and the teaching method is 'developing [the student's] feeling of responsibility to understand his rights and duties [...] and planting in him the love of his country and loyalty to his rulers.'[46] Schoolbooks consistently

[41] *Al-hadith*, 2nd grade, intermediate (1st part), girls, p. 36 and *Al-tarbiyya al-wataniyya*, 3rd grade, secondary (1st part), boys, p. 27. Unless stated otherwise, references to Saudi textbooks refer to schoolbooks in circulation during the 2002 academic year and do not take into consideration the revisions made in 2003.

[42] See for instance, *Al-hadith*, 2nd grade, intermediate (1st part), girls, p. 36 and *Al-tarbiyya al-wataniyya*, 3rd grade, secondary (1st part), boys, p. 27.

[43] *Al-hadith*, 1st grade, secondary (2nd part), boys, p. 105.

[44] *Al-tawhid*, 3rd grade, intermediate (2nd part), girls, p. 102.

[45] *Ta'rikh al-mamlaka al-sa'udiyya*, 6th grade, elementary, boys, 1999 and *al-ta'rikh*, 3rd grade, intermediate (2nd part), girls, p. 88.

[46] Adel A. E. al-Sharaf, 'A Comparative Study of the Development of the Primary Stage of Religious Education in the State of Kuwait and the Kingdom of Saudi Arabia', PhD thesis, University of Sheffield, 1992.

emphasise obedience as an important duty of the citizen: 'Obey Allah and his Prophet and those with authority.' This obedience has several levels: obedience to the rulers, obedience to the teacher as well as to the head of family. Disobedience is equated with trying to create *fitna* (dissension),[47] an accusation also used to discredit and delegitimise critics of the regime. The ulama and *umara* (tribal shaikhs) are those charged with authority. While the ruler must uphold Islamic law, the ulama should support him, but only as long as he does follow Islamic law. Obedience to authority is contingent upon the latter's adherence to Islam: 'A Muslim should listen and obey [...] unless he is ordered not to obey God.'[48]

Fear and obedience are further reinforced by the teaching method, which places a heavy emphasis on rote learning and repetition. By suppressing questioning, creativity and initiative, the philosophy of teaching imports passivity and dependence, an *a priori* respect for authority and an unquestioning attitude. Interaction between the teacher and his/her students is limited, debate often absent, as the sources of knowledge, the *Qur'an* and *Sunna*, are considered inviolable. As Prince Khaled al-Faisal, Governor of Asir and President of the Foundation for Arab Thought expressed it: 'We accustom our children not to know how to engage in dialogue, but to obey blindly. [...] Our educational system is sterile, because we do not make room for experience. We should not fear to take from the West what can be useful for us, as it did from us in the past.'[49]

The Context

Contextual factors, such as teacher personality, attitudes and values, prevailing classroom dynamics, social background or place of residence heavily influence, if not determine, the way the message is received and interpreted. There is likely to be a different experience between students in public and private schools and between the very conservative areas of the Najd and the more open coastal cities of the Hijaz or the Eastern Province. The contradictory messages leave a

[47] *Al-hadith*, 2nd grade, intermediate, boys, p. 23 and *Al-hadith*, 1st grade, secondary (1st part), boys, p. 58.
[48] *Al-tawhid wa al-hadith wa al-fiqh wa al-tawhid*, 6th grade, elementary (2nd part), boys, p. 23, Riyadh: Ministry of Education, 1999.
[49] *Arab News*, 3 December 2003.

wide margin of interpretation, thus teachers' and mosque preachers' attitudes play an instrumental role in shaping the mindset of the young generation.

Exposure to sermons in the mosques or to opposition discourse is equally important. Even government-paid and sanctioned religious authorities expressed often very parochial and anti-Western sentiments. Such as the former Grand Mufti, Shaikh Ibn Baz, in relation to the presence of expatriates:

> It is not permissible to employ a non-Muslim servant, male or female, nor a non-Muslim driver, nor a non-Muslim labourer in the Arabian Gulf, because the Prophet, peace be upon him, ordered the removal of all Jews and Christians from it, and he ordered that none should remain in it except Muslims [...]. This is because bringing male and female disbelievers is a danger to the Muslims, their beliefs, their morals, and the upbringing of their children, so it should be forbidden.[50]

This *fatwa* from the highest official religious authority bears some resemblance, not in means but in ends, to the radical ideologies espoused by Al-Qa'ida or other groups opposed to the presence of 'infidels' on Arabia's holy soil. Although resort to violence and rebellion against the rulers is not part of the curriculum, the duty to disobey a ruler that has departed the right path is very clearly articulated in opposition discourse: Muslim rulers have, through their military connections and political alignments become 'puppets' of the West and its Zionist allies and thus became like the unbelievers. For the most radical, the Al Sa'ud, by inviting 'infidel' forces to defend the 'Holy Land of Islam', have thus become like foreign occupiers and Muslims have the duty to rise up, engage in a jihad and rectify the situation.[51]

In its efforts to combat 'deviant' thinking, the government is trying to encourage more moderate thinking. At the opening session of the Islamic Fiqh Academy in Mecca in December 2003 King Fahd called upon the religious scholars to 'highlight the dangers which

[50] Quoting hadith Muslim no. 1767, Abu Dawud no. 3030 and At Tirmithi nos 1606/1607, 'Verily, I will expel the Jews and Christians from the Arabian Peninsula, until I leave none but Muslims', from *Fatawa Islamiyah: Islamic Verdicts*, vol. 1, Riyadh: Darussalam, 2001, p. 260.

[51] Quintan Wiktorowicz, 'The New Global Threat: Transnational Salafis and Jihad', *Middle East Policy*, VIII, 4 (December 2001), p. 27.

extremism poses to Muslim faith and conduct', to 'correct the flaws in the thinking of some Muslims through dialogue in seminars, conferences and via the media' and to use religious arguments to annul 'aberrant' *fatawa* that legitimised militancy or suicide bombings.[52] Similarly, Shaik Saleh bin Abd al-Aziz Al ash-Shaikh, Minister for Islamic Affairs, Endowments, Guidance and Call proclaimed,

> reviling and abusing others is un-Islamic and Prophet Muhammad (PBUH) has prohibited it. Dialogue is the best way for dealing with those whose ideas and convictions are different from ours and there are Islamic schools of thought that are within the parameters of Sunnah and general consensus, and there are others like Shi'ism, which are outside the Sunnah and consensus, but reviling them is irreligious and hence undesirable.[53]

Learning experiences of the individual are also continually modified by the impact of the global information flow. Access to foreign sources of media through travel and satellite television has opened new channels of information circumventing the tightly controlled Saudi media. While officially illegal, satellite dishes are widespread and in 1998 the government legalised the use of the internet. However, while it has invested heavily in blocking 'objectionable' web sites ranging from politics to pornography, fewer efforts have been made to block extremist Islamic sites.[54] Chat rooms have become popular outlets for political discontent and debate. Issues such as 9/11, the war in Afghanistan, the Palestinian *intifada* and the occupation of Iraq feature prominently in the discussions online.

According to a survey, Saudi children spend an average of 3.1 hours a day on weekdays and 4.9 hours at the weekend watching TV, particularly popular among children being the Disney channel,[55] a trend with serious implications for the way children perceive the gap between what they are taught in school, the heavy stress on upholding morality and tradition, and TV reality exposing them to the Western 'corruption of the minds'. Some observers have referred to this discrepancy as social or cultural dissonance or schizophrenia.

[52] 'King Fahd Calls for Streamlining Fatwas', *Arab News*, 14 December 2003.
[53] 'Riyadh project to eliminate extremism', *Gulf News*, 24 September 2003.
[54] Human Rights Watch Report, 'Saudi Arabia', 2002.
[55] The survey was conducted by Merlin, an American consumer research firm, involved 800 Saudi children in the 5–12 age group and 400 parents. *Arab News*, 6 January 2004.

There are limited outlets for social frustrations for the young generation as entertainment remains strictly controlled and segregated. Reports of drug and alcohol abuse have augmented and feature regularly in the Saudi media. A survey of more than 2,000 students in Jeddah, aged 13 to 25 revealed that 65 per cent of boys and 72 per cent of girls showed symptoms of depression, 7 per cent of girls admitted that they had attempted suicide (twice the rate of boys), drug use was nearly 5 per cent for both sexes, as was the rate of alcoholism.[56]

Education as a Foreign Policy Tool

Similar to the Kingdom's education policy, its self-proclaimed foreign policy role emphasises the importance of 'Islamic solidarity in the face of opposing ideological currents' and 'to combat all ideas, currents, and ideologies that contradict the Islamic creed.' It stresses the country's 'unique role in leading the Islamic world. This role is the result of the Kingdom having been entrusted by Allah with the protection of Islamic Holy sites, their custody and supervision, and on the whole of the Islamic world acknowledging this important status.'[57] Every citizen has a duty to participate in spreading the message.[58]

Religious and political power projections, i.e. the rivalry for leadership of the Muslim world, have often provided the rationale for the Kingdom's support of missionary activities abroad while the massive influx of petrodollars provided the pecuniary means. In the 1950s and 1960s efforts were aimed at containing the influence of Arab nationalism, Nasser's popularity and to ward off military coups that plagued most of Saudi Arabia's neighbours. Competing Islamic

[56] Lawrence Wright, 'The Kingdom of Silence', *The New Yorker*, 5 January 2004.

[57] Abdullah Saud 'Al-Gabba', *As-siyasa As-sa'udiyya Al-kharijiyya* (the Saudi Foreign Policy), 1407, p. 90.

[58] It can been argued, however, that this Islamic *motif* has been instrumental at least as much as, if not more than, a genuine determinant in its own right: see James Piscatori, 'Islamic Values and National Interest: the Foreign Policy of Saudi Arabia' in Adeed Dawisha (ed.), *Islam in Foreign Policy*, London: Cambridge University Press, 1983, pp. 33–53. Such a view is compatible with some of the evidence presented below. For the broader context of Saudi foreign policy, see the chapter by Nonneman in this volume.

organisations were set up, each claiming leadership of the Muslim world and denouncing the 'others' as having strayed from the right path, the Islamic University in Medina as a counterweight to Al-Azhar in 1961, the Muslim World League in 1962 followed by the World Assembly of Muslim Youth in 1972. After the 1979 Iranian revolution, the Islamic Republic became the main adversary and competitor. Contesting the very legitimacy of monarchical rule, the Iranian revolutionary message, broadcast throughout the Muslim world via tapes and radio, posed a direct threat to the House of Sa'ud. Iran also tried to foment unrest amongst the Saudi Shi'a community in the Eastern Province. The strong anti-Shi'a messages in the Saudi textbooks reinforced the suspicion of the Shi'a as a potential fifth column and thereby also helped to prevent the revolutionary message from spilling over to discontented Sunni. The competitive fervour was toned down somewhat in the aftermath of the 1990 Gulf War, in line with the general rapprochement between Saudi Arabia and Iran and a more conciliatory stance of the Saudi Shi'a opposition.

For many years the Saudi regime was able, by exporting the message and its messengers, to contain, control and divert the attention of potential opponents away from the Kingdom, its 'unholy alliance' with the West and allegations of corruption and profligacy. This practice of 'exporting' potential dissenters began to backfire when many of the so-called 'Arab Afghans' returned to the Kingdom after the Soviet withdrawal from Afghanistan. The return of the 'Arab Afghans' to the Kingdom coincided with the Iraqi occupation of Kuwait and the ruling family's decision to invite the 'infidels' to defend the Kingdom. The Saudi regime and its Western allies thus became the new focus of criticism and the new target against which jihad should be waged.

The Kingdom's involvement in the educational sphere abroad ranges from building and funding mosques, Islamic cultural centres, schools and universities, the provision of generous scholarships for study in Islamic institutions, assistance to perform the *hajj* (pilgrimage to Mecca), to the diffusion of the Qur'an in local languages and religious textbooks as well as the publication and distribution of works of Islamist intellectuals. Migrant workers who often spend extended periods in Saudi Arabia and whose children often attend

Saudi schools are also 'carriers' of the religious message back to their own country. Schools and mosque centres funded by the government, charities or individuals recruited their students from all over the globe and trained a new generation of mosque leaders and clerics who, once returned to their countries, opened schools or religious centres especially in rural areas where unemployment is high and economic development lacking, factors that facilitate the spread of the Wahhabi-inspired worldview from Morocco to Central Asia, from Bosnia and elsewhere in Europe to parts of Africa and Asia.

Activities abroad, similar to the message pervading the schoolbooks, reflect the preoccupation with the onslaught of 'false ideologies', the encroaching Westernisation and secularisation of the Muslim world. To further the 'Islamisation of knowledge' the Kingdom, for instance, sponsored events such as the First World Conference on Muslim Education in 1977 to 'Islamise knowledge and to make it viable for the present and future development of Islamic scholarship leading to the reconstruction of an Islamic worldview.' The conference *inter alia* recommended the establishment of an International Islamic School of Literary Criticism that would 'scrutinise alien values inculcated in Muslims by the study of foreign literature.' The thinking of the conference was to contain the 'unchecked onslaught on Islam of the secularist and anti-faith theories' emanating from the West.[59]

The puritan Wahhabi message is alien to the Islam prevalent in most of the countries to which the message is exported, hence the influx of money and Arab missionaries often caused friction with the local religious authorities and community leaders. While the message may not have taken root among mainstream Muslims in many countries, it did resonate among those groups or individuals in opposition to the authorities and thereby often fuelled latent tensions. Dagestani authorities, for instance, have accused the Wahhabis and their financiers in the Gulf of fomenting unrest and launching a jihad.[60] Similarly Uzbek officials have blamed Pakistan and Saudi-financed *madrasas* (religious schools) for fuelling unrest, particularly

[59] Ghulam Nabi Saqeb, 'The Islamisation of Education since the 1977 Makkah Education Conference', *Muslim Education Quarterly*, 18, 1 (2000), p. 41.

[60] Robert Ware, 'Why Wahhabism went wrong in Dagestan', *The Analyst*, September 2000.

in the Fergana Valley. The local authorities and religious leaders often use the term 'Wahhabi' in a derogative manner to connote its external, i.e. Saudi, origin, and for all who oppose its tight control on Islam.[61] The requirement of women to veil completely (often including face veil) is alien to societies who under the Soviet government had become largely secularised. There are many reports from Central Asia, the Balkans and the Arab world that schools funded by Saudi charities or the Saudi government require female students to wear the veil and that Saudi Arabia is paying for the religious garb.[62]

It is necessary to differentiate between those schools that provide education and religious teachings and those that use religion to incite hatred towards others and that have been used by some individuals or groupings for political aims. Education in *madrasas* has been the main method of teaching throughout the Islamic world for many centuries. It continues to provide many students, who otherwise would not have had the opportunity, with the means to read and write.[63] Some of the *madrasas* at the Pakistan/Afghanistan border, that received funding from Saudi Arabia and other Muslim states, differ from traditional *madrasas*. Students were particularly trained and ideologically indoctrinated to become political tools in the conflict in Afghanistan, against the Hindus in Kashmir or in other locations where Muslim interests were perceived to be threatened.[64] Saudis constituted the largest national grouping of Arab fighters thus accelerating the spread of Wahhabi thought.[65] These schools provided religious and military training that heavily influenced the religious understandings of thousands of volunteers from all over the world, particularly in Egypt and Algeria. In the aftermath of 9/11 many countries in which these schools and religious institutions are located have become more alert and have taken precautionary measures while Saudi authorities have instituted controls on funding. However, much remains to be done to create alternatives and job opportunities for the disadvantaged and disenfranchised 're-

[61] 'The Crusade against the Wahhabis', *The Economist*, 7 April 1998, p. 36.

[62] Interviews in various Arab countries with students and teachers, 2002.

[63] This is true also in Pakistan, for instance, where the illiteracy rate, according to the *UNESCO Statistical Yearbook 1998/1999*, remained above 60 per cent.

[64] Jessica Stern, 'Pakistan's Jihad Culture', *Foreign Affairs*, December 2000.

[65] Quintan Wiktorowicz, 'The New Global Threat: Transnational Salafis and Jihad', p. 23.

cruits' in order to address the underlying political and economic dynamics.

Playing with the Future of the Young Generation

In 1979, after the first serious Islamist challenge to the Al Sa'ud regime, the Kingdom possessed the means to pay for the economic 'side-effects' of its concessions to conservative religious forces: the heavy emphasis on religious education and rote teaching methods. Even during the mid-1980s when oil revenues plummeted, funds for religious institutions kept flowing generously, domestically as well as internationally. However, with revenues to be shared amongst a rapidly growing population, the price for this trade-off is increasingly borne by the young generation. Approximately 60 per cent of the population is below the age of twenty, and more than 100,000 young Saudis enter the job market every year, while unemployment estimates range between 10 and 30 per cent.[66]

Saudi Arabia's unemployment problem and the lack of skilled employees, necessitating the presence of a large expatriate community, can partly be attributed to the Kingdom's educational policies including its exclusion of half of the population from participating fully in the workforce. The development of the educational system in the 1970s emphasised quantitative expansion and physical infrastructural development over qualitative improvements.[67] As a consequence, there is a huge gap between the outputs of the education system and the requirements of the domestic labour market. Between 1995 and 1999 only 10,000 out of 120,000 students graduating from Saudi universities had a degree in technical subjects, accounting for only 2 per cent of the total number of Saudis entering the job market.[68] The Sixth Development Plan (1990–5) estimated that 41.6 per cent of Saudis complete their education before reaching secondary schools and that 27.9 per cent of the new entrants to the labour market are dropouts from elementary and adult vocational

[66] In 1999 the total population was estimated at 21.4 million (including 5.7 million non-Saudis) and is expected to increase to 29.7 million by 2020 (*Seventh Development Plan*, Ministry of Planning, p. 160).

[67] See also Delwin Roy, 'Saudi Arabian Education: Development Policy', *Middle Eastern Studies*, 28, 3 (July 1992), pp. 477–508.

[68] 'People Pressure', *The Economist*, 21 March 2002.

training programmes.[69] The products of the Saudi education system, particularly graduates from religious universities or those with a degree in social sciences and humanities, are often ill-equipped to perform in a competitive environment. Until the late 1980s the governmental apparatus absorbed most of the graduates from foreign, secular and religious institutions, often regardless of actual qualifications and capabilities engendering the expectation that once graduated or once leaving school, a job was secure. Facing mobility closure, expectations of particularly the younger generation tend to remain at a level based on what the older generation was accustomed to. As the state can no longer provide positions for all, and once the differences in levels of education start to reflect more in the recruitment practices, this could lead to a significant increase in the levels of resentment and feelings of marginalisation that are already in evidence, particularly among those with a traditional educational background.

Demographic and economic pressures provide the main driver for reforming the education system and teaching methods. The government has moved towards emphasising qualitative improvements and continues to give education a high priority. Education is the only category of civilian expenditure that has not suffered from significant budgetary cuts in the last couple of years and whose share in the total government budget has actually increased. The focus of the 2004 budget is on education and employment creation and envisages the funding of new universities, colleges, vocational training centres, a professional military training centre and allocations for the construction of new schools for boys and girls.[70] Several new technical and vocational institutes have been opened to attract Saudi students to support the Saudisation policies. Attendance, however, is below expectations as the prestige and tradition associated with government positions contribute to the failure to attract students into the technical and vocational streams in the required numbers.

Combating 'Deviant Thinking': The Challenge of Reform

As mentioned, reform efforts in Saudi Arabia predate 9/11. In March 2002 the Saudi Minister of Education stated that the first

[69] *Sixth Development Plan*, Ministry of Planning, p. 179.

[70] *Al-Riyadh*, 23 December 2003 and *Arab News*, 16 December 2003. The 2004 budget allocates SR63.65 (US $16.97) billion for general education, higher education and manpower training, an increase of SR 6.2 bn on the previous year.

phase of a two-phased educational development plan that 'focused on ridding books of the unnecessary materials and correcting errors' had already been completed while the second phase aimed at encouraging creative thinking, self-learning and providing students with the skills and materials necessary in modern life was ongoing.[71] For the 2003/04 academic year the Education Ministry announced the revision of thirty-two textbooks including *tawhid* and history books and the continuation of efforts to revise controversial chapters.

While there is widespread consensus that the education system has to be reformed to better cater to the demands of the employment market, reform initiatives so far have largely shied away from controversial issues such as reducing the overall percentage of religious education. In introducing the reforms, Prince Sultan, chair of a committee composed of prominent scholars for reviewing the education system, emphasised that the 'reforms aim to strengthen morality, flexibility, openness to dialogue and respect of other opinions while retaining religious subjects as the basis of our education system.'[72] The recommendations of the National Dialogue Forum on 'Excess and Moderation: A Thorough Review', held at the end of 2003, outline a few key elements that could provide a roadmap for reforming the education system. In a rare and very recent official acknowledgement of the diversity of religious interpretations, the Forum brought together religious leaders from various Islamic schools of thoughts, the Shi'a, Isma'ili and Sufi as well as official ulama and several Islamist activists. The Forum discussed the effect of religious curricula, the role of teachers and the social milieu in achieving moderation, and the role of education in bringing about sound ways of thinking and creating a balanced personality. Its recommendations also included a call to modernise the religious message to conform with contemporary developments and encouraged the young generation to engage in dialogue 'by opening the doors to responsible free speech'. Suggestions were also made to develop

[71] 'Saudis Will Not Allow Changes Imposed on National Curricula', *Gulf News* (Dubai), 7 March 2002.

[72] 'Education System Reform to Promote Moderation: Sultan'. Members include the chairman of the *Shoura* Council, Minister of Justice, Islamic Affairs, Education, Higher Education, Water and Electricity, Secretary-General of the Muslim World League and prominent academics. *Arab News*, 5 December 2003 and 15 February 2004.

educational programmes for spreading the spirit of tolerance and moderation, to develop a spirit of innovation and to support youth programmes and youth centres.[73]

There are strong forces that would prefer a policy of withdrawal and stagnation, while projecting hostility and rejection to changes considered as 'imposed' from outside as part of a conspiracy against Islam. The recommendations, albeit in their infancy and far from being translated into concrete measures, have already aroused strong condemnation. In January 2004 156 Saudi religious scholars and university professors issued a warning against changing the school curriculum fearing that it would take 'the Kingdom along the path of infidels': 'any omission or mutilation of what was written by the Islamic scholars [...] contradicts the national unity the state is calling for, as this unity is based on our religious creed.'[74] They called on teachers and parents to oppose reform, accused the government of conceding to American pressure and proclaimed that 'defence of our curriculum is a defence of our existence and identity.'[75] Many observers caution that imposing change from the outside would backfire as the religious opposition may view any revision of the curriculum as a sign of weakness on the part of the rulers and another sign of its subservience to America.[76] Saudi officials vehemently deny that curriculum changes are due to external pressure, some also keep denying any link between education and extremism. At the beginning of 2004 Prince Nayif, for instance, declared: 'Most people in the Islamic world have studied the same curriculum but their thoughts and ideas have not been corrupted like this small number of terrorists who were the product of deviant thoughts, alien to Islam.'[77]

One of the main dilemmas confronting the Al Sa'ud in moving the reform agenda forward is their heavy reliance on the conser-

[73] 'Saudi Arabia: Text of Final Communiqué and Recommendations of the Second National Intellectual Dialogue', *Middle East Economic Survey*, XLVII, 2, 12 January 2004.

[74] Reuters, 3 January 2004. The warning was *inter alia* signed by Safar al-Hawali, a prominent dissident cleric and Shaikh Abdullah bin Jibrin, a member of the Senior Council of Ulama.

[75] *The Economist*, 24 January 2004, p. 42.

[76] *Mideast Mirror*, 16 October 2001, p. 13 from *al-Rai*. Interview with Sa'd al-Faqih, Movement of Islamic Reform in Arabia (MIRA) in London, February 2002.

[77] 'Educational Reform not Under Foreign Pressure', *Arab News*, 22 January 2004.

vative religious establishment in fighting 'deviant' ideas and dissenters, the very forces that obstruct the social, cultural and economic reforms that Saudi Arabia needs to confront to deal with today's economic and social realities and aspirations of the public at large. In the wake of the 2003 bombings, the ulama have been instrumental in persuading several scholars to recant and withdraw controversial fatawa, and have relied on their support in removing several hundred, some even claim thousand, clerics for inciting and preaching intolerance and in initiating training or 're-education' in more moderate religious interpretations.

In the 'war of ideas', it is the young generation's future that is at stake. Cosmetic changes and cutting out the most 'offensive' parts of the textbooks are not enough to deal with the multiplicity of challenges facing the Kingdom. A concerted effort of structural economic reforms combined with a progressive opening of political and social space is required. Educational reform that stops short of encouraging debate, critical thinking and a reduction of the time dedicated to religious studies will not be able to address the economic and social malaise of the young generation. Continuing the parochial, even if toned down, Wahhabi message while preventing the articulation of different Islamic interpretations, will also not be able to bridge the sectarian and regional divisions. The impact of changes to the content of teachings will take years if not generations to take effect and will not only necessitate retraining of teachers but also the introduction of a methodology of teaching that allows for tolerance and understanding of the 'others'. The legacy of years of indoctrination, suppression of any creative and innovative spirit and the fear of change instilled into the minds of generations may prove to be the main obstacles to change.

Part II. POLITICAL ECONOMY

SAUDI ARABIA'S ECONOMY: THE CHALLENGE OF REFORM

*Monica Malik and Tim Niblock**

The Dynamics of Economic Reform since 2000 and the Creation of New Administrative Structures

The paradox of recent measures towards economic reform in Saudi Arabia is that they have been put forward at a time when the immediate financial pressures are less than they had been. Higher oil prices since 2000, and especially since the beginning of 2003, have meant that the immediate financial imperative driving economic reform—the need to reduce costs so as to balance the budget—has been weakened. With oil prices reaching $55 dollars per barrel for Brent crude in 2004, against a low point of $10 dollars per barrel in 1998, the Saudi government has had the resources to stave off structural reform. Growth in real GDP rose to 7.2 per cent in 2003, and is expected to have achieved a similar level in 2004.[1] Yet it has been precisely over this period that the pace of reform has quickened. And while there is a significant prospect of these reforms changing the relationship between the Saudi state, the private sector and the wider society, this may not be sufficient to resolve the underlying problems.

A number of reasons may be put forward as to why reform has advanced just when the immediate financial pressures have eased. First, domestic political unrest has become more open and explicit,

* Some of the material in this chapter is drawn from the forthcoming book by Tim Niblock, *Saudi Arabia: Power, Legitimacy and Survival*, London: Routledge, 2006.

[1] International Monetary Fund, 'IMF Concludes 2004 Article IV Consultation with Saudi Arabia', Public Information Notice no. 05/3, 12 January 2005.

such that the government has felt impelled to re-shape its policies. Although the government may be earning more from oil revenues, the problems facing the population have not necessarily eased. Key factors behind the growing political discontent in the country are unemployment levels, which have continued to rise—in part through the high population growth—and living standards, which have fallen.

Second, since 9/11 Saudi Arabia has been subject to much greater international pressure, especially since elements in the United States have suspected Saudi Arabia's domestic conditions of feeding the forces of international terrorism. The domestic and international pressures relate as much to political as to economic issues, yet there is a rationale for prioritising economic reform since, for the Saudi government, it is less controversial and problematic, and indeed to some extent provides a cover for the failure to pursue radical political reform.

Of critical importance in the new dynamic towards economic reform has been Saudi Arabia's application for membership of the World Trade Organisation (WTO). In 2005 Saudi Arabia was still one of the largest economies operating outside the WTO. Although the Saudi Arabian government entered into negotiations in 1996, the critical issues impeding membership did not begin to be seriously addressed until 2002. The issue of WTO membership has in practice become one of the main drivers of economic reform in the Kingdom and to some extent has been used by those intent on reform to provide a rationale for forcing the pace. Indeed many of the legal changes discussed in the next section stem directly from the need to satisfy WTO conditions of membership. Admission to the WTO would certainly ensure greater transparency in the trade regime, and make the economic environment more accommodating to non-resident business.

The need to undertake economic reform has also led to the creation of new administrative structures to carry the process forward. The development of these new institutions began in August 1999 with the creation of the Supreme Economic Council (SEC), which was given responsibility for evaluating economic, industrial, agricultural and labour policies so as to assess their effectiveness. The focus of the SEC has been on opening up Saudi markets and attracting investment.

Furthermore, in 2000 a series of organisations were created covering economic policy in areas that were critical to the process of economic reform. In January the Supreme Council for Petroleum and Minerals (SCPM) was established, with responsibility for policy-making on the exploitation of the Kingdom's hydrocarbon resources. The Council was to give particular attention to the attraction of international investment in this field, starting with the natural gas sector. In April 2000 the establishment of the Supreme Council of Tourism (SCT) was announced, with responsibility for fostering tourism and encouraging investment in this sector. The notion that the Kingdom should actively encourage both tourism in different parts of the country and international investment in new projects, rather than simply respond to the annual flood of pilgrims to the holy places, marked a significant departure. In September 2003 the Secretary-General of the SCT announced a twenty year plan for the development of tourism, which envisaged the employment in tourism of as many as 2.3 million Saudis by 2020.[2] April 2000 also saw the establishment of the Saudi Arabian General Investment Authority (SAGIA), which was given the task of attracting foreign investment and serving the interests of the business community as a 'one-stop shop' for licences, permits and other administrative procedures relevant to business. SAGIA was to work closely with the SEC and the SCT, playing a mediating role between investors and the government.

Reforming the Legal Framework to Encourage Foreign Investment

Central to the government's plans for economic reform—and to influencing the perceptions of international financial institutions concerned about the potential for sustainable development in Saudi Arabia—have been measures designed to attract foreign investment, which is seen as necessary if the needs of Saudi Arabia's rapidly rising population and workforce are to be met. The law on foreign direct investment provides the main framework for governmental attempts to boost foreign investment, but legal changes affecting taxation, capital markets, intellectual property rights and insurance are also important.

The Law on Foreign Direct Investment

Prior to April 2000 foreign investment was only permitted in the Kingdom if it fulfilled three conditions: undertakings had to be 'de-

[2] The plan was announced during the annual meeting of the governors of the IMF, September 2003.

velopment projects'; investments had to generate technology transfer; and there had to be a Saudi partner with at least 25 per cent equity. Applications for licences tended to take a long time, except for those in which the government was a partner. Furthermore, foreign companies and individuals, apart from other GCC (Gulf Cooperation Council) citizens, could not own land or engage in internal trading and distribution activities.

The new law was endorsed by the Council of Ministers in April 2000 and became effective the following June.[3] A framework for future legislative and regulatory activities was established by the law, intended to enhance the country's investment climate and attract capital. Critical elements of the new law, and of the executive rules of the law which were enacted at the same time, were:

- Companies could now be 100 per cent foreign owned (except in certain specified sectors), and foreign and Saudi companies were to be treated on an equal basis. Previously, the Foreign Capital Investment Committee had usually demanded 51 per cent Saudi ownership. Under the new law, foreign companies could apply for low-cost loans from the Saudi Industrial Development Fund (SIDF), on the same terms as Saudi companies, and these could cover up to 50 per cent of a venture.
- Foreign companies were now allowed to own land for licensed activities and for housing employees. Previously, the Saudi partner had been required to hold the land.

However, perhaps most significant of all was the role given to SAGIA as a facilitator for foreign investment, speeding up investment decisions and reducing bureaucracy. SAGIA was mandated under the new law to make a decision on all investment applications within thirty days, and in the event of failing to meet that deadline was required to issue the licence forthwith. Moreover, explicit directions were given regarding the basis on which licences were to be issued, with investment permitted in all areas except those specified on a 'negative list'. Minimum investments required for the issue of licences were also specified: SR 25 million for agricultural projects; SR 5 million for industrial projects; and SR 2 million for service projects.

[3] Foreign Direct Investment Law 2000, accessed at the SAGIA website at www.sagia.gov.sa/innerpage.asp?ContentID, 12 December 2004.

Guarantees against the full or partial confiscation of investments were also made more explicit than they had been, as were the arrangements for foreign investors to repatriate funds and transfer money so as to fulfil contractual obligations. For the first time, foreign companies were given authority to act as sponsors for non-Saudi staff.

As a corollary to the Foreign Direct Investment Law, the Council of Ministers enacted a Real Estate Law later the same year.[4] The law, which was sub-titled 'The System of Real Estate Ownership and Investment of Non-Saudis', gave non-Saudis the right to own real estate for their private residence.

Tax reform

Attracting more foreign investment also required changes to the taxation levied on such investment. Prior to 2000 the overall rate of corporate tax for foreign investors stood at 45 per cent. In the light of the low rates of corporate tax in the smaller states of the Gulf, this acted as a strong disincentive for foreign investors. Moreover, the comparison with tax regulations covering Saudi companies—an obligation to pay the 2.5 per cent *zakat* contribution, which even in practice was not rigorously or consistently enforced—emphasised the disadvantage to foreign investors.

In 2000 the overall rate for foreign investors was reduced to 30 per cent, and with the introduction of a new Corporate Tax Law in July 2004 the rate was reduced further to 20 per cent.[5] However, for investments in the hydrocarbons sectors a higher rate was maintained: 30 per cent in natural gas investment activities, and 85 per cent in oil and hydrocarbons production. In practice foreign investors could still only enter the latter field in conjunction with Aramco.

Although the taxation changes improved the environment for investors, the level of taxation on foreign businesses was still substantially more than in other Gulf countries. In the UAE and Bahrain, for example, no corporate tax is levied. Therefore, the decision to reduce corporate tax was unlikely to lead investors to shift investment from the smaller Gulf states to Saudi Arabia. Consequently,

[4] Real Estate Law 2000, accessed at the SAGIA website at www.sagia.gov.sa/innerpage.asp?ContentID, 20 December 2004.

[5] Corporate Tax Law 2004, accessed at the SAGIA website at www.sagia.gov.sa/innerpage.asp?ContentID, 27 December 2004

there was some danger that it would cut the government's non-oil income without necessarily leading to a major boost in foreign investment. Nonetheless, the new law did clarify the regulations and procedures with regard to tax, and as such could be expected to increase confidence among potential investors.

Regulating the capital markets

Foreign investment can also be conceived in terms of returning back to the Kingdom investments currently held outside the country by Saudi citizens themselves. The reform of the capital markets was intended to encourage such a capital movement and to encourage Saudis with money to invest to look to domestic rather than foreign investment. It has been estimated that in 2004 Saudi citizens held some $600 billion in holdings outside the country (with some estimates putting the figure as high as $1 trillion).

Prior to the adoption by the Council of Ministers of the Capital Markets Law in June 2003,[6] Saudi Arabia did not have a stock exchange. It had been possible to trade shares through the national securities depository centre, but there was no regulatory framework facilitating such trading or protecting the interests of investors. The Law formally established the Saudi Arabian Stock Exchange (SASE), whose activities were to be regulated by a Saudi Arabian Securities and Exchange Commission. The latter, now named the Capital Markets Authority, was duly set up in June 2004. It was made responsible for organising the capital market, protecting investors from unfair practices, achieving efficiency and transparency in securities transactions, and developing and monitoring all aspects of the trade in securities.[7] Trading in the Saudi Arabian Stock Exchange was limited to GCC nationals, but non-GCC nationals could participate through investing in mutual funds offered by Saudi Arabian banks.

With a well-regulated market, it was believed that capitalisation would increase. It would be easier to float companies, who would in turn have more incentive to gain a listing on the stock market. They would also benefit from being able to issue corporate bonds. Inter-

6 Capital Markets Law 2003, accessed at the SAGIA website at www.sagia.gov.sa/innerpage.asp?ContentID, 27 December 2004.

7 See the home page of the Capital Markets Authority at www.cma.org.sa, accessed 22 January 2005.

national banks would also be able to win licences for investment banking in the country. However, these benefits might not come quickly. Even with the full implementation of the law, Saudi Arabia's capital markets will remain weak. A range of institutions are needed if a capital market is to constitute an effective financial instrument, channelling funds from those who wish to invest and putting it in the hands of those who are developing economic projects. The potential impact of the Saudi Arabian Stock Exchange is limited by the absence of investment banks, independent brokerage firms, asset management firms etc, and by the inadequacy of venture capital.[8] At the end of 2004, there were still only 71 companies listed on the Saudi stock exchange, and in some sectors only one company was represented.

Nonetheless there was a marked increase in share dealings in 2002–3, even before the detailed procedures of the new law had become effective. The value of share dealings grew approximately three-fold over the period between the end of December 2002 and the end of December 2004.[9]

Intellectual property rights

Foreign investors need to know that they are operating in a market where copyrights on their products are respected. In June 2003 the Council of Ministers approved a new Copyright Law,[10] replacing the previous 1990 law. The 2003 law, which came into effect six months after publication in the official gazette, protected intellectual property rights in the fields of literature, arts and sciences, computer programmes, audio recordings and visual displays. The legal change was consistent with the requirements of the WTO's Agreement on Trade Related Aspects of Intellectual Property Rights (TRIPS).

[8] See Khan Zahid, 'Investment Challenges Facing Oil-Rich MENA Countries: The Case of Saudi Arabia', paper presented to the OECD conference Mobilising Investment for Development in the Middle East and North Africa Region, Istanbul, 11–12 February 2004.

[9] Details of the rise and fall of total share dealings on the Saudi Arabian Stock Exchange can be found at www.ameinfo.com.financial_markets/Saudi_Arabia. The information given here was accessed 31 December 2004.

[10] Copyright Law 2003, accessed at the SAGIA website at www.sagia.gov.sa/innerpage.asp?ContentID, 27 December 2004.

However, there remain doubts as to whether the Saudi government will enforce the law effectively enough. In 1995 Saudi Arabia was placed on the US's 301 Priority Watch List, and at the time of writing the country remains on the list despite the new law. The List comprises the countries which, in the view of the US Trade Representative, 'do not provide an adequate level of Intellectual Property Rights protection or enforcement' and are pursuing 'the most onerous or egregious policies that have an adverse impact on US right holders.'[11]

A new Patent Law was passed by the Council of Ministers in July 2004,[12] covering integrated circuits, plant varieties and industrial designs. Formulated with a view to meeting the requirements of TRIPS, the law may improve Saudi Arabia's position with regard to the 301 Priority Watch List.

Regulating the insurance sector

In July 2003 the Council of Ministers approved a new Insurance Law[13] to regulate the insurance sector in the Kingdom. The law opened the sector to foreign investors and created a legal framework for the many insurance companies operating in the Kingdom.

The Impact of Legislation on Actual Investment

As has already been indicated, the passing of the new legislation will not necessarily have the effect of increasing the level of investment in Saudi Arabia. Much depends on the way in which government bodies handle the new legal frameworks, and on how the new investment structures compare with those in surrounding countries.

Up to March 2004 SAGIA had issued some 2,220 licences, for projects whose total value came to $15 billion.[14] About three-quarters of these were wholly foreign-owned. If this were followed by

[11] As described on the official website of the US Trade Representative, accessed at www.ustr.gov/Document_Library/Reports_Publications/2004/2004_Special_301, 20 December 2004.

[12] The full text of the Patents Law 2004 can be accessed at www./laws/saudi/p.htm.

[13] See the statement of the Saudi Oil Minister, Ali Naimi, reported in *Middle East Economic Survey*, XLVII, 49, 6 December 2004.

[14] *Ibid.*, p. 9.

actual investment on a similar scale, Saudi Arabia would be benefiting from a major boost in foreign investment. However, obtaining a licence does not necessarily lead into investment. By the end of 2003 there was little hard evidence that Saudi Arabia was attracting a substantial scale of investment. UNCTAD's *World Investment Report 2004* ranked Saudi Arabia as 31st in the world for investment potential, but 138th for actual investment performance.[15] The performance indicator measures the extent of foreign direct investment relative to the size of the economy. 140 countries were compared, with only Indonesia and Suriname ranking below Saudi Arabia. Thus a wide gap exists between potential and performance. In fact over the period 2001 to 2003 the flow of investment registered a negative figure of $387 million. More funds were leaving Saudi Arabia through the repatriation of profits on investment than were entering the country in new investment. Although a positive figure of $208 million was registered for the year 2003 alone, suggesting a change in the trend, it is too early to draw such a conclusion.[16]

The extent to which the Saudi investment law can be seen as attractive to investors is, of course, greatly dependent on the scope of the 'negative list' referred to above—i.e. the sectors where foreign investment is barred. In February 2001, in the immediate aftermath of the law's promulgation, the SEC produced a 'negative list' of twenty-two sectors in which 100 per cent foreign ownership was not allowed.[17] These included oil exploration and production, fisheries, electricity distribution, insurance, telecommunications, printing and publishing services, education, trade, and land and air transportation. The list was extensive and initially gave the impression that the scope for foreign investors was narrow—at least for those wanting 100 per cent ownership of any scheme. The SEC seems to have been under pressure, from parts of the private sector supported by some elements within the government, to restrict the scope of foreign investment. However, SAGIA itself favoured shortening the

[15] United Nations Conference on Trade and Development, *World Investment Report 2004*, Geneva: UNCTAD, 2004, Annex, tables A.1.5. and A.1.7.

[16] United Nations Conference on Trade and Development, 'Country Fact Sheet: Saudi Arabia', accessed at www.unctad.org/fdstatistics, 15 December 2004.

[17] See http://www.sagia.gov.sa/innerpage.asp?ContentID, accessed February 2002. The SAGIA website has since been updated, covering only the sectors currently on the negative list.

'negative list'. In February 2003 the SEC duly removed six sectors from the list, either fully or partially.[18] The bans on foreign investment in education, transmission and distribution of electrical power within the public network, and pipeline transmission services were totally removed. The fields of printing and publishing services, telecommunications, and insurance services were partially opened up. In February 2004 more areas (including mobile phone services) were removed from the partially-restricted list, and insurance was removed totally, which still left three industrial and fifteen service sectors on the list.[19] Some of the restricted fields remaining relate to defence and to the provision of services in the holy cities, where the exclusion of foreign companies is to be expected. The restrictions on foreign investment in oil exploration and production, trade, and land and air transportation are, however, significant—cutting off important parts of the economy from foreign investment. Nonetheless, an extensive list of areas are now open to foreign investors.

An instructive case showing the problems that foreign investments still encounter, despite the new law, is the *Saudi Integrated Gas Initiative* (SGI). The gas sector did not fall within the ambit of the 'negative list', and indeed the development of this sector was planned around the attraction of foreign investment on a massive scale. The initiative was critical to the country's ability to meet its future energy requirements. The SGI included a range of industrial projects dependent on gas either as a power supply or a feedstock: electricity generation plants, water desalination facilities and petrochemical plants.

Both the international oil companies and the Saudi government appeared eager for a major partnership to exploit the country's gas resources within the framework of the SGI.[20] The conception, announced in December 2000, was that ten international oil companies, under an arrangement coordinated with Aramco, would form a consortium to carry through the huge projects that had been envisaged. The international oil companies were expected to inject

[18] See www.sagia.gov.sa/innerpage.asp?ContentID=87, accessed March 2003.

[19] SAGIA, *Negative List*, accessed at www.sagia.gov.sa/innerpage.asp?ContentID=87, 20 December 2004.

[20] Information on the IGI can be found on the website of the US Energy Information Administration, accessed at www.eia.doe.gov/emeu/cabs/saudi.html#gas, 15 December 2004.

some $30–40 billion of investment into the Saudi economy over a twenty year period. This would constitute the first major reopening of Saudi Arabia's upstream hydrocarbons sector to foreign investment since the sector was nationalised in the 1970s, and the centrepiece of the country's whole foreign investment strategy. With new discoveries having raised Saudi Arabia's gas reserves to the fourth largest in the world (after those of Russia, Iran and Qatar) much was at stake in this initiative. Moreover, the gas initiative was expected to prompt wider reforms in the economic system, given that it would force the government to review the tariff rates for power and water, removing subsidies in these sectors.

Negotiations with the international oil companies proceeded through 2001, 2002 and the first half of 2003, but in June 2003 the Saudi Oil Minister announced the termination of negotiations.[21] The SGI, as originally conceived, was abandoned. It appears two major stumbling blocks had caused the breakdown of negotiations. First, the companies were dissatisfied with the extent of the gas reserves that would be opened up for foreign investment, and specifically the exclusion of the Saudi Aramco Reserve Area. Second, they found the offered rate of return unattractive.

The abandonment of the SGI constituted a major setback for hopes of attracting substantial foreign investment into the development of this crucial sector. The project has now been re-packaged as a number of smaller and more limited undertakings. The new scheme is less ambitious than the original, and relies substantially less on foreign investment. The first major contract (and the largest so far) was signed in November 2003. This was worth some $2 billion and involved a consortium between Royal Dutch/Shell, Total and Aramco. The three companies would undertake gas exploration and develop gas production in a 209,160 square kilometre area of the Empty Quarter. Not all of the $2 billion constituted foreign investment: 30 per cent was Aramco's share of the total cost.

Saudi Arabia signed three more agreements under the relaunched gas development package in early 2004, with Lukol (Russia), Sinopec (China) and a consortium of Eni (Italy) and Repsol YPF (Spain), to explore and develop gas reserves in the northern zone of the

[21] See the website of the US Energy Information Administration, *ibid*.

Empty Quarter. Aramco was a 20 per cent partner in each of the three joint ventures. The three companies' initial investment in the first exploration phase was expected to total less than $1 billion.[22]

Some foreign investment may also be attracted into the banking sector as a result of the new law. In October 2003 SAMA announced that it would allow Deutsche Bank AG to begin independent operations in the Kingdom, and in the course of 2004 similar announcements were made with regard to the American bank JP Morgan Chase and the French BNP Paribas. This was the first time such banks had been allowed in since the 1970s, when the banking industry was nationalised.[23]

The WTO and Trade Liberalisation

As noted earlier, negotiations with the WTO have been under way since 1996. By the end of 1999 it was possible to identify where the main problems lay. On the Saudi side, there was an insistence that the United States and European Union lift customs duties on Saudi petrochemical products as a condition to Saudi Arabia opening its own markets. On the WTO side, there were requirements that the Saudi government place upper limits on tariffs, remove protective barriers to trade, open service sectors (such as banking) to greater foreign participation, liberalise regulations on foreign investment, and improve the business climate in such areas as the protection of intellectual property rights. The legal changes outlined above have satisfied many of the WTO's requirements for structural reform, and to some extent were designed specifically to do that, even though they were also responses to a wider need for reform.

Saudi Arabia has also pressed ahead with another measure necessary for WTO membership that requires agreeing arrangements with its main trading partners on market access and cutting customs duties. These must then be widened to all other WTO countries. Saudi Arabia's main trading partners in recent years have been the European Union and the United States. A trade agreement with the

[22] For further information on the agreements see http://www.sagia.gov.sa/innerpage.asp?ContentID=7&Lang=en&NewsID=238, accessed 5 January 2005.

[23] Dun and Bradstreet, *Country Report: Saudi Arabia*, London: Dun and Bradstreet, 2004, p. 50.

European Union (the Kingdom's leading trade partner) was reached in August 2003.[24] This required Saudi Arabia to reduce import tariffs on most EU agricultural and industrial products (although 165 items in the agricultural, dairy and poultry sectors won a greater degree of protection).[25] The agreement with the European Union was facilitated by the creation in January 2003 of a common external tariff in the GCC countries, thus forming a customs union. The tariff was set at 5 per cent on most goods, and an internal duty-free market was established. There were further plans to establish a monetary union in 2005, a common market in 2007, and a unified currency based on the US dollar in 2010. The Saudi agreement with the European Union stipulated that the Saudi Arabian service sector would be further opened up to include the banking, insurance, construction and telecommunications sectors. Saudi Arabia would also end the practice of selling gas cheaper on the domestic market than on the international market. Following the conclusion of the agreement, the EU trade commissioner gave the European Union's formal backing to Saudi Arabia's application for WTO membership. By the end of 2004 Saudi Arabia had also signed trade agreements with thirty-two other countries/trading blocs.[26]

However, the one major trading partner with which an agreement had not been reached by the end of 2004 was the United States. Although it had been clear, since mid-2003, that the US government was intent on Saudi Arabia joining the WTO, seeing this as integral to President Bush's Greater Middle East project,[27] the US government seemed to have been more demanding in its requirements than the European Union. The United States was said to be seeking greater concessions from Saudi Arabia in areas such as intellectual property rights, fuel price discounts, non-tariff measures and financial service sector reform. Moreover, at the end of 2004, when agreement had seemed close, the situation was further complicated by the impact of the Free Trade Agreement reached between the

[24] See 'EU Backs Saudi Arabia Joining the WTO', accessed at www.eubusiness.com/afp/030829173232.fnyapsil, 28 December 2004.

[25] See www.ictsd.org/weekly/03-09-25/inbrief.htm, accessed 22 January 2005.

[26] Dun and Bradstreet, *Country Report: Saudi Arabia*, p. 50.

[27] See 'Can Saudi Arabia Ever Join the WTO?', accessed at www.ameinfo.com/news/Detailed/42278.html, 20 December 2004.

United States and Bahrain.[28] This agreement envisaged the removal of all tariffs in trade between the United States and Bahrain, thus undermining the GCC's plan to standardise all its tariffs at 5 per cent following the 2003 formation of the GCC customs union. The US–Bahrain FTA would make it difficult for Saudi Arabia to prevent US goods entering the country duty-free through Bahrain. This undermining of the Saudi negotiating position vis-à-vis its own trade agreement with the US, therefore, created a new cause for delay.

Once the US–Saudi trade agreement is reached, most of the obstacles hindering Saudi accession to the WTO will have been resolved—given the changes to Saudi law and economic policies that have already been made. The WTO Working Party on Saudi accession met three times between October 2003 and April 2004, presumably indicating that negotiations had reached the final stages. Among the critical elements that remain, however, is Saudi Arabia's current practice of giving certain merchants the sole right to serve as agents of foreign companies. Changing the law on this may not be easy, given the politically powerful lobby of merchants that will resist it. However, the WTO is unlikely to accept continuation of the practice as it significantly constrains competition. Changes to the labour law (to increase labour mobility) and the introduction of a new competition law (enabling foreign companies to compete on an equal basis with local firms) may also be required.

Since 2000 Saudi Arabia has moved slowly but steadily towards fulfilling the conditions for membership of the WTO. This has involved introducing a number of reforms that were overdue for various reasons. Although membership will enable the Kingdom to expand the market for its petrochemicals exports—a necessary move in the light of the investment the government has put into this sector—it will also present a number of challenges. For one, Saudi companies will have to improve their productive efficiency in the face of greater international competition.

Privatisation

Privatisation moves are closely linked to two dimensions of economic reform that have already been discussed: the attraction of

[28] See 'US–Bahrain Free Trade Deal Draws GCC Ire', accessed at www.dailystar.com.lb/article.asp?edition_id=2&article_id=11182, 29 December 2004.

foreign investment, and the satisfaction of conditions for WTO membership. The Washington Consensus[29] regards privatisation as providing two major benefits for economies. First, it increases productivity by reducing the role of the 'bureaucratic' public sector. Second, it encourages the growth of private sector-led investment, a significant proportion of which will be from foreign sources. The latter, it is contended, will increase efficiency and introduce new technology. Both arguments have been used in justifying an extensive privatisation policy in Saudi Arabia.

Following years in which only limited privatisation occurred, a new push towards privatisation was initiated in 2001. The formal basis for this programme came from a plan created by the Council of Ministers on 6 August 1997. The plan laid down eight objectives for privatisation: improving the efficiency of the national economy and enhancing its competitive ability; encouraging private sector investment; enlarging the productive assets of Saudi citizens; encouraging domestic and foreign capital to invest locally; increasing employment opportunities; providing services to citizens and investors; rationalising public expenditure and reducing the burden of the government budget; and increasing government revenues. These objectives, and the description given of the policies needed to achieve them, were well-conceived. However, the next stage of the process did not take place until February 2001, when the SEC was given responsibility for supervising the privatisation programme, determining which activities were to be privatised, developing a strategic plan and timetable for the privatisations, and monitoring the implementation. In August 2001 the Supreme Economic Council created a Privatisation Committee to take charge of the process, with members representing relevant ministries and economic bodies.[30]

In June 2002 the SEC accepted the privatisation strategy that had been drawn up by its Privatisation Committee, and in November of

[29] This term was coined to describe the lowest common denominator of policy advice being addressed by the Washington-based financial institutions. The publications of the International Monetary Fund contain descriptions of the elements which are usually regarded as being key to this approach. For one article on this subject which is on the IMF web-site, see www.imf.org/external/pubs/ft/seminar/1999/reforms/Naim.htm.

[30] See 'Privatisation Objectives and Policies', accessed at www.sec.gov.sa/english/list.asp?s_contentid=22&s_title+&ContentType=&Cat, 30 December 2004.

that year the Council of Ministers approved the listing of public utilities and activities targeted for privatisation.[31] The listing was extensive: water and drainage; saline water desalination; telecommunications; air transportation; railways; some roads (expressways); airport services; postal services; flour mills and silos; seaport services; industrial city services; government shares in some government corporations (including the Saudi Electric Company, banks, Saudi Basic Industries Corporation (SABIC), the Saudi Arabian Mining Company, the Saudi Telecommunications Company, and local oil refineries); government shares in paid-up capitals of joint venture companies in Arab and Islamic countries; hotels, sports clubs, and a wide range of municipal, educational, social, agricultural and health services. The scope of what was being proposed was impressive.

Close consideration appears to have been given to devising a framework for privatisation that would ensure the economy benefited fully. In a document entitled 'Basic Issues to be Dealt with in the Privatisation Process', which formed part of the privatisation strategy, stress was laid on creating a proper regulatory framework for the privatised sectors, with the establishment of regulatory agencies; devising a systematic method for setting tariffs for services that were previously subsidised through government corporations; creating procedures for some public enterprises to be restructured prior to sale; bringing in strategic partners to cope with the largest privatisation projects; and fostering the correct business environment for privatisation by ensuring the proper functioning of capital markets and promoting human resource development among the Saudi population.[32] Privatisation, then, was not being regarded primarily as an easy way for the government to meet its budget deficit, but as a process involving structural transformation.

The main measures of privatisation were initiated in the later part of 2002, after the guidelines had been laid down. The most important such measure taken so far has been the initial public offering for 30 per cent of Saudi Telecom Company (STC) (the country's sole fixed line and GSM service provider), which was held between 17 December 2002 and 6 January 2003. This was the first major

[31] See 'Privatisation Announcements', accessed at www.sagia.gov.sa/innerpage.asp?ContentID, 20 December 2004.

[32] See 'Basic Issues to be Dealt with in the Privatisation Process', accessed at *ibid*.

government sell-off since the part privatisation of SABIC in the early 1980s. There was strong demand for the sale: according to the finance ministry, the government generated a net US $4 billion from the sale of 90 million shares. Around one third of the shares were sold to two state-run pension funds, the Retirement Pension Directorate (RPD) and the General Organisation for Social Insurance (GOSI), which together hold some 65 per cent of total government debt. The remainder of the shares were sold to Saudi citizens. With the public offering of STC shares, STC rapidly became the largest publicly traded company in Saudi Arabia.[33] However, since the government retains majority control of the corporation, the broadening of the share ownership seems unlikely to change the way the corporation is run.

Two other initial public offerings have been announced, both involving companies playing substantial roles in the economy. In May 2004 the SEC approved the long-awaited sale of the government's stake in the National Company for Co-operative Insurance (NCCI). The initial public offering duly took place in December 2004 and January 2005, with 7 million NCCI shares being put on the market at SR 205 each. This was equivalent to about 70 per cent of the company's total capital. The offering was oversubscribed by 11.5 times.[34] In May 2004 the SEC also approved the privatisation of the Saudi Arabian Mining Company (Maaden). Wide-ranging restructuring of the company has already begun, to facilitate selling it off in different parts. According to the company, the precious metals business will be the first to be sold off. There is also expected to be an initial public offering for the government's 50 per cent shareholding in the National Commercial Bank.[35]

Privatisation of services in a number of fields has been advancing. The privatisation of the management and operation of local and international airports has been announced; the postal services are now being operated privately; plans for the privatisation of urban transport systems and of some medical care facilities are also being discussed.

33 SAGIA, 'Foreign Direct Investment in Saudi Arabia', presented at the OECD conference Mobilising Investment for Development in the Middle East and North Africa Region, Istanbul, 11–12 February 2004.

34 See www.zawya.com/Equities, accessed 22 January 2005.

35 Dun and Bradstreet, *Country Report: Saudi Arabia*, p. 25.

Elsewhere privatisation remains more a matter of conjecture and discussion than of practical planning. Long-standing candidates for sale, where detailed discussions are now said to be underway, include the petrochemical and steel producer SABIC, which is still 70 per cent owned by the state, and Saudi Arabian Airlines. In both cases the discussions still relate to partial rather than total privatisation. The sale of more of the government shares of SABIC would be particularly significant. The company accounts for about 10 per cent of world petrochemical production, a percentage that will increase with new projects it has in hand.[36]

However, perhaps of greater significance than privatisation has been the evidence that opening up fields of investment to private investors has actually had results. In other words, government policies do seem to be expanding the private sector even in the absence of significant privatisation. Governmental plans at present envisage that capital investment of $117 billion in power and $80 billion in water is needed before 2020, with most of the money coming from the private sector.[37] Power projects worth $15 billion were put up for offer in January 2004, to private investors both inside and outside the Kingdom. In August 2004 the Council of Ministers licensed a foreign company (the UAE-based Etisalat) to establish and operate the second mobile phone network in the country. In June 2003 the Supreme Economic Council opened up the Saudi aviation sector to private enterprise, making it possible for Saudi-owned private companies to operate domestic airline services. And private health clinics, hospitals and educational facilities are all developing.

Measuring the Reforms against the Needs

The implications of all this for the future of the Saudi political economy now need to be considered. The main issue is to what extent the reforms that have been undertaken will help achieve two critical objectives: to create an economy that will be viable when oil revenues decline; and to provide productive employment for Saudi

[36] Embassy of the United States, Riyadh, 'Saudi Arabia: Economic Trends 2004', accessed at www.usembassy.state.gov/riyadh, 5 December 2004, p. 13.

[37] *Ibid.*

Arabia's growing population. Governmental estimates in 2002, based on 1999 data, put the country's overall unemployment figure at 9.6 per cent.[38] The Saudi American Bank put the male unemployment rate in 2002 at 11.9 per cent.[39] However, these figures probably underestimate the true level of unemployment. A more accurate figure would be 15–20 per cent among the male population, with some unofficial reports suggesting a figure as high as 30 per cent overall.[40] To attain the two objectives, a higher level of investment is needed, targeted towards increasing production and productivity. Greater public investment will be needed in some fields, but alone will not be enough. More private investment will be needed, some of it from foreign investors.

The Saudi government's achievements in moving towards these ends in the last four years should not be underrated. As shown above, the government has made legal and policy changes that are mostly worthwhile and well-conceived. Moreover the government deserves credit for forging ahead with the reform agenda despite the respite offered by higher oil prices.

However, the need to reform the economy and provide productive employment has an urgency that requires a more radical approach. The reforms undertaken so far suffer from two problems. First, they have mostly been implemented slowly and partially. There is the danger, already apparent in the country, that economic reform may become more difficult the longer it is left. Rising unemployment and deteriorating social conditions, fed by one of the highest rates of population growth in the world (almost 4 per cent during the 1980s and 1990s), will intensify political unrest and social disruption.

Second, the reforms are still inadequate. The wider reforms that are needed are in many ways the most difficult, and will require a greater social and political transformation than has so far been envisaged. Greater transparency and accountability will be needed, and the educational and social facilities offered to Saudis must enable

38 Saudi American Bank, 'Saudi Arabia's Employment Profile', Riyadh: SAMBA, 2002, p. 2.

39 *Ibid.*

40 The 30 per cent figure has been given in a number of newspaper reports, within Saudi Arabia and outside. Prince Al-Walid bin Talal was quoted as one source for this in Economist Intelligence Unit, *Country Report: Saudi Arabia*, London: EIU, May 2004, p. 22.

Saudi labour to be as productive as migrant/expatriate labour. While the problem of unemployment may gain temporary redress through the imposition of Saudi labour on unwilling employers, this will not create a productive economy for the long term. Saudi labour must be able to compete with expatriate/migrant manpower. The balance needs to be re-adjusted on both sides: making Saudi labour more productive and less expensive to employers; and improving the working conditions of migrant labour, thereby making it more expensive.

To explore both these dimensions requires first looking at the manner in which current economic reforms needed to be extended/furthered, then considering the social requirements of carrying such reforms to successful conclusion.

Ways in which the reforms need to be extended/furthered

The ways in which the reforms need to be extended/furthered, can be grouped under five points.

- *Completing accession procedures for WTO membership.* This is required not simply because of the benefits that Saudi Arabia could draw through greater access to international markets for its petrochemicals, but to provide the impetus for legal and policy changes needed for the long-term viability of the economy. WTO membership would increase transparency and predictability in the commercial environment. It would also enable Saudi Arabia to pool its strength with that of other developing and industrialising countries within the WTO (led at present by Brazil, India and China) seeking to shift the advantage of international trading practices away from the interests of the developed industrialised countries.
- *Developing further the legal framework affecting private investment.* The government has already taken important steps to open the investment environment and make it more attractive, but it still remains less favourable than in the other GCC states, who have, for example, lower tax regimes; Bahrain and the UAE levy no corporate tax on either domestic or foreign investment. This in itself may not be decisive: companies could accept a higher tax regime if it is accompanied by other advantages. Saudi Arabia has a larger domestic market, Saudi hydrocarbon resources are considerably

larger, and the overseas holdings of its citizens are much more substantial. However, some of the other aspects of the commercial environment emphasise, rather than diminish, the disparity. Despite the setting up of SAGIA to act as a one-stop-shop for foreign investment, establishing a business in the Kingdom remains time-consuming and bureaucratic. A recent report co-sponsored by the World Bank and the IFC notes: the minimum capital requirement for setting up a business in Saudi Arabia is fifteen times the average income; there are fifteen procedures that need to be completed; and the average time needed to complete these procedures is sixty-four days.[41] Even by the standards of the bureaucratically-heavy Middle East, these figures are unusually high.

Governmental ability and determination to follow through initiatives is equally important. The introduction of the integrated gas initiative was a sign that the government was open to foreign investment. It appeared to usher in a new era in the reform process. Yet after three years of negotiation the scheme was abandoned. The contrast between Qatar's success in developing its own integrated gas scheme, and the Saudi government's dilatory approach is stark.

- *Undertaking a more far-reaching privatisation of state corporations and services.* As noted above, the pace at which privatisation has been carried forward so far has been slow. To some extent this has been justified by the absence of regulatory frameworks for the sectors concerned. Certainly the frameworks need to be in place before privatisation is undertaken to ensure the process does not involve the stripping of state assets, the establishment of privately-owned monopolies, or the exploitation of consumers. The creation of competitive markets is essential. However, the elaboration of the regulatory frameworks has been too slow, with a number of public corporations (e.g. those in the electricity, mining and insurance sectors) having spent several years awaiting privatisation. Even if the government continues to hold a majority stake in the companies, it should allow the corporations to be run on a commercial basis. Also, the government has sometimes indicated that jobs should not be cut following privatisation.[42] However, this

[41] See www.rru.worldbank.org/doingbusiness, accessed 25 January 2005.

[42] See Monica Malik, 'The Private Sector and the State in Saudi Arabia', University of Durham, PhD thesis, 1999, p. 258.

removes one of the major benefits of the privatisation process—to improve efficiency.

- *Reshaping government finances: re-directing expenditure and generating new revenue.* The Saudi economy requires substantial new public investment. A recent report suggests that over the next twenty years a total of $267 billion of investment will be needed to cover the development of the power, telecommunications, petrochemical, oil and gas, and water and sewage sectors.[43] However successful the government may be in attracting private investment, a substantial portion will still have to come from the public sector. Funding of the country's social infrastructure (health, education and welfare services) also needs to increase (see below). However, the government should not count on rising oil revenues to provide the funds for new investment, both because this source is uncertain, and because a substantial portion of new oil earnings needs to be put into a 'fund for future generations', for the country's non-oil future. Therefore, the money will have to be raised both by redirecting existing expenditure, and by finding new sources of revenue.

  There are three areas where expenditure can be reduced. First, military expenditure is currently excessive, making up about 40 per cent of central government expenditure. Even by Middle Eastern standards this is very high. The regional average in the Middle East is 21.5 per cent, as against 14.5 per cent for the developing world, and a global average of 10 per cent.[44] There is little evidence that the high expenditure has brought security. On the contrary, the major threat to security appears currently to come from the domestic environment, and is perhaps better treated by effective socio-economic policies and political understanding than by sophisticated weaponry. Second, there is widespread acknowledgement that resources are being wasted, partly through expen-

[43] National Commercial Bank, *Saudi Arabia: Business and Economic Developments*, Riyadh: NCB, 2004. Report by Said al-Shaikh. Accessed at www.saudieconomicsurvey.com/html/reports.html, 20 January 2005.

[44] See Anthony Cordesman, *Saudi Arabia Enters the 21st Century: The Political, Economic and Energy Dimensions*, Westport, CT: Praeger, 2003, p. 391. The figures are based on the last year for which global comparative information is available from the US Department of State's database on World Military Expenditure and Arms Transfers, 1999–2000.

diture that has no formal controls and partly through corruption. A strict system of financial accountability for all monies raised and disbursed would help to limit the wastage. At present not all the revenue from oil sales appears in the budget. National accounts need to document the whole revenue and expenditure process. Third, general subsidies that do not target specific parts of the population that are in particular need should be curtailed. Although such expenditure has been reduced in recent years, significant sums are still spent on general subsidies.

New sources of revenue also need to be developed. Pressure on the Saudi government to 'diversify fiscal revenues' has recently been exerted by the IMF,[45] and there is good reason for this to be done as membership of the WTO will reduce customs revenues. The IMF has suggested the introduction of a Value Added Tax on certain goods, which other GCC states have also discussed, and the introduction of income tax for Saudi citizens and corporate tax for Saudi companies. Currently, as noted above, Saudi companies only pay *zakat*, and Saudi citizens do not pay income tax.

- *Making Saudi labour competitive.* Government policy at present seeks to impose Saudi labour on private employers. While the policy's intentions are commendable, it is (under current conditions) incompatible with moves towards increasing the international competitiveness of the Saudi private sector. This incompatibility will become increasingly apparent with Saudi Arabia's incorporation into the WTO framework. The operation of the Saudi labour market in effect guarantees Saudi labour higher wages/salaries than those offered to expatriate/migrant labour—except at the highest levels of technical professional expertise. This operates not through legal regulation but through understandings that Saudi labour employed in the private sector should benefit from similar conditions to those employed in the public sector. The feather-bedding of labour that exists in the public sector thus feeds through to the employment of Saudis (but not migrants) in the private sector. Statistics from 2000 indicate the scale of the divergence in remuneration between Saudi and non-Saudi labour: the average monthly income of Saudis in jobs requiring qualifi-

[45] International Monetary Fund, 'IMF Concludes 2004 Article IV Consultation with Saudi Arabia', Public Information Notice no. 05/3, 12 January 2005.

cations up to secondary school level was approximately three times greater than that of non-Saudis with the same qualifications; for those with university qualifications, earnings were about twice that of non-Saudis.[46] Given that Saudi labour also benefits from stronger contractual regulations on dismissal and redundancy, and often lacks the experience and technical/educational training of migrant labour, the freeing of the labour market (as favoured by the WTO) would reduce the employment of Saudis in the private sector.

Current regulations forcing the private sector to employ more Saudis may have short-term benefits, but will not be viable or effective in the long term. Long-term resolution of the problem must come from enabling Saudi and non-Saudi labour to compete on an equal basis. On the one hand this entails raising the competitiveness of Saudi labour. There are two dimensions to this: improving the quality of Saudi labour through training; and reducing the extra cost to employers of employing Saudis (in effect, lowering salaries and expectations). On the other hand the cost to employers of migrant labour needs to be increased by improving their wages and labour conditions (or, if necessary, imposing taxes on companies for every non-Saudi employed). This need not follow from government *diktat* (apart, perhaps, for setting and enforcing a minimum wage). Better conditions of employment for foreign labour in the private sector may emerge naturally by allowing more scope for labour organisation. Any reduction in international competitiveness resulting from this needs to be met with increased governmental support for private sector operations, and by encouraging service and industrial sectors to adopt higher levels of technology (thereby also reducing the need for migrant labour).

Massive investment in some policies aimed at achieving change in these fields have already been initiated by the government.

Recognising the social costs of economic reform and responding to the resulting problems

The measures mentioned above will not, in the short-term, reduce Saudi unemployment. Indeed, the immediate short-term effect of

[46] Saudi American Bank, 'Saudi Arabia's Employment Profile', Riyadh: SAMBA, 2002, p. 5.

adopting them would be to increase unemployment. The contention is that their adoption will create a basis for long-term employment growth, within a viable economy. However, the strategy is only viable if the resources currently used to support the employment of Saudi labour in unproductive jobs is used to improve the conditions of Saudi citizens in other ways. Massive new investment in improved training facilities, better health services and education, welfare support etc. is needed. The transition will be difficult, especially in politically-troubled times. Positive results can only be achieved if the state plays an active role in two key areas:

- *Providing the welfare and support arrangements necessary to protect the livelihood of the population during the transition.* Contrary to the views expressed by some economists,[47] the state should not be reducing the level of social support it offers its population. As indicated above, welfare expenditure will need to increase to carry through the major changes that are required. The new expenditure must be carefully targeted at those who are in greatest need, although a general improvement in the health and social facilities will also support the economic transition. Government expenditure should not be used to support wages/salaries in excess of their market value, but to support people until they can find productive employment.
- *Ensuring Saudis have the skills and training to exploit the jobs that will be created in the long term.* In this field too, substantial new expenditure is required. The Saudi government is already spending some 25 per cent of its overall budget on education, for which it deserves credit. Expenditure on education does not have immediate results, so it may be that the effects of this expenditure are not yet apparent. Nonetheless, private sector sources continue to insist that Saudi graduates do not meet the needs of the sector. Moreover, the greatest need may be for training (both prior to, and during, employment) rather than general education. A governmental initiative to increase funding for training was announced in January 2005. A closer liaison between educational organi-

[47] See Robert Looney, 'Can Saudi Arabia Reform its Economy in Time to Head off Disaster?', *Strategic Insights*, III, 1 (January 2004), p. 8. The same view is expressed in most publications recommending economic reform in the Kingdom.

sations and employers is required. Government subsidisation of training schemes within private sector companies would be beneficial. Providing governmental support (in training, facilities and regulation) to enable more women to enter the employment market is also critical.

A radical agenda of the kind proposed above requires a new social contract between the state and the population. A significant level of trust is needed, built on governmental transparency and a stronger commitment to socio-economic equity and greater popular accountability. Privileged access to the resources of the state must be limited. Taxation will need to be used to reduce inequalities. A clear dividing line must be drawn between the state and the private sector, such that private sector gain is not dependent on governmental favour.

The debate on economic reform in Saudi Arabia, both within the country and in international circles, has been governed too much by the limited concerns of the Washington Consensus. The reform measures that have been proposed in such circles are no doubt useful. However, the creation of a viable economy for the long term requires more profound structural changes, focused most crucially on making Saudi labour competitive nationally and internationally. The Saudi state will need to relax its control over some economic activities, but greatly expand its role in others. To bring this about, a new social contract is needed between the state and the population, encompassing political and economic dimensions.

SEGMENTED CLIENTELISM: THE POLITICAL ECONOMY OF SAUDI ECONOMIC REFORM EFFORTS

Steffen Hertog

Saudi politics sometimes has a circular quality to it: similar debates and ideas have recurred time and again; issues fade away just to reappear some years later. The same is true of the debate on the Saudi political economy: orthodox 'rentier state theory' has been declared obsolete many times, and each budget crisis in the Kingdom is closely followed by announcements that the Saudi 'distributional' system has reached a breaking point, or is at least under immense pressure—pressure which leaves no choice but radical reform and a redefinition of the Saudi 'social contract'. Pressure to reform Saudi economic structures has indeed been mounting, but the outcome of reform efforts has been highly mixed—apparently without endangering the overall functioning of the system. Although the socio-economic fundamentals have changed significantly since the oil boom years, a true redefinition of the Saudi political economy has yet to happen.

This chapter seeks to explain why perceived pressures have not thus far translated into significant systemic economic or political reform—or indeed crisis. More precisely, it attempts to trace the structural reasons why key economic reform projects were either implemented in a highly partial fashion or not at all. There have of course been a few successes in economic reform, and on many counts of institutional and economic performance, Saudi Arabia outpaces most other states in the Middle East. Even so, fundamental and trans-sectoral reform has been limited, and an examination of the obstacles may bring theoretical insights.

The thesis is that a pattern of 'segmented clientelism' explains both the resilience of the current set-up of institutions and political coalitions, and their witting or unwitting capability to scupper wide-ranging reform projects. The main body of the Saudi polity, it is argued here, consists of a large number of parallel, often impermeable institutions which have grown on oil income, are suffused with informal networks, and coordinate and communicate little. In a path-dependent process of state expansion, stakes have been created which, depending on the issue at hand, can give effective veto power to a great variety of factions, royal, bureaucratic and other. An expanded space for debate and apparent top-level willingness to reform are not by themselves sufficient for inducing structural change.

Initially in this chapter, the ways in which the ideas proposed here depart from rentier state theory are profiled, following which those ideas are developed in some detail. A number of case studies are then outlined to corroborate the argument. Some possible alternative explanations of the observed results are briefly discussed, before sketching how the 'segmented clientelism' approach, relative to other approaches of comparative political sociology, may add value to the debate about distributive states, and indeed tell us something about the prospects for reform in Saudi Arabia.[1]

A Note on Rentier State Theory

This section positions the arguments of the chapter vis-à-vis 'rentier state theory' (RST), the dominant paradigm in the study of Saudi Arabia's political economy.[2] The central tenet of RST is that the main political function of a commodity-rich state like the Kingdom is distribution of wealth, which implies that no effective political power sharing is necessary. 'Freed from its domestic economic base'[3]

[1] Many of the observations in this chapter are informed by in-country participant observation and extensive informal exchanges over the period 2003–4.

[2] For a fuller statement of RST see Giacomo Luciani, 'Allocation vs. Production States: A Theoretical Framework' in Giacomo Luciani (ed.), *The Arab State*, London: Routledge, 1990, pp. 65–84; See also Terry Lynn Karl, *The Paradox of Plenty: Oil Booms and Petro-States*, Berkeley, CA: University of California Press, 1997; Dirk Vandewalle, *Libya Since Independence: Oil and State Building*, Ithaca, NY: Cornell University Press, 1998; Jill Crystal, *Oil and Politics in the Gulf: Rulers and Merchants in Kuwait and Qatar*, Cambridge University Press, 1995.

[3] Luciani, 'Allocation vs. Production States', p. 71.

through external income, the state operates on the principle of 'no representation without taxation'. Individual strategies of sharing in the rent dominate political strategies of organisation, and distribution is a more important state function than regulation or economic policy in a strict sense.

It can be argued that there was a 'window of autonomy' for the Saudi state when oil income rose rapidly in the 1970s and early 1980s, with corresponding freedom to distribute, create dependent groups, and structure alliances. However, demands by societal actors towards the state have adapted and increased over the last two decades—witness the general tone of the Saudi press in recent years: whereas criticising the royals remains taboo, one mantra of its enhanced critical posture is the call for efficient and wide-ranging state services. The repeated withdrawals of subsidy cuts since the mid-1990s also demonstrate there is, at least, a strong perception of societal resistance to curtailed distribution. It appears that the Saudi state cannot mete out its riches at will anymore, but to the contrary is catering to strong and persistent demands.

Moreover, distribution is not neutral but discriminatory by its very nature and hence tends to induce politics, just like *re*distribution in other states does. As in any other systems there are potential group interests, say of agriculturalists, industrialists, commercialists, bureaucrats, the lower urban strata etc. Especially under fiscal strain, the discriminatory nature of a distribution state becomes clear, and interests of different groups are more salient.

The rentier theory response here may be that 'the state' does not mind: it is still autonomous in its policies as no tax deals are necessary, and distribution is still a one-way interaction. If certain groups may feel deprived, they have little bargaining leverage, not least as they have been formed, and their organisation is controlled, by the state itself.

There is some truth in the 'group formation' argument, as we will see. However, taxation, although a crucial form of state-society interaction, is not the only lever which gives society access to and influence over the state and its agencies. The taxation argument derives from a simplified macro-view of Saudi state and society. Links and alliances between state and societal actors can exist on many levels, and can define the very nature and capabilities of the state.

Co-option of groups in society means state agencies and actors can get 'tied down' in numerous lopsided, but still reciprocal relationships. A regime is not only dependent on income, but also on quiescence, cooperation, information and even organisation on the societal side. Stability and cohesion in Saudi Arabia are built on numerous formal and informal networks all of which want to be attended to. These networks often have an autonomous quality which can prevent coordinated top-down policies, be it of austerity or of institutional and regulatory reform.[4]

A 'soft' distributive state like the Saudi one tends to get tied down in society in specific ways: Chaudhry has demonstrated the importance of informal coalitions in Saudi policy-making.[5] Close ties of bureaucrats and businessmen in the 1980s, often based on kinship, prevented austerity policies and meaningful economic regulation. State capacity and regulation problems of rentier states are due not least to their distributional nature, which provides space for slack and the pursuit of particular interests in state agencies, and frequently leads to their concomitant penetration by society on a smaller scale. Historically, the Saudi state has co-opted considerable chunks of society 'into itself', most saliently through more or less indiscriminate provision of employment. Little consideration appears to have been given at the time to the impact of such policies on state capacities. Today, however, the rapidly grown state apparatus is often hard to control even for those formally in charge.

State autonomy hence appears to be much lower than RST posits.[6] As the Saudi regime is not willing to employ large-scale sup-

[4] The extent to which networks are shaped by the state or, by contrast, have autonomous qualities (for instance penetrating state agencies through kinship networks) remains a subject for further research.

[5] Kiren Chaudhry, *The Price of Wealth: Economies and Institutions in the Middle East*, Ithaca, NY: Cornell University Press, 1997.

[6] 'Autonomy' is a contentious and difficult term. Suffice it to say that there is a difference between the autonomy to decide certain measures and the autonomy to implement them. Both are lower in Saudi Arabia than RST would have one expect, and the latter arguably is lower than the former. Autonomy to implement relates to the issue of 'state capacity', which is similarly contested; here it simply means capacity to regulate, to enforce and monitor rules in economic life. Broader—and possibly opposite—meanings like repressive capacity, capacity to satisfy needs (however defined), capacity to react to crises etc. are bracketed out.

pression, it needs to engage and bargain with societal actors to maintain stability. Society matters.

Although distribution, as posited by RST, is still a defining feature of Saudi politics, there is a much greater need for social, historical and institutional specifics to explain economic policies and their limits. State-society links and interaction have become more complex than the lean original RST model allows. Disaggregation of 'state' and 'society' is in order, and more micro-oriented approaches of comparative political science can help here. The state, for our purposes, should not be understood as a unified actor with unified interests, but rather as an institutional conglomerate which, although strongly hierarchical in many respects, creates sets of different, 'local' material stakes within itself and between parts of it and societal actors. It creates a 'political field' in and around which politics is negotiated.[7]

The Thesis

The concept of 'segmented clientelism' allows us to capture such institutional specifics within a broader distributive framework. Chaudhry has provided a more precise picture of state capacities and types of state-society links. But her work does not fully capture the fact that the state itself is not only soft and shot through with informal links and structures of authority, but also strongly *segmented*: oil-based growth allowed the parallel creation and expansion of institutions and networks with various sets of clients within state structures and society.

'Clientelism' here refers to unequal, exclusive, diffuse and relatively stable relationships of exchange and mutual obligation, both on micro and macro levels.[8] It is 'segmented' because of the parallel

[7] For the notion of 'political field' see Sami Zubaida, *Islam, the People and the State*, London: I. B. Tauris, 1993, pp. 145–52.

[8] The use of 'clientelism' is inspired by the patron-client literature, but as I am also dealing with aggregates here, it is used much more loosely. This may make anthropologists cringe, but I find the term useful to denote inequality of relations and vertical, more or less localised, often exclusive structures of communication and authority. Usually an exchange of broadly material favours against loyalty of one kind or another is involved. The relationship normally is more stable and diffuse than a mere market transaction. It clearly is a more specific term than 'group' and

and often strongly divided existence of clienteles, which in many cases are not consistently brought together or orchestrated at the top of the system anymore.[9]

Juxtaposed groups of stakeholders tend to have different patrons within the state and the political elite, and clientelist relationships are also reproduced within these groups. One may argue that this is not specific to rentier states. But the fact that the Saudi state was predominantly a distributive institution meant there was little need for *communication* between different sets of institutions and actors, and hence the *horizontal integration* of the system was very low, as 'clientelism' denotes vertical structures of communication and exchange. The imperatives of growth and expansion were allocative, not regulative, hence different institutions and networks could blossom and coexist. This institutional inheritance from the oil-induced period of state growth explains the fate of economic reform projects and more broadly, patterns of political negotiation and state capacities.

At its most extreme, the system has created a number of institutional, regulative and distributive 'fiefdoms', sometimes with strongly overlapping areas of jurisdiction. This increases the number of stakeholders and channels of formal or informal access, but makes the creation of 'reform coalitions' a formidable task—as opposed to *de facto* veto coalitions which do not have to be organised, but often exist by default in the given structures, if only through diffuse bureaucratic resistance. As we will see, segmentation can be played out on various levels, and can create strong *de facto* resistance to implementation at lower levels even if the regime leadership appears united.

Segmented clientelism describes the internal structure of the state, but it also describes both the scattered nature and the simultaneous strength of state-society links. It is, moreover, reflected both at a formal level (e.g. in the set-up of ministries and other public insti-

---

more useful for Saudi Arabia than 'class' or, in most cases, 'coalition'. For a broad, political understanding of clientelism, see Luis Roniger, 'Clientelism and Civil Society in Historical Perspective', paper prepared for the workshop 'Demokratie und Sozialkapital', organised by the German Political Science Association, Berlin, June 2002.

9 All systems based on clientelism tend to be segmented, but the parallelism of structures, including modern state structures, is especially stark in the Saudi case and its impact on macro-issues of policy making and implementation particularly pronounced.

tutions, public employment patterns etc.) and informally (in the manifold personal structures of authority in public institutions and beyond). In both cases one can broadly speak of clientelism, as the functions are similar: individuals are part of a network of distribution and patronage which gives them a stake in particular sections of the system. Informal structures often provide the actual glue of the clientelist links, although they can contradict formally assigned functions. Admittedly, the Saudi political economy has moved beyond mere nepotism and exploitation of personal links, and there is an array of stable rules and administration. However, these stable rules themselves can be part of the segmented and particular set-up.

In terms of policy outcomes, segmented clientelism structures impair the horizontal coordination of policies, create a plethora of potential veto players in the process of policy negotiation and implementation, and make central steering difficult. At the same time, however, it integrates many actors into the system in a fragmented fashion, which reduces the overall pressure on state and regime, not least as coherent interest formation is vitiated.

The approach should be seen as a correction and complement to RST, not a replacement. Distribution remains central to the functioning of the system; it still mostly emerges from the state, access to which has not ceased to be the central prize; distribution is still used in the craft of politics, which is more immediately 'material' than oriented towards setting abstract political rules. The segmented clientelism approach especially bears out the implicit 'group formation effect' of RST, i.e. it documents the power the state has to shape groups through its distributive policies, beyond the more straightforward 'spending' and 'taxation' effects.[10]

The main adjustment to RST argued for here is a fundamentally historical one: the creations of oil wealth—institutions, rules and

[10] For this differentiation, see Michael Ross, 'Does Oil Hinder Democracy?', *World Politics*, 53 (April 2001), pp. 325–61; The 'group formation effect' is the main reason why expectations towards the 'new middle class' have proved empty, as even those with 'modern' education (and potentially modernising demands) often use traditional, personal, exclusive channels of access or are at least caught up in a system which segments their class into a plethora of different sub-groupings and institutions. For an example of implicit 'new-middle-class' assumptions see Mordechai Abir, *Saudi Arabia: Government, Society and the Gulf Crisis*, New York: Routledge, 1993.

networks—have their own dynamic and, though perhaps brought into being more or less by *fiat*, can decisively constrain future state action. Institutional developments and reform options are path-dependent; the state does not stay autonomously above the fray for long. Conventional RST can only deliver a snapshot of what happened when the oil income hit the Kingdom; for subsequent political options and limits, one has to look more closely at the historical trajectory and entanglements of institutions.[11]

Historical Roots of Segmented Clientelism

Patron-client relationships broadly defined played a large role early on in Saudi state formation. Shaikhs and notables became the clients of King Abd al-Aziz and were themselves the patrons for strata which the state could not access directly. By creating local patrons, regionally or bureaucratically speaking, state power can be mediated, inclusion increased and a 'softening' of the state achieved. Especially in early stages of state formation, intermediation can make the state, as an otherwise alien entity, accessible. Illiterate peasants or tribesmen can access the state via *omdahs* (village headmen) or shaikhs as brokers. State expansion does not always involve a tearing apart of old structures. Yet intermediation also comes at a cost in terms of state capacity and nationwide coherence of policies.

The onset of oil meant a crucial historical juncture of state formation. The state developed a much higher ability to engage with its subjects immediately. However, to some extent, old and new patterns of clientelism were articulated into the growing state itself. Expansion of the state meant cooptation of groups at least as much as enhancement of administrative capability.[12]

The creation of the 'dependent bourgeoisie' is an example of a newly created societal clientele: a business class thriving on state

[11] This line of thought is, in different ways, explored by Chaudhry; cf. also Gwenn Okruhlik, 'Rentier Wealth, Unruly Law, and the Rise of Opposition: the Political Economy of Oil States', *Comparative Politics*, April 1999, pp. 295–315; and Paul Aarts, Gep Eisenloeffel and Arend Jan Termeulen, 'Oil, Money and Participation: Kuwait's *Sonderweg* as a Rentier State', *Orient*, 32, 2 (1991), pp. 205–16.

[12] Ayubi speaks of a 'privatising' effect on state agencies: Nazih Ayubi, *Overstating the Arab State: Politics and Society in the Middle East*, London: I. B. Tauris, 1995, p. 250.

contracts, licenses, subsidies etc., granted through a plethora of different institutions. The growth of bureaucracy itself in many cases represented the creation of large-scale clienteles within the state. Employment in different government branches and agencies represented institutionalised—and relatively equitable—distribution of wealth at least as much as functional considerations. It was more 'granted' than a result of political bargaining over legal or regulatory objectives. Rent circulation became increasingly sophisticated and created 'cascades' of brokers and sub-patrons within administration and the private sector. At this point, the 'inability to discriminate clearly among economic and social goals'[13] did not appear salient, as the state was not in need of economic policy.[14]

Oil wealth provided the basis for the growth of separate, rather isolated institutional recesses, sometimes called 'fiefdoms'. One important source of segmentation of the body politic was repeated political balancing between royal family factions, neatly analysed by Michael Herb in several Gulf states.[15] It frequently resulted in the creation of additional posts and institutions; the administration became a site and provided instruments for family politics.[16]

Herb has stressed the stabilising function of such bureaucratic proliferation enabled by oil riches, but does not discuss its potential impact on state manoeuvrability and capacity. There are largely impenetrable conglomerates with vast, often parallel jurisdiction, like the ministries of defence and interior. Many top-level bodies have their own health and educational systems attached; examples include the Ministry of Foreign Affairs, the National Guard and to some extent the Ministry of Finance. There is large-scale parallelism of state functions. Institutions like the Al-Riyadh Development Authority (ADA) have the requisite high-level backing to pursue policies in their jurisdiction which are partially independent of what the responsible line ministry or even the Council of Ministers says. To

[13] Vandewalle demonstrates this inability with the Libyan example, which admittedly is a crasser one in terms of lacking state capacity: *Libya Since Independence*, p. 162.

[14] This was Giacomo Luciani's contention in 'Allocation vs. Production States'.

[15] Michael Herb, *All in the Family: Absolutism, Revolution, and Democracy in the Middle Eastern Monarchies*, New York: SUNY Press, 1999.

[16] Gary Samore, *Royal Family Politics in Saudi Arabia (1953–1982)*, PhD Harvard, Cambridge, MA, 1983, p. 199.

some extent, there are even parallel foreign policies that skirt the Ministry of Foreign Affairs. Due to the enormous financial means available to the royal elite, welfare policies are to some degree pursued on a 'private' basis.[17] Segmentation of assets is also reflected in the structure of landholdings in the Kingdom; many valuable plots in strategic locations do not belong to the state anymore, but to individuals attached to various segments of patronage.

However, the institutional sprawl also had a dynamic of its own. It is most closely intertwined with family politics on the highest level, but institutions run by commoners also developed in parallel and often acquired an insular quality. The explanation lies in the primarily distributive nature of the state and the accompanying vertical structures of authority; there was no pressing necessity for horizontally integrated policies or regulative 'outreach' into society. Moreover, in technical matters, the integrative capacity at the very top of the system was often weak.

The Recent Salience of Discriminatory Clientelism

With the demographic explosion and lower oil revenues since the mid-1980s, it became obvious that this system's performance was declining. Existing stakes of rent seeking, bureaucratic power, state support and employment were usually defended successfully, but the discriminatory nature of the compartmentalised system became increasingly obvious. Relative to the population, the distributive reach of the state has declined and new entrants have found it increasingly hard to get access; there are growing differences between those who are well-connected and positioned within the various clienteles and those who are not. Competition for resources and discrimination have become fiercer.

To be sure, the royal ethics of 'care' for the Saudi 'citizens' are still strong,[18] and subsidy cuts, if happening, tended to be directed against those with larger incomes. However, the benevolent patrimonialism in the Kingdom began to break down by default, due to limited

[17] Examples include Crown Prince Abdullah's and Defence Minister Sultan's engagement in housing projects, land donations for hospitals etc.

[18] See e.g. various speeches by the King and the Crown Prince in the *Majlis al-Shura* and on other occasions.

overall resources.[19] Public employment is no longer sufficient to provide millions of young Saudis with jobs; there, as in other areas of life—including mundane things like having a water line fixed or your new house quickly supplied with electricity—success in receiving state or other support often depends on the '*wasta*', which some have and others do not.[20] In a situation of scarcity, when relations are personalised and structures of access segmented, networks tend to become more discriminatory and exclusive. Rapid social ascendancy, still possible in the 1970s and '80s, is largely a thing of the past. The same is largely true of the business sector, where there is little space for new entrants, who find it hard to obtain loans and where state support—lower overall—is largely apportioned to established players.

However, the private sector has matured a great deal since the 1980s and is relatively less dependent on the state.[21] It has been demanding more opportunities to become active by itself, through privatisation, with a leaner regulative environment and less state interference. This seems to accord with the emerging position of the government that more responsibility for employment generation, economic growth and service provision has to be delegated to Saudi business.

The growing strain on the state-based distributive system and a general demand for domestic economic liberalisation is the background against which a serious economic reform debate slowly emerged in the mid-1990s. This gained momentum towards the end of the decade under Crown Prince Abdullah's stewardship, when he himself publicly declared that the fat years of the oil boom were over for good and that economic growth would require real effort. The

[19] Contrary to the perception that Saudi Arabia is converging on a global neoliberal path, there is no deliberate state policy of exclusion or of deliberately condoned inequality through privatisation and economic liberalisation. The limited austerity since 1994 has targeted big actors rather than small fry (agricultural subsidy cuts hit big investors, for instance, and electricity tariffs were mostly increased for higher consumption brackets). Emerging inequalities rather are a result of soft, clientelist state structures at lower levels and the sheer pace of demographic growth.

[20] Personal examples abound; Mai Yamani gives an account of personal complaints of young Saudis who feel shut out of the networks: Mai Yamani, *Changed Identities: The Challenge of a New Generation in Saudi Arabia*, London: Royal Institute of International Affairs, 2000.

[21] See the chapter by Giacomo Luciani in this volume.

projects envisaged included a general shaping up of the bureaucracy, a new labour law, a stock market law, the privatisation of public services and assets, and other regulatory reform enabling more autonomous private wealth creation. World Trade Organisation (WTO) membership and a new foreign investment code, while slightly more contentious (at least in the private sector), were emblematic aims. The most symbolic project—though one in which the Saudi private sector was to play only a supporting role—was the opening up of the upstream gas sector for foreign investment.

In parallel to these generally liberalising efforts, the government attempted to pursue the 'Saudisation' of private sector labour markets, which have been strongly dominated by expatriates. Finally, the most revolutionary and disputed project of all was an income tax to tap private wealth (of expatriates at least) for state coffers.

'Political' and 'Administrative' Clientelism in the Saudi Political Economy

The outcome of such reform efforts has been patchy at best. At the time of writing in late 2004 most of the above projects were not at all or not fully implemented; several remained in gestation; at the very least, several self-imposed deadlines had passed. The long-term outcome of the reform moves is not predictable, but that eventual success in implementation most likely will be mixed at best as long as the Saudi state—and by implication, its structure of clienteles—does not witness a fundamental restructuring. Reform moves thus far have become tangled in segmented state and societal structures, the apparent consensus for reform notwithstanding.

Within the broader framework of segmentation, this chapter differentiates two forms of clientelism: political and administrative. The first, political, level of analysis deals with large clienteles. It involves aggregate groups or leading actors at a systemic or at least regional level.[22] This type of clientelism is played out in negotiations and

[22] This includes leading princes, ministers, segments of the bureaucracy, and (as leading groups or important individuals) 'retailers', 'bankers', 'contractors' etc. Even on such a general level, clientelism usually is a more useful perspective than class analysis, as it reflects asymmetry, particularism of exchange, the segmental structure of polity and the *potential* role of personal patrons.

decisions about broader policy issues.[23] The second, 'administrative', level consists of more personal, micro-political entanglements, mostly between bureaucrats and businessmen, sometimes also involving individual princes. It involves daily dealings of the Saudi administration, also at lower levels, rather than broader political questions. The boundary between the two is not wholly clear-cut, but the distinction will help to analyse separate causal processes.

Political clientelism

Political clientelism occurs both within the state and between state and society. One could say the Saudi polity consists of various parallel and staggered pyramids of clienteles: partners and followers of princes and their institutions, ministries, public enterprises, policy-making bodies etc., both through formal and informal links.[24] These are not static, and individuals or groups can belong to and move between several clienteles.[25]

Within state structures, there is patronage between elite members (e.g. senior princes protecting and positioning their offspring and younger full brothers), between elite members and institutions (for instance, senior princes are known to be close to certain ministers or ministries), and also within institutions (various forms of bureaucratic patronage and internal segmentation of departments and sections; patterns of kinship or regional background sometimes play a role here).

A crucial aspect of this set-up, many facets of which are not unique to Saudi Arabia, is that vertical links are much more strongly developed than horizontal ones. The historical reasons related to dis-

[23] 'Negotiations' is broadly defined here as any kind of interaction where political interests are uttered either explicitly or through actions.

[24] Within broader segments, patrons can be clients of larger patrons, patronage can be wielded by individuals and groups etc. Spelling out all possibilities would create too many categories and be unduly formalistic. The concept needs to be spelled out and historicised from case to case.

[25] Such suppleness admittedly makes the concept somewhat fuzzy, but due to the inequality of relations and the vertical, often exclusive structures of communication and authority, it still combines wide reach with relative specificity. In some cases, we do have to speak of 'coalitions', but these often have internal clientelist structures and tend to be more ephemeral, context- and policy-dependent phenomena.

tribution-based state growth have been alluded to above. Today, just as in the days of rapid administrative expansion, the authority and power of distribution which sustain institutions emerge from the centre of the system, which in itself is to an extent segmented.

The size of the royal family plays an important amplifying role in this context; the number of princes in government and business has been steadily rising, and there is a prevailing sense of personal entitlement for them.[26] Although some are committed public servants, the overlapping of informal structures of neo-traditional authority and formal bureaucracy can induce incoherence in the implementation of official policies and increase the isolation of agencies. The growth in royal bureaucrats has also led to an additional proliferation of administrative structures.

The extent to which institutions are working in isolation, mostly communicating with their superiors in the elite, is reflected in the low degree of information sharing between equivalent bodies: on almost any economic issue, conflicting sets of figures are available from different ministries or organisations. The Saudi press has been carrying repeated complaints that concerned ministries were not consulted about policies by other bodies which clearly pertained to their jurisdiction too. Due to the high degree of formal centralisation, enhanced by the royal power of the purse, senior bureaucrats are more likely to compete for access to the top than coordinate among themselves.

Structures meant for horizontal integration—e.g. inter-ministerial committees—often only reproduce such cleavages. Although there are centres of administrative excellence,[27] like the Saudi Arabian Monetary Agency (SAMA) or the Ministry of Petroleum and Minerals, these usually have an even more insular character limited to their sector.

Because clients compete for top-level access, controlling the overall administration is easier; this is a pattern reproduced on a smaller scale within institutions. Against this background, rent-seeking and

26 See Hazem Beblawi, 'The Rentier State in the Arab World' in Giacomo Luciani (ed.), *The Arab State*, London: Croon Helm, 1990, pp. 85–98, at p. 91.

27 'Insulated agencies', in the parlance of public administration researchers; cf. Barbara Geddes, *The Politician's Dilemma*, Berkeley, CA: University of California Press, 1994.

maximising institutional fiefs often appear easier and more rewarding for senior bureaucrats than pushing coherent policies. The latter demand true top-level commitment and understanding and often require cross-cutting coalitions that are not easy to engineer. Political caution is often rewarded, as a premium is put on control. Engaged and critical policy advocacy is often substituted by the convenient technocratic illusion that policy questions can be depoliticised through scientific research—which tends to lead to the commissioning of endless studies; 'analysis paralysis' in the words of a Western banker. There is limited capacity at the very top to deal with policy details, although this is what the formal centralisation would demand. This also means that supervision of technical competence and success through the leadership, even if genuinely desired there, is strictly limited.

A crucial variety of large-scale political clientelism *within* the state is embodied by public employment itself. Salaries have been gobbling up a growing share of the Saudi budget since the 1980s, whereas capital expenditure—more relevant for long-term economic development—has been progressively squeezed. In many cases, overstaffing in public bodies is so obvious that the distributive purpose is hard to dispute. Against a background of rising unemployment, job provision through the state is a highly sensitive political issue. The conflict between job guarantees in various institutions and imperatives of administrative reform is evident.[28]

The benefits of employment reach well beyond those directly employed to much larger numbers, so in this sense state employment already touches upon the second main area of political clientelism: patronage over groups in Saudi society. 'Society' and 'state' in Saudi Arabia are in many ways interwoven, so the distinction is blurred. We will concentrate here on patronage over private sector actors.

On the face of it, the independence of the Saudi private sector as an actor on the Saudi political scene would seem to have much increased. Institutions like the regional Chambers of Commerce and Industry and their overarching national council (CSCCI) seem to enjoy increased say and input when it comes to policy discussions. The private sector has also successfully used the *Majlis al-Shura* as a

[28] Ministries are often forced to take on new graduates with non-relevant degrees from a roster that is imposed upon them.

conduit of its interests. The financial autonomy of Saudi merchants has expanded tremendously due to years of rent accumulation, and their degree of organisation and managerial professionalism has improved markedly. The state has a stronger need for the private sector nowadays, mainly for its contribution to growth and employment, but also in some cases for its expertise in economic matters, for quick and flexible policy input, and information on sectors which the soft, segmented administration itself cannot obtain. The most highly qualified Saudis are now usually found in the private sector; the fairly egalitarian public sector pay schemes, frozen over many years, are far less attractive for top graduates than they used to be.[29]

The voice of Saudi business has hence become much more audible, and many complaints have been made in recent years against obtrusive and obstructive bureaucracy. The state does indeed dish out much less materially, but still interferes with business through what may be called predatory regulation (the reluctance to give up control incidentally is one main reason for the stalled privatisation process). Privately, some Saudi businessmen also complain vehemently about the expansion of princes into business, which tends to tilt the playing field against them.[30] The business-state relationship has become somewhat more equal and certainly more confrontational, as the cake is relatively smaller and competitors are more numerous.

Yet none of this makes the private sector a key opponent of segmented and clientelist political structures, nor will it be able easily to take over where the state fails. First, Saudi capital retains an international exit option, and second, Saudi business remains too much a creation of the Saudi system, and too embedded in it. To the extent that Saudi investors have gained real autonomy in terms of capital and expertise, a globalised economy makes exit options more easily available. Moreover, although opinions are strong, the corporate coherence of Saudi business is still undermined by games of public favours from different sides. Though these favours often are less immediately material than they used to be, they still create individual or small-group clients. Examples include public works tenders which are less than transparent, individual licenses, favourable regulatory

[29] See also the chapter by Giacomo Luciani in this volume.

[30] See e.g. Abir, *Saudi Arabia*; personal interviews in Riyadh, 2003–4.

decisions and support policies, discretionary information on public policies etc. Personal links between leading businessmen and administrators or royals loom large here. The system gets vastly more complex and opaque through the occasional involvement of persons who are beyond the reach of the Saudi judiciary.[31]

The lack of legal security and the uneven playing fields can be reason for complaints, but they can also contribute to the fragmentation of the private sector. As the number of actors who matter in Saudi business is relatively small, this effect is reached fairly quickly. Those who seek individual gain can actually profit from local intransparency and segmentation. There is no need for a grand conspiracy theory here: segmentation and favouritism can reproduce themselves quite well without a grand scheme of divide and rule in the background. One is nevertheless led to speculate that in many cases the lack of transparency is tolerated for good reason.[32]

A related point undermining the coherence of Saudi business as a whole is that the Majlis al-Shura and the CSCCI have often been used by big, established business actors—precisely those relatively few who are likely to be well-connected. This has been changing only slowly.[33] In business as in other areas, there has been a certain sclerosis: the private sector has seen few new entrants since the 1980s, and there has been little mergers and acquisitions activity or sectoral consolidation. Entrenched monopolies and oligopolies are hard to budge. The 'dependent bourgeoisie' at the highest level remains close to the state and its leadership. Most family conglomerates are involved in many sectors and company boards at the same time, indicating privilege and, one suspects, making their policy interests somewhat more diffuse. There has not been much mean-

[31] In the parlance of recent scholarship on state-business relations, reciprocity, credibility and trust are often lacking at least a broader scale; Ben Ross Schneider and Sylvia Maxfield, 'Business, the State, and Economic Performance in Developing Countries' in Schneider and Maxfield (eds), *Business and the State in Developing Countries*, Ithaca, NY: Cornell University Press, 1997, pp. 3–35.

[32] Compare the recent survey by Transparency International, available on www.transparency.org, and the commentary in *Gulf News*, 2 October 2004, which notes that Saudi Arabia still ranks very low.

[33] In recent years, more policy-minded figures have entered the boards of chambers and their sectoral committees, not all of them from the very highest stratum of business.

ingful Small and Medium Enterprise (SME)[34] development which would make markets more dynamic and contested, and interests potentially less individualised.

The private sector appeared to be the strongest collective actor when it came to orchestrating veto coalitions, e.g. against income tax plans, attempts to remove national privileges in commercial distribution, or hikes in electricity rates. Generally the private sector is willing to speak, but not to openly confront the system which has brought it into being. How coherent it or its sectoral components are as a lobby depends on the issue at hand and on how strongly its interests are individualised and segmented by the Saudi political economy. To return briefly to RST, it is less distribution as such, than *the structure of ties and groups involved in distribution* which determines political action.

Administrative clientelism

The final aspect to be addressed is lower-level or administrative clientelism.[35] The difficulties which Saudi economic reforms have faced cannot be completely understood without looking at the fabric of the Saudi state itself: the way its bureaucracy operates and interacts with society on a daily basis. Even larger interests and group delimitations are often rooted in the micro-politics of Saudi administration. Administrative structures have not been sufficiently analysed so far by RST, although they are intimately related to the distributive nature of the state. They determine state capacities and define important aspects of the state-society relationship.

As indicated, the functional integration of most Saudi administrative agencies is low. This is true for inter-agency relations, but also for agencies themselves. Historically, there were few pressing incentives for cogent information-gathering and regulation—functions which tend to meet stiff societal resistance and require major effort if not coercion. There is strikingly little information available on important sectors like agriculture or retail, on businesses in general, or

[34] As opposed to the sprawling, low-margin and low-innovation micro-enterprises in commerce and services.

[35] 'Lower-level' is not lowest level: a stiff hierarchy means that below upper management, in many agencies, there is little leeway for personal discretion (and often little to do in general).

on personal incomes, which could, for instance, be used for taxation. Only recently have there been efforts to enhance business regulation; the courts are generally perceived to be weak and at least until 2004 there was no such thing as a competition policy.[36] Society has not been strongly penetrated by the state in these regards, as oil removed the historical necessity to undertake such painful tasks.

When legislation and regulation are drawn up in ministries, outreach efforts are usually limited, although the Majlis al-Shura and the increasing inclusion of the chambers of commerce and industry have brought considerable improvement at least for more important projects.[37] State-society communication at a *policy level* has traditionally been limited; where it occurred, it was more a personality- and issue-driven phenomenon than the result of well-established communicative structures.

At the same time, at an *individual* level, there has been extensive interpenetration between administration and business (or society). The ubiquitous favouritism which spread with the growth of the Saudi state has already been mentioned. Unclear, overlapping regulations and jurisdictions often provide leeway for personalised dealings at lower, less political levels, involving not only contracts, but also licenses, certificates, registrations, utilities, business information etc.[38] Considerable inventive talent has been invested in providing rent-seeking opportunities to oneself and one's kin, friends or clients; inflated or fictitious sub-contracting has proved especially popular. Clientelist fiefs and segmentation can exist even within ministries; some administrative units have disproportionate influence and budgets because of the personal standing of their bosses.

The *'wasta'* needed for many interactions with the Saudi administration follows the broader segmentation: a plethora of applications

[36] Regulatory institutions generally tend to be weak in distributive states; Vandewalle, *Libya Since Independence*, p. 8.

[37] According to a prominent *Majlis al-Shura* member, laws are no longer simply drawn up by a small number of consultants and bureaucrats in the back room of a ministry; interview with Abdalrahman al-Zamil, Riyadh, June 2003.

[38] In the current apparatus, responsibilities are often diluted between agencies. Water management is a good (and vital) example, which is located somewhere in the vacuum between the ministries of agriculture, electricity and water, and municipalities and rural affairs.

and documents is necessary to open a business; many different agencies have to be approached, sometimes issuing conflicting requirements.[39] Even without nepotism, the system can prove cumbersome. But although this inhibits the functioning of markets, it also helps to keep foreign competitors in check, and gives the 'insiders' a stake in the system as it is. It helps to reproduce informal and exclusive networks, based on favouritism and secrecy, which inhibit broader group formation. The general secrecy in which the Saudi bureaucracy operates is integral to the segmentation of clienteles and institutions.

Business attitudes to such procedures may be ambiguous, but most bureaucrats involved certainly have an interest in defending them. Although bureaucrats, especially at lower levels, have little aggregate active policy power or agency, a tremendous diffuse veto and obstruction capacity can emerge from their ranks. Even if there is genuine commitment to structural change at senior levels, higher bureaucrats often prove powerless against a diffuse mass of employees which can hardly be sacked and have little incentive to perform in a non-meritocratic setting—strong hierarchies notwithstanding. Reform coalitions, as far as they exist, are often top-heavy; but over-centralisation and limited capacity at the top, together with a lack of effective sticks and carrots means that diffuse resistance can be quite effective. Mid-ranking bureaucrats have even been observed to conspire against engaged colleagues who were willing to push certain standards of performance and output.[40]

In addition to the broad obligations the Saudi state has incurred through political clientelism, it gets bogged down on a small scale through administrative clientelism, especially when it comes to implementation of policies that have been agreed at a higher level. Whereas overarching interest aggregation, dispute resolution and policy communication are frequently deficient and state and society appear juxtaposed on a larger scale, the two are often closely intertwined on a micro scale.

[39] One could argue that many of these and other links are not 'clientelist' in a strict sense, as there is no clear hierarchy between the parties involved, who rather act like partners or friends. However, the broader structure in which such relationships are embedded tend to be hierarchical, and by and large societal partners function as clients of the bigger institution involved.

[40] See note 1.

Case Studies[41]

The case studies that follow, focusing on WTO accession issues, the foreign investment law, Saudisation, and plans for a personal income tax, exemplify how policies are played out in a segmented clientelist setting. They show that strong top-level backing is needed for any significant policy project, as the system is hierarchical and potential interest groups tend to be fragmented. Input from society is only selective and the system does not offer an integrated field for negotiating policies. When it comes to implementation, policies tend to lose momentum at lower levels and, if they have a transversal nature, become lost between 'fiefdoms' and informal networks. In most cases, the overburdened leadership has limited follow-up capacity.

WTO accession

The decision to apply for WTO (then GATT) accession was taken in 1993, at a point when it was becoming obvious that membership would soon be nearly universal. It seemed a prerequisite for being a serious international economic player. However, the Saudi authorities did not seem fully aware of the extent of regulatory changes that would have to be discussed—if not necessarily implemented fully—in the course of the accession process. The principle of non-discrimination, implying the opening of sectors to foreign or domestic competition, the abolition of monopolies and exclusive agencies etc., went against the tradition of Saudi business policies.

The private sector was in large parts unenthusiastic about the implications of WTO membership. Its interests were determined by stakes in formally legitimate rent-seeking (e.g. exclusive retail 'agencies'), but, it appears, also by stakes of many individual actors in administrative clientelism, which explains part of the resistance against WTO-induced transparency. The lukewarm response to the WTO idea demonstrated that significant parts of the Saudi private sector still had a rather cosy position in the current system, highlighting the still considerable importance of various protection mechanisms and favours.

The lack of debate and information on WTO within the Kingdom demonstrated the absence of a powerful public forum to settle policy

[41] These are based on in-country research over the periods from April to June 2003 and from October 2003 to July 2004.

debates. As far as debate occurred, it did so in a dispersed and patchy fashion in different fora. The push behind the accession long appeared rather timid; there were no broad developmental elites pressing the issue; and no strong coalition partners in society. WTO negotiations also appeared to show the limited capacity of the Ministry of Commerce, which appeared to be responsible for WTO matters in a rather isolated fashion and long failed to reach results—the successful conclusion of negotiations was repeatedly announced, only to be delayed again briefly later. The Majlis al-Shura was allowed to enter the debate only very late in 2003, and there appeared too little adjustment of other agencies and regulations to shape up the legal environment. Too much seemed to be at stake, with too little coordinated capacity, for any important adjustment to happen quickly. Only in autumn 2003 were the important bilateral WTO negotiations with the European Union concluded, and as of late 2004, US–Saudi negotiations appeared at an advanced stage. How far eventual membership will really force changes in business and regulative practices in the Kingdom remains to be seen (the evidence from neighbouring cases like Egypt or Jordan is mixed at best).

Foreign Capital Investment Law

At least as much as WTO membership, the foreign investment law of April 2000 appeared to be largely a top-down project. The Crown Prince had put his full weight behind it and although it was issued somewhat later than announced, the active gestation period of the project seemed limited to a period of not more than two years, quite brief by Saudi standards. Still, its initiation demonstrated the existence of political factions and clienteles within the state, although in this instance, the most obvious case was one of reform-oriented patronage: of the Crown Prince over Prince Abdullah bin Faisal bin Turki, the later head of the Saudi Arabian General Investment Authority (SAGIA). As one Saudi banker had it, the law was a 'personality-driven project'.[42]

Significant parts of the private sector were sceptical about the undertaking, which by allowing 100 per cent foreign-owned ventures was likely to erode Saudi privileges in a number of markets, and by

[42] Interview with chief economist of a Saudi bank, Riyadh, May 2003.

putting remaining protected sectors on a 'negative list' for periodical review created a possible gateway for further foreign encroachment (especially in the commercial sector). Although one hears conflicting statements on the issue, Saudi business was certainly not the driving force behind the law and did not appear as a unified actor. It was, however, granted opportunity to comment on drafts of the law, which were circulated in 1999 and 2000. At least in some sectors, administrative clientelism tended to create stakes in intransparency and lack of competition, whereas foreign entrants were perceived as likely to undercut established favouritist structures through superior technology and management. At the very least, Saudi businesses were clients of various forms of regulatory protection.

Strong political leadership was needed to push the issue, and this was probably induced by the oil price crisis of 1998/9. The law brought the creation of an additional institution—SAGIA—which was responsible for regulatory follow-up and for dealing with future investors. The resistance of most other Saudi institutions was epitomised by the first draft of the 'negative list', to which ministries in the course of drafting had added so many additional sectors that the Supreme Economic Council under the Crown Prince eventually intervened to curtail it.

SAGIA, though a genuinely reform-oriented body, has often proved unable to break into the turf of other institutions,[43] which still can create enormous obstacles on the ground for foreign investors who need documents and clearances from a plethora of opaque and slowly working bodies. The ideal of creating a 'one stop shop' in SAGIA has not been fulfilled (puckish commentators call it the 'one more stop shop'). This shows how implementation of cross-cutting policy projects is likely to become bogged down in old patterns of segmentation and in the vertical structures of authority in and around the Saudi state. Saudi business often acquires its competitive edge through access to exclusive networks which help to 'get things done' within this system, operating through networks and brokers in numerous agencies. Administrative clientelism in institutions like the Ministry of

[43] In this it is different from otherwise comparable reform bodies in places like Brazil and Tunisia, which had the power to undercut other agencies. In Saudi Arabia, these apparently have much more staying power; for Brazil see Geddes, *The Politician's Dilemma*; for Tunisia see Eva Bellin, 'The Politics of Profit in Tunisia', *World Development*, 22, 3, pp. 427–36.

Interior—which has a broad administrative reach even into business—means that many markets are far from 'level playing fields'. Foreign actors often have to tap the networks of local Saudi intermediaries.

If SAGIA represents an attempt to skirt the bureaucratic thicket, so does the Supreme Commission for Tourism and even the Supreme Economic Council itself, which was founded in late 1999 as a kind of mini-cabinet for economic policy issues, skirting the bigger and more sluggish Council of Ministers. Beyond these major bodies, numerous additional committees have been called into being for new policy questions. Some of these bodies are lively, insulated from the rest of bureaucracy, and do more than reproduce existing cleavages.[44] Such institutions can indeed help in finding clarity over issues of principle, but often do not effect the necessary changes in existing bodies and the administrative nitty-gritty which stays unchanged, uncoordinated, segmented and opaque. State capacity cannot be created by *fiat*, or at least not without great effort and hurting large numbers of stakeholders in the system. The creation of new bodies in the course of reforms may reflect a historical rule of thumb: since the onset of oil wealth, the Saudi system has mostly changed through expansion. This has its limits.

Saudisation

State employment is perhaps the area where the limits of expansion have become the most obvious. The sensitive issue of rising Saudi unemployment has become so pressing that it has even found its way into the semi-official Saudi press. Saudisation of labour markets is a notion that has been around for more than two decades. However, only in recent years have serious administrative moves been made to force the private sector to contribute to job creation for Saudi nationals (as of 2004, around 7 million expatriates were resident in the Kingdom, a majority of them actively employed; an estimated 90 per cent of private sector labour was expatriate).

The government has attempted to impose annually rising quotas of Saudisation on private companies since the mid-1990s, ceased

[44] The jury is still out on many of them; as of early 2005, the new sectoral regulators were still empty shells. This is also part of a pattern of announcements not being followed through at the level of implementation: this requires restructuring (which may be painful), attention to detail, capacity building and often coordination between various bodies at lower levels.

issuing new work visas in certain areas of employment, and has stipulated the complete Saudisation of others, including vegetable markets, gold souks, and taxis at various points since 2000. There appear to be political divisions among the leadership about pace and instruments of the policy, and different princes are known to be for and against. This may have contributed to the declaratory nature of at least the first few repeated attempts at imposed Saudisation. The measures in the second half of the 1990s seemed to have little will or capacity of enforcement behind them. When enforcement progressively happened, it tended to be selective. Administrative clientelism allowed some businesses to skirt the regulations, whereas others, often foreign, were penalised. A prominent technique somewhere in between was to reduce the number of overall employees by outsourcing certain tasks; not by coincidence the companies who did the outsourced work tended to be particularly well-connected.[45] Such accounting tricks and the use of *wasta* meant the private sector's opposition to a theoretically costly policy in the 'soft stage' of Saudisation was muted, as individual strategies of finding one's way were often preferred.

When pressure for meaningful Saudisation from both elite and society increased, the loopholes became fewer, and the resistance of the private sector became more vocal. Implementation remains patchy and rules are badly communicated to the sectors concerned, reflecting both the customary low coordination of involved agencies and their limited outreach capabilities. Different agencies and senior princes seemed to pursue various parallel Saudisation policies, decreeing often contradictory quotes and prohibitions, and a lively informal trade around 'Saudisation certificates' has evolved on an administrative level. But whatever the eventual degree of implementation of the policy, it seems to have demonstrated that the specific setting in which actors move influences the political salience of issues and the will to act on them collectively. Administrative clientelism seems to individualise strategies.

Income tax

The project of an income tax on expatriates was one of the few issues that met a strong collective response. The tax was meant to diversify public revenue away from volatile oil income. Most schemes

[45] Interview with senior banker in Riyadh, November 2003.

under debate were aimed at expatriates first, but for many Saudi observers, a tax on nationals loomed in the background.[46] This is an issue at the very heart of the RST debate. Two attempts to introduce a tax have been made, in 1988 and 2003. Both failed. Attempts to redefine the distributional system are most likely to induce a broad *veto* coalition, as a fundamental systemic feature of the rentier state is in question, a feature in which almost everybody regardless of his particular position has a stake.

In 2003 it was the Majlis al-Shura that brought down the proposal; the business representatives there played a prominent role, as a tax on their expatriate employees was a potential indirect cost factor. The implicit exit threat of Saudi capital helped to drive home the point that under current political circumstances the income tax idea is dead. Transparency of government finance was an important implicit issue, probably more so than representation, as the general sense was that nobody is willing to contribute money to a system which does not generally open its books. In this case, even those with a relatively privileged position tended to agree. The private sector is more alienated—and vocal—in this regard than it used to be.[47]

Summary of Findings

Other case studies might have been used, including issues of legal transparency, labour and company laws, and various privatisation projects. More examples could be fielded to illustrate the role of royal actors and high-level spheres of influence, specific patronage structures within the state and state and society, and the interplay of formal and informal structures. Yet several basic points should by now be clear. Strong top-level backing is needed for an important

[46] Recently, collection of certain fees and revenues has been outsourced to private companies in some municipalities; this is a possibly paradigmatic development that merits in-depth research.

[47] Conversely, open books are anathema for Saudi business itself, which hedges its information tightly. Should a tax materialise one day—perhaps a sales tax instead of one on personal income—the state would be challenged to develop information-gathering and enforcement capacity which, as the lack of data on most sectors shows, it does not have (to be sure, there is an Islamic 'Zakat' tax on Saudi business, but the uneven and oblique application of its rules rather supports the point).

policy project to enter serious debate. There is little 'bubbling up' of projects either from the hierarchical and segmented bureaucracy or from a society that is also still fragmented in many regards. The private sector, although enjoying more voice and autonomy, is still tied up in a system of partial protection, perks and favours, both formal and informal; its input is selective.[48] Access in segmented clientelism is often via specific and parallel channels, not general, aggregate or public ones. As indicated above, this tends to inhibit class formation and the emergence of more 'political' as opposed to 'distributional' interests, as visible in the policy debate. Segmented clientelism in this sense has a stabilising effect. Although there is an exit threat for private capital—whether concerted or not—this does not threaten the system with imminent collapse, and is executed without fanfare.

Broader state-society communication about policies has improved, but there is still no comprehensive framework for it. The Majlis al-Shura serves to articulate interests of at least certain parts of society, but is not powerful enough to act as a central clearing and 'pacting' institution for really difficult decisions. It has helped to give some legitimacy to moderately contested projects, but it is at the same time another layer of decision-making which—as several of its members admit—can slow things down even more.[49]

Nevertheless, when crucial high-level players agree, reform decisions are sometimes taken. But when it comes to implementation, trans-sectoral projects run the risk of getting stuck between several agencies and spheres of jurisdiction and influence. Most parts of the Saudi administration have not historically developed high capacities to consistently regulate business (or society in general), and due to their insular quality do not coordinate much. Many remain groupings of clienteles as much as functional units.

The formal centralisation in the Saudi state—an aspect of the vertical structures of power built up around the royal family as 'arch-distributor'—ends up increasing the implementation stalemate, due

[48] Admittedly, on other more limited, legal issues than the case studies examined here, demands and input of Saudi business have been more clearly articulated and were more strongly oriented towards regulatory reform and state withdrawal. Yet the point is that its stance depends on the issue at hand, and hence a broader political position is slow to emerge.

[49] Interviews with Saudi bureaucrats and *Majlis* members in Riyadh, May and June 2003.

to both the overburdening of leaders with tasks of decision and monitoring and their role as senior patrons with numerous clienteles they do not want to hurt.

This often leaves considerable *de facto* autonomy to holders of 'fiefs' below them to distribute, regulate and manipulate on a small scale. These actors have less leeway for meaningful reform projects that would require powers of restructuring and setting rules—often rules that other institutions would have to adhere to. It is true that a number of policies arguably *were* successful at all stages, most prominently the corporatisation and partial privatisation of Saudi Telecom.[50] But these were precisely those that could be acted out under high pressure on a limited field, with relatively few stakeholders and agencies involved.

It should be said that the distributional structures and social services in Saudi Arabia are on many accounts still a success: the Saudi regime has largely been able to avoid becoming the sort of 'fierce' regime represented by the examples of Saddam's Iraq, Syria under Hafez al-Asad and Sudan: violent oppression did not become the central tool for survival. The overall stability of the system is remarkable, and the emerging exclusion from economic and social networks is a relatively benign phenomenon compared to what is going on in some other parts of the Middle East. Yet clientelist stability has come at a price for the manoeuvrability of the Saudi state.

A Note on Alternative Explanations

While the explanatory power of the concept of segmented clientelism seems clear from the above, it is worth engaging with two alternative explanations for the lacklustre reform results.

'The Saudi leaders could if they wanted, they are just too careful.' Proponents of this view often emphasise the importance of consensus in Saudi political culture. It is true that senior princes usually want everybody on board. It is a somewhat moot point whether this is their choice in each instance or to what extent the extensive Saudi

[50] Other successes include the privatisation of ports management, making SABIC a world player in petrochemicals, and managing and expanding the industrial cities of Jubail and Yanbu.

system of stability management simply demands it. But the evidence examined here shows the leadership has in fact tried to push certain initiatives, even if there was some resistance, and failed, at a cost to their credibility. If they withdraw from projects or stop pushing them, this may well be an expression of their caution, but the problems their projects run into in the first place are better explained by segmented clientelism than by the political culture of the leadership alone.[51]

A broader counterargument to a culturalist explanation is that it was the political economy of oil which enables consensualism and a game of positive pay-offs for everyone in the first place. As late as the nineteenth century senior princes were in the habit of killing each other. This could also counter the closely related argument about a 'culture of care and inclusion'. There is some merit to this, but it does not explain the whole pattern of reform politics and is in itself in need of elucidation (in part, precisely by showing how it became 'operationalised' in a framework of segmented clientelism).

'It is all a result of senior-level infighting.' This would be a strongly curtailed version of the segmented clientelism argument, looking only at its upper end. But projects have become bogged down at lower levels, and the power base of senior actors derives from the segmented institutions and groups they control—groups they also have to cater to.[52] There is strong anecdotal evidence that Saudi bureaucrats are not easily forced to perform. How much senior level segmentation matters compared to lower level state structures—some of which are perhaps tolerated as a result of senior level disunity—may become more transparent if Crown Prince Abdullah emerges as a full king. A serious acceleration of reforms on the

[51] A similar argument is that reform moves are only meant as public relations exercises. This may be partly true, but it is clear that in several instances senior princes have put their reputation as policymakers on the line with specific projects; it is in any case hard to deny that demographic and other pressures have created an interest in economic reform and decreasing the burden on the distributional state.

[52] For a particularly strong general argument of how societal structures of authority can grow into the state and incapacitate it, see Joel Migdal, *Strong Societies and Weak States: State-Society Relations and State Capabilities in the Third World*, Princeton University Press, 1988.

ground would reduce the power of a broader structural argument. But soft state structures, administrative clientelism and low capacities most probably cannot be swiftly removed by a unified leadership, as this would mean redefining crucial parts of the system.

To summarise, lack of momentum in economic reform is not (only) a personality and top-level issue, but more of a structural phenomenon explained by the institutional history in the Kingdom. Putting it crudely, fiefs are more than just their holders.

Saudi Arabia and Political Science

How does the present approach relate to broader theoretical perspectives in political science? The case against using conventional RST for analysing Saudi economic policy has already been made. But what about using and elaborating 'corporatist' or 'neopatrimonial' approaches, which comparativists beyond the confines of Middle Eastern Studies may well favour. Admittedly, Saudi Arabia is a strongly authoritarian, highly centralised system where societal and functional groups are controlled and arrayed by the state: a prime suspect for 'corporatism'. Yet, while apposite for analysing certain features of segmentation and political negotiation, this approach is less useful for capturing the limits of autonomy of the Saudi state, and for analysing the specifics of oil-based institution building.[53] Moreover, the Saudi state is certainly not a unitary and insulated actor.[54] So if politics has more of a network character, why not em-

[53] Martin Carnoy speaks of groups with distinct economic positions which are orchestrated by a powerful, independent state; this does not quite fit the Saudi picture. Martin Carnoy, *The State and Political Theory*, Princeton University Press, 1984, p. 39; on different types of corporatism (none of which quite fits the Saudi reality of limited control through the leadership) see Peter J. Williamson, *Varieties of Corporatism: a Conceptual Discussion*, Cambridge University Press, 1985. Recent attempts to formalise political interest representation have followed a corporatist mould, but are often hamstrung by the low level of formal organisation of Saudi society (see. Steffen Hertog, 'Building the Body Politic: An Emerging Corporatism in Saudi Arabia?', paper presented at the Sixth Mediterranean Social and Political Research Meeting of the Mediterranean Programme of the Robert Schuman Centre for Advanced Studies at the European University Institute, Montecatini Terme, March 2005).

[54] 'Bureaucratic authoritarianism' may also be suggested as a candidate, but this is too obviously development-oriented and predicated on needs of 'production states'.

ploy 'neopatrimonialism', a well-established explanatory framework for non-Western politics, with a specific focus on access to resources and informal linkages? Much of what is described here fits neopatrimonial models, where politics dominates economics and personal relations (as opposed to, for instance, abstract class relationships) explain a great deal of politics.[55] But rules and formal policies do matter in many areas in Saudi Arabia; despite limited state capacities, the level of 'stateness' and bureaucratic legality is higher than in many other developing countries. Arguably, segmental clientelism is in many ways a sub-case of neopatrimonialism, which is not a very specific model.

This chapter has tried to suggest a specific combination of different approaches—rentier and distributive state theory, patron-client analysis, neopatrimonialism—as, by themselves, they are inadequate for capturing the dynamics of the Saudi political economy and thus presumably that of other countries too. While Saudi Arabia has some very specific features, important aspects can certainly be compared: one objective of this exercise was precisely to bring the Kingdom back into the remit of general comparative politics. The research agenda should include examining other, comparative examples of segmented clientelism, to discover which aspects may be generalised.[56]

The findings of this chapter also provide an empirical illustration of some of the themes in the debate about 'the state' which has been raging in political science since the 1980s. First, they may help to differentiate separate aspects of state 'autonomy', qualifying and specifying a concept that has often been used too loosely. As far as economic policies in the Kingdom go, one should distinguish decisional autonomy of the leadership—which can be rather high if unity is reached—and implementation autonomy, which is pretty low in case the policy has some kind of regulatory or cross-cutting character.[57] Generally, as Gourevitch has pointed out, a far reach of the state does not mean it is autonomous in its actions, and 'more' state also means more interests in its actions, both in that more

[55] For a succinct statement see Jean-Francois Medard, 'The Underdeveloped State in Tropical Africa: Political Clientelism or Neo-patrimonialism?' in Christopher Clapham (ed.), *Private Patronage and Public Power*, London: Pinter, 1982, pp. 162–92.

[56] Syria, Iran and Venezuela may be candidates.

[57] See note 6 for a discussion of state 'capacity'.

numerous interests are involved and that the level of interest tends to be higher.[58] This is as true for an expanding distributive system like Saudi Arabia as it is for any other state and in that sense limits the use of conventional RST.

This chapter was also an attempt to historicise the rentier state, and show its development options and limits over time by analysing the consequences of path-dependent institutional development. In quite a different context—a comparative analysis of state-led industrial development in mostly non-rentier states—the sociologist Peter Evans has made an argument similar to the present one: 'The class structure that emerged as a result of state action changed, in its turn, the political condition for future state action.'[59] Substitute 'structure of clienteles' for 'class structure' and this summarises the bind in which the Saudi state finds itself.

Conclusions: The Future of Saudi Economic Reform

The above discussion has implications for the future of economic reform in Saudi Arabia. Gourevitch has used Western historical examples to show that increased struggle over policy leads to stronger organisation of interest groups; this may be necessary for new reform deals to materialise.[60] One may add that fragmented or segmented societies are less likely to produce strong sectoral and functional group organisations. Groups in Saudi Arabia are not sufficiently united and autonomous to negotiate a new deal, and the policy debate remains incomplete (thus, budgetary transparency is still a public no-go area, although it would have to be part and parcel of many reform policies; it is also the central issue on which almost all of the otherwise heterogeneous critics of the leadership agree).

Evans directs our attention to the state side of the equation: to create powerful developmental coalitions, he suggests, a state has to develop new types of links to society.[61] The mechanisms for this do not appear to be there in present-day Saudi Arabia. There is no level

[58] Peter Gourevitch, *Politics in Hard Times: Comparative Responses to International Economic Crises*, Ithaca, NY: Cornell University Press, 1986, pp. 230, 231.

[59] Peter Evans, *Embedded Autonomy: States and Industrial Transformation*, Princeton University Press, pp. 35–6, 228, 238–9.

[60] Gourevitch, *Politics in Hard Times*, p. 232.

[61] Evans, *Embedded Autonomy*, p. 228.

field for negotiation, aggregation of interests and legitimate dispute settlement which would enable the necessary reform deals—usually painful for parts of society.[62] In this respect the state needs more equal, policy-oriented links, not institutionally and personally segmented downward ones. This does not appear to be in prospect: the structural underpinning for it, this chapter has argued, is largely lacking.

62 I am indebted for this idea to Giacomo Luciani; it emerged in one of many discussions in Riyadh.

FROM PRIVATE SECTOR TO NATIONAL BOURGEOISIE: SAUDI ARABIAN BUSINESS

Giacomo Luciani

The literature on the Arab states, and specifically on the state in the oil-producing countries, has insisted on the paramount role that the state plays, and its considerable autonomy with respect to society. This approach is still fundamentally valid: Saudi Arabia remains a rentier state, in which the state enjoys almost total fiscal autonomy, and is able to engage in distributive politics to ensure political support. However, this chapter will argue that the rentier development model followed by the Kingdom has also nurtured and allowed the development of a strong private sector, which has reached a stage where it is by and large itself autonomous from the state, and has turned into a national bourgeoisie. This means that there now exists a dialectic between the state and the national bourgeoisie, whose main object is the size and allocation of investment, and consequently the result in terms of economic growth.

The outcome of this dialectic—i.e. how much is invested, in which activities, how much growth is generated—is politically important. In this sense, the national bourgeoisie has acquired political leverage, and its actions, though normally non-political, end up acquiring political significance.

Definitional Problems: Bourgeoisie, Private Sector, Business Sector, Entrepreneurial Class

The first problem faced in discussing Saudi Arabia's 'private sector' is definitional. The expression 'private sector' currently used in the

Kingdom has a technocratic connotation, and is in tune with the Washington consensus with respect to privatisation and playing down the role of the state. Yet it is not neutral from the point of view of political analysis, and must be treated with caution.

As we engage in political analysis, the obvious primary alternative would be to speak of the bourgeoisie, i.e. the class of owners of capital. The main problem with this is that in several of the Middle East countries the private sector includes significant economic activities that are owned directly or indirectly either by the ruler or King, or by various members of his family. Bourgeoisie is normally understood in contraposition to aristocracy, but in this case the boundary between the two classes is problematic: whether or not a businessman is a member of the royal family, his interests will often be primarily related to his business activities—which arguably would define him as a 'bourgeois'.

Yet the problem lies primarily with considering the ruling families an aristocracy—because they do not share the characteristics of feudal aristocracy, i.e. that of being primarily a landed class. The ruling families of the Gulf may be said to be a (real or pretended) tribal or religious aristocracy, but they are not an aristocracy from the point of view of political economy. In fact, it is tempting to describe most or all of the ruling families as being essentially bourgeois, representing (and in some cases being themselves originally) merchants, nowadays capitalists and financiers. It is therefore not altogether clear why the concept of bourgeoisie has been so rarely used with reference to these states and Saudi Arabia in particular.[1]

[1] Robert Springborg is an exception. In his seminal article 'The Arab Bourgeoisie: A Revisionist Interpretation' (*Arab Studies Quarterly*, 15, 1 [winter 93]) he sets out to re-evaluate the role of the bourgeoisie in the Levant and Egypt before the wave of nationalist, etatist military regimes. Yet the article says very little about the bourgeoisie today: the case in favour of a prominent role of the bourgeoisie in the countries that Springborg has in mind is asserted but not fully made. Moreover, Springborg essentially ignores the Gulf states, which I would argue is where the Arab bourgeoisie is found today. Finally, he includes the landowners as part of the bourgeoisie, while they are probably more correctly considered a tribal aristocracy turned landed class (see Batatu on Iraq: *The Old Social Classes and the Revolutionary Movements of Iraq*, Princeton University Press, 1979, chapter 6), not primarily a merchant or capitalist class. Of course there are exceptions, and some merchants must also have been landowners—although industrialists more rarely so. The Gulf bourgeoisie is not a landed class: it is a merchant class turned industrialists and

In this chapter the term 'private sector' shall be used either in its statistical meaning (e.g. in national accounts), or to mean the initial status of the universe of business people in the Kingdom, which was characterised by dependence on government largesse and lack of political profile.[2] The chapter will argue that this universe has progressively transformed itself into a (cosmopolitan) national bourgeoisie, which is today largely autonomous from the State, increasingly class conscious and ready to play a political role.

A distinction should also be made between 'private sector' and 'corporate' or 'business sector'. In fact, the term 'private sector' is frequently used to mean the corporate or business sector, as it is defined to include economic activities that are corporatised or conducted on purely commercial criteria, yet are not private at all, but are either majority or wholly owned by the government. So, in the national accounts of Saudi Arabia, companies like SABIC or the National Commercial Bank are included in the private sector, although they are in fact controlled by the government. Some fundamental institutions of the business sector, such as the stock market, are therefore in fact dominated by state-owned interests: all the largest companies traded on the Saudi stock market are majority-owned by the government.

Nevertheless, to overlook the difference between the logic and behaviour of a business corporation, albeit state-owned, and that of the bureaucracy would be a mistake. In this sense it may, depending on the context, be appropriate to speak of the private sector and also include in it certain state-owned entities. It is thus normally accepted that the telephone services sector has been privatised, in the sense that it used to be a section of the Ministry of Post and Telecommunications, and was first set up as a corporation, which was then partially floated on the stock exchange. Therefore, although the

---

financiers. In Saudi Arabia some of the major merchant families have benefited from the distribution of agricultural land especially in the Najd—see below.

2 Some of today's leading bourgeois families (Alireza in Hijaz, Qusaibi in the Eastern Province) had a significant political role when they bankrolled King Abd al-Aziz to the tune of hundreds of thousands of pounds before the oil riches kicked in. Muhammad Alireza was one the first commoner ministers (commerce) in the 1950s. Full state dependence most directly applies to the Najdi merchants through all of Saudi Arabia's modern history.

government still owns 70 per cent of the stock, a transformation has taken place. Politically, however, we would not include the managers of the majority state-owned enterprises in the national bourgeoisie.

Finally, the term 'private sector' is ambiguous because it includes genuine entrepreneurs as well as financiers and pure rentiers. The distinction should be clear enough, although at times the same individual/company may simultaneously possess all of these traits.

Entrepreneurs are individuals or companies that initiate the creation and establishment of new activities, be they large or very small, and be they in industry, commerce or services. They can do this independently or in joint venture with established international companies—as long as they are actively involved in the business they deserve to be called entrepreneurs.

Financiers, on the other hand, provide funding for business enterprises, but are not actively involved in the business. They were rare in Saudi Arabia until recently, because most business enterprises had only marginal recourse to outside financing, and business families were closely knit. But in more recent years companies have been established that have sought outside financing, and the original family business groups have witnessed a growing differentiation between managers and owners; in addition, the development of an active and buoyant stock market very much encouraged the emergence of financiers.

Thus the distinction between financiers and active entrepreneurs has until now attracted little interest or analysis, because the two aspects frequently coincided in the same person or, at least, family; but it is bound to become more important as successive generations follow the original founder of the family business, and roles become more diversified. As this process unfolds, the role of financial intermediaries is also likely to become more important than it has been so far, with some significant implications that will be discussed below.

Finally, the pure rentiers are those who cash in on their position as mere citizens or as citizens with variable degrees of *wasta* available to them, to extract revenue from expatriate workers, foreign companies, or more entrepreneurial fellow citizens. Several members of the ruling family would fit into this category, although you do not need to be a prince to carve out a rentier niche for yourself. Sponsors of immigrant labour, for example, may be very small fish: they frequently do not actually employ the worker, but receive an income stream for providing an *iqama* and holding the worker's passport (this of course being illegal, but frequent nevertheless). Conversely, not all business people from within the ruling family conform to the description of the pure rentier—in fact the best known among them certainly deserve to be considered real entrepreneurs and/or world-class financiers.

While the distinction between entrepreneurs, financiers and rentiers has become totally outmoded with reference to the industrial countries—where even hedge fund speculators are praised for their contribution to the proper functioning of markets—it is often referred to in the context of the oil-producing countries. Indeed the Saudi private sector is still often described, even at times within the country, as being peopled essentially by such parasites—but this is a blatant misconception.

Clearly, when we speak of the national bourgeoisie we mean the entrepreneurs. The pure financiers or rentiers may be wealthy, but they are neither economically nor politically part of the national bourgeoisie.

Obstacles to Knowledge

It is difficult to conduct serious empirical research on the private sector in Saudi Arabia—as indeed in most other Arab countries. The primary obstacle is that the process of corporatisation and transformation of the original family business groups into publicly traded companies is just beginning.

It is a common trait of Arab (and Mediterranean) culture that one does not boast about one's fortune.[3] In many parts of the world, openly discussing one's wealth only serves the purpose of attracting the attention of the taxman. Therefore, no privately held business group publishes financial or indeed industrial data that may allow estimating aggregate indicators of the private sector's capabilities and results. This may change with time, but it is to be expected that resistance to stringent disclosure rules will persist. For the time being, the best information is available from state-owned enterprises that are publicly traded on the stock market—but of course, as men-

[3] In this sense business people that are members of the ruling family stand out from the rest, being often atypically ostentatious.

tioned above, whether they should be included in the private sector is quite dubious.

Ownership is also frequently confused by the use of multiple trademarks—i.e. only some of the family business groups identify their activities by using a common name, either the family name or some other business name—or by the use of intermediaries and proxies. The latter is normal practice for royal and some princely interests—although of course not all.

Thus we have only incomplete knowledge of the interrelationship between political and economic power—this being the case, of course, not just in the Gulf countries but also in Jordan, Morocco and, for that matter, Egypt and Tunisia. Rumours abound, but to what extent should we allow such rumours to influence our scientific evaluation?

In addition, economic statistics in general are still highly inadequate in the Gulf countries, including Saudi Arabia. We have no proper and reliable series for industrial production, and investment figures are quite uncertain. Statistical coverage is improving, but the lack of a proper fiscal function—both direct and indirect taxes, corporate and personal—means the kind of consistency checks that help keep economic statistics on track are not possible or reliable in this environment. Therefore, we can not use economic statistics to check aggregations of corporate information either.

Generally business activity is gauged at the moment when a license is requested: we have information about the number of licenses granted, the authorised capital the expected number of workers etc. However, this information is a notoriously inaccurate picture of actual reality. Not only is some of the licensed investment in fact never turned into a working business; more important, with time those businesses that started working and have prospered will increasingly diverge from the parameters in their original license, which will soon become totally irrelevant.

Finally, but certainly no less important, we obviously lack information on Saudi investment abroad. As the argument unfolds here, it will become clear that this is a very significant limitation, because the importance of this investment is at the heart of the analysis.

So, how can we make any progress? There is no alternative to relying on the scant and insufficient information available, and making the best of it. The alternative to this very imperfect approach is to follow Wittgenstein: 'Whereof one cannot speak, thereof one must be silent' (*Tractatus Logicus-Philosophicus*, proposition 7)—and terminate here. Nevertheless, some observations on the private sector shall be put forward, with the hope that fresh research will in future improve our knowledge of this important element in the Middle East puzzle.[4]

Origins of the Private Sector: Representation, Land, Agriculture, Government Procurement

What are the origins of today's business families? Their wealth has largely been made possible thanks to the process of circulation of the oil rent, based on government expenditure. However, it is important to recall that some of today's prominent business families were prominent and active well before oil came to the fore. A number of merchant families, some with important international ties, were established in the Hijaz before the Saudi conquest. Indeed, some of them financed Abd al-Aziz even before the conquest, and welcomed his triumph over the Hashemites.

Historians have discussed the causes of the ascendance of the Al Sa'ud, and have interpreted Wahhabism and Saudi rule as an essentially urban movement aimed at establishing a state and means of control of the nomadic tribes.[5] In this sense Saudi rule has always aimed at protecting the settled population, i.e. primarily the merchants. The pro-business attitude of the Saudi monarchy is therefore deeply ingrained, and is the key difference in terms of political economy between the Saudi and other GCC (Gulf Cooperation Council) regimes on the one hand, and the military-revolutionary regimes of other Arab countries on the other: the latter destroyed or fundamentally weakened their respective national bourgeoisies, while in

[4] In addition to the sources listed, observations are based on close to two decades of direct engagement with, and in-country observation of, a wide spectrum of Saudi economic actors. Nevertheless, the evidence remains anecdotal even if extensive, rather than the truly systematic kind one would ideally need.

[5] See Abdulaziz al-Fahad 'The 'Imama vs. the 'Iqal: Hadari-Bedouin Conflict and the Formation of the Saudi State', *EUI Working Papers*, 11 (2002), Badia Fiesolana: Robert Schuman Centre, European University Institute, 2002.

the Gulf countries the objective always was to nurture a strong domestic private sector (see below).

The mechanisms through which the oil rent, initially accruing to the state, was transformed into private wealth are well understood and documented. It is possible to distinguish essentially five main channels:

(1) Representation of foreign companies;
(2) Land distribution and real estate speculation;
(3) Promotion of extensive agriculture;
(4) Government procurement;
(5) Government support to industry.

To say which was most important is of course impossible, but individual family fortunes are quite clearly linked to either one or the other.

Representation of foreign companies has possibly been the most widespread method. Initially, some of the major import deals were 'assigned' by the King to specific princes or merchants or bureaucrats, in order to reward them for their services and loyalty. However, the law simply stated that foreign enterprises needed a local partner to be in business in the Kingdom, a 'sponsor', not that the sponsor should be appointed by the King. This stipulation opened the door to a 'market for sponsorships', foreign companies looking for the best sponsor, and local business people looking for foreign companies that might succeed in the Kingdom, and whom they might attract and represent. This 'market' was only partially controlled by the state.[6]

The sponsorship business is extremely varied. Some local sponsors or representatives simply sign the required papers once a year or provide formal cover for a fee, and take no interest at all in the business. In a few notable cases, foreign companies have grown frustrated by the ineffectiveness of their local sponsors, and have divorced from original sponsors to seek new ones—although this is generally not at all well regarded.

[6] Strictly a Sponsorship is needed if a company wants to operate on Saudi soil. For exporting to Saudi Arabia a foreign company needs an 'agent'. Both sponsorships and agencies provide opportunities for local 'middlemen' to profit from the business.

But in several other notable cases the local importer has progressively established a significant business in its own merit, especially in areas which require after sale service, such as automotive, domestic appliances, machinery, computers and consumer electronics and so on. The local content of these business enterprises is quite significant: they have absorbed important investment, and accumulated significant managerial and technical know-how. In a growing number of cases they have begun manufacturing locally some components or segments of the product range, if the economic rationale for doing so exists. Thus, while it is certainly true that these companies are not truly independent, there is no reason to belittle their significance and capabilities: they are big businesses in their own right.

Land distribution and real estate speculation are extremely important sources of wealth creation, in a land in which population grows rapidly and the major cities are expanding relentlessly. Originally public land was granted by the ruler either to members of the ruling family (by far the most frequent case) or to individuals having acquired special merits. Whatever the original pattern of distribution, it is increasingly clear that what made the difference was the use that was made of the land. Some of the original owners simply quickly cashed in on their bounty, others have sat on their property without doing much with it (this being the origin of the empty lots of land, including in prime urban areas, that are such a striking feature of some Gulf cities); others, finally, have more or less successfully developed or redeveloped what they received or acquired.

Today real estate speculation is an activity that is no longer primarily dependent on the ruler's largesse, but animated by the initiative and intelligence of a vast number of entrepreneurs who buy and sell, develop or re-develop, rent etc. Thanks to the fact that foreigners are prohibited from owning real estate (a prohibition which only recently has started to be eroded[7]) the business of providing housing for expatriates, or offices for foreign companies, has always been very lucrative; but it also became increasingly competitive, as

[7] The new law regulating Foreign Direct Investment approved in 2000 allows companies investing in the Kingdom to own the land and real estate required for their own activities, including employee residences. See chapter by Malik Niblock in this volume. Individual foreign residents cannot buy property on their own, at least for the time being.

supply outpaced demand. Therefore, in this field as elsewhere, not everybody was equally successful, and success is not purely, and no longer primarily, a function of closeness to the government.

Promotion of extensive agriculture has been an important episode, which, however, has quickly ebbed and lost importance. The combination of subsidies for the digging of wells and the installation of pumps, subsidies for diesel, no charge for fossil water utilised, and subsidised prices for wheat and barley, led to a boom in agricultural production in huge agricultural estates in formerly desert land that was distributed by the state either to members of the ruling family or to others having acquired special merit.[8]

However, this pattern of extensive agriculture has proven unsustainable, and the government has reviewed or eliminated the various subsidies. Sooner or later limitations will be imposed on the use of fossil water, and only those agricultural businesses that will have managed the transition to new crops and more advanced technology will be able to survive. This selection process is presently underway, and may be expected to result in a substantial reduction of the size, and redrawing of the map of the agricultural sector. Of course incumbents resist the change, but they are fighting a losing rearguard battle.

Government procurement deserves special scrutiny as the most direct link between the oil rent and private-sector fortunes. In the early days of the oil boom, up until the mid-1980s, the urge to spend was such, and the government's ability to manage and control its spending so seriously strained, that contracts were easily handed out to 'politically' selected contractors, and allowed for the realisation of excessive profit margins on the part of both the local and the foreign

[8] Such land distribution occurred primarily in the Najdi heartland—which received the vast majority of agricultural funds, to the relative detriment of the country's traditional agricultural areas in the Asir and Tihama in the West, and in the al-Hasa oasis in the East. This is possibly the one aspect for which Chaudhry's interpretation—seeing rent circulation as a tool to favour an emerging Najdi business clientele to the detriment of the longer established Hijazi business families—is more relevant (Kiren Aziz Chaudhry, *The Price of Wealth: Economies and Institutions in the Middle East*, Ithaca, NY: Cornell University Press, 1997). In industry and finance, the Saudi bourgeoisie is national: although individual families obviously originate from somewhere, be it the East, Najd or Hijaz, an insistence on regional origin would be in most cases artificial.

suppliers. Some fundamental political targets were pursued in this period, most notably the rebalancing between the Hijazi and the Najdi business interests, which was achieved to a large extent through the shift of the capital from Jeddah to Riyadh.[9]

However, the situation has very much changed since those times. Funds available for so-called Chapter-4 expenditure have dwindled—as total expenditure has been constrained and a growing share of the budget has been eaten up by recurrent expenditure. Of course obtaining a contract with the government is still considered good business, like in almost all countries; and the various groups compete for this business. Of course proximity to government officials or individuals in power is considered to be an advantage in bidding for government business. And finally, there are certainly occasions in which corruption, i.e. the private interest of government officials, plays a role in determining the selection. Again this is true in almost all governments.

At the same time it is noteworthy that the government and the bureaucracy have reacted with increased vigilance and professionalism in the management of government procurement to the growing challenge of achieving results with limited means. As any contractor will confirm, government contracts currently on offer are not as 'fat' as they used to be. The better managed branches of public administration—especially such atypical or hybrid entities as Saudi Aramco and SABIC—run some very sophisticated and well-reputed procurement systems, based on competitive bidding from approved suppliers. The perception that the bids being offered were too high has led to the cancellation of several tenders—notably in connection with investment projects for which the government did not have sufficient funds and tried the BOT (build-operate-transfer) alternative.[10]

[9] This process has been studied and documented in detail by Chaudhry, *The Price of Wealth*: today one can see clearly that the Hijazi business community, although in a sense it may have been offered fewer opportunities to prosper, nevertheless remains in many respects important in the country.

[10] SABIC and Saudi Aramco are specific institutional islands, exceptions rather than the rule. Elsewhere in the system, procurement has not improved very much. Sometimes cost criteria are indeed adhered to rigidly, to the detriment of quality. Procurement methods are often archaic and prescriptive, with little performance orientation. Yet the example of SABIC or Saudi Aramco is very important.

It seems fair to state that a fundamental transformation has taken place, inasmuch as in the past contracts were allocated to parties that had no relevant know-how, and started acquiring or looking for the required know-how only *after* receiving the contract, while today most contracts are subject to competitive pressures, and although it may not always be the case that the best offer is accepted, at least incompetent bidders will hardly have a chance. This means that individual private sector actors must strive to acquire the knowledge and know-how, either directly or through partnership with foreign enterprises, to be able to successfully bid for government business.

There is little doubt that providing for the government's needs will continue to be an important avenue of business success, and on some occasions a tool for the government to reward key supporters, but the extent to which this is the case has drastically diminished relative to the past. The situation that exists at present is certainly far from the transparent and even playing field that the economic literature advocates. However, one gets the impression that the extent of non-transparency is not really under the control of the political authority, but increasingly used by middle and lower level bureaucracies to benefit other links—regional, kinship or plain friendship.[11] In this respect, the private sector feels freer to object to non-transparent procedures, and the holders of political power may conclude (and in some cases have) that they need to enforce transparency in order to re-establish their control.[12]

Finally *government support to industry* should be mentioned, though it has been of lesser importance in the nurturing and consolidation of the Saudi 'private sector'—not because it has not been generous enough, but because the various benefits available have accrued primarily to majority state-owned companies, such as SABIC. Nevertheless there are numerous smaller, genuinely privately owned industrial enterprises that have benefited of the ability to locate in one of the serviced industrial cities, to receive favourable loans from

[11] See the chapter in this volume by Steffen Hertog.

[12] The assessment of their ability to do so is to some extent subjective. On all major deals, which may attract the personal attention of the top political leadership, transparency will be enforced. Of course, when it comes to the myriad of smaller transactions, there is some merit to the argument by Hertog (this volume) that it may be harder to turn the desire for transparency into reality.

the Saudi Industrial Development Fund (SIDF), to enjoy competitively priced power. As the presence of private enterprises in petrochemicals grows alongside SABIC (see below), the availability of natural gas (methane) and NGLs as feedstock will also become increasingly important. Thus, if historically policies in support of industry have been a relatively minor pillar in the overall strategy of support to the private sector, they are bound to become increasingly important, compensating for the decline of promotion of extensive agriculture and the reduced importance of government procurement.

Not Everybody is Equally Rich: Some Prosper More, Some Less

The growing competitiveness of access to government procurement, the progressive closing down of the agricultural boom, the expansion of cities and growing supply of real estate and urban land, all point in the direction of the decreasing importance of governmental favour, and the growing importance of the managerial skills of the entrepreneur. While in the past it could be concluded that the only important condition for becoming wealthy was proximity to power, as time goes by a process of natural selection amongst those that initially benefited of the government's largesse is set in motion, and fortunes diverge. The more or less accidental origins of a company or family business group are progressively forgotten, and their ability to manage their own affairs and pursue growth becomes more important.

The initial largesse of the rentier state has benefited many whose names are entirely forgotten. Their families and descendants may be personally well off, but they are not active and recognised businessmen in any sense. We tend to notice and know only the very successful ones, who have masterminded the growth of their initial business and branched out into numerous successful parallel ventures. Sheer luck of course also plays a role—i.e. whether you happen to be the representative of a successful foreign product, whose quality and success is to a large extent independent of your efforts. But this is true in many situations in all parts of the world, not just in Saudi Arabia.

To underrate the savvy and business acumen that is required to make the best of the initial opportunity that may have been offered by the process of circulating the rent is a mistake. As time goes by and the business continues to grow, as the founders grow older and die, as the management of the business becomes increasingly complex, we have some very clear cases of remarkable success; but there are also cases of people simply 'sitting' on their fortune and not making the best of it, and a few cases of mismanagement leading to (relative) demise.[13]

Today's Saudi business leaders certainly continue to value proximity to the government, and would only wish to have a positive relationship with the key power brokers in the royal family; but would not accept that their success is due exclusively to such contacts as they may enjoy.

The attitude has very much changed. Of course, if the government offers opportunities, they are sought after. But all major business groups know perfectly well that their prosperity and growth should depend less and less on the government, and more and more on their being able to serve markets competitively. They in fact complain constantly that the State, in order to defend state monopolies or bureaucratic privilege, is barring them from pursuing business opportunities that they believe would be highly profitable. Although the net balance of advantages and disadvantages that each business group derives from its various contacts with the government and the bureaucracy is likely to be positive in some cases and negative in others, if such a statistic could be compiled (profits realised vs profits foregone because of government regulations and procurement) it would almost certainly show a negative aggregate sign—or so at least the business community firmly believes.

The State as Protector of the Business Sector: From the Origins of the Saudi State to the Present

Nevertheless, the state remains, as it has always been, the protector of the business community—from the origins of the Saudi state itself. The urban origins of the power of the Al Sa'ud are clear, and their constant search for the support of the merchant community and

[13] Kahlid bin Mahfouz remains a very wealthy businessman but he lost control of the National Commercial Bank. The Maghrabi family lost very substantial assets due to infighting after the death of the founder—a case often referred to with respect to the need to corporatise—see below. More generally, there are plenty of unknown faces that simply never came to the fore, though they had their opportunity.

attention to the prosperity of the latter are unequivocal. The Saudi state—different from most other Arab states outside the Gulf, never sought to assert its power by curtailing the influence and wealth of the major merchant families; and did not have to deal with a foreign (non-Arab) bourgeoisie or colonial class as it existed in other Arab countries (where it was ousted after independence). In other words, the Saudi state never engaged in a process of destroying a pre-existing class order in order to open the door to a new one—it simply integrated and remoulded what it found. The business community integrated into its ranks several 'foreign' families or entrepreneurs, which in some cases had established themselves in Saudi Arabia from several decades before the formation of the Saudi state, and in other cases were attracted by the oil boom. Not all of the newer ones were granted citizenship and naturalised, but they were nevertheless allowed to prosper, in some cases accumulating very significant wealth.

The fact that the state progressively expanded its direct role in the economy is not due to the desire of limiting the role of private entrepreneurs, but rather to the wish of supporting the private sector by undertaking those investments, which it was felt the private sector could not undertake. There are some very clear episodes showing this: for example, the state did not nationalise the originally private electricity companies, but underwrote increases in their equity capital so that they could expand their generation capacity in line with demand; in this way it acquired the vast majority of the equity. Furthermore, because electricity was for several years sold below cost to check increases in the cost of living, the private equity holders were guaranteed a minimum return on their equity notwithstanding the fact that the companies may have been operating at a loss. Overall, it was a sweet deal for the original owners.

A reorganisation of the electricity sector has come only recently, with the formation of a national electricity company, SEC, purportedly as the first step towards privatisation of the sector. However, for the time being no second step has followed.

Especially in the 1970s, the Saudi state had to cope with multiple bottlenecks that threatened to choke economic growth and led to severe inflation. Ports, airports, roads, electricity, telephones, cement—everything had to be expanded in a hurry in order to accommodate the wave of investment made possible by the explosion of the oil rent. In this phase the private sector was inevitably crowded out of many activities which the state undertook directly frequently facing very high charges for implementation at emergency speed. The private sector benefited as the purveyor and contractor for the extraordinary appetite of the state. Hence the expansion of the state apparatus, far from being a move against the bourgeoisie, really greatly contributed to its enrichment and consolidation.

However, when the tide receded the opportunities for catering to the state decreased, and the private sector has so far found it difficult or unprofitable to enter sectors from which the state had crowded it out. But as subsidies are scaled down, prices are realigned, and excess availability of certain capital goods is reabsorbed, the private sector is again increasingly attracted to those activities that it had engaged in in the past, but had subsequently relinquished. The resistance to this re-privatisation is more bureaucratic than ideological, and does not presuppose a radical change of course for the Saudi regime.[14]

The Wealth of the Private Sector

Thanks to the various mechanisms for rent circulation discussed above, and to the benevolent treatment it has received from political power, the Saudi private sector has engaged in very significant investment abroad. It is hardly necessary to stress that the Saudi economy always enjoyed complete freedom of capital movement—not an indifferent consideration in international comparison. The Saudi business people and financiers have always had, and continue to have, a considerable attachment to their country, and one cannot speak of a 'capital flight' out of Saudi Arabia at any moment in time (occasionally, there have been runs on the Saudi riyal, but these have generally been short-term phenomena). Nevertheless, the size of available profits and the limited availability of investment opportunities at home has led to a natural desire for diversification, which has translated into massive investment in real estate and financial assets abroad; occasionally, specific industrial or service companies

[14] Increasing utility prices to the consumer is not an attractive course of action for the leadership, yet it is done if it is perceived as necessary—this is no different than in any other country. As elsewhere, the calculation changes when it is discovered that privatisation offers an opportunity for disengaging the political leadership from unpopular decisions.

have been acquired by Saudi entrepreneurs, but this has been the exception rather than the rule.

Once again we lack reliable statistical information on the extent of wealth accumulation abroad, and anything better than an educated guess is unlikely ever to be available. In part this is because of the sheer difficulty of estimating the value of all assets that are not publicly traded financial instruments. Nevertheless, we know that Saudi investors have bought prime real estate in the major cities of Europe and the United States (much of it in London), and have greatly benefited from the bull equity market of the 1990s. They may have seen a partial decline in the value of their assets since 2000, but their losses have probably been limited, because they were not seriously caught in the new-economy frenzy.

In this light, the generally convergent estimates that are put forward appear credible. For example, according to Abd al-Rahman Al-Jeraisy, chairman of the Council of Saudi Chambers of Commerce and Industry, 'Saudi investments abroad are estimated at between $800 billion and $1 trillion and most of these funds are concentrated in the United States and Europe.'[15] In 2003 I estimated that Saudi accumulated wealth abroad was probably at least $600 billion.[16] All such estimates probably undervalue real estate holdings, or ignore them altogether.[17]

Even if we assume a margin of error of plus or minus 30 per cent, our qualitative conclusion does not change. On such an asset base, the annual income accruing internationally to Saudi investors must be in the order of $30–35 billion at least. To put this figure in perspective, we may recall that in 2004, which was an extremely good year from the point of view of oil revenue, the Saudi Arabian Monetary Authority increased its total international reserve by $26 billion,

[15] *Arab News*, 10 November 2004.

[16] On the basis of an estimate of GCC assets held internationally put forward by international banking sources: my intervention at the SWP/EUROMESCO workshop 'Looking Ahead: Challenges for Middle East Politics and Research', convened by Volker Perthes in Berlin, 5–7 December 2003 (published as EUROMESCO, paper no. 29).

[17] The Institute of International Finance (IIF) estimates that between the beginning of 2004 and the end of 2005 the total foreign asset holdings of the six Gulf Cooperation Council countries will grow by at least $150 billion (*Arab News*, 23 February 2005). This presumably also includes official reserves.

to reach an accumulated $85 billion. Total government expenditure was about $79 billion. This means that, thanks to the rapid increase in oil revenue, the state has regained ground since 2000, but previously for some years had commanded financial resources smaller than those available to the private sector. In terms of accumulated assets, the private sector still by far surpasses the official government reserve.

Another interesting way to look at financial realities is to recall that in the course of the first eleven months of 2004 the increase in the value of stocks traded on the Saudi stock exchange created a wealth effect of $235 billion.[18] The state, being the largest owner of the stock of Saudi publicly traded companies, has in theory gained almost as much from this capital appreciation as from oil revenue. The private investors have of course also gained very substantially.

When we add all sources of income of the private sector, the returns on their international and domestic financial investment, the appreciation of real estate domestically and internationally, the profits made by the private companies, it becomes abundantly clear that the direct dependence of the Saudi bourgeoisie on the government's largesse is very much reduced. Clearly, if the government were to substantially decrease expenditure, this would precipitate the national economy in a recession, which would hurt the bourgeoisie—but this is a macroeconomic effect entirely different from having access to government contracts. Direct access to government spending, that is, to the primary injection of the oil rent into the national economy, today accounts for a fraction of the total financial resources available to the bourgeoisie.

It would therefore appear that the Saudi bourgeoisie has substantially ceased to be dependent on the state, and is now autonomous. Autonomous does not, of course, mean that it is indifferent, even less hostile—simply that it can survive and prosper independently of direct recourse to the state. The latter is required to maintain law and order, receive the oil rent and judiciously inject it into the economy, but it should not do so by competing with the private sector or shutting it out from profitable opportunities.

At the level of individual entrepreneurs this autonomy means that the state cannot undermine them, although it can selectively withdraw

[18] See the discussion of the stock market below.

favour. Of course it is always preferable to have an excellent relationship with political power; but you no longer need to be waiting at its door to be the first to capture the opportunity of the day.

The Private Sector Commitment to Investing in the Kingdom

The interesting aspect of the Saudi private sector is that, notwithstanding the very substantial accumulation of assets abroad, and the ease with which capital can be exported out of the Kingdom (or possibly because of it), Saudi investors appear to be strongly committed to investing in their country.

This is a very important trait, which distinguishes the Saudi situation from that of other Arab countries outside the GCC (and possibly to some extent some within the GCC as well) and many other oil-producing countries. It is a trait that results from the combination of a lack of complete trust in the level playing field offered by the international investment environment, coupled with a feeling of trust and confidence in the respect of property rights at home. Because of this attachment to investment at home and the development of their own country, the Saudi bourgeoisie deserves to be characterised a national bourgeoisie.

The lack of complete trust in the international investment environment was already present before September 11th and the deterioration in US–Saudi relations. Saudi investors generally shy away from playing the role of entrepreneurs in the major industrial countries. This is the reason why so few have established companies in the United States or in Europe, or acquired substantial stakes in existing companies. Even some of the major corporate investors, such as SABIC or Saudi Aramco, have been extremely cautious in acquiring foreign companies or downstream assets. The implicit or explicit fear is that they will not be allowed to effectively control their investment, because they are not truly acceptable investors to the host country. Of course this feeling is not entirely unwarranted: one only need recall that Kuwait was forced in 1988 to reduce its 21.6 per cent stake in BP to 9.9 per cent, and this by the most economically liberal of all governments, that of Margaret Thatcher.[19]

[19] See: The Monopolies and Mergers Commission, 'The Government of Kuwait and the British Petroleum Company plc.: A Report on the Merger Situation', London: HMSO, October 1988.

Consequently, Saudi entrepreneurs know that in the international arena they will be welcomed as prized clients of banks and real estate agents, as they will always be welcome to pay their registration fee and hotel room to attend the World Economic Forum in Davos, but this will not be enough to be regarded as first-rank players in the global business scene. Their political and business influence is closely tied to them being Saudi and major business players in Saudi Arabia, and Saudi Arabia being the largest exporter of oil in the world.

From this point of view, engaging in profitable investment worldwide is viewed by many Saudi business people (one is tempted to say: by most—but there may be many more who do not very much care and who are invisible to us) as second-best to establishing a prosperous business empire at home. It is their position as entrepreneurs in their home country, and the direct ties with major international companies that frequently come with that position, that determines their rank and influence.

Hence, Saudi entrepreneurs constantly complain that they do not find sufficient investment opportunities at home. The perceived need for the Saudi government to deliver a better economic growth record than has been attained in 1985–2000 is tied on the one hand to the growing number of unemployed youth, but on the other to the dissatisfaction and criticism coming from the business community. The Saudi national bourgeoisie commonly views the state's glacial decision-making process, excessive red tape, and penchant for control as the main obstacle to increased private investment at home and higher growth rates. The success of Dubai and other emirates, which compete with Saudi Arabia and have attracted substantial Saudi investment and business initiatives (the other GCC countries, followed by other Arab countries, being viewed as the second-best solution, after investing in Saudi Arabia itself), is an implicit indictment of Saudi government immobilism[20].

[20] See e.g. 'Riyadh Forum to Probe Flight of Saudi Capital', *Saudi Gazette*, 12 April 2005. 'Why are Saudis taking their capital out of the Kingdom and investing it in the neighbouring Gulf states? This will be one of the topics to be addressed at the Riyadh Economic Forum (REF), said Abdulrahman Al-Jeraisy, Chairman of Riyadh Chamber of Commerce and Industry (RCCI). (...) According to reports, around 4,000 Saudi investors have already left the Kingdom to set up their businesses in other Gulf states, where the investments laws are comparatively attractive. (...) RCCI has reportedly studied 126 obstacles to investing in

It is important to note that unemployment is not necessarily the main driving force behind seeking a higher rate of growth. In a country like Saudi Arabia, where the number of expatriate workers employed is vastly superior to the number of nationals unemployed, the temptation of solving the unemployment problem by 'Saudising' a certain number of expatriate jobs is obviously very strong. Saudi business people always strenuously resisted this solution, because it would increase their costs and reduce their competitiveness. Instead, they argue in favour of higher growth, which, however, is not at all certain to translate into more jobs for unqualified and sometimes unemployable Saudis.

Hence the national bourgeoisie, in its desire to find more numerous investment opportunities and invest relatively more at home, is simultaneously pushing for higher growth rates and for a selective retrenchment of the state, which may again leave to the private sector a long list of investment opportunities which the state occupied when all the money was in its hands and the private sector was weak, and which it has since been reluctant to relinquish.

In fact, the public sector, which was an essential promoter of growth in the 1970s and early 1980s, has today become an obstacle to, rather than a driver of, growth. This is not a necessary outcome: we have the example of other, admittedly smaller, Gulf countries in which the state continues to be the main promoter of growth, continuously creating opportunities for private sector profit. One could not rule out that the same might happen also in Saudi Arabia, and indeed to some extent growth requires a more entrepreneurially-minded state. However, again for the state to promote growth, greater strategic clarity and leadership at the top would be required. In the absence of these, the painfully slow decision-making process translates into long delays in the adoption of measures that are widely recognised as necessary, and growth is inevitably slowed down.[21]

Saudi Arabia and found that at least 14 of them can be done away with in order to motivate Saudis to keep their capital in the Kingdom.'

[21] I believe that the weak leadership resulting from an ageing and ill absolute ruler also facilitates the emergence of other degenerative phenomena such as the segmented clientelism which Steffen Hertog discusses in his chapter in this volume. If strong leadership came to the fore, this pattern could theoretically be reversed; in practice, however, that is not a very likely scenario.

An accelerated growth agenda therefore requires a considerable redistribution of assets and responsibilities from the government to the private sector, although the role of the state in the economy is bound to remain important. The issue is not so much availability of investment funds—although this will remain limited notwithstanding higher oil revenues—as the need to respond more promptly to market signals and competitive opportunities, in an economy, which is diversifying both nationally and regionally.

The national bourgeoisie not only favours a renewed growth agenda, but also knows that it is indispensable to its realisation. It views itself as a not fully utilised asset for national prosperity, stability and regional influence, and claims from the government that it should make better use of its potential. Thus the main expectation concerning the government has shifted: the focus used to be on the distribution of the oil rent—and the pursuit of development was simply a way to justify certain distribution channels; today, wealth accumulated in private hands, the bourgeoisie is conscious of its considerable capabilities, and national development is the prerequisite of its continuing prosperity and regional influence.

The Capabilities of the Bourgeoisie

The Saudi bourgeoisie consists not just of the very large families, each worth several billion dollars, and whose names are easily recognised, but also of a myriad of smaller entrepreneurs, businessmen and women, of considerable weight. The number of families whose net worth is above $100 million certainly runs into several thousand, and smaller entrepreneurs are very numerous indeed. The Saudi bourgeoisie as a class may now be estimated at well over 500,000, or 3–4 per cent of the population at the very least.[22]

By comparison to the average composition of the workforce in either developing or industrialised countries, Saudi society (i.e.

[22] A rough estimate of the numerical importance of the bourgeoisie can be based on the number of members of the Chambers of Commerce and Industry, which is in excess of 100,000 for the Kingdom as a whole (40,000 in Riyadh alone). This must be expanded to include their family members, leading to an estimate of the bourgeoisie as a social class well in excess of 500,000. But many smaller entrepreneurs probably do not bother becoming members of the Chambers of Commerce.

nationals, not including foreign workers) is characterised by the almost total absence of a national blue collar class; by the comparatively small size of the white-collar labour force employed in the private sector; and by the comparatively larger proportion both of those employed by the public sector, and of the self-employed or entrepreneurs; and frequently the two roles are simultaneously found in the same individual (i.e. the government employee also runs a private business).

The major business families, but also the second layer of families whose net worth may be above $100 million but below $1 billion, have frequently developed some remarkable capabilities. They have prospered because of their international contacts and are, comparatively speaking, very cosmopolitan and well equipped for understanding and participating in the globalisation process. These people are frequently very well travelled and have experience of how business is done in Japan and in Europe or the United States. The older generation did not always have an opportunity to acquire an international education, but certainly 'speaks better English' than their average equivalent in continental Europe or Japan. The newer generation frequently is issued from the best American or European schools, and is perfectly at ease in the environment of Global Big Business.

The combination of accumulated 'soft' assets with remarkable financial capabilities creates an environment in which entrepreneurs are constantly scouting for investment opportunities, and use the best consultants and business partners to guarantee the quality of projects they engage in. Indeed, sometimes the insistence on always having the best quality (the best product, the most established producer as partner) may become a bit of a self-limiting factor—but pragmatism is also on display.

The old idea, according to which the business community is composed largely of greedy speculators that will only invest in projects with very quick returns, and will not take any large or long-term risk, has increasingly proven totally unwarranted. Of course any entrepreneur will prefer a high rate of profit and quick return of his invested capital, but this does not necessarily mean they are unwilling or unable to invest in more substantial ventures.

This is shown very clearly by the fact that private companies have recently entered the field of petrochemicals with several large-scale projects, requiring investment of the order of billion of dollars. The Saudi International Petrochemical Company (SIPC), the National Petrochemical Industrialization Company (NPIC), the Saudi Chevron Phillips Company and the Sahara Petrochemical Company among others, stand for the increasing know-how and capabilities of private investments in downstream chemicals and other value-added products.[23]

In 2004 the Sahara Petrochemical Co. evolved from the former Al-Zamil Petrochemical Co. The aim of the company is 'to invest in industrial projects, especially chemical and petrochemical ones, to produce propylene, polypropylene, ethylene, polyethylene and other petrochemical and hydrocarbon products.' It will also 'own and carry out projects necessary for meeting the company's demand for crude

[23] The following list may be instructive:

- The Saudi International Petrochemical Company (SIPC) has been initiated by the Zamil Group in 1999 as a Saudi joint stock company to produce and market Maleic Anhydride (MAN), Butanediol (BDO) and Methanol through three limited liability companies being established through joint venture agreements with international partners.
- The National Petrochemical Industrialization Company (NPIC) was established by the National Industrialization Co. (NIC) in 2000 as a joint stock company. NIC owns 51 per cent of NPIC, while other private Saudi and Gulf investors hold the remaining shares. NIC is part of the Kingdom Group of Prince Al-Walid bin Talal.
- The Saudi Chevron Phillips Company is owned jointly by Chevron Phillips Chemicals and the Saudi Industrial Investment Group, a consortium of leading Saudi businessmen and several Saudi public joint-stock companies, which is focused on industrial investment in the petrochemical industry in Saudi Arabia.
- The Saudi Formaldehyde Chemical Company Ltd. (SFCCL) began operations in 1991 already and has since developed into a major producer and international supplier of Formaldehyde and derivative products. SFCCL is a private sector enterprise developed and financed by a group of industrialists from the GCC countries.
- In 1986 XENEL Industries Group (family of Alireza) founded the SAFRA Co. Ltd., a producer of aliphatic and aromatic solvents (110,000 t annual capacity) located in Yanbu, being the first privately owned petrochemical plant in the Middle East. XENEL Industries and Alujain Corp. are major shareholders in the National Petrochemical Industrial Co. (NatPet) building the 'TELDENE' polypropylene project in Yanbu with a planned capacity of 420,000 t/year, scheduled to come on stream by late 2006.
- In early 2004 the Gulf Farabi Petrochemicals Co. promoted by the Al-Rajhi Group commissioned the building of a plant to produce n-Paraffin and Linear Alkyl Benzene.

resources and facilities,'[24] and market its products inside and outside the Kingdom. The founders have underwritten 80 per cent of the shares, and the remaining 20 per cent were offered to the public.[25]

In June 2004 the IPO of Sahara Petrochemical Company 'made history in shares flotation when it raised a record amount of over SR37.5 billion (US $10 billion), with its shares oversubscribed 125 times'.[26] In March 2005 NPIC, Sahara and Basell (a joint venture of Basf and Shell Petrochemicals) jointly undertook a project worth $1.6 billion in Jubail.

The outstanding success of the launch of the Sahara Petrochemical Company is significant in many respects. First, it shows how the ability of the private sector to undertake larger projects is enhanced by the transformation of family businesses into corporations, some of which are beginning to be publicly traded. The transformation of an informal family business into proper corporations is encouraged by the difficulty of maintaining a loose and informal structure in the face of the progressive disappearance of the founding fathers of the business, and enlargement of the families. As is natural, it becomes increasingly difficult to maintain the unity of the family in the face of sometimes divergent interests as families grow bigger and bigger. Corporatisation is therefore a tool to prevent possible family squabbles that may have disastrous consequences on the busi-

24 *Middle East Economic Survey*, 47, 35, 30 August 2004, p. A12.

25 The first Board of Directors of the company included: Abd al-Aziz al-Zamil (former Minister of Industry) chairman; Abd al-Rahman al-Zamil; a representative of the General Organization for Social Insurance; a representative of the General Establishment for Retirement; Rashid al-Gharir (representative of al-Jazeera Petrochemicals Company); Sultan ibn Khalid ibn Mahfuz; Sa'd al-Za'im (representative of Riyadh Cables); Sa'id al-Aisani; Abd al-Rahman Sa'id; Tariq al-Mutlaq (representative of al-Mutlaq Group); and Fahd al-Zamil (managing director).

26 *Arab News*, 5 June 2004. The article quoted Abdulaziz al-Dukheil (head of the firm that managed the flotation of shares), who underlined that a 'distinctive feature of the flotation was the transparency in the flotation process, with datewise subscription details available to the shareholders.' At the same time, he pointed out, the overwhelming subscription underlined the acute shortage of investment channels for the huge liquidity in the private sector. 'This phenomenon should engage the attention of the Saudi Arabian General Investment Authority (SAGIA) in opening up the market to investors,' he said. The CCFI chief also underlined the need for curbing the monopoly of some major shareholders.

ness. In other cases it has been a tool for the qualitative transformation of the business, as when the al-Rajhi network of moneychangers was transformed into a proper bank, and more recently a group of smaller moneychangers have been encouraged to merge and form the Al Bilad Bank,[27] whose initial public offering (IPO) was even more successful than Sahara's.

In these and in other cases, the corporatisation and flotation of new or existing business enterprises has allowed the original owner or initiator to realise some very considerable capital gains. This constitutes a very powerful example and precedent for all Saudi business families, and we may expect a rapid process of progressive transformation of the existing businesses, especially in areas in which there is greater potential for expansion, and therefore need for capital strength.

The Ascendance of the Stock Exchange

The transformation of Saudi capitalism has been encouraged by the equity market boom (not just in Saudi Arabia: in other GCC countries and in Egypt as well), and in turn the equity market benefits from the increasing supply of attractive assets.[28]

The extraordinary upturn in the major Arab equity markets is commonly attributed to the desire of regional investors to diversify their portfolio out of the United States, following the 11 September 2001 terrorist attacks. The extent of actual divestment of American

[27] The Al Bilad Bank was formed in November 2004 from the merger of eight money exchange businesses. The owners of the original money exchange companies retained 50 per cent of the capital of the new bank, while the rest was floated in an IPO in March 2005. The eight founders are: Muhammad Abdullah Ibrahim Al-Subaie Company (42%); Al-Muqairen Money Exchange (18%); Al-Rajhi Commercial Foreign Exchange (16%); and Al-Rajhi Trading Est. 14%; Muhammad Saleh Sairafi Est. (5%); Injaz Money Exchange (Yousuf Abdul Wahab Niamatullah Company) 3%; Abdul Mohsen Saleh Al-Amri Est. and Ali Hazza Partners for Trade and Money Exchange, 1 % each. The IPO of Al Bilad was an extraordinary success: a total of 8.3 million subscribers bought shares (i.e. 50 per cent of the Saudi population, including infants), contributing 7.51 billion riyals one day before the closure of the offer.

[28] The pace of IPOs accelerated in 2003–4. It remains well below potential, and the UAE market has been more dynamic in this respect. The recent trend will have to be sustained to make a real difference, but this is likely to be the case.

assets is unclear: some shifting of balances from the United States to British and European markets must have occurred, motivated also by the persistent weakness of the US dollar relative to the Euro. More likely, what has taken place is simply a redirection of additional flows: the previous regular outflow of liquidity from the GCC countries has been reduced or possibly even reversed, and profit is not reinvested in the United States. This would be sufficient to create a run in the Gulf equity markets, whose size is relatively small.

The increase in the price of oil may have contributed to the positive results, creating a climate of optimism, eliminating the government's need to borrow, and finally also increasing government expenditure, which, however, has been much smaller than the increase in revenue. All in all, in 2003 and 2004 all indicators have encouraged the bull run.

The Tadawul All Share Index (TASI) rose by 84.9 per cent in 2004, outperforming the growth of 76.2 per cent recorded in the previous year. The increase continued in the early months of 2005, soliciting mixed comments from analysts.[29] Obviously, if the stock market were to crash, investors' confidence might be seriously undermined and the process of transformation of the Saudi bourgeoisie temporarily stopped.

[29] TASI started 2004 at 4,450 points, only to almost double its value by the end of the year, closing at 8,206 points. It crossed the 10,000 points mark in March 2005. TASI's capitalisation, which was around $140 billion at the beginning of 2004, has also more than doubled to reach $375 billion. Some analysts saw the increase as fully justified, others warned that the price/earnings ratios of major Saudi stocks appeared to be high, and thought a correction inevitable.

It should however be noted that the Saudi companies have been very profitable. The combined net profit of 72 out of 74 listed companies rose by 45.4 per cent in 2004 (the two missing companies are Sahara Petrochemical and Etihad Etisalat, which have not been in existence for the entire year). The strongest performance in 2004 came from Saudi Basic Industries Corp. (SABIC), which declared a record 112 per cent increase in net profit to SR14.2 billion, making it the most profitable petrochemicals firm in the world. According to a Market Review and Outlook report prepared by the National Commercial Bank in April 2005, the combined cash dividend payments alone are estimated to have totalled SR24.78 billion, on a total market capitalisation which touched a new high of SR1.47 trillion in March 2005. NCB's Chief Economist Dr Said Al ash-Shaikh said 'Profitability growth among the Saudi listed companies has been a key reason for the steamy Saudi equity market last year and during the first three months of 2005.' (*Arab News*, 11 April 2005).

However, a virtuous scenario is also possible, in which the rapidly increasing liquidity is absorbed by the flotation of new companies or the progressive sale of existing companies currently owned by the government. Indeed, the current state of the market constitutes a golden opportunity for the acceleration of the process of privatisation, especially with respect to assets that have long been targeted for sale by the Saudi Government. In May 2005 the flotation of the National Commercial Bank, which the Government took over from the Mahfouz family, after Khalid Bin Mahfouz stepped down from the chairmanship in 1999, appeared to be imminent. The major question is whether finally the Government will sell some of the 70 per cent of the stock it owns in SABIC, a move that was announced already in the Fourth Development Plan in the second half of the 1980s but never implemented; or some of the 70 per cent that it owns in the telecommunications company STC, as well as an initial tranche of the electricity company SEC.

Why, notwithstanding these favourable circumstances, is privatisation proving so difficult? The answer points to one of the important fault lines in Saudi society. It is easy to say that the slow pace of privatisation, in the face of an officially proclaimed policy, is due to bureaucratic resistance—but this is not enough. Bureaucratic resistance is substantially reinforced by a current of thought insisting that a few private 'sharks' should not be allowed to benefit from the entrepreneurial capacity of the state, which created such jewel companies as SABIC. The idea is that if these companies are privatised, a few major private sector investors will be able to accumulate large participations, even if in the beginning the flotation is conducted in a transparent and 'democratic' fashion. Furthermore, it has been said (although this argument has probably lost ground in the light of the recent increase in share prices) that SABIC shares were undervalued and should not be sold at such a bargain price. Finally, it has in the past been informally suggested that a flotation would not be conducted in a transparent manner, and, specifically, that some princes might take advantage of the circumstances to achieve substantial capital gains.

In other words, there is a (political/intellectual) current in the country, which we may term vaguely populist, that defends state ownership against what is perceived as the excessive greed of the major business characters, or of some members of the royal family. This is why the transparency and wide participation in some of the recent

IPOs is extremely important to establish the credibility and acceptability of any privatisation process.[30]

More generally, the transparency of other key state-business transactions also is worth noting, and has contributed to establishing a new business climate in the Kingdom. In the early stages of the so-called gas initiatives, international oil companies were invited to visit the Kingdom and present their proposals for involvement in the oil and gas sector. When one after the other did so, the visiting delegations were received by the Crown Prince, who explicitly and directly recommended that they should abstain from seeking allies or partners within the Kingdom.[31] When, after various vicissitudes, three gas exploration and production concessions were granted in early 2004, the Saudi authorities made a point of publishing the bids of all companies, including the losers, to prove that the process had been impeccable. The same procedure was followed in other important cases, notably for the adjudication of the second mobile telephone concession: in the latter case, eleven international consortia entered the field, many including prominent princes among their partners, and six were invited to submit bids. The cynical talk of the town was that one of the princes would necessarily win the concession, but in the end that proved unfounded. The consortium led by the UAE's Etisalat won by a significant margin,[32] and included no member of the royal family.[33]

30 One should also not forget the IPO of Ettihad Etisalat, the second mobile telecommunications network, which was fifty times oversubscribed; on the first day of trading the company's shares rose five-fold, from 50 to 300 SR; one should also mention the IPO of the National Company for Cooperative Insurance, which had a more moderate impact because of Islamic reticence with respect to the insurance business.

31 The author was present at one such 'admonition', and was told that the same message had been given to all companies.

32 The Etisalat Consortium offered SR12.21 billion ($3.25 billion), followed by the consortium including South Africa's MTN, which offered SR11.05 billion ($2.94 billion). Egypt's Orascom (Sawiri family) came third, offering SR9.8 billion ($2.61 billion); the consortium including Kuwait's MTC was fourth, at SR9 billion ($2.4 billion); the Samawat Consortium (Telecom Italia Mobile) was fifth, at SR8.7 billion ($2.32 billion). The consortium in which Prince Al-Walid bin Talal bin Abd al-Aziz partnered Spain's Telefonica Moviles made the lowest bid at SR6.7 billion ($1.78 billion).

33 Etisalat's Saudi partners in the consortium are the General Organization for Social Insurance (a Government agency), Riyadh Cables Company, Abdul Aziz

In July 2004 the government also moved to improve the governance of the equity market, by establishing the Capital Markets Autho rity to overlook trading. One thing is very clear: by now the attention and interest that the stock market receives in the country is such that the Saudi state cannot afford to be indifferent to its continued growth and stability. Preserving a healthy equity market has certainly become one of the key testing grounds for the government's performance and legitimacy—just as preserving monetary stability has been for a long time. For two decades the Saudi government has insisted that it wanted to protect the country from a repetition of the Suq al-Manakh crisis (1982), which seriously undermined the credibility of the Kuwaiti state and ruling family. Managing the equity's market boom and piloting a soft landing will be no trivial challenge, but the steps required are clear: offer government-owned equity on the market, encourage corporatisation and IPOs of family enterprises, enforce better transparency and information requirements, widen the ownership base by allowing access to foreign investors (Qatar did so in April 2005). All of these steps are frequently advocated in the press and failure to take them would be reproached to the government if it resulted in a collapse of the market. At the same time taking the required steps for managing a soft landing will radically transform the relationship between the Saudi state and private sector.

The Politics of the Saudi Bourgeoisie

There is little point in trying to identify political convictions of the Saudi business leaders as a class: just as elsewhere, and given that this is a relatively numerous group encompassing very diverse interests and life experiences, there are all sorts of political opinions among Saudi business leaders. A more meaningful question is whether and how businessmen are active in politics; and on which issues they are likely to converge and be motivated by their class interests.

Certainly a majority of the business leaders have no political profile, but the exceptions are interesting. In some rare cases, they take

---

Al-Sughayyer (industrial) Group, Al-Rana Investment Company and two groups—Al-Jomaih and Bin Zager—with both industrial and commercial arms.

side on issues of political importance; more frequently they engage in 'political games', i.e. in behaviour that, while not immediately political per se, nevertheless has clear political undertones and symbolism.

Two contrasting cases may be used in illustration. The first is Prince Al-Walid bin Talal, individually the most powerful and visible businessman in the country, and one of the richest men on earth. Al-Walid is in theory in the line of succession to the throne, but in practice his chances of getting there by virtue of simple seniority are very small. He is number five on *Forbes*' list of global billionaires in 2005, with an estimated net worth of $23.7 billion. *Forbes* categorises billionaires according to how they got there, and Al-Walid is listed as 'self made'.

Al-Walid has called his business group 'Kingdom'. He has built the tallest tower in Riyadh, visible from all sides of town, and has called it Kingdom Center (the Arabic may just as well be understood to mean the Center of the Kingdom) from where he conducts his business as the 'CEO of the Kingdom'. In addition to such obvious symbolism, he is constantly in the news with his activities and political meetings. He visits heads of states and governments abroad and receives those that call on him in Riyadh—and the news is announced just as if he were a high government official.[34] He displays royal behaviour, primarily by being generous and giving publicly to several worthy causes.[35] One month after the 9/11 attack he travelled to New York and publicly presented Mayor Rudolph Giuliani with a $10 million donation to a September 11th relief fund. At the same time, in a written statement circulated by his office, he declared: 'At times like this one, we must address some of the issues that led to such a criminal attack. I believe the government of the United States of America should re-examine its policies in the Middle East and

[34] See for instance the report in *Arab News* on 2 January 2004 on his visit to Palestine and Palestinian officials.

[35] *Middle East Intelligence Bulletin*, 4, 9 (September 2002) has a good summary of Al-Walid's charity activities. A more recent example appears in a long article on poverty in Saudi Arabia published in *Saudi Gazette*, 30 January 2005, where it is said: '...Custodian of the Two Holy Mosques King Fahad donated SR50 million at the beginning of a major fundraising campaign. In a separate move, Crown Prince Abdullah also set aside SR200 million for emergency housing for the country's poor. Prince Al-Waleed Bin Talal pledged to donate 10,000 houses over the next decade.' No one else is mentioned.

adopt a more balanced stance toward the Palestinian cause.'[36] In reaction, Giuliani returned the donation. Later, Al-Walid blamed Giuliani's decision on 'Jewish pressures'; although apparently a blunder, the whole episode probably enhanced his political stature in the Kingdom.

He manifested his desire for political recognition when he bid to replace Rafiq Hariri as Prime Minister of Lebanon (he carries a Lebanese as well as a Saudi passport, being half-Lebanese on his mother's side: his grandfather was Lebanon's first post-independence prime minister, Riadh al-Solh).[37] In 2002 Emile Lahoud attempted to play the card of Al-Walid bin Talal to undermine Hariri. The possibility of Al-Walid replacing Hariri continued to be mentioned intermittently until in September 2004 he declared to a group of Lebanese businessmen in the presence of Lahoud that the Lebanese opposition (which was resisting the extension of Lahoud's mandate and advocating international pressure for the withdrawal of the Syrians) 'oversteps the limits' and should be 'brought to heel'.[38] This provoked a wave of criticism from various sources. Following Hariri's assassination, and the turn of events in Lebanon, Al-Walid's bid to take the Prime Minister's job may have been forgotten.

Al-Walid's stance in Lebanon contrasts with the position that he has taken in Saudi Arabia, where he has publicly advocated direct election of the *Majlis* based on universal suffrage.[39] He has also advocated women rights, notably the right to drive; and in a *coup de theatre* in November 2004 he hired the first Saudi woman pilot to fly the private planes of Kingdom Holding.[40] He has attacked the Govern-

36 *Middle East Intelligence Bulletin*, 4, 9 (September 2002).

37 See *ibid*.

38 'Lebanese Opposition Cries Foul over Saudi Prince's Remarks', *Agence France Presse*, 10 September 2004.

39 *New York Times*, 28 November 2001. More recently he was quoted as saying the decision to hold municipal elections had put Saudi Arabia in the company of developed countries that have adopted universal suffrage.(...) 'Municipal elections are stepping stones for major elections,' he added, calling on all potential voters to register vote (*Arab News*, 5 December 2004).

40 *Saudi Gazette*, 24 November 2004: 'In a historic move, Prince Alwaleed Bin Talal announced that he has hired Hanadi Zakariya Hindi, the first female Saudi pilot, to fly the company jets of Riyadh-based Kingdom Holding, the multi-billion-dollar company he chairs. I'd like to see Saudi ladies working in all fields, Alwaleed told the Saudi Gazette (...). Step by step, for sure I'll hire more female

ment's oil policy and the conduct of Oil Minister al-Naimi in unusually harsh terms, accusing him of mismanaging the gas initiative originally launched by Crown Prince Abdullah.[41] He has advocated reform of the education system and has invested in model schools of excellence.

Although he has invested in the National Industrial Company (NIC), which is active in industry including petrochemicals, his business interests are concentrated in banking, in real estate and hotels, in the media and in large-scale retail trade. His assets are abroad as well as in Saudi Arabia: the jewel of the crown is his participation in Citicorp, but his investments are also in Europe and in several Arab countries (Dubai, Kuwait, Lebanon, Syria, Palestine...).

The profile of his investment is not so different from that of many other Saudi business families or individuals (Al-Walid is a business individual, not part of a family), he certainly cannot be considered as representative of the Saudi bourgeoisie. This is so not just because of his flamboyance and very public profile, which no other Saudi bourgeois would imitate, but also because of his ambiguous position as a businessman and member of the royal family. On the one hand his profile is that of a pure businessman, having by all accounts made very little use of his royal lineage to enhance his business success;[42] he is, as *Forbes* says, a self-made man, more so than many other businessmen of his age that have inherited a family business established by their fathers. Yet at the same time he is a royal and behaves like

---

Saudi pilots, he said, hoping that the national carrier, Saudi Arabian Airlines, would follow suit. And about women not being allowed to drive in Saudi Arabia, Alwaleed said: I hope the campaign will begin in the air, women in the air are safe and they will be found safe on the ground as well.'

41 On 11 November 2003 *Gulf News* reported that Al-Walid had 'launched a virulent attack on the kingdom's oil minister and state-owned Saudi Aramco, accusing them of torpedoing a multi-billion-dollar gas deal and undermining the country's credibility,' and described the cancellation of the $25 billion original Gas Initiative early this year as a farce that would scare off other foreign investors: 'Frankly, it was obstructed by Aramco as it represents the oil bureaucracy in the kingdom...I mean that the oil minister and Aramco have wasted this deal,' damaging 'Saudi industry which is in a bad need of products provided by gas...don't forget the thousands of jobs which could have been provided to our youth.' No similar item was published in the Saudi press.

42 Not everybody agrees with this assessment: *The Economist* has repeatedly attacked him.

one, meaning that he would never pass as a representative of the bourgeoisie. In this he suffers from the same limitation of other princes that are very distant from the top of the succession line, are good technocrats, yet nevertheless have little chance of being appointed ministers in 'technocratic' ministries—i.e. those other than the *sulta* (political power) ministries—since the rule in the Kingdom is that those are given to non-royals who can be dismissed.[43]

That said, he is an asset for the Saudi bourgeoisie, just like the other less visible businessmen princes, because he guarantees that the ruling family will never turn against business, and there will always be a continuity of interests between the bourgeoisie and political power.

The second example is Dr Abd al-Rahman al-Zamil, a spirited older man who runs the al-Zamil group from an unassuming two-storey building in a formerly fashionable and now much rundown section of Riyadh,[44] in association with his brother Abd al-Aziz, formerly Minister of Industry and Electricity, who as the head of the family normally plays the role of Chairman and stays out of the limelight. Abd al-Rahman is probably the most important industrial entrepreneur in the country, in the sense that his interests are primarily in various branches of manufacturing industry, as opposed to finance or real estate.[45] Abd al-Rahman al-Zamil is also quite out-

[43] This applies less to princes from minor branches of the family (who can be more easily dismissed), but these are unlikely to be given senior ministries in any case. An example of a prince closer to the centre of the family would be Prince Abd al-Aziz bin Salman, the Deputy Minister of Petroleum, who is unlikely ever to become the minister. On the other hand, *sulta* ministries like Interior, Foreign Affairs Defence or Intelligence, do go to princes—who then invariably build a fiefdom of their own. In this sense Saudi Arabia differs from the other GCC states.

[44] The main headquarters of the Zamil group are in Dammam.

[45] In 2004 Zamil Industrial Investment Company (ZIIC) announced a rise in its net profits by 39.7 per cent to SR70.2 mn ($18.7 mn), after Zakat contributions. ZIIC posted a turnover of SR1.96 bn ($523 mn), a 25.6 per cent increase over 2003. The company's exports increased by 62 per cent, reaching SR889 mn ($237 mn) and amounting to 45 per cent of the company's annual turnover. In 2004 the Sahara Petrochemical Company was added to the list of petrochemical companies and joint ventures owned by ZIIC. (*MEES*, 48, 4).

ZIIC was founded in 1998. It employs about 5,000 people in fifty countries. ZIIC exports to more than seventy-five international markets and derives 35 per cent of its revenues from outside Saudi Arabia.

spoken, and, as a member of the *Majlis al-Shura*, frequently expresses his views on a variety of issues. Nevertheless the style is entirely different from that of Al-Walid.

On issues of corporate governance, the Zamil group has pioneered corporatisation, and Dr Abd al-Rahman has made public statements to point to the fact that the old guard in the group has passed the responsibility of day-to-day management to the younger generation. One of the members of the younger generation, Abdullah al-Zamil, has taken up the role of chief operating officer of Zamil Industrial Investment Company (ZIIC). Speaking at the *Leaders in Dubai* conference in November 2004, Abdullah al-Zamil insisted on the need to benchmark corporate governance to international standards.[46]

Dr Abd-al Rahman is Chairman of the Saudi Export Development Center (SEDC) of the Saudi Council of Chambers of Commerce and Industry, a position that recognises the pioneering role of Zamil Industries in promoting non-oil exports. As such he has been arguing in favour of the establishment of a Supreme Commission for Exports Promotion and for other measures for export promotion, but has also blasted Egypt for its trade with Israel and been threatening implementation of the boycott to Egyptian products.[47]

When the Ettihad Etisalat IPO was launched, the al-Zamil group offered loans to its employees to facilitate the purchasing of shares, a clear statement in favour of 'popular capitalism' in the Kingdom.[48]

In a strong speech at the *Symposium on the Long Term Vision for the Saudi Economy* convened by the Ministry of Economy and Planning in November 2002, Dr Abd al-Rahman criticised Saudi Aramco for the delay in developing the Kingdom's gas resources, which was blocking further investment in petrochemicals (including for the projects that later were undertaken by Sahara).

[46] 'A large proportion of Arab businesses are family-owned and many have become formidable forces over the years. In today's global economy it is essential for them to conform to the new ways in which businesses across the world are now expected to operate. This means providing effective leadership to implement the measures necessary to adopt a level of corporate governance that is on a par with international counterparts and in particular, competitors.' Abdullah Al-Zamil became a member of the board of directors of ZIIC in May 2004. He was appointed chief operating officer in January 2004, responsible for Zamil Air Conditioners, Zamil Glass Industries and Corporate Shared Services.

[47] *Arab News*, 7 January 2005.

[48] *Arab News*, 23 October 2004.

More recently he has been expressing himself on more strictly political matters. Thus for example he praised Bashar al-Asad's decision to withdraw from Lebanon.[49] And on the eve of the March 2005 Algiers Arab Summit he expressed the hope that the creation of a pan-Arab Parliament would become a reality.[50] At the same time he has opposed an enhanced role for women in business, attracting criticism from male and female businesspeople.[51]

There are several other cases of members of the bourgeoisie expressing themselves in politically significant ways, which space does not permit to be listed here. But at least the case of Lubna Ulayan must be mentioned, who has been the CEO of the Ulayan group for several years, but initially took a very low profile, so that the wider public was not necessarily aware of the fact that the Ulayan group had a woman as top executive. Lately, however, she has very much been in the news, especially since she took the podium at the Jeddah Economic Forum in January 2004, unleashing a storm of major proportions and attracting the virulent condemnations of the conservative *ulama*. Yet political intent need not be so blatant to be evident. For example, the implicit political message of Al-Walid investing in Citicorp is clearly quite different from that of Salah Kamel or Abdullah and Muhammad al Faisal establishing, respectively, the Dallah al Baraka Islamic Bank and the Faisal Islamic Bank (both *outside* Saudi Arabia because they never received a license to operate inside), or of al-Rajhi promoting Islamic banking within the Kingdom.

The bourgeoisie is not a political party, and there exists no political formation that can be said to be its 'class expression'. Yet the major Chambers of Commerce and Industry (in Riyadh, Jeddah and Dhahran) have large memberships and run democratic, hotly contested elections to appoint their respective leaderships. Chambers of

[49] *Saudi Gazette*, 7 March 2005.

[50] 'What is now required [for the Arabs] is confidence-building measures by being frank and honest and by genuinely discussing the root causes of their problems, Zamil said. He appealed for a comprehensive and practical mechanism on Arab reforms to be included in the final communiqué. We should concentrate on how much our [Arab] nation can benefit, he said, doubting the possibility of consensus on political issues because of the external pressures on the summit. We should concentrate on the requirements of the Ummah.' *Saudi Gazette*, March 22 2005.

[51] *Gulf News*, 22 April 2005.

Commerce are service structures, and will not take openly political positions; nevertheless both the Jeddah and the Riyadh chambers organise Economic Forums that are opportunities for wider-ranging and non-technical statements by Saudis as well as carefully selected non-Saudi speakers. Leaders of the Chambers are co-opted in more political positions: for example, Amr Dabbagh, who was the organiser of the Jeddah Economic Forum, was appointed to head the Saudi General Investment Authority (SAGIA) in 2004; and Adel Faqeeh, Chairman of the Jeddah Chamber of Commerce and Managing Director of Savola, was appointed to the delicate position of Mayor of Jeddah briefly before the first partial municipal elections took place in the city in 2005.[52]

In the partial municipal elections several businessmen were candidates,[53] but none had great success. This points to the fact that the bourgeoisie may experiment with democratic ways in the Chambers of Commerce, and promote the democratisation of the Saudi state, but is very unlikely to win the elections.

Conclusions: Reform and the Bourgeoisie

A silent transformation has taken place in Saudi Arabia in the long aftermath of the first oil boom (1973–82). While the state was retrenching in order to survive the long slump in oil prices and production, and the considerable regional political and military turmoil, the private sector dependent on the government's largesse has mutated into a national bourgeoisie whose financial assets outstrip those of the government, whose capabilities are remarkable by international standards, and whose class consciousness (expressed primarily in the contraposition with the bureaucracy and the latter's instinct for imposing all sorts of controls) and assertiveness is clearly increasing. There is no opposition between, on the one hand, the state and ruling family—whose power is based on access to an oil rent that remains very large and has been growing again—and, on the other, the bourgeoisie. The two are very closely intertwined in a variety of

[52] *Arab News*, 7 March 2005.

[53] In Riyadh several real estate entrepreneurs (or speculators, depending on the viewpoint) ran some very visible and equally unsuccessful campaigns; in Jeddah the candidates included members of prominent business families, such as Batterjee and Jamjoum: they too did not get elected.

ways, and tied in a continuum of interests; yet they are distinct and engaged in a dialectical relationship. The state must take into account other corporates[54] in the Saudi society, and sometimes resists the demands of the bourgeoisie; nevertheless the bourgeoisie is needed to deliver economic diversification, growth and quality jobs, all of which are essential to the legitimacy of the system.

Democracy may or may not be a priority for the bourgeoisie. One suspects that as long as the system delivers what the bourgeoisie needs on the basis of a system of *shura*, the issue of democracy will continue to be pursued in slow motion. Well-known entrepreneurs have been candidates in the recent partial municipal elections, with very uneven success, showing that the bourgeoisie does not enjoy automatic popular support. However, the situation might change if the bourgeoisie saw its interests seriously threatened—for example by a mismanagement of the financial markets, or a break-up of the GCC, or repeated episodes of opaque management of state-business relations. But fundamentally the bourgeoisie is patient: to the extent that it will not get what it wants from the Saudi system, it will get it from neighbouring countries: the game of competition in governance is very clearly on. The bourgeoisie remains attached to, not trapped in Saudi Arabia.

On other issues, one can only speculate. The Saudi bourgeoisie has extensive investment in the United States, so it will probably favour maintaining good relations notwithstanding the hostility it might have towards specific US policies, notably towards Israel. The bourgeoisie also has extensive investment in the other GCC and Arab countries, so it is keen on closer integration, firstly within the GCC then in the pan-Arab dimension. It is obviously keen on privatisations, and fundamentally also on trade liberalisation, although on the latter point attitudes are more nuanced.

On issues like the role of Islam in politics and the economy, attitudes are more likely to be divided. It is interesting to note that, to the extent that certain traditional ways of political expression, such as notably charity giving, are becoming more difficult in the aftermath of 9/11, the bourgeoisie may feel the incentive for more open and direct political expression.

[54] See Steffen Hertog, 'Building the Body Politic: Emerging Corporatism in Saudi Arabia' in Abdelhadi Khalaf and Giacomo Luciani (eds.), *Constitutional Reform and Political Participation in the Gulf*, Dubai: Gulf Research Center, 2006.

Part III. REGIME AND OPPOSITION

CIRCLES OF POWER: ROYALS AND SOCIETY IN SAUDI ARABIA

Madawi Al-Rasheed

Turbulence in the Kingdom

Throughout the twentieth century outside observers, academics and insiders commented on Saudi political stability, believed to derive from a combination of traditional authority, economic prosperity and an Islamic tradition encouraging obedience to rulers.[1] Most commentators on Saudi politics agreed that, with the exception of a few successfully contained moments of turbulence in the twentieth century, the regime is resilient and capable of overcoming any minor opposition erupting as a result of the interconnection between internal politics and the regional context.[2] The ability of the government

[1] Some analytical work even shows a measure of admiration for the resilience of the Saudi regime: see M. Herb, *All in the Family: Absolutism, Revolution and Democracy in the Middle Eastern Monarchies*, Albany, NY: State University of New York Press, 1999; G. Gause III, 'The Persistence of Monarchy in the Arabian Peninsula: A Comparative Analysis' in J. Kostiner (ed.), *Middle East Monarchies: The Challenge of Modernity*, Boulder, CO: Lynne Rienner, 2000. The resilience of the Saudi monarchy was reasserted during the centennial celebrations in 1999 in the context of several local and international conferences. For example, a conference at Georgetown University was held under the auspices of the Saudi Embassy. See *Saudi Arabia: One Hundred Years Later*, Proceedings of a Conference at the Centre for Contemporary Arab Studies, Georgetown University, 28 April 1999. On other centennial celebrations, see M. Al-Rasheed 'The Capture of Riyadh Revisited: The Shaping of Historical Imagination in Saudi Arabia' in M. Al-Rasheed and R. Vitalis (eds), *Counter Narratives: History, Contemporary Society, and Politics in Saudi Arabia and Yemen*, New York: Palgrave, 2004, pp. 183–200.

[2] For example, in the late 1930s the *ikhwan* rebellion, which challenged the authority of Ibn Sa'ud, the founder of the Kingdom, was crushed with the help of

to contain several cases of 'threats' led many to believe that Saudi Arabia remains politically stable and that its leadership is capable of dealing with domestic opposition and even political violence.

However, the end of the twentieth century brought about a major shift in academic discourse on Saudi Arabia, and arguments celebrating the resilience of the regime are difficult to come by in more recent years.[3] A combination of internal and external factors has contributed to this change of perception. Internally, economic misfortune (the end of the 1970s oil boom and the austerity of the 1980s), social and demographic problems, violence starting in the 1990s and increasing in frequency and intensity throughout 2003–4 and the crystallisation of a strong indigenous Islamist opposition have led many to believe that the twenty-first century may bring a serious rupture between state and society. Today the apparent vulnerability of the Saudi regime and its inability to effectively provide solutions to domestic social problems and respond to political pressure for reform are polarising scholars. Those who would like to see the regime go consider these conditions the seeds of the fall of the House of Sa'ud. Their discourse challenges the illusion of security and stability, which the regime is active in promoting both at home and abroad.[4] Such accounts of Saudi politics forecast a seething cauldron of dissent and chaos replacing previous acquiescence and prosperity.

There is ample evidence to support the view that tension within Saudi society has become acute. One manifestation of this is the

---

Britain. In the 1960s the regime faced a different kind of opposition, mainly of Nasserite and Ba'thist persuasions, all borrowed from neighbouring Arab countries. The ruling group contained the internal opposition by deploying a variety of mechanisms so that by the 1970s the voices of dissent were pacified and eventually silenced. Similarly, under pressure from the Iranian revolution in 1979, the Saudi Shi'a found inspiration and staged an uprising in the Eastern Province where the majority live. The Islamic revolutionary rhetoric of this opposition subsided after clashes with Saudi security forces. On these episodes, see M. Al-Rasheed, *A History of Saudi Arabia*, Cambridge University Press, 2002, pp. 106–62.

[3] See A. Cordesman, *Saudi Arabia Enters the Twenty-First Century: The Military and International Security Dimensions*, Westport, CT: Praeger, 2003; and J. Peterson, *Saudi Arabia and the Illusion of Security*, Adelphi Paper 348, Oxford University Press, 2002.

[4] Some authors went as far as to forecast the expected date for the 'fall of the House of Sa'ud'. See S. Aburish, *The Rise, Corruption and Coming Fall of the House of Saud*, London: Bloomsbury, 1994.

increase in violence in all major cities and towns, which in 2003–4 led to death, devastation and serious unrest in the country.[5] Furthermore, the crisis manifested itself in increasing pressure on the government to reform the political system. In 2003 six petitions were handed to the rulers, all demanding radical reforms, which if implemented would lead to serious changes at governmental level. One of the most important petitions demanded the establishment of a constitutional monarchy in Saudi Arabia. In January 2003 103 intellectuals, liberals and moderate Islamists signed the National Reform Document, submitted to the Crown Prince.[6] This brought together a wide range of signatories, including some Islamists, and was followed up in December 2003 by a further major petition including a larger number of Islamists. Whether these documents reflect the emergence of a united coalition of Islamists and liberals or a temporary alliance between ideologically incompatible partners remains to be seen, but in any case the December initiative met with a hard-line response: in March 2004 several reformers were arrested and, although most were later released, the poet Ali al-Dumaini al-Ghamdi, political scientist Dr Matruk al-Falih, and Dr Abdullah al-Hamid remain in jail at the time of writing.[7]

Speculations about whether the regime will overcome the wave of violence and demands for reform are difficult to make. At one end of the spectrum are those who consider the current violence a passing summer cloud, which can be overcome by deploying behind-the-scenes negotiations, co-optation and reactivation of the social pact between rulers and society.[8] It is believed that such mechanisms

5 See the chapters by Abdulaziz Sager and Roel Meijer in this volume, for details of these attacks, which occurred throughout the country and targeted judges and officials as well as foreign interests and government targets.

6 For a discussion see the chapter by Stéphane Lacroix in this volume.

7 For more details on the petitions and their signatories, see [no author], *rabi al-sa'udiyya wa mukhrajat al-'unf: duat al-islah al-su'udi*, Beirut: Dar al-Kunuz al-Adabiyya, 2004; and Ali al-Dumaini, *zaman al-sijin..azminat al-hurriyya*, vol. 1, Beirut: Dar al-Kunuz al-Adabiyya, 2005. Also the chapter by Stéphane Lacroix in this volume.

8 The Saudi–US Relations Information Service, the Saudi-American Forum and the National Council on US-Arab Relations are Washington-based pro-Saudi websites that mix academic discourse with lobbying on behalf of various commercial and political groups interested in a smooth relationship between the United States and Saudi Arabia. Articles by retired US Ambassadors, ex-CIA

have previously been successfully deployed by the ruling group during times of crisis and that the present one should not be any different. At the other end of the spectrum are those who argue that the current Islamist opposition, combined with a general politicisation of society and the changing international and regional context, for example the US-led Coalition's invasion of Iraq, will make it difficult to survive the storm.

Instead of elaborating futuristic scenarios regarding the survival of the regime, this chapter will concentrate on an interpretation of a number of observations. It argues that Saudi Arabia faces two challenges at the level of leadership. First, as it enters the twenty-first century, the ruling group fails to live up to popular cultural and religious notions relating to leadership, notions that have been constructed and perpetuated by the ruling group itself. This failure erodes the basis of legitimacy that the Saudi ruling group propagated throughout the twentieth century, which in turn has prompted a serious rupture in state-society relations, a manifestation of which is the high level of violence, terrorist attacks and government violation of human rights witnessed in 2003 and 2004.

Second, the ruling group is today lacking a supreme head and is beginning to resemble an acephalous tribal group with several princes representing several circles of power, simultaneously competing and co-operating to perpetuate the group's rule. The royal family itself is best seen as a headless tribe within which several groups have competing claims to leadership.[9] Given the age of the contenders (most senior princes are over seventy years old) and the horizontal principle of succession (since 1953 succession has passed from brother to brother), there seems to be a sense of urgency to occupy the

---

analysts, journalists, scholars, businessmen and oil experts propagate an image of Saudi Arabia as floating in a sea of stability and celebrate government initiatives to contain terrorism and Islamic radicalism in the Kingdom and abroad. See news@saudiusrelations.org. Similar internet sites include news@saudi-american-forum.org. For newsletters (*Gulf Wire*) and *Saudi–US Relations Information Newsletter* see www.arabialink.com.

[9] This argument draws on anthropological theory relating to the segmentary model, first developed by Evans Pritchard in the context of his ethnography on the Nuer of the Sudan. The theory was later refined by a second generation of anthropologists. See M. Al-Rasheed, *Politics in an Arabian Oasis: The Rashidi Tribal Dynasty*, London: I. B. Tauris, 1991, pp. 24–8.

throne; hence competition among brothers tends to be fierce. Since the mid-1990s Saudi Arabia has been governed by five circles of power, each comprising a core, a prince and other important actors. The five circles are those of King Fahd (through his sons); Crown Prince Abdullah; the Minister of the Interior, Nayif; the Minister of Defence, Sultan; and the Governor of Riyadh, Salman. While these are the ruling factions, there are others which might be considered as aspiring to rule, for example the circle comprising King Faisal's sons. This chapter will describe three of these ruling circles and an aspiring one.

This approach challenges conventional wisdom relating to royal politics, inaccurately presented in terms of a cleavage between the so-called Sudairi seven on the one hand (Fahd, Nayif, Sultan, Salman, Ahmad, Turki and Abd al-Rahman) and Crown Prince Abdullah on the other.[10] This interpretation is grounded in a concept of binary opposition which falls short of accounting for the demographic and political changes within the ruling group. Binary opposition arguments are based on the assumption that matrilineal solidarity (descent from a Sudairi mother) is a foundation for political solidarity, but miss the point that kinship solidarity, in the form of both matrilineal and patrilineal genealogical links, is always manifested in specific historical and political contexts, which determine the articulation and expression of such links.

Following this misconception of royal politics, scholars and observers project an image of Crown Prince Abdullah as a 'pioneer reformer' while Minister of the Interior Prince Nayif is seen as a 'bastion of conservatism'. This is reminiscent of the discourse of the 1960s when Faisal and Sa'ud were depicted in those terms, but does not fully capture the situation today.[11] This chapter shows that royal reputations are constructed, and are subject to change over time. Competition between several circles of power leads to a clash of reputations in the quest for political supremacy.

[10] This division is delineated in J. Kechichian, *Succession in Saudi Arabia*, New York: Palgrave, 2001. More recently divisions within the royal family are discussed in M. Scott Doran, 'The Saudi Paradox', *Foreign Affairs*, 83, 1 (January/February 2004), pp. 35–51.

[11] S. Yisrael *The Remaking of Saudi Arabia*, Tel Aviv: Moshe Dayan Centre for Middle East and African Studies, 1997.

Such leadership problems are unfolding at a critical time in Saudi Arabia. A series of regional military conflicts has put Saudi Arabia in the frontline. The 1991 Gulf War, the two Palestinian uprisings, the 2001 Afghan War and the 2003 US-led invasion of Iraq, combined with a volatile regional context dominated by the US Global 'War on Terror', further aggravate the leadership problem. These wars were not remote conflicts, but are sources of tension in which both Saudi leadership and society have been directly involved.[12]

Notions of Leadership

Today the legitimacy of the Saudi leadership is questioned by two important sections of Saudi society: those with (a variety of) Islamist orientations and those with liberal leanings. While these two camps have several platforms to express discontent and voice criticism, both overt and covert,[13] the 'silent majority' is no longer silent thanks to

[12] In the 1991 Gulf War Saudi Arabia hosted American forces and allowed its territory to be used to liberate Kuwait. It also financed the war against Ba'thist Iraq. Saudi Arabia played an important role in the liberation of Afghanistan from the Soviet Union through money and *mujahidin*. The US war on the Taliban regime and Al-Qa'ida in 2001 and the occupation of Iraq in 2003 put Saudi Arabia in an awkward position internally and internationally. For a review of the tension in Saudi Arabia since 2001, see P. Menoret, *L'Enigme saoudienne: les Saoudiens et le Monde 1744–2003*, Paris: La Decouverte, 2003, pp. 212–31. On Saudi-Iraqi relations and the US-led Coalition's war on Iraq, see M. Al-Rasheed 'Saudi Arabia: The Challenge of the American Invasion of Iraq' in Rick Fawn and Raymond Hinnebusch (eds), *The Iraq War: Causes and Consequences*, Boulder, CO: Lynne Rienner, 2005.

[13] Since 11 September 2001 Islamists and liberals have been allowed to engage in debate in official media channels. So far this debate has focused on social, political and economic problems. The loosening of the restrictions on the press gave a false impression, namely that the country was experiencing freedom of expression. Analysis of the exchanges between Islamists and liberals in various media forums reveals that the debate takes place according to strict rules, which exclude any direct critical comments on the performance of the ruling group during the successive crises of the last three years. Intellectuals (both Islamists and liberals) and journalists are allowed the freedom to criticise each other and to point out the failure of government policies which are implemented by high-ranking civil servants in the ministries, but no direct criticism of the role of the Al Sa'ud in government and decision making is allowed. Journalists use metaphors but avoid direct criticism for fear of losing their jobs, arrest or other means successfully employed in silencing opposition and open criticism. In

anonymous electronic discussion boards or forums, which in recent years have become the only outlet for an increasingly politically frustrated, socially marginalised and economically deprived young population, lacking the basic and most rudimentary channels for expressing opinions. A reading of Saudi internet discussion boards gives us a window from which to observe Saudi expectations of their leadership and the frustration resulting from the failure of this leadership to live up to the challenge and meet popular demands for greater political participation, freedom, social justice and economic reform.[14] Another source from which one can assess the opinion of 'disenchanted' Saudis is Radio al-Islah, the communication arm of the London-based Movement for Islamic Reform in Arabia,[15] and Radio al-Tajdeed, of the Party for Islamic Renewal. These radio channels alarm the Saudi leadership, which is unsuccessfully struggling to silence them. In December 2004 the Saudi regime managed to block radio al-Islah from broadcasting on Hotbird; however, at the time of writing this channel remains available in a limited capacity on Helas-Sat and on the internet.

Historically the Al Sa'ud were able to rule as a result of the manipulation of a cultural ideal related to leadership which they were

---

addition to Israel, the United States has recently been targeted by the official media, especially after 11 September when American media expressed unprecedented hostility towards Saudi Arabia. The negative tone of the Saudi press vis-à-vis the United States has recently been toned down. After the Riyadh bombings in May and November 2003 there were attempts to portray both Saudi Arabia and the United States as victims of terrorism. Harsh criticism of the United States has recently subsided, but has not disappeared from the Saudi press altogether. Criticism resurfaced in 2004 after the scandal of the torture and abuse of Iraqi prisoners by American soldiers in Abu Ghraib prison.

[14] For liberal web sites see www.tuwaa.com (discontinued in 2004) and www.daralnadwa.com. For Saudi Islamist sites, see www.yaislah.org, www.wasatiyah.com and www.islamtoday.net.

[15] Under the directorship of Sa'd al-Faqih, Radio al-Islah communicates the movement's political agenda and invites Saudis to call and comment on current affairs in a chat programme broadcast every day. Monitoring of the programmes since October 2003 has revealed that while most callers offer their allegiance to the movement, an increasing number of participants, who may or may not be core members, are drawn from a wide cross-section of Saudi society. Both core members and sympathisers challenge the Saudi leadership from different angles. All callers focus on the ruling group and discuss the behaviour of individual princes.

active in constructing over the last century. This cultural ideal draws on notions specific to Saudi Arabia and the manner in which the state was established. As a conquest state, the notion of leadership is very much dependent on a historical narrative which celebrates certain attributes, for example chivalry, vitality, generosity, youth and vigour, in addition to diplomacy, forgiveness, negotiation and political wisdom. Such constructions are embedded in biographies of the founder of the Kingdom, Abd al-Aziz ibn Sa'ud, and his successors.[16] These biographies represent the official vision of leadership, which is reiterated in the media, classroom teaching material and all cultural events, for example poetry recitals and heritage festivals.[17] Furthermore, televised appearances of key political figures and live encounters with members of the royal family tend to reinforce these constructions which aim to enhance the legitimacy of the ruling group and reiterate its compliance with the cultural ideal.

Other notions of leadership are rooted in Islamic interpretations specific to the country. Historically only a small minority of Saudi religious scholars theorised about the appropriate characteristics of *wali al-amr* (leader of the Muslim community) and the nature of *imama* (the rightly guided Muslim polity);[18] the majority of Wahhabi religious scholars seem to be less concerned with these important questions in Islamic studies. The official Saudi religious tradition, represented by the Grand Mufti and other prominent state religious scholars, consider these questions as *min umur al-dunya* (matters relating to this world). In a televised show one Saudi religious scholar argued that the role of the *ulama* (religious scholars) is to engage

[16] Several biographies of the founder of Saudi Arabia, Ibn Sa'ud, are published under the sponsorship of the Saudi Ministry of Information and other government research centres. See Ministry of Information, *A Brief Account of the Life of King Abd al-Aziz (Ibn Saud)*, Riyadh: Ministry of Information, 1998. The themes in the official biographies repeat other narratives, for example R. Lacey, *The Kingdom*, London: Hutchinson Co., 1981; and L. McLoughlin, *Ibn Saud: Founder of a Kingdom*, Basingstoke: Macmillan, 1993.

[17] See Al-Rasheed, *A History*.

[18] Muhammad ibn Abd al-Wahhab, the Salafi reformer whose religious treatises are revered in Saudi Arabia, did not dedicate substantial effort to the topic of *imama* (leadership of the Muslim community). His biographer Abdullah al-Uthaimin confirms that Ibn Abd al-Wahhab and his followers did not discuss this topic in an elaborate way. See Abdullah al-Uthaimin, *ash-Shaikh Muhammad ibn Abd al-Wahhab hayatuhu wa fikruhu*, Riyadh: Dar al-Ulum, 1992, 2nd edn, pp. 152–3.

only in theological debates relating to *ibada* (orthopraxy) and *fiqh* (jurisprudence). He sees the role of the ulama as educators in matters relating to ritual behaviour and Islamic practices, i.e. *umur al-din* (matters relating to religion proper).[19] He argued that a society can live without scientists—for example, doctors and engineers—but it cannot survive without the ulama who are responsible for educating the populace in religious matters. The same scholar is more than happy to leave the question of Islamic leadership untheorised. He argued that the ulama have limited capacity and time; therefore, they cannot engage in inessential matters such as the nature of Islamic leadership, which he considered to belong to *umur al-dunya*. It seems that there is an implicit recognition of the separation between state and religion, at least in the official Wahhabi circles, which is willing to support government policies out of pragmatism, regardless of whether these policies correspond to religious interpretation.

Given this official religious position, the majority of Saudis have developed an understanding of leadership as a result of socialisation into a cultural tradition which is by nature diverse, oral and highly subjective. Only a small but influential minority—for example, dissident ulama, Islamists and their followers—are preoccupied with questions relating to the nature of the Islamic leadership.[20]

It seems that since the 1970s many Saudi Islamists have relied on alternative contemporary Islamic sources which discuss the question of Islamic leadership. While some Saudi religious scholars have returned to the classical Sunni sources on Islamic leadership,[21] others

[19] Shaikh Muhammad al-Uraifi on Saudi owned satellite television channel *al-Arabiyya, Violence in the Land of the Two Holy Mosques*, 17 November 2003.

[20] No substantial monograph deals with the tension and accommodation between contemporary traditional ulama, dissident ulama and Islamists in Saudi Arabia, although the topic has been addressed in other Muslim countries. A comparative note by religious studies specialist Zaman is illuminating. See M. Q. Zaman, *The Ulama in Contemporary Islam: Custodians of Change*, Princeton University Press, 2002, pp. 152–60. For a general discussion see also D. Eickelman and J. Piscatori (eds), *Muslim Politics*, Princeton University Press, 1996; and F. Burgat, *Face to Face with Political Islam*, London: I. B. Tauris, 2003. See also the chapters by Guido Steinberg and Abdulaziz Sager in this volume.

[21] The classical text which informs Wahhabi understanding of Muslim leadership and politics is Taqi al-Din Abu al-Abbas Ahmad ibn Taymiyya, *as-Siyasa ash-shar'iyya fi islah al-ra'y wa ar-raiyya*, Beirut: Dar al-Jil, 1988 edn. For a concise review of the Wahhabi idea of the Muslim polity, see A. Al-Azmeh, *Islams and*

rely on contemporary interpretations of the Islamist movement, for example the writings of famous members of the Muslim Brotherhood (both Egyptian and Syrian) and other Islamist literature. A contemporary Syrian Salafi scholar who is believed to have inspired contemporary Saudi Islamists and religious scholars since the 1960s, including Safar al-Hawali and Salman al-Awda,[22] summarises his view on the legitimate Islamic leadership. Shaikh Muhammad Surur Zein al-Abdin argues that five characteristics must be demonstrated by the legitimate ruler according to *ahl al sunna wa al-jama'a* (followers of the Prophet's tradition and consensus): (1) he must be a male; (2) he must be an adult with all his reasoning capacities intact; (3) he must be free (not a slave); (4) he must be able to act as a judge who can issue religious rulings; and (5) he must be a Muslim, a category which excludes the *kafir* and *murtad* (the blasphemous and the apostate).[23] This position summarises the widely acceptable principles of leadership dominant within the Sunni tradition. Many ordinary Saudis are today familiar with this theorising which is regularly reproduced in electronic discussion boards and other media outlets. Since the 1990s Saudi Islamists have remained divided on whether the Saudi political system as a whole represents an 'Islamic leadership'.[24] They are even more divided over how to reform it:

Modernities, London: Verso, 1993, pp. 104–21. For recent challenges to the traditional Wahhabi view on Islamic leadership, see T. Asad, *Genealogies of Religion Discipline and Reasons of Power in Christianity and Islam*, Baltimore, MD and London: Johns Hopkins University Press, 1993.

[22] See Al-Rasheed, *A History*; and M. Fandy, *Saudi Arabia and the Politics of Dissent*, Basingstoke: Macmillan, 1999.

[23] Muhammad Surur ibn Nayif Zein al-Abdin, *al-Salafiyya bayn al-wulat wa al-ghulat*, MS, n.d., p. 75.

[24] For example, Saudi dissident Muhammad al-Mas'ari, Director of CDLR (Committee for the Defence of Legitimate Rights in Saudi Arabia) and since 2004 of *Harakat al-Tajdid al Islami* (Movement for Islamic Innovation), considers the Saudi system an illegitimate government from the point of view of Islam. See Muhammad al-Mas'ari, *al-Adilla al-shar'iyya 'ala 'adam ahariyyat ad-dawla as-sa'udiyya*, London: Dar ash-Shar'iyya, 1995. For a similar view from a radical Islamist angle, see Abu al-Bara al-Najdi, *al-kawashif al-jaliyya fi kufr ad-dawla as-sa'udiyya*, London: Dar al-Qasim, 1994. For a middle-ground view, see Saad al-Faqih (Director of MIRA [Movement for Islamic Reform in Arabia]), *an-Nizam as-sa'udi fi mizan al-islam*, London: Movement for Islamic Reform in

while some try to achieve reform by 'advising' the leadership, others use violence to overthrow it. A third group promotes political activism and education as means to overthrow the regime from below.

In Saudi society today two of the most important leadership qualities discussed by a cross-section of society are *hinka* (an ability to judge situations and act accordingly) and *hikma* (general wisdom). These attributes must be demonstrated together with chivalry and vitality, qualities that resonate with people and are normally associated with young leadership. Given that the Al Sa'ud founded a state on the basis of conquest, the chivalry demonstrated in the process of the unification of Saudi Arabia has always been a central dimension in the state's foundation narratives and oral poetry. Unification by the sword gave the regime a certain legitimacy, especially in the first half of the twentieth century. Invoking the sword is also a regular feature of political speech, especially of Crown Prince Abdullah and Interior Minister Nayif in the context of the 'War on Terror'. Moreover, a reputation for *karam* (generosity) constitutes an important attribute which functions to bind ruler and ruled. However, according to many Saudis these qualities do not seem to be sufficiently demonstrated at the top level. The ability to judge situations and act accordingly is seriously undermined as Saudis witness the consequences of royal policies. To mention a few examples, supporting Saddam Hussein throughout the 1980s during his war with Iran antagonised substantial sections of Saudi Arabia, especially those who regard Saddam and his Ba'thist ideology as the antithesis of the Islamic *umma*, the community where faith rather than race is the binding principle. Religious scholars, including the highest religious authority in the country, Shaikh Abd al-Aziz ibn Baz (d. 1999) regarded Arab nationalism in its Ba'thist version a form of *jahiliyya* (pre-Islamic age of ignorance) to be fought alongside Communism and Westernisation.[25] According to religious interpretations, politi-

Arabia, 1996. Al-Faqih states that the Saudi political system does not '*yahkum bima anzala allah*' (rule according to the divine revelation). However, he does not invoke the concept of *takfir* (the practice of considering fellow Muslim blasphemous) when discussing the Al Sa'ud princes.

25 M. Al-Rasheed, 'Political Legitimacy and the Production of History: The Case of Saudi Arabia' in L. Martin (ed.), *New Frontiers in Middle East Security*, New

cal pragmatism could not justify the alliance with Saddam Hussein, which eventually led to subsidising his war and the draining of Saudi economic resources.

Saddam's invasion of Kuwait in 1990 and Saudi Arabia's alliance with the West in the Gulf War (1990–1) precipitated a serious assessment of royal politics, especially the ability of senior princes to judge situations and act accordingly. In the eyes of many Saudi Islamists, Saudi Arabia's invitation to American troops to fight Saddam and liberate Kuwait in 1991 amounted to a violation of the principles of *istiana* (the principle of calling for assistance).[26]

The Islamic notions of leadership, for example *taqwa* (piety and good general Islamic conduct) are also being undermined. While state-controlled media continue to propagate images of a pious and just leadership, alternative sources of information, which are now abundant and easily accessible, undermine these images. Today the state has no control over the flow of information. The personal conduct of members of the royal family is regularly scrutinised and any deviation, scandalous behaviour, corruption and other misdemeanour is rapidly exposed on the internet and heatedly discussed in electronic forums and opposition radio channels. In the absence of venues for open public discussions of royalty, a mixture of fact and fiction thrive. As royalty remains a taboo, a prohibited field, society stretches the limits of human imagination. In official media channels, royalty assumes a sacred status. In contrast, in unofficial channels, especially opposition sources, the personal conduct of members of the royal family, including holiday destinations, private purchases and excessive consumption, inflame the imagination. Saudis search for such stories and circulate them among close relatives and trusted friends. An unusual example was the publication of a semi-autobiographical novel by a member of the Saudi royal family itself, Saif al-Islam ibn Sa'ud ibn Abd al-Aziz, one of the sons of deposed King Sa'ud. The novel, entitled *Qalb min Banqalan* (A Heart from Banqalan) narrates the story of his Baluchi slave mother in the Harem of

---

York: St Martin's Press, 1999, pp. 25–46; and E. Doumato, 'Manning the Barricades: Islam According to Saudi Arabia's School Texts', *Middle East Journal*, 57, 2 (2003), pp. 230–47.

26 For Islamist debates on these issues, see Al-Rasheed, *A History*; and Fandy, *Saudi Arabia*.

King Sa'ud. The novel moves between the personal and the political, in a way deemed unacceptable to senior princes. The novel was withdrawn from bookshops in Beirut, where it was published by Dar al-Farabi, allegedly as a result of pressure from a senior prince.[27]

This obsession with the personal conduct of members of the royal family occupies not only ordinary citizens but also established opposition groups.[28] Members of the royal family themselves are fascinated by the behaviour of other members.[29] In this early phase of political opposition, it is common to dedicate substantial energies to unveiling royal intrigues and misdemeanours, which distract potential opponents from concentrating on developing alternative political visions. This situation is a product of the sacralisation of royalty, while at the same time it is a reflection of the infant history of political activism and opposition in Saudi Arabia. Obvious restrictions on freedom of expression allow the development of an alternative discourse, with 'hidden transcripts' erupting in peripheral spaces such as on the internet and exiled opposition media.[30]

The sacralisation of royalty, combined with a strong belief among Saudis that princes are above the law or are subject to a law of their own, fuels interest in their personal conduct and generates disenchantment with the ability of the system to apply the Islamic principle of *hisba* (establishing accountability of a ruler). Several well-publicised cases,[31] together with a whole range of minor offences involving

[27] Saif al-Islam bin Saud bin Abd al-Aziz Al-Saud, *Qalb min Banqalan*, Beirut: Dar al-Farabi, 2004.

[28] The on-air chat programmes of the radio channel of the Movement for Islamic Reform in Arabia (Radio al-Islah) allows Saudis to phone and express their grievances against the regime and the princes. A survey of the topics discussed between January and June 2004 indicates that criticism of the personal behaviour of princes remains an important preoccupation of the callers.

[29] On one occasion the author was asked by a friend to purchase a popular book about a series of scandals by an important member of the Al Sa'ud. The book was sold in London in typical bookstores/supermarkets which specialise in this kind of literature. My friend explained that a Saudi prince had asked him to purchase this book for his own use. He said that the prince is very interested in the 'bad behaviour' of a relative, the subject of the book.

[30] On 'hidden transcripts' see J. Scott, *Domination and the Arts of Resistance: Hidden Transcripts*, New Haven, CT: Yale University Press, 1990.

[31] Saudis cite three cases in particular for confirming their suspicion that the royal family is subject to a law of its own, historically enforced by the head of the family, the King. In 1947 Nasir ibn Abd al-Aziz organised a party in which seven

royalty and commoners which remain subject to royal will, enforce a sense among Saudis that their rulers are above the *shari'a* Islamic law, which they claim to guard and uphold.[32] This sense is exaggerated as a result of the apparent lack of an obvious supreme moral authority figure, commanding respect or engendering discipline among the royal family.

Today the traditional authority of Al Sa'ud, historically based on an appeal to religious and cultural notions of legitimacy, is threatened as a result of political impotence accelerated and exaggerated by the leadership's old age. In a society where the chronic failing health of old men is often not talked about publicly, that of the King can only help diminish his stature and undermine his masculine persona, which is not conducive to enforcing his authority. In a society where the leader is meant to convey youth, virility and vitality, expressed in the common tradition among senior princes of dying grey facial hair black, the body of leadership must be manipulated in such a way as to maintain these cultural notions. In some Salafi circles, prolonged illness and mental or physical incapacity are grounds for *khal'*, the removal of the leader of the community, either by force or by peaceful withdrawal of *bay'a*, oath of allegiance.[33]

---

guests including members of the deposed Al-Rashid family of Hail died of alcohol poisoning. Rather than subjecting his son to the ruling of an Islamic court, as demanded by the ulama, Ibn Sa'ud came up with a compromise. He removed his son from his position as Governor of Riyadh and promised to exclude him from future official posts. In 1951 Mishari ibn Abd al-Aziz killed the British Vice Consul and sexually assaulted his wife. Rather than being subject to the rulings of an Islamic court as normally practised in the country, the prince took refuge with his brother Faisal until the death of his father in 1953. In the 1980s the death of a Saudi princess at the hands of her grandfather after being caught eloping with a commoner demonstrated that *shari'a* law was suspended in this case. The princess and her lover were executed in public. The decision over this case was left to a close circle of royalty who applied what they regarded as punishment appropriate to their status. The Saudi judiciary was not involved in this case.

[32] Imprisoned poet Ali al-Dumaini tells the story of his father who struggled unsuccessfully for years to get compensation for the confiscation of his land by the government. His father died and the case is still unresolved. See Ali al-Dumaini, *zaman al-sijn…azminah lil huriyyah*, Beirut: Dar al-Kunuz al-Adabiyyah, 2004.

[33] Zein al-Abdin, *al-Salafiyya*.

While old age is normally associated with moral authority in Saudi society, King Fahd does not seem to enjoy this kind of prestige. Since the mid-1990s the King's televised appearances, in a wheelchair and looking frail, distracted and weak, can hardly inspire confidence in the leadership in general. Such images bring to mind the last years of his father, Ibn Sa'ud, whose deteriorating health was known but not televised.[34] Despite Ibn Sa'ud's prolonged illness, he continued to enjoy the status and prestige associated with being the conqueror and founder of the Kingdom, a status which King Fahd cannot claim.[35]

In the opinion of many Saudis the ailing body of King Fahd has become symbolic of the ailing political system over which he presides. The regular appearance of the King on Saudi television screens greeting guests in highly ritualised ceremonial contexts generates debates among viewers who speculate about the state of his health and his ability to rule. Most royal decrees and speeches are read by the King's son or the Crown Prince. Televised appearances are often seen as a burden inflicted on an old man by other members of the royal lineage, who have a stake in keeping him in office as long as possible. According to some analysts, fear of succession disputes between several sons of Ibn Sa'ud contributes to the urgency of perpetuating a united façade. Today the Saudi royal family gives the impression that the King is still in charge, but the situation attests to a different reality.

Circles of Power within Royalty

The Saudi state continues to be seen as a state of personalities rather than institutions. Despite prestigious institutions such as the Council of Ministers, the 120-member Consultative Council (increased to 150 in 2005) and the proliferation of regional government bureaucracies, decision making at the very top level remains the prerogative of a handful of senior princes. The King is supreme commander and decision maker. Legislation is by royal decree. However, given the absence of an obvious 'kingship' due to King Fahd's illness, the decision-making process is dominated by several princes. However,

[34] Saudi Arabia established a television station in the 1960s, almost ten years after the death of Ibn Sa'ud.

[35] On Ibn Sa'ud's failing heath in the 1950s, see Al-Rasheed, *A History*, pp. 104–5.

today there is no conclusive evidence to suggest that the royal family can be broken along matrilineal lines, thus creating two opposed groups (Abdullah with other princes on the one hand and Nayif and his brothers on the other), each with common interests. While it is doubtful whether matrilineal cleavages were behind the succession crisis in the 1960s that resulted in the overthrow of King Sa'ud in 1964, it is equally implausible that such links are behind the leadership crisis over who should succeed King Fahd in the twenty-first century. The problem of succession is a product of the existence of the five 'circles' that aspire to rule the country.[36]

Since the mid-1990s the failing health of King Fahd has precipitated a *de facto* vacuum, temporarily occupied by various factions revolving around individual princes, which compete and co-operate, creating in the process hesitancy, incompetence and contradictory visions. Since 1953 Saudi Arabia has followed a horizontal pattern of succession with no serious commitment to the principle of seniority. As a result, competition among the most senior princes tends to be fierce and is exacerbated by the fact that they are very close to each other in age.

In the twenty-first century, the state consists of five circles of power established by individual princes. Each circle often includes a core, i.e. a senior prince, his own sons and a wide network of commoners, drawn from specific regions and communities. Each senior prince occupies the core of the circle, often anchored in a ministerial office, which forms its social, military, economic and bureaucratic basis. The most important of these ruling princely factions are the Al Fahd, Al Abdullah, Al Nayif, Al Sultan and Al Salman.

There are other circles, less dominant but with aspirations for power, for example that of Al Faisal.[37] Other less prominent princely circles include those of Abd al-Rahman, Turki[38] and Ahmad. Although

[36] For comparison see Volker Perthes (ed.), *Arab Elites: Negotiating the Politics of Change*, Boulder, CO: Lynne Rienner, 2004, in which the editor and the case study contributors—including Iris Glosemeyer on Saudi Arabia—apply a model of three circles.

[37] The word 'Al' inserted before the names of the princes refers to the cluster (the close 'family') around one senior individual, even if deceased, as in the case of the Al Faisal—the children of King Faisal. The Al Fahd is the cluster that consists of the King and his sons.

[38] Although Turki ibn Abd al-Aziz is a full brother in the Sudairi seven circle, common rumour has it that he was marginalised reportedly as a result of the

most accounts of Saudi royal politics emphasise that these princes represent a cohesive group,[39] often attributed to their common matrilineal descent from Hussa bint Ahmad al-Sudairi, a descendant of a loyal family whose members were elevated to princely status as a result of matrimonial connections with and deep loyalty to Al Sa'ud, in reality the above-mentioned princes do not form a cohesive group whose solidarity derives from the Sudairi matrilineal connection. Less prominent princes tend to attach themselves to the major five circles mentioned above.

The coexistence of several princely ruling groups makes it difficult to analyse the Saudi royal family as a single entity or the state as a single state. Instead, it is more accurate to describe royal politics as consisting of several circles of power within a headless tribe, creating in the process a quasi-pluralistic system of government, woven around individual princes and their entourages.

The first circle of power is that of the Al Fahd. Although King Fahd is now incapacitated, it seems that his circle remains operative. It operates through his controversial young son Abd al-Aziz and other influential sons. Since his father's illness, Abd al-Aziz has played the role of spokesman for the *diwan* (the King's court). His youth and perceived extravagance have invited unflattering portrayals by some in the country, added to by a number of other allegations: even if possibly inspired by an anti-regime agenda, such rumours and perceptions in themselves present a difficulty. Whatever the facts, in the mind of many today, the King's circle of power is associated with political manoeuvring and possibly criminality. As such, it would seem to have been considerably discredited and has had to resort increasingly to coercion to enforce authority.

---

behaviour of his wife, a member of the Fasi family. In June 2003 unconfirmed opposition allegations claim that his son Sultan was kidnapped from a hotel in Geneva and returned to Saudi Arabia, following a series of statements in the press about the corruption of the royal family. See http://www.yaislah.org/more.php?id=325_0_1_0_M4. Another 'dissident' prince is Talal ibn Abd al-Aziz who is associated with the post-1960s movement for constitutional monarchy. On the latter see Al-Rasheed, *A History*, pp. 109–10.

39 In a review of Kechichian's book on succession in Saudi Arabia, Gregory Gause III rightly questions whether there is any evidence that neat divisions within the royal family can be attributed to genealogy. See G. Gause III review of Kechichian in *International Journal of Middle East Studies*, 35, 4 (2003), pp. 646–7.

The second most important circle of power revolves around Prince Nayif, the Minister of the Interior. Given the importance of this ministry, Saudis are convinced that Nayif governs the country while his ministry operates as a quasi-independent clique capable of blocking decisions and policies that undermine his hold over domestic issues of concern. The Al Nayif circle is consolidated by the kinship of loyal civil servants and a powerful security force. Nayif appointed his son Muhammad to the key office of Deputy Minister in the Interior Ministry. In addition to junior royal key figures, who are deputies and assistants to their fathers, a wide range of civil servants, advisers and consultants assist in implementing measures introduced at the top level. Civil servants are responsible for the daily functioning of the circle created by Nayif. Like other major institutions of the Saudi state (for example, the army and the National Guard), Nayif's ministry allocates the top positions in the Saudi security forces (intelligence and police, which are contained within the Interior Ministry) to loyal Qasimis and southern Najdis (for example, inhabitants of the small towns around Riyadh who were historically the most loyal supporters of the Saudi leadership), while low-ranking policemen and intelligence personnel are drawn from historically impoverished and peripheral tribal groups in the Hijaz, Asir and Najd. According to a Saudi reformer who is currently in prison, interrogators in the intelligence services include Ahmaris, Harthis, Ruwaylis, Zahranis and others.[40]

The daily lives of Saudis seem to be affected above all by the Interior Ministry, the largest employer in the Saudi government. It has more than 500,000 employees, almost one-third of whom hold security-related jobs.[41] The lives of both employees and citizens are directly influenced by the ministry and those who control the decision-making process. Since Saudi Arabia started a vigorous campaign against Islamist groups following the events of 11 September 2001, the Interior Ministry and its security arms, the police, the emergency forces and the intelligence services (*mukhabarat*), have increasingly been associated with harsh policing practices. The internal 'War on Terror' contributes to the development of a strong sense of mistrust between society and Nayif's policing agents. Sections of

[40] Dumaini, *zaman al-sijn...azminah lil huriyya.*
[41] See Peterson, *Saudi Arabia*, p. 30.

Saudi society today accuse the ministry of a whole range of injustices carried out against individuals who may or may not be part of terrorism networks.

The problem of *mafqudin* ('missing people'), possibly over 5,000, remains unresolved. These are young men whose families simply do not know their whereabouts. Some are believed to be among those who responded to calls for *jihad* in Afghanistan in the 1980s and never returned home. According to some accounts more than 30,000 Saudis joined the jihad campaign and around 10,000 returned in the early 1990s after the Soviet withdrawal.[42] In the absence of an exit strategy by the American administration and the Saudi government, both of whom had encouraged the departure of Saudis for jihad in Afghanistan, the Saudi Afghans found themselves without a clear way out of Afghanistan or a coherent policy from their own government as to how to reintegrate into Saudi society. From the early 1990s the Saudi Afghans began to be portrayed as 'fanatics' in public discourse and media channels.[43] It is believed that those who did not return to Saudi Arabia moved to other locations such as Bosnia, Chechnya and Iraqi Kurdistan, while a small minority dispersed in the West. Other *jihadis* returned to Afghanistan when the Taliban regime was established in 1996. Afghanistan continued to be a destination for Saudi jihadis. It has been estimated that several thousand travelled to Afghanistan after 11 September 2001 as the American invasion became inevitable.

It is estimated that more than forty-five Saudis were killed and at least 240 were captured during the US war in Afghanistan in 2001.[44] Others fled to Pakistan and Yemen. Some were among the dispersed Al-Qa'ida members. Today between 125 and 150 Saudis are prisoners in Guantánamo Bay, almost one-third of the detainees. Their

[42] On the experience of the Afghan Arabs, including Saudis, see A. Anas, *Wiladat al-afghan al-'arab*, London: Saqi, 2002; A. Zaydan, *Bin Ladin bila qina*, Beirut: al-Sharika al-Alamiyyah lil-Kitab, 2003; and M. Salah, *Waqa'i' sanawat al-jihad*, n.p.: Khulud li al-Nashr, 2002.

[43] Saudi Arabia ceased its glorification of the *mujahidin* immediately after they objected to the invitation of American troops to Saudi Arabia following the Iraqi occupation of Kuwait in 1990. Objections were expressed by young ulama who were strong supporters of the jihad in Afghanistan. For further details, see Al-Rasheed, *A History*, pp. 176–87.

[44] Peterson, *Saudi Arabia*.

cases are being considered by a committee of Saudi lawyers.[45] Others are in Saudi prisons following the arrest of suspected Islamists. In August 2003 the Ministry of the Interior urged families to register the names of all missing individuals. However, many parents were reluctant to come forward and give their sons' names in case this information is used against them in the future. Not knowing the purpose of the register and having a deep sense of alienation from Nayif's circle of power, people hesitate before offering information relating to missing relatives. Furthermore, the lack of an independent judiciary makes it difficult for families to trust the courts. Recently, a number of Saudi lawyers and religious scholars publicly declared that the judiciary 'is not independent and as such it fails to respond to the needs of society'. The committee claimed the judiciary 'is out of touch with the modern context; the judges are corrupt and ignorant of the law. More seriously, the judges' rulings are often against the *shari'a*.'[46]

This perhaps explains why not many so-called terrorists responded to the call of a group of Saudi ulama and Islamists, including Shaikh Safar al-Hawali and Muhsin al-Awaji, who announced their readiness to mediate between the government and the jihadis on the assumption that these suspects would be given a fair judicial hearing leading to their public repentance. This was announced by moderate Islamists in an attempt to engage in dialogue with radical Islamists. However, so far only a handful have taken up this offer.

A third ruling circle of royal power revolves around the Crown Prince. Abdullah, who is also Commander of the Saudi Arabian National Guard, resorts to similar mechanisms to perpetuate his circle by relying on close kin. His son Mit'ab is Deputy Commander of the National Guard. The Crown Prince's control of this predominantly tribal paramilitary body is seen as a counter-force to the regular army, which is drawn from a wide circle of Saudis with a substantial proportion coming from the north, west and south-western parts of the country. The foot soldiers of the National Guard are predominantly drawn from the major tribal groupings in Saudi Arabia, for example Utaybah, Mutayr, Shammar, Sebay', Ajman, Qahtan and

[45] *al-Hayat*, 15 November 2003, p. 4.

[46] Abd al-Aziz al-Qasim, statement on *al-Jazeera*, 15 November 2003. Al-Qasim is increasingly described as a 'liberal Islamist'.

others, while the top officers are recruited from loyal families in Qasim and southern Najd. Abdullah's circle of power impinges directly on the lives of many Saudis, especially those who work in the National Guard and their families. Expanding the National Guard also expands Abdullah's budget and power. The National Guard operates a patronage system whereby employees benefit not only from salaries but also from schools, hospitals and welfare funds. One source estimates that the National Guard supports up to one million Saudis by providing income, medical support and education,[47] while others claim this figure is exaggerated. Nevertheless, regardless of the accurate size of this paramilitary institution, important networks of loyalty and patronage are woven through the National Guard, and substantial funds are dedicated for their maintenance and perpetuation. The beneficiaries tend to be the traditional tribal groups who either demonstrate strong allegiance to the Saudi regime or were co-opted through generous subsidies during the oil boom in the 1970s. The ability of this military organisation to absorb the growing number of young Saudis is increasingly limited; so is the ability of the regular army. What is perhaps more worrying for Crown Prince Abdullah is the recent allegation that members of the National Guard were implicated in the May 2003 attack on one of the residential compounds in Riyadh.[48] If this allegation is proved, it would mean the loyalty of this important tribal force can no longer be taken for granted.

Like the Al Fahd and the Al Nayif, Crown Prince Abdullah surrounds himself with a group of advisers, consultants and high-ranking civil servants, the majority of whom are from southern Najd and Qasim, mainly the cities of Unayzah and Buraydah. The Al-Tuwayjiris of al-Majma'ah have produced a number of educated supporters who give Abdullah the necessary guidance for the functioning of his increasingly bureaucratised circle of power. Some of the Qasimi families also have strong connections with groups that have produced generations of Islamic scholars, preachers and judges. This gives Abdullah an entry into the religious field. While he is yet to demonstrate his ability to function as a *de jure* ruler, he is thought to be a centre around whom other disenchanted princes converge.

[47] Cordesman, *Saudi Arabia*.

[48] Reports that members of the National Guard facilitated the attack appeared in *The Independent on Sunday* on 16 May 2004.

While the scope of this chapter does not allow full coverage of the other two circles of power, that is the Al Salman and the Al Sultan (the first would appear to concern itself mainly with the control of old and new media and communication technology, the second with defence and the armed forces), it is important to include an 'aspiring royal circle', that of the Al Faisal. This revolves around the sons of King Faisal (assassinated in 1975), and consists of the Foreign Minister, Sa'ud; the Saudi Ambassador to Britain, Turki; and the Governor of Asir, Khalid. Although Faisal's sons belong to the second-generation princely group, some are close in age to their paternal uncles. So far their prestige is a reflection of their descent from King Faisal. In addition, they have acquired a reputation for education, moderation and the promotion of charitable work through several foundations, which carry the name of their father. Their patronage of culture and research—for example, the King Faisal Foundation and the Arab Thought Foundation—and Islamic charities assures them a reputation for benevolence, which can be beneficial in Saudi Arabia and among Muslims worldwide. However, in some quarters—especially the United States—the post-9/11 climate meant that their association with global Islamic charitable organisations and Islamic Youth associations has come under scrutiny, giving rise to some negative press and public perceptions. Inside Saudi Arabia the Al Faisal cluster of power exercises influence through informal channels of charity and the co-optation of academic research and learning. Although the Al Faisal princes have maternal kinship links with the Al ash-Shaikh, the descendants of the eighteenth-century reformer Muhammad ibn Abd al-Wahhab, their 'Islamic modernity' (*hadatha islamiyya*), believed to be a function of combining Western and Islamic education, somehow distances them from the old guard of the religious establishment, which is increasingly diversified in terms of composition and background and in which the Al ash-Shaikh, although still in control of the very top religious posts, are no longer the key figures. The Al Faisal circle draws on support from a collateral branch of the Al Sa'ud, the Al Thunayan, members of which are royalty but without a claim to the throne. In the daily running of their circle of power, the Al Faisal depends on a network of supporters historically drawn from the Hijaz, perhaps a reflection of the fact that their father King Faisal was based in this region before becoming King. One famous case of a Hijazi support was Oil Minister Zaki Yamani, who played a crucial role in shaping Saudi oil policy until his marginalisation by King Fahd in 1986. King Faisal's sons continue to perpetuate patronage networks with the Hijazi families, for example the Naqshabandis, Khashoqjis and others. The Saudi Ambassador in London, Prince Turki ibn Faisal, surrounds himself with a number of Hijazi media advisers and consultants.

The Al Faisal circle of power projects an image of royalty as bastion of Islamic modernity. This image was somewhat undermined in the West as a result of the post-9/11 atmosphere. Outside Saudi Arabia, and specifically in the Western media, the reputation of Prince Turki al-Faisal, who was previously Head of Intelligence, for a while came under attack with allegations of negotiations with the Taliban and possibly Bin Ladin, and the transfer of funds, even though official investigations discovered no hard evidence of anything untoward.[49] Prince Turki dismissed the allegations in an interview published by a Saudi magazine four months after the 9/11 attacks.[50] Since then he has, as ambassador in London, striven to polish the image of Saudi Arabia and the royal family. In media briefings he depicts the royal family as the guardian against the 'Talibanisation' of the country, a prospect much feared in the West. His brother Prince Khalid al-Faisal does the same domestically through *al-Watan* newspaper. Most important, Prince Sa'ud al-Faisal, the Foreign Minister, remains the face that Saudi Arabia projects to the outside world, perhaps with the exception of the United States where Saudi Ambassador Prince Bandar ibn Sultan retains the trust of the Bush family, even if his reputation too came under attack in some of the post-9/11 media coverage.

In the presence of highly personalised networks of patronage that revolve around individual core princes, ordinary Saudis oscillate between total obedience to and hatred of key royal figures. A loyal client within a princely power circle easily moves from unquestioning support to harsh criticism. In a personalised patron-client relationship, the thread between love and hate is very thin indeed.

[49] A lawsuit by some of the families of the victims of 9/11 that also involves Turki al-Faisal, further added to the problems of public perception.

[50] See interview with Turki al-Faisal in the Saudi magazine *al-Rajul*, 111 (February 2002), pp. 16–29.

Those who enjoy the prestige and material benefit of being 'close' or part of a prince's circle of power can demonstrate extreme loyalty. A client is incapable of engaging in an objective evaluation of the prince's power or its abuse while he remains firmly embedded in the circle. In contrast, those who are suddenly excluded from princely circles or are not part of the network at all (their numbers are increasing as a result of demography, urbanisation and inaccessibility of princes) tend to switch to extreme hatred. An ex-editor of a Saudi magazine moved from being a loyal supporter of royalty to being one of the most critical opponents of the regime within a very short period of time.[51] Political dissent and opposition to royalty focus on individual princes for criticism. 'Hating' a prince is cathartic as it absorbs general public discontent and grievances. When individual critics do not extend their negative evaluations of a prince to the whole royal group, thus challenging their right to rule, royal authority is more likely to be perpetuated, as one can hope to find a 'good and benevolent prince' who can restore faith in the royal family. However, whether this possibility will remain available to the Al Sa'ud in the long term is uncertain.

Clash of Reputations

Away from the public sphere, private meetings where family members and friends gather, internet forums and opposition radio channels tend to be the context for debating the role of the Al Sa'ud princes, the various circles of power, and the merit of their leadership. These 'behind-the-scenes' or 'off-stage' contexts are arenas for comparing circles of power and evaluating the attributes of their cores.

Opposition based on dissatisfaction with the policies of one prince and his circle tends to absorb wider discontent and divert attention from important general questions relating to the royal family as a whole. Therefore, the multiplicity of power circles at the level of royalty can act in favour of the royal group in the short term. This 'pluralism' allows the evaluation of individual princely factions, whose

[51] This is the case of Abd al-Aziz al-Khamis, the editor of Saudi-owned magazine *al-Majal*. After he was sacked for unacceptable reporting, he became very critical of the Saudi regime and various princes. He established *al-Markaz al-Saudi li Huquq al-Insan* (the Saudi Centre for Human Rights) in London.

merits and faults are identified by the constituency without threatening the royal group as a whole.

On the other hand, the multiplicity of power circles within the royal family can lead to a stalemate and weaken the royal group in the long term. At the level of policy, contradictory statements and lack of a coherent vision at a challenging time have characterised public political discourse in Saudi Arabia for the last three years. The language of reform dominates the rhetoric of one prince, only to be undermined by statements of others. Contradictions became especially apparent after 9/11 when fifteen Saudis were named by the United States as having taken part in the attacks on New York and the Pentagon. The initial denial of the responsibility of the fifteen Saudis by Prince Nayif was followed by a plea for 'self-examination' and 'self-criticism' by Foreign Minister Sa'ud al-Faisal.[52] Contradictory statements of this kind are discussed regularly by Saudis. Contradictions and differences between princes are commented on and exposed not only in real social contexts but also 'off-stage'.

At a more general level, the opinion of one prince, regardless of his seniority or public role, undermines the reputation of the whole royal group. For example, statements by an alienated prince, Turki ibn Abd al-Aziz, ex-Vice Minister of Defence, from a self-imposed exile in a Cairo hotel, delivered by his son, Sultan, were vigorously discussed by Saudis searching for cracks in the royal family. Society holds the royal family responsible for the conduct of its members, a tradition reminiscent of the tribal ethos at the heart of the Saudi value system and cultural heritage. The head of the royal group, normally the King, needs to be seen as the source of discipline 'among his own family'. This tradition was understood and valued by Ibn Sa'ud who was known to have disciplined one or two of his sons after he sensed their unacceptable behaviour had become public knowledge. The image of the ruler as father is perpetuated by Shaikh Safar al-Hawali, an eminent scholar associated in the 1990s with ulama *al-sahwah* (the ulama of the awakening), who has recently tamed his criticism of the government. In a televised show, al-Hawali asserted that '*wali al-amr ab wa nahnu usratuhuh*' (the ruler is

[52] Contradictory statements on important policy were also evident during the US-led Coalition's war on Iraq. For further details, see Al-Rasheed, 'Saudi Arabia: The Challenge of the American Invasion of Iraq'.

the father and we are his family).[53] However, the root of the problem is 'multiple paternity', a fact al-Hawali cannot acknowledge in public. With no apparent head and with the royal family undergoing a demographic explosion, it is not clear who is in charge of it. What is evident is that the state consists of five circles of power.

Pluralism at the top can potentially benefit the royal group. It diverts attention from discussion of the whole group and its leadership role, while at the same time it offers several models of political behaviour and persuasions. Individual princes develop reputations for a whole range of political attitudes and inclinations, such as 'moderate reformers', 'Arab nationalists', 'conservatives', 'Westernised modernists', 'constitutional monarchists' and 'tribal patriarchs'. Other reputations derive from personal conduct and relate to morality and individual qualities. In general the reputation of princes is often seen in terms of binary qualities. So there are 'corrupt' and 'pious' princes, 'mean' and 'generous' princes, 'humble' and 'arrogant' princes, and 'educated' and 'ignorant' princes. Princely reputations are created through a complex process whereby internal and external agencies are active in the construction process. This dual quality perpetuates the rule of royalty in Saudi Arabia.

To give an example, the reputation of Crown Prince Abdullah evolves and is built on contradictory attributes. In the mid-1990s he was constructed as a 'tribal patriarch', upholding bedouin values. This image stemmed from his association with the National Guard and its festivities, such as the *Janadiriyya*, an annual event previously dedicated to celebrating culture and heritage, mainly that of the tribal and bedouin past, but has now widened its interests. As his mother was a member of the Shammar tribe, he was also presented as protector of tribal interests. As such he was considered a 'conservative' and possibly a defender of wider regional Arab interests, through his association with Syria's president Hafiz al-Asad. This image was dominant throughout the 1990s but recently some opposing qualities have been associated with him in certain domestic and external circles. Today, in official Saudi media, the Crown Prince is projected as '*rajul al-hiwar wa rajul al-islah*' (the man of dialogue and reform). This reputation for willingness to listen to calls for reform was sealed with the establishment in August 2003 of the King Abd

53 Safar al-Hawali in *Bila hudud*, al-Jazeera, 5 November 2003.

al-Aziz Centre for National Dialogue, a government body where selected professionals, religious scholars and intellectuals meet and debate current issues. The fact that he failed to intervene on behalf of imprisoned reformers (for example Abdullah al-Hamid, Ali al-Dumaini and Matruk al-Faleh) who were associated with demands for a constitutional monarchy, has undermined his reform-oriented reputation in the eyes of many and was viewed as an illustration of the weakness of his circle of power.

Secrecy, remoteness and lack of transparency fuel speculation about the eligibility of this prince or that prince to succeed to the throne. Furthermore, the sacralisation of royalty inhibits open debate and objective assessment of their characters and suitability as public figures. While the royal family suppresses any discussion of the suitability of its own members, Saudi society is apprehensive as the consensus over royalty seems to be undermined in the face of both internal and external pressure.

Conclusions: Impaired Authority and Royal Strategies

Royal authority is seriously impaired in Saudi Arabia. It would appear that the royal family does not inspire due respect, nor does it command total obedience and loyalty. The consensus that enabled it to rule unchallenged throughout the twentieth century can no longer be taken for granted in the twenty-first. While each prince draws heavily on a wide circle of civil servants and beneficiaries, together with co-opted ulama who reiterate the need to respect leaders of the community, there are many voices calling for drastic reform which, if implemented, may eventually lead to the marginalisation of royalty, and even its overthrow. Hence today the state increasingly resorts to direct coercion to enforce law and order, while at the same time pursuing a vigorous policy of co-optation, negotiation, and slow and superficial reform. It creates an atmosphere of fear of imminent terrorist attacks to rally the population and distract it from any radical political demands.[54]

[54] In response to an Al-Qa'ida videotape broadcast on al-Jazeera in February 2004 (*Badr al-Riyadh*) in which two Saudi suicide bombers celebrate their coming martyrdom before the bombing of the al-Muhayya complex in November 2003, the Saudi Interior Ministry issued a warning, almost a week later, alerting the population to a black four-wheel-drive car loaded with explosives that had gone

The royal family plays a well-known game; it projects itself as a mediator between social and political groups, in this case the liberals and the Islamists, the old religious establishment and the new *Sahwi* ulama, the Sunnis and the Shi'a, the tribal and the non-tribal, the Najdis and the Hijazis etc. Historically the royal family played one group off against the other. Official media often exaggerate the divisions in society, for example, those between liberals and Islamists. In 2003 these two groups united to present a petition demanding a constitutional monarchy within three years. This surprised the government, hence the harsh reprimand dealt out to a select number of signatories by a senior prince, which was followed by the arrest of some of them in 2004.[55] It remains to be seen how long the royal family can claim to mediate between various Saudi pressure groups, now that it has resolved itself into five factions, all split between competition and co-operation to claim legitimacy from an increasingly disenchanted constituency.

The erosion of the leadership's cultural and religious credentials should not be interpreted as a sign of the demise of the Al Sa'ud. In fact, so far the segmentation of the leadership has acted as a source of strength. The fact that Saudi Arabia is now endowed with 'multiple paternity', a 'clash of reputations' and 'quasi-pluralism' at the very top level may well perpetuate the overall stability of the regime in the short term.

However, it is important to point out that the survival of the regime at the beginning of the twenty-first century is not a function of royal wisdom and vision, or a function of the weakness of political opposition, or lack of social and political awareness among Saudis. The regime survives, in large measure, because it is authoritarian and coercive, while at the same time using indirect pressure and measures to contain opposition through bribes, co-optation and other means. The 1990s witnessed the most repressive measures to be implemen-

---

missing. The car was similar to the one shown on the Al-Qa'ida video. It seems that Al-Qa'ida terrorism generates counter-terrorism of a psychological nature exercised by the state. Both are part of the misfortune inflicted on the Saudi and foreign population in the country.

[55] For further details on the 2003 various petitions to the government, see H. Dekmejian, 'The Liberal Impulse in Saudi Arabia', *Middle East Journal*, 57, 3, pp. 400–13.

ted by the Saudi regime throughout its short history. Critics from a wide circle of religious scholars, intellectuals and reformers were imprisoned for long periods. The state does not seem to distinguish between different opposition groups. Under the pretext of the 'War on Terror', it imprisoned Islamists of all persuasions. Even reformers who called for constitutional monarchy in 2003 found themselves in prison. In August 2004, the state accused them of undermining national security and royal authority.

Today the Saudi state is reaping the results of its own repression. By imprisoning important and popular individuals following the Gulf War of 1991, the government created a political, social and intellectual void, which was occupied by the most uncompromising elements in society. The pre-eminence of radical religious scholars such as the deceased Shaikh Humud al-Shu'aibi and Ali al-Khudair, in addition to young scholars such as Nasir al-Fahad and Ahmad al-Khalidi, among others, should be assessed in the light of state repression in the 1990s and the imprisonment of a circle of more established dissident religious scholars. In addition to the co-optation of important sections of society mentioned earlier (families, tribal groups, religious scholars, commoners, technocrats and professionals) who are integrated in each royal circle of power, the state constantly co-opts those who potentially represent an independent source of leadership, which in turn causes them to lose their credibility among their constituencies. Whether a state can continue to function as a coherent and efficient institution with five circles of power, each having at its disposal several networks of patronage in addition to a military force, remains to be seen.

CHECKS, BALANCES AND TRANSFORMATION IN THE SAUDI POLITICAL SYSTEM

Iris Glosemeyer

The Saudi monarchy is currently undergoing a process of transformation. During this process the ruling elite is losing some of the sources of power and legitimacy it used to rely on. Consequently the Saudi rulers will lose some of their political instruments, especially those that are based on rent distribution and the exploitation of societal divisions. Thus the ruling family has to look for alternatives. This is not to suggest that Saudi Arabia is about to democratise, but that it is modernising, i.e. overcoming a state of artificial equilibrium and adjusting to a changing internal and external environment.

Since the core question revolves around the (re-)distribution of power, the checks and balances in the Saudi political system—those affecting the rulers and those affecting society—need to be considered. This chapter first analyses the development of those restrictions and constraints affecting the leadership. The term 'checks and balances' usually applies to the formal built-in mechanisms in a political system that prevent the emergence of a ruler who controls all branches of government or all state institutions. However, as formal political institutions in Saudi Arabia are weak, compared to the personal networks created by influential political actors, the concept is here broadened to include any informal mechanism or division of power that prevents the emergence of an absolute ruler. Stretching the concept even further allows the analysis of another set of checks and balances, made up from societal divides, that is affecting society while providing the rulers with a particular form of legitimacy.

Finally, because the process is still ongoing, different scenarios will be suggested in lieu of a conclusion. In the best case scenario, the political system becomes more transparent, formalised and efficient without the occurrence of a major crisis. In the worst case scenario, the process results in civil war. In the most likely case, the steps already taken towards reform of the system will be followed by more courageous ones that are met with resistance from those who cannot adjust.

Checks and Balances on the Leadership

With regard to those checks and balances placing constraints on the leadership, two different sets of constraints exist, each of which consists of different elements.

First, there was—and still is—a division or separation of power among different segments of the ruling elite, leading to a system of checks and balances along functional lines between the royal family and the *ulama*.[1] In Sunni theory, an Islamic state—which the Kingdom of Saudi Arabia claims to be—is to be ruled by a ruler (*wali al-amr*) advised by the ulama. They are to complement each other and are restricted by the supremacy of Islamic law, i.e. they have to run the affairs of the community according to the *shari'a*, which leaves some space for interpretation. In correspondence with the teachings of Muhammad ibn Abd al-Wahhab, the Najdi ulama who, during the first decades of the Saudi kingdom, dominated all state institutions, outside of direct ruling family control, chose an interpretation that was exclusive towards other Muslims and hampered the modernisation of social and governmental systems.[2]

The founder of the current Saudi state, Abd al-Aziz Al Sa'ud (Ibn Sa'ud), had a special position as he inherited the title *imam*, indi-

1 The ruling elite is defined here as those actors who have a direct influence on decision making on the national level. See Volker Perthes, 'Politics and Elite Change in the Arab World' in Volker Perthes (ed.), *Arab Elites: Negotiating the Politics of Change*, Boulder, CO: Lynne Rienner, 2004, pp. 1–32. For a survey on the different segments of the politically relevant elite in Saudi Arabia see the article by Iris Glosemeyer, 'Saudi Arabia: Dynamism Uncovered' in *ibid.*, pp. 141–69.

2 However, at times they chose to follow a rather pragmatic approach. See the contribution by Guido Steinberg in this volume. For a more comprehensive discussion of the concept of leadership see the chapter by Madawi Al-Rasheed in this volume.

cating religious authority, from his father in 1915.[3] This meant he was not only *wali al-amr* but also the leader of the Wahhabi community in religious affairs. King Abd al-Aziz remained the near-undisputed Imam of the expanding community that finally comprised a heterogeneous Muslim population until his death in 1953. He is still described as an Imam by many Saudis.[4] However, Saudis are much more circumspect regarding the question of whether the ruler of Saudi Arabia is to be considered the Imam *ex officio*.[5] This has especially been the case since the mid-1990s when King Fahd fell ill. While Fahd is still King, his half-brother Crown Prince Abdullah is regarded as the *de facto* ruler of Saudi Arabia. This is of some importance, as the Imam would be the highest religious institution that can decide, for example, which *fatwa* should be considered binding for the whole community.[6] However, since the death of Abd al-Aziz, the ruler has been considered the *wali al-amr*, the ruler who has no religious authority, but who has the right to rule unless his rule is considered un-Islamic. Instead, the function of religious authority has, over time, been completely absorbed by the ulama, most clearly by Shaikh Abd al-Aziz ibn Baz who died in 1999, leaving a gap yet to be filled.[7] Left to the ruling family was the function of defender of the holy places of Islam and, especially when Islam was attacked in Western media after 9/11, defender of the faith against what was perceived as an anti-Islamic campaign.[8]

While, in the days of Abd al-Aziz, the ruler's power was *de facto* restricted by the presence of other powerful actors on whose co-operation or acquiescence the ruler depended, such as tribal leaders, ulama, wealthy townspeople—and the British colonial power in the immediate neighbourhood of the emerging state—the setting chan-

3 Gudrun Krämer, 'Good Counsel to the King: The Islamist Opposition in Saudi Arabia, Jordan, and Morocco' in Joseph Kostiner (ed.), *Middle East Monarchies*, Boulder, CO: Lynne Rienner, 2000, pp. 257–88, at p. 260.

4 Interviews with Saudis inside and outside Saudi Arabia between 2001 and 2003. The only noteworthy exemption was in the late 1920s when the Ikhwan rebelled against Abd al-Aziz and thus challenged his position.

5 Author's interviews.

6 This was especially relevant at the height of the Saudi 'war against terrorism' in 2003.

7 On the distinction between the different forms of Islamic legitimacy—religious authority being one of them—see Krämer, 'Good Counsel to the King', pp. 258 ff.

8 Glosemeyer, 'Saudi Arabia', pp. 147–8, 153.

ged with the demise of the British empire and the advent of the oil era. With the rise of the rentier state after World War II, many formerly independent actors became clients of the royal family. Simultaneously, King Abd al-Aziz—deliberately or not—introduced a system of checks and balances into the royal family by deciding that his son Sa'ud should follow him on the throne, but was to be assisted by Sa'ud's younger brother Faisal. However, this did not resolve the problem of Sa'ud's weakness as a ruler. Rather, the fight for the throne between Sa'ud and Faisal in the late 1950s and early 1960s allowed the ulama to regain some of their influence, because their compliance was needed when the ruling family finally deposed King Sa'ud in 1964. Hence, the ulama acquired, for the years to come, the role of 'kingmakers', inadvertently bestowed upon them by the ruling family. When the succession question regained importance in the mid-1990s, the ulama again benefited from the stalemate between several influential princes. However, a few years on, the climate has changed and they can no longer fully exploit the situation because of the absence of a charismatic leader (as Shaikh ibn Baz had been), the precarious situation they found themselves in after 9/11 and the rise of popular scholars outside the establishment.

Second, as a result of the horizontal succession rule,[9] those checks and balances within the royal family that had shaped and finally aborted King Sa'ud's reign have, since the reign of King Khalid (1975–1982), recurred in a different form. Because the sons of King Abd al-Aziz and their offspring are said to compete with each other for the throne, we may assume they exert a fair amount of control on each other. However, these checks and balances appear in different forms simultaneously and are not formalised.

On the one hand, one of the features of King Khalid's rule was the emergence of several power centres restricting the king's autonomy of decision making and constituting a new functional element of checks and balances within the family. In the 1960s and 1970s Crown Prince Abdullah, Prince Sultan and Prince Nayif, to name only the most powerful princes, were all given influential ministries,

[9] In Saudi Arabia the throne has been passed on to the numerous sons of the state founder since his death in 1953. The succession question attracted a lot of attention in the late 1990s. See Joseph A. Kechichian, *Succession in Saudi Arabia*, London: Palgrave Macmillan, 2001.

and thus money and other political resources. King Khalid permitted them to bolster their own power bases, so when Fahd took over in 1982, stripping his brothers and half-brothers of their power was neither possible nor recommendable. By the early 2000s influential princes like Sultan and Nayif had staffed their ministries with their younger brothers as vice-ministers and their sons as assistant ministers.

Sometimes, competing structures evolved, for example the Saudi army and the Saudi Arabian National Guard. While the Saudi National Guard (SANG), commanded by Crown Prince Abdullah since 1963, is slightly smaller than the regular army, it is nevertheless the more important force. Unlike the regular army, whose task is to protect the country against an external enemy, the SANG safeguards sensitive domains like the oil installations and the royal family.[10] A military conflict between the two forces would obviously plunge the country into a civil war that could not be won by either side. Thus, in the case of aggravated internal competition within the royal family, this balance of military power might prevent a palace coup.[11]

Moreover, many princes, reaching beyond their positions in the state institutions, established power bases in the economic and social subsystems. The 'fiefdom' of an influential prince or a family branch might include a bureaucratic (ministry), a security (intelligence service, military or SANG), a social (hospitals, welfare services or foundations) and/or an intellectual domain (research centres, libraries and newspapers). In other words, while a prince has one particular official function within the state apparatus, he may also lay claims on other areas dominated by another family member. Consequently, on this level some princes compete not only within the government but also in different societal systems, thus checking and balancing each others' influence.

Also, there are government agencies headed by a member of one branch of the family with the deputy belonging to a competing branch. The most prominent example being King Fahd holding the

[10] Anthony H. Cordesman, *Saudi Arabia Enters the 21st Century: The Political, Foreign Policy, Economic, and Energy Dimensions* (vol. 1); *The Military and International Security Dimensions* (vol. 2), Westport, CT: Greenwood Press, 2003.

[11] A dangerous situation is said to have emerged during the struggle between Faisal and Sa'ud. For this period see Sarah Yizraeli, *The Remaking of Saudi Arabia: The Struggle between King Saud and Crown Prince Faysal, 1953–1962*, Tel Aviv University, 1997, Dayan Center Papers, 121.

position of Prime Minister while Crown Prince Abdullah is the First Deputy Prime Minister.[12] Another example is found within the Saudi General (Foreign) Intelligence Service, which was headed by Prince Turki ibn Faisal until he was replaced by Prince Nawef in August 2001, both of whom are regarded as rather close to the Crown Prince. Nawef, who resigned from his position in January 2005, can be expected to be followed by another confidant of the Crown Prince. However, Prince Sa'ud ibn Fahd, a son of King Fahd and thus a member of the Sudairi branch of the family, remained deputy chief of the Service. In such cases, different branches of the family are in the position to apply checks within the same institution, thus balancing each other's influence.

Although a fair amount of competition among the different family branches certainly exists, this should not be misunderstood to be the sole determining feature of the family, as internal coherence is maintained through intermarriage and political attitudes shared by members of the diverse branches. Abdullah and Nayif concur in blaming 'the Zionists' for Saudi Arabia's problems with internal security and foreign relations.[13] And although the Crown Prince is said to be supported by the offspring of the late King Faisal, Prince Khalid ibn Faisal wrote poems praising Prince Sultan,[14] and Princess Haifa bint Faisal is married to Prince Bandar ibn Sultan, Saudi ambassador to Washington. Obviously, there are some in-built moderating mechanisms at work, and competition is limited by the rule that it must not endanger the political survival of the family. These mechanisms not only solved the struggle between Sa'ud and Faisal in the early 1960s, but also, since the 1970s, helped to create a kind of collective leadership, increasingly so since King Fahd fell ill in the mid-1990s.[15]

[12] Fahd is the oldest living son of King Abd al-Aziz and Hassa bint Sudairi whose offspring are called the Sudairi bothers or the Sudairi Seven. Fahd's full brothers are: Fahd, Sultan, Abd al-Rahman, Nayif, Turki, Salman and Ahmad. Abdullah is the son of al-Fahda bint Asi al-Shuraim (Shammar tribe) and has no full brothers.

[13] Compare for example MEMRI Special Dispatch no. 706, 3 May 2004 and MEMRI Special Dispatch no. 446, 3 December 2003.

[14] See Khalid Al-Faisal, *Poems*, translated by Alison Lerrick, Riyadh: King Faisal Foundation, 1996.

[15] For the function of the Royal Family Council see Glosemeyer, 'Saudi Arabia', pp. 151–2.

However, the informal checks and balances within the royal families seemed to have reached the limits of their functionality by the late 1990s. Some observers have concluded there is a stalemate between different factions of the family that hampers decision-making. Indeed, the development of the political system and the implementation of economic reforms have made little progress during the last decades. Even though appropriate strategies had been developed as early as the 1970s and 1980s, not until the late 1990s were political measures implemented to prepare the population for a future in which oil income would no longer keep pace with the population growth rates. With the increase of oil prices since 1999, the Saudi government has started to settle its domestic debts. Nevertheless, the current increase in oil income is likely to provide only temporary relief for the government's budgetary constraints. Moreover, the need for a more transparent royal budget in the foreseeable future might affect the royal fiefdoms and force the royal family to look for other options to secure their position.

Checks and Balances on Society

For a long time in Saudi Arabia the ruler has also checked the strength of societal actors and political forces and balanced them against each other. Lisa Anderson notes that strengthening existing loyalties is an essential characteristic of monarchies in the Arab world: 'Monarchical rule requires a household to supervise, clients to satisfy, and constituencies to balance.'[16] Ibn Khaldun had already described this function several centuries earlier when he portrayed the ruler as the one who prevents his subjects from fighting each other.[17] King Abd al-Aziz certainly had to apply this in the early years of his rule to keep Najdi zealots, striving for application of the Wahhabi version of *shari'a* law, out of the religiously and culturally rather heterogeneous Hijaz, gaining the reputation of a 'trusted mediator among all societal groups'.[18]

[16] Lisa Anderson, 'Dynasts and Nationalists: Why Monarchies Survive' in Kostiner, *Middle East Monarchies*, p. 61.

[17] This is the function of the king (*malik*) as 'the one who restrains'. *Muqaddima*, section 3.23. It is beyond the brief of this chapter to discuss the relation between tribalism, the concept of *umma* as a superstructure and the fear of *fitna* in this context.

[18] Joseph Kostiner, 'Transforming Dualities: Tribe and State Formation in Saudi

To rule in this way requires keeping ascriptive identities, traditional roles and social divides alive and even, to a certain degree, strengthening them—be they regional, sectarian, tribal or sexual. However, a divide-and-rule strategy if pushed too far or in the hands of an incompetent ruler, might lead to civil war or the separation of specific groups, especially if concentrated in particular regions.

At least since the early 1970s outside observers have expected that with the process of modernisation and its associated processes of economic and social functional differentiation, traditional identity patterns and loyalties would be re-adjusted by the inclusion of identities based on common economic or political interest. According to these assumptions Saudi society would increasingly organise along horizontal lines, finally evolving as a class-based society in a nation state.[19] Thus modernisation was expected to weaken the social divides, which are one of the bases of power for the monarchical rulers in the Arab world. However, modernisation theory, assuming linear development towards democratisation, did not take into account factors such as the impact of oil rents on the process of political development.

Political development in Saudi Arabia (and elsewhere) hence took a different course, supported by rent-distribution, rent-seeking behaviour and the lack of incentives to reorganise societal divisions. The 'new elites' or the 'new middle class' did not develop into a forceful political actor.[20] But although during the 1990s the rulers perfected their strategy based on the 'divide and rule' paradigm, in the early 2000s they suddenly appeared eager to replace it with a strategy based on the 'unite and survive'—or 'congregate and discuss'—paradigm, thus undermining their own position. A brief look at the setting in the early 1990s and an analysis of the situation in the early 2000s indicates the ruling family was trying to adjust the political system to changing circumstances.

Arabia' in Philip S. Khouri and Joseph Kostiner (eds), *Tribes and State Formation in the Middle East*, London/New York: I. B. Tauris, 1991, pp. 226–51, at p. 233.

19 See Anderson, 'Dynasts and Nationalists', p. 63.

20 See for example Mark Allen Heller and Nadav Safran, *The New Middle Class and Regime Stability in Saudi Arabia*, Cambridge, MA: Harvard University Press, 1985; or Mordechai Abir, 'The Consolidation of the Ruling Class and the New Elites in Saudi Arabia', *Middle East Studies*, 23, 2 (April 1987), pp. 150–71.

The Situation in the Early 1990s

With the massive deployment of US troops in Saudi Arabia after the Iraqi invasion of Kuwait in August 1990, an unusually high number of actors with sometimes contradicting and sometimes similar demands appeared on the political scene for about two years. Different groups of intellectuals sent open letters and petitions to the rulers demanding better governance and more transparency.[21] Petitioners with a classical Islamic education, led by young religious Sunni shaikhs who were aghast at the presence of American troops in the land of the two Holy Places of Islam, justified their demands by referring to the *shari'a*. Those who had a Western style education couched their demands in Islamic terminology, but were more obviously inspired by Western discourse on good governance and political participation.[22] Moreover, women demonstrated for their right to drive cars, and Usama bin Ladin is said to have offered the support of Afghanistan returnees to defend the country etc.[23] The rulers reacted—with the usual delay—by promulgating the Basic Law of Governance in 1992, establishing a Consultative Council (*Majlis al-Shura*) which convened in 1993, by striking a deal with the organised Shi'a opposition in the same year, and by finally arresting, in 1994, those Sunni Islamist activists who had not left the country and could not be silenced otherwise.

The rulers' strategy was a combination of appeasement and dual containment, based on the paradigm of divide and rule: The most dangerous and persistent challengers to the legitimacy of the ruling family—the Sunni Islamists—were jailed, while those who provoked other groups and thus disturbed the internal balance—women demanding the right to drive cars—lost their jobs. All others were appeased by fulfilment of some of their demands expressed in the different petitions, but warned not to go any further. Moreover, by employing the partially contradicting demands of the petitions as a

[21] In the category 'intellectuals' we subsume ulama, traditionally educated and Western educated academics.

[22] For detail on the petitions, see the chapter by Abdulaziz Sager in this volume; also Mamoun Fandy, *Saudi Arabia and the Politics of Dissent*, New York: St Martin's Press, 1999; Joshua Teitelbaum, *Holier than Thou: Saudi Arabia's Islamic Opposition*, Washington, DC: The Washington Institute for Near East Policy, 2000; and Kechichian, *Succession in Saudi Arabia*.

[23] Prince Turki in an interview with *Arab News* and MBC, *Arab News*, 7 November 2001.

shield to fend off demands for a substantial reform of the system, the rulers justified their refusal to make any additional concessions. Under such conditions the reforms could not unfold a dynamic that would have resulted in a comprehensive modernisation of the political system.

The Situation in the Early 2000s

Ten years later, in the early 2000s, a completely different picture is revealed. One may suggest that 9/11 was the turning point: not so much because the events themselves as the behaviour of outside actors—the government of the United States, political advisors and the international press—brought about a change in strategies.

External and Internal Threats Following 9/11 Saudi Arabia was attacked in the international media as never before, probably even more so than in 1973 when it proclaimed the oil embargo. Saudis—and others—complained that US government agencies treated those Saudis (and other Arabs), who wanted to visit, work or study in the United States, rather rudely. Thus Saudis felt attacked as Saudis, not as Najdis, Hijazis, Asiris or as Shi'is or Hanbalis or as men or women. This discriminatory treatment made no distinction between them. Saudis started reacting as Saudis and published their experiences in the Saudi press. Unintentionally, therefore, the US government contributed to the growth of a nascent Saudi national identity—and not only among those who travelled abroad.

Furthermore the US government, by leaking to the press suggestions, made by political advisors, to split up Saudi Arabia into several smaller states, threatened the territorial integrity of the Saudi state.[24] This may well have pleased those Saudis who were not happy to be ruled from Riyadh, but it motivated the leadership to look for support in their own country against a possible threat from the same external actor it had turned to for protection in 1990. Therefore, in order to counter the attacks against the policy of discrimination against minorities and women, the rulers had to ensure their loyalty and, if possible, mobilise them to their defence. In order to prevent

[24] Laurent Murawiec, Daniel Pipes, Alex Alexiev and Daniel Brumberg, 'Symposium: The Future of US–Saudi-Relations', led by Jamie Glazov, *FrontPageMagazine.com*, 11 July 2003. For the effect of the leakage on the Saudi public see also Toby Jones: 'Seeking a "Social Contract"' *Middle East Report*, 228 (fall 2003).

the Shi'a in the oil rich Eastern Province from becoming the 'fifth column'—not, as was usually suspected, of Iran, but of the United States—the rulers had to listen to their complaints. And to counter the accusation that the Saudi state was a relic of medieval times, it had to mobilise its male and female modernists and engage them in the Saudi 'charm offensive' that began in late 2001. For the first time, therefore, the rulers found themselves in a situation where they needed the active co-operation of a variety of societal groups that had hitherto played no role in securing the Saudi state and its political system.

The Riyadh bombings of May and November 2003 added to the situation. The bombing of three expatriate compounds in Riyadh in May 2003 caused a group of ulama to denounce such attacks in an open letter published in *al-Hayat*, a newspaper distributed throughout the Middle East, published in London and owned by members of the Saudi ruling family.[25] Among the authors were the shaikhs Salman al-Awda and Safar al-Hawali, who had co-authored a petition and a more comprehensive 'Memorandum of Advice' to the rulers in the early 1990s, and had spent some years in jail in the mid-1990s. Apart from considering these attacks a violation of Islamic law, the author's feared the United States would use such events as a pretext for invading the country in order to re-establish security. The invasion of Iraq had just occurred and had obviously left a deep impression on the shaikhs.

The November attack was another blow to the alliance of *status quo* oriented political forces. By targeting the Muhayya residential complex in Riyadh, which was inhabited by Arab and other Muslims, the militants gave the Saudi public an idea of what the alternative to the current leadership would look like. In stark contrast to the situation in the early 1990s, by the end of 2003, both leadership and society (or at least vocal parts of it) were pulling the same string—moulded into a coalition by the combined threat of external interference, terrorist attacks and the invasion of Iraq.[26]

Exercises in Citizenship In 2002 Saudi intellectuals had already published a series of open letters, some of them addressed to the rulers

[25] *al-Hayat*, 20 May 2003.
[26] See also the chapter by Meijer in this volume.

and peoples of the region and others addressed to a Western—particularly American—audience. Many of these writers had been involved in the petitions of the early 1990s. However, unlike in the early 1990s, male and female intellectuals and activists of very diverse regional backgrounds and political attitudes signed the same letters.[27] The Shi'a was initially excluded from this exercise of citizenship, but not for long. Only days after Crown Prince Abdullah had announced in January 2003 the Charter for Reform of the Arab Condition (originally a proposal for the Arab League summit in Bahrain) calling for broader political participation,[28] the royal family received a first petition. Emphasising their respect for the rulers, the authors suggested elections to the Consultative Council, decentralisation, judicial reform, more respect for human rights and a national dialogue on controversial issues, in short: mechanisms for better governance. This was only the first in a series of petitions and most of their authors were received by the Crown Prince. Some of these letters were submitted by groups explicitly defined by their religious or regional identity, like the petition of the Shi'a of the Eastern province (signed by men and women) in April and the one from the 'People of Najran' under the title 'The Homeland for all and all for the homeland' in June, asking for equal rights in return for their proven loyalty to the Saudi state. Other letters and petitions, e.g. the ones of January, September and December 2003, were supported by very heterogeneous groups, sometimes comprising male and female Saudis, indicating that shared political demands allow for cutting across religious, regional and even sexual divides.

Riding the Wave While political activists prepared open letters and petitions, the royal family decided to change its strategies towards domestic and international actors. The year 2003 in particular was marked by steps that were long overdue and must have been considered by the rulers for quite some time. After publishing the Charter for Reform in January, Crown Prince Abdullah wasted no time

[27] See Iris Glosemeyer, 'Saudi Arabia', pp. 162 f; and Stéphane Lacroix, 'Between Islamists and Liberals: Saudi Arabia's New "Islamo-Liberal" Reformists', *Middle East Journal*, 58, 3, pp. 345–65, as well as his chapter in this volume.

[28] *Arab News*, 15 January 2003. In the end, Crown Prince Abdullah did not submit the Charter for Reform. Instead the summit was dominated by discussions over the pending war on Iraq.

and within a month, a member of the royal family pronounced plans to hold municipal elections following the withdrawal of the American troops from Saudi Arabia.[29] In April 2003 this bone of contention—having provoked much domestic anger since 1990—was eliminated when the US government announced the imminent withdrawal of its troops. By September 2003 only a few hundred were left in Saudi Arabia.[30] Hence, in October 2003 plans to elect half of the 178 seats of the municipal councils were made public, indicating the regime was ready to embark on the reform process and permit limited popular political participation. Whether women would be allowed to run and vote was kept quiet till September 2004. Elections for the Consultative Council were also mooted as a possibility for a not so distant future, and in November the Council was allowed to set its own agenda without having to wait for the King to agree.[31] This small but significant step not only made the Council less dependent on the ruling family, it also accelerated its quasi-legislative proceedings, a function that had more or less been ascribed to the Council of Senior Ulama (*Hay'at Kibar al-'Ulama*) until the establishment of the Consultative Council in 1993. But while the Council of Higher Ulama is dominated by septuagenarian Najdi ulama, the Consultative Council is staffed with professionals in their fifties from all parts of the country, including members of the Shi'a minority.

Starting in the summer of 2003, Crown Prince Abdullah took the lead in a series of national dialogues, thus putting himself at the head of the various reform initiatives that were about to clash with traditionalist elements of society. The Crown Prince thereby fulfilled his role as the ruler who mediates between conflicting elements of society in a rather sophisticated form; instead of keeping the different groups apart he brought them together. A national forum for dialogue—one of the proposals of the January petition—was held with the participation of scholars of all prevalent Saudi religious sects and currents in Riyadh in June 2003. Its recommendations touched on a number of sensitive issues, prominent among them being the issue of national unity.[32] In August a centre for national dialogue was

[29] *New York Times*, 10 February 2003.

[30] *Frankfurter Rundschau*, 7 December 2004.

[31] *Saudi Press Agency*, 29 November 2003.

[32] *al-Hayat*, 22 June 2003.

established under the auspices of the Crown Prince. Thus the rulers seized on the national dialogue, institutionalising it under their guidance. To drive home the point, the centre was attached to the King Abd al-Aziz library, the 'intellectual domain' of the Crown Prince. However, the public debate prompted a number of conservative ulama to take action in order to regain their dominant position over public discourse and to defend their official monopoly on advising the rulers.[33] Already in September 2003 a group of 130 conservative ulama and academics had sent out a strong warning. They protested against the emerging discussion about women and women's rights, which they saw as yet another 'vicious campaign from the (Muslim community's) enemy, led by the American government, to divert it from its faith'.[34]

At this point the rulers did not pay much attention to such reactions, and a few months later, at the end of December, the second forum for national dialogue was held. At this meeting the sexual divide was bridged for the first time: Nine women participated in the Mecca meeting (albeit seated in a separate room), and the third meeting was announced, intended to concentrate on the issue of women and their role in society as a whole. Holding the second meeting in Mecca, and not Riyadh, indicated the rulers were now ready to pay attention to regional sensitivities, primarily to the traditional competition between the Najd and the Hijaz regions. Even the idea of having the forum move through the different regions of the Kingdom was openly discussed[35]—important as it implied a crosscutting of regional boundaries.

Thus within less than a year three 'demarcation lines' were cut across with the support of the Crown Prince—the sectarian line, the regional line and the sexual line—suffusing the process of Saudi nation building with new energy. However, the rulers would not allow the process to spin out of control, that is, to challenge their position or upset conservative scholars to an extent that they would withdraw their support from the ruling family. When in autumn the opposition-in-exile called for demonstrations against the regime,

[33] In fact this monopoly never existed. All Saudi rulers including the founder of the current state have had advisors other than the ulama.

[34] *Associated Press*, 11 September 2003.

[35] Saudi press and interviews in Riyadh, December 2003.

only a few Saudis took to the streets. But the mere possibility of demonstrations taking place has always been interpreted as a major security problem by the Minister of the Interior, Prince Nayif.[36]

In December a group of intellectuals received a clear warning from the ruler. While they were preparing their petition, they were told that Crown Prince Abdullah would not be the one inviting them for a meeting, as he had done with various petitioners throughout 2003. Rather, Prince Nayif, Minister of the Interior, dealt with the petitioners and reportedly left them in no doubt that whoever called for a constitutional monarchy would go to jail.[37]

Mid-2000s

One year later, the developments that had seemed set to unfold their own dynamics had basically dissolved. There are indications that the rulers felt they were about to lose control over the path and speed of reform. Obviously they decided they had made enough concessions and that further input into the reform process from outside the royal family was not desirable. State officials—including university professors, many of whom had supported various petitions—were explicitly forbidden to engage in any kind of criticism of the government.[38] Also, by early 2004, there was a measurable degree of resistance to reforms in various fields, especially with regards to education and women's public appearance.[39]

The rulers made clear that while they accepted the need for limited reform under their guidance, they would not tolerate open disobedience or provocation of their traditional allies. The group of reformers who, in spite of a clear warning, had called for a constitutional monarchy in late December 2003 was arrested at the end of March 2004, a time when the G-8 member states had decided to include on their summit agenda the issue of reform in the Arab

[36] See his comments on two (attempted) demonstrations that were not directed against the ruling family in 2002, *Saudi Press Agency*, Riyadh, 12 May 2002.

[37] *Financial Times*, 17 January 2004.

[38] *Financial Times*, 16 September 2004.

[39] On 1 January 2004 150 Saudi intellectuals signed a document protesting the change of school curricula, http://www.as-sahwah.com/viewnews.php?newsID=555 (19 January 2004). For the struggle about the curricula see the contribution by Michaela Prokop in this volume. For the issue of women's public appearance see below.

World, and most other Arab governments were trying to prove their reform capability to the West. Most of the detainees were released after a few days, but some who refused to apologise and to promise to abstain from involvement in further petitions remained in custody at the time of writing, awaiting the outcome of their trial.

According to some reports the petitioners were preparing another open letter when they were arrested, while other reports indicate they were about to set up a human rights organisation. This would have challenged the National Human Rights Association (NHRA), an organisation the rulers had just approved in early March 2004,[40] little more than a year after Human Rights Watch had been invited to Saudi Arabia for the first time in January 2003.[41] Dealing with complaints, including those against government agencies, on such a broad level had so far been the prerogative of mainly the Board of Grievances, dominated by Najdi ulama.[42] Nevertheless, the NHRA, which counts three women among its forty-one members,[43] started work immediately, receiving complaints about human rights abuses from various corners of society—including foreigners who constitute one third of the Saudi population.[44] However, the chairman of the NHRA, a member of the Consultative Council, made clear that the association would cooperate but not enter into an alliance with international human rights organisations,[45] thus ensuring the organisation's findings would not be used to the disadvantage of the regime.[46]

On the other hand, the decision about how much protest from the conservatives (mainly but not exclusively ulama) was tolerable, remained with the rulers. In September 2004, after the matter had

[40] See e.g. Human Rights Watch, *Overview: Saudi Arabia*, http://www.hrw.org/english/docs/2005/01/13/saudia9810.htm.

[41] However, Human Rights Watch was not allowed to do fieldwork (*Arab News*, 21 July 2004), and Amnesty International did not get an invitation, due to its 'hostile position towards the kingdom'. Interview with a member of the Saudi Foreign Ministry, *al-Hayat*, 12 March 2004.

[42] For the function of the Board of Grievances see Nathan J. Brown, 'Arab Judicial Structures (A Study Presented to the United Nations Development Program)', http://www.pogar.org/publications/judiciary/nbrown/saudi.html.

[43] *Financial Times*, 11 March 2003.

[44] *Arab News*, 21 July 2004.

[45] Interview with Abdallah bin Salih al-Ubaid, *al-Hayat*, 12 March 2004.

[46] Consequently the organisation was allowed entry into the country's prisons. *al-Hayat*, 26 September 2004.

been left to speculation for about one year, the election committee announced that women were officially banned from taking part in the local elections.[47] Back in January 2004, Lubna Ulayan's style of wearing her headscarf, combined with the fact that she gave the opening speech at the Jeddah Economic Forum, had already caused such an uproar among conservatives that the Grand Mufti had had to intervene.[48] He thereby reassured the conservatives that the behaviour of one of the most prominent and successful Saudi businesswomen was considered improper by the highest official religious authority, who usually renders the rulers' opinion. The style and content of the discussions at the third national dialogue meeting on women's issues in Medina in June 2004 re-emphasised both that the issue of women's rights is highly controversial and that women are not yet allowed to cross the dividing line that keeps them from full participation in the public sphere because of stern resistance from traditionalists, inside and outside the conference rooms.[49] Thus the elections for the municipal councils went ahead without the participation of female voters and candidates,[50] but their participation has been announced for the next elections.

Following this period, during which the new limits had been clearly defined, the more daring petitioners had been put in their place and the resisting conservatives had been mollified, the rulers went on with their programme of national dialogue. The fourth dialogue meeting took place in December 2004 in Dhahran, in the Eastern Province, with 600 male and female young people invited to discuss concepts of citizenship. Its final statement again stressed the need for 'promoting the culture of dialogue, tolerance, respect and acceptance of each other's opinions'.[51]

[47] *Financial Times*, 24 October 2004. However, registration figures of voters for the municipal elections are likely to be rather low, indicating either that there is little acceptance of or interest in this kind of procedure or that figures in the population statistics are higher than the actual number of eligible voters.

[48] *al-Hayat*, 21 January 2004.

[49] For the clash between a (male) head of the Teacher Training College in Riyadh and a (female) former employee of UNDP at the conference, see *Arab News* between 15 June and early July 2004. A group of 100 ulama reportedly addressed an open letter to the conference refusing to accept the most basic women's rights. The letter is summarised in *Neue Zuercher Zeitung*, 16 June 2004.

[50] *Arab News*, 19 September 2004.

[51] *Arab News*, 10 December 2004; *al-Hayat*, 10 December 2004.

Summing Up and Scenarios for the Future

Summing up the evidence so far

The two systems of checks and balances discussed above are undergoing change. With regard to the leadership, several mechanisms of parallel and functional checks and balances could be identified. However, none of them comprised the typical clear division of labour characterising checks and balances in other political systems. The developments following 11 September 2001 seemed to have mitigated competition inside the royal family and increased its decision-making capacity by 2003.

Informal checks and balances might prevent the emergence of an absolute ruler, but they lack transparency and can result in deadlock when they proliferate to an extent that blocks decision-making. In the Saudi case, a foreign government, a transnational terrorist organisation and its local followers destroyed the state of paralysis by strengthening those political actors who opted for reform of the political system and by convincing the rulers that steering the process rather than resisting it would be advisable.

While the rulers are ready to give up playing social forces off against each other and to promote a supervised and limited form of political participation, they nevertheless follow a paternalistic approach in doing so. They still assume the role of a mediator and will keep conceding to the conservative ulama as long as they see no alternative way of legitimising their rule—even though the Saudi populace no longer defines itself as belonging to the Wahhabi community, but increasingly as citizens of the Saudi state. Thus checks on, and balances among, societal actors have weakened, but have not disappeared.

Challenging and provoking the rulers to the extent that they fear for their position—by calling for a constitutional monarchy or public demonstrations—is a double-edged sword. On the one hand it makes the rulers look for more moderate allies, but on the other it prolongs the process of substituting Najdi Wahhabi scholars with a broad coalition of citizens, as it inevitably triggers pre-emptive measures on the part of the rulers.

Future scenarios

As of early 2005, several scenarios for the future of the Saudi political system are possible, the following present themselves as the best, worst and most likely.

Best case-scenario: successful nation building and increased political participation The negative experiences with the current system translate into the development of the political system in the narrower sense of the word, i.e. in political institution building within the next five years. Informal checks and balances are substituted by formal and transparent mechanisms. An elected Consultative Council comprising men and women acquires full control of the budget. The rulers continue to follow their inclusive approach and negotiate a new social contract no longer exclusively based on rent distribution and mediating functions. These measures support the nation building process and silence or calm external criticism. As a consequence, society and state institutions become more independent of the rulers. Therefore, internal crises, for example caused by succession matters, have less impact on society and political decision-making. Moreover, unpleasant but necessary reforms are carried out by political institutions (e.g. the Majlis al-Shura) and can therefore not be blamed primarily on the royal family. Thus negative feedback is less dangerous for the legitimacy of the ruler(s).

Worst case-scenario: state failure The cross-boundary rallying for political goals does not gain momentum, and violence in Iraq or other parts of the Middle East spills over to Saudi Arabia. The pro-reform actors (rulers and political activists) might lose cohesion and/or cannot convince the majority of the population, who want to preserve the status quo in such an insecure environment. The Najdi-Wahhabi establishment regains its position. This might satisfy the conservative majority of Saudis. But their inability to adjust to a changing internal and external environment brings about more uncertainty that creates broad discontent. This in turn leads to political violence, with militants targeting pro-reform actors, including members of the royal family, and heavy security measures provoking further discontent. Simultaneously, generational change in the royal family affects their degree of cohesion, leads to the collapse of informal checks and balances and the decay of domains and thus the different socio-political networks before alternatives can be successfully established. As a result, the militant opposition gains weight, the US military intervenes, the level of violence rises and externally supported separatism prevails.

Most likely scenario: accelerated gradual change Provided there is no intervention by an outside actor, and the question of who will succeed Abdullah does not become acute in the next few years, a period of calm sets in. After the rather eventful and exciting period of 2002–4 the rulers will try to optimise the existing checks and balances within the family, but they will not be able to return to the former system of checks and balances on society. Generational change within the ruling family will not start at the top level (King, Crown Prince), but within core ministries (Interior, Defence).

Efforts at establishing or strengthening new institutions like the Consultative Council or the National Human Rights Association, representing different social groups, indicate that the existing institutions like the Council of Senior Ulama or the Board of Grievances dominated by the Najdi-Wahhabi (male) establishment will be at least substituted if not sidelined in the long run. The conservative ulama are running the risk of being excluded from an integrating society because of their own exclusiveness and their inability to provide answers to the questions that preoccupy the Saudi populace.[52]

Sidelined by new institutions, the Najdi-Wahhabi establishment will successively lose its functions—but not without resistance. Reform within the ulama establishment—encouraged by the rulers—will turn out to be the only viable option. A younger generation of scholars will embark on reinterpreting Shaikh Muhammad ibn Abd al-Wahhab's texts.

Social integration and institutional reform will make progress, and the quality of governance will improve, but the rulers will stop the process whenever it threatens to get out of control, thus joining the club of other liberalising autocracies in the Arab World. They will be supported by an international community eager to secure its energy supplies.

[52] None of the author's Saudi interview partners has ever depicted the Council of Higher Ulama (or similar institutions) as an authority that provides guidance in these turbulent times. To the contrary, they referred exclusively to scholars who are not members of any of these institutions. The websites of Saudi ulama, not members of the establishment, on the internet give a rough idea about the real concerns of major parts of the Saudi population.

POLITICAL OPPOSITION IN SAUDI ARABIA

Abdulaziz O. Sager

Exploring the nature and scope of Saudi political opposition does perforce involve the discussion of several other issues that bear closely on the nature and structure of the Saudi political system and state apparatus. In this respect, a number of questions come to mind: What is the fulcrum that sustains the political legitimacy of the Saudi regime and what is the extent of the force and consolidation of the lever of legitimisation? How efficient are state institutions in coming to grips with socio-economic problems? In other words, what is the level of the 'performance legitimacy' of the state? What agenda informs and upholds Saudi foreign policy? What type of relationship does Saudi Arabia really entertain with the United States? How do regional and international developments affect the domestic politics of the Kingdom?

Other chapters in this volume address those questions in some depth. While inevitably touching on them, this chapter aims more narrowly to highlight the main facets of political dissent in Saudi Arabia and to provide a net assessment of the current performance of political opposition as well as a prospect for its future. The aim of this chapter (as of some of the others, even where accents and interpretations differ) is to stimulate further research towards a comprehensive map of opposition forces, their social roots, and their sectarian and/or political creeds. It is important in this context to steer clear of embracing Wahhabism as the single explanatory factor, in a broader analysis of the ideologies that drive Saudi opposition groups, their organisational structures, the strategies they follow in their dealings with state authorities and the behaviour of the regime vis-à-vis such forces of political opposition.

A Glimpse into the Opposition

The state formation of Saudi Arabia was based in part on defending 'orthodox', or 'pure', Islam. The founder of the state, King Abd al-Aziz bin Abd al-Rahman Al Sa'ud (often referred to in the western literature as Ibn Sa'ud) fought his rivals with the use of these justifications. Therefore, Islamic opposition is not new; it has been the main political driving force in the polity now known as Saudi Arabia since the advent of the twentieth century (and arguably before). It is no wonder, then, that much of the current opposition embraces the same tools and discourse. The other opposition trends, such as nationalists and leftists, who were active in the 1950s and 1960s, had little impact on either state or society, and the current resurgence of opposition in the country has been confined basically to Islamists, with a small margin left to the 'liberals'.

Islamist criticism of the monarchy grew dramatically following the 1990–1 Gulf War. This was caused by a combination of factors, amongst them the financial difficulties that limit the government's continued use of a strategy of welfarism, diminishing the ideological threat of the Arab left, and the trans-boundary experience the Islamists have had in Afghanistan, Chechnya and Bosnia. The rift was heightened by the direct presence of American troops in the country. The presence of thousands of Western, non-Muslim troops in close proximity to the holy cities of Mecca and Medina was seen as heretical. Moreover, reliance on foreign troops for defence highlighted the vulnerability of the monarchy and seemed to insinuate that, in view of the billions spent, the defence of the Holy Land had been mismanaged. Thus, in the eyes of the religious opposition, the Islamic credentials of the monarchy had been called into question. When, following the Gulf War, some Western troops remained in Saudi Arabia, the radical opposition viewed them as a prop for what had become an illegitimate government.[1]

[1] See also Mordechai Abir, *Saudi Arabia: Government, Society and the Gulf Crisis*, London: Routledge, 1993, pp. 55–8.

Increasingly austere economic conditions have curbed prosperity, highlighted fissures within Saudi society, and exposed the royal family to charges of waste and corruption. Since the mid-1980s the standard of living has fallen precipitously. Critics charge that the government has done too little to diversify an economy that is overwhelmingly dependent on oil revenues. Population growth is robust, but the economy is stagnating, further straining the social welfare net.[2]

The religious opposition reflects this myriad of problems. A cross-section of prominent opposition personalities demonstrates a strong mix of academic backgrounds and religious training. By and large they are well-educated and have had significant exposure to the Western world. Perhaps of more importance, they are largely drawn from the urban middle class, a segment of society that has been excluded from the decision-making process.[3]

Among the opposition movements and figures, Al-Qa'ida is the most radical and activist, and with the exception of the Movement for Islamic Reform in Arabia, headed by Sa'd al-Faqih, currently exiled in London, few other opponents are calling for the regime's downfall. These more moderate groups, whether Islamist or liberal, stress evolutionary reform. The Islamists among them accept that Saudi Islamic society will have to accommodate the modern world in some respects. They wish to mitigate the more problematic influences of modernity through a revival of traditional Islamic values. They accept the royal family as a political institution, but object to the indulgence and corruption of its more free-wheeling members.

The Saudi record of governance and response to opposition challenges has often been contradictory. The rules of the game were set two and a half centuries ago,[4] but the game has changed. The strict adherence to orthodox Islamic tenets provided the regime with a credible ideology and self-avowed identity. In the past the govern-

[2] Compare Richard H. Dekmeijan, 'The Rise of Political Islamism in Saudi Arabia', *Middle East Journal*, 48, 4 (autumn 1994), pp. 627–43.

[3] Mamoun Fandy, *Saudi Arabia and the Politics of Dissent*, New York: St Martin's Press, 1999, p. 24. Arguably the term 'middle class' does not properly reflect the socio-economic developments in Saudi Arabia. Classes in the classical Western sense have not yet become clearly defined; therefore, 'social strata' might be a more appropriate term. We will use the more familiar term as that has become established usage—but would urge the reader to keep the above qualification in mind.

[4] Wahba, Hafiz, *Arabian Days*, London: Arthur Barker, 1964, pp. 98–100.

ment has sought to co-opt Islamists through the support of groups both home and abroad. Elements of the opposition that have proven less susceptible to this strategy have been ruthlessly suppressed.[5] However, while this strategy has continued to bear results, it has arguably become less successful. Tentatively many of the circumstances that preceded Islamic revolution in Iran exist today in Saudi Arabia: an authoritarian government; an unbalanced economy heavily dependent on oil revenues; problematic demographic growth; income distribution gaps; and political persecution. Nonetheless, there are still important missing factors—not least the strong independent institutions of the Iranian Bazaar, the independent religious establishment of Iranian Shi'a Islam, and the middle class. In contrast, Sunni Islam's official institutions rely on the state and have no independent, secure sources of wealth. Indeed, over the centuries the Sunni religious establishment has had a close relationship with the ruling establishment.[6] These differences lessen the readiness of Sunni Islam as a vehicle for revolution, as compared to its Shi'a counterpart. In addition, one striking and crucial contrast between the Shah of Iran and the Al Sa'ud has been the latter's conscious effort to project an image in tune with local cultural (including religious) tradition both in policy and the portrayal of the regime.[7] As a result, the regime remains, for the time being, intact. But the quest for stability in Saudi Arabia is ongoing.

Causes and Actions

Saudi Arabia remains in essence a rentier state that depends almost exclusively on oil revenue to keep running the state's agencies and

5 David Long, *The Kingdom of Saudi Arabia*, Gainesville, FL: University of Florida Press, 1997, p. 117.

6 The Sunni religious establishment has by and large served the ruling regimes since the end of the reign of the 'rightly-guided Caliphs' (*al-khulafa' al-rashidun*) thirty years after the death of the Prophet. This became especially clear in the early middle ages after expansion of the empire had ceased and taxation was having to be imposed on Muslims as well as non-Muslims. See Nazih Ayubi, *Political Islam*, London: Routledge, 1988. This pattern continues today, as illustrated by the Council of Islamic Affairs in Saudi Arabia and Al-Azhar in Egypt.

7 See Nikki Keddie, *Debating Revolution*, New York University Press, 1995; and Bernard Lewis, 'Islamic Revolution', *The New York Review of Books*, 21 January 1988.

activate various business and economic sectors.[8] This has implications both for the resilience of the system under changing economic circumstances, and for the nature and possible outlook of opposition forces.

No proper approach to political opposition in Saudi Arabia is possible without a clear understanding of the complex web of increasing domestic problems, whether political, economic, social or even administrative. These mounting problems have been accumulating since the mid-1980s (oil prices dipping below $10 per barrel in 1986). The depletion of Saudi assets was the result also of the contribution to the exorbitant cost of the Second Gulf War and the $45 billion owed by Iraq. Military spending, moreover, increased at an annual rate of $18 billion per annum for the period 1990 to 2002.[9] The Saudi government can no longer afford the over-generous welfare schemes of the past. From 1983 until 2003 (with the exception of the year 2001) the public budget was racked by chronic deficit at a time when public spending for development never exceeded 7 per cent of the budget. Indeed, Crown Prince Abdullah has pointed out that the oil boom is a thing of the past.[10]

This financial straitening has coincided with (and has partly worsened) growing unemployment among Saudi youth. Teens and the young comprise around 55 per cent of the demographic pyramid of Saudi Arabia. Some social analysts talk of a real 'youth explosion' in

[8] For a clear discussion of the political economy of rentier (or 'allocation') states see Giacomo Luciani, 'Allocation vs. Production States: A Theoretical Framework' in Giacomo Luciani (ed.), *The Arab State*, London: Routledge, 1990. A range of more unexpected consequences of the rentier state model are dealt with in Gwenn Okruhlik's, 'Rentier Wealth, Unruly Law, and the Rise of Opposition: The Political Economy of Oil States', *Comparative Politics*, April 1999, pp. 295–315.

[9] Lawrence Wright, 'The Kingdom of Silence', *The New Yorker*, 5 January 2004 and Michael Doran, 'The Saudi Paradox', *Foreign Affairs*, January/February 2004. According to reports published by the International Institute for Strategic Studies the gross value of Saudi military expenditure stands today at $234 billion.

[10] This is despite the surge in oil prices in 2004: in comparison with the first oil boom in the 1970s and by taking into account the devaluation in the US dollar and global inflation rate, the current increase in oil prices does not reflect a meaningful boom, and in essence merely adjusts the recession in the oil market. This can be clearly seen by comparing the increases in prices of manufactured goods and raw materials including oil, since the 1970s.

the Kingdom.[11] The combination of a high population growth rate (estimated to average around 4.3 per cent annually for the period 1980–97[12]) and high unemployment is hugely problematic. Such rapid population growth is destabilising because of the tremendous economic pressure it generates: it automatically decreases per capita wealth in the absence of extraordinarily high economic growth, and strains infrastructure and social services. Individual incomes, indeed, have decreased and living standards are palpably affected. This bleak economic situation made it easier for extremist groups to draw disaffected young people into their ranks.

It should be noted that despite serious difficulties, the Saudi economy is hardly on the verge of collapse. But the social implications of economic stresses will accentuate problems, not least because of the unequal distribution of wealth. Gulf youths today expect more from the government than did previous generations; the evidence now coming from Saudi Arabia suggests a combination of high expectations with frustration. More realistic socioeconomic expectations appear to be gradually gaining prevalence, alongside a growing recognition that the government cannot, and perhaps even should not, present a career and a comfortable lifestyle on a platter.[13] But, paradoxically, socioeconomic and political expectations may enjoy an inverse relationship: accepting lower socioeconomic expectations may prompt demands for political development and greater political participation, reversing the undeclared social contract, which has

[11] See for instance Anthony Cordesman, *Saudi Arabia Enters the 21st Century: IV, Saudi Arabia: Opposition, Islamic Extremism, and Terrorism*, Washington: CSIS, 31 December 2002, available on http://www.csis.org/burke/saudi21/S21_04.pdf, p. 13. See also Lisa Anderson, 'Absolutism and the Resilience of Monarchy in the Middle East', *Political Science Quarterly*, 106, 1 (winter 1991), pp. 1–18.

[12] See World Bank, *World Development Report 1998/99: Knowledge for Development*, New York: Oxford University Press, 1999, p. 195. Saudi population statistics, like most when it comes to Saudi Arabia, are 'suspect'. On inaccurate figures and the difficulty of obtaining information in general, see also Fred Halliday, 'Review of: *Saudi Arabia: Government, Society and the Gulf Crisis* by Mordechai Abir (1993)', *Middle Eastern Studies*, 30, 3 (1994), pp. 691–2. Saudi academics, too, complain that reliable information is sometimes scarce, inaccessible or unavailable.

[13] Daniel L. Byman and Jerrold D. Green, 'The Enigma of Political Stability in the Persian Gulf Monarchies', *Middle East Review of International Affairs*, 3, 3 (September 1999). See also J. E. Peterson, *Saudi Arabia and the Illusion of Security*, Adelphi Paper, no. 348, Oxford University Press, 2002, p. 68.

been in place since the 1973–4 oil boom, whereby the Al Sa'ud support a generous 'welfare state' in return for political quiescence.[14]

Against this background, political reform programmes moving ahead in Qatar, Bahrain, Oman and, of course, Kuwait have conferred clout and cogency if not urgency to some of the demands, particularly political and administrative demands, proclaimed by some opposition groups in the Kingdom, as shown in Table 3 (see appendix). Moreover, demands of reformers and opposition activists in the Kingdom have been buttressed by the increased worldwide interest in democratic practices and human rights, the IT revolution and the role of mass communication media.

As indicated, much of the expression of grievances has taken an Islamist form. Quite apart from the local Saudi historical background, there is a wider context that needs to be reckoned with. All Arab countries, with the notable exception of Lebanon, have constitutions that explicitly proclaim Islam as the official religion of the state as well as the main, if not sole, source of legislation. This is an essential issue as far as political development in the Muslim world is concerned. It has much to do with the politicisation of religion by both regimes and opposition groups.

[14] See Anthony H. Cordesman, *Saudi Arabia: Guarding the Desert Kingdom*, Boulder, CO: Westview Press, 1997, pp. 47, 73–6; Helen Lackner, *A House Built on Sand: A Political Economy of Saudi Arabia*, London: Ithaca Press, 1978, p. 216; Peter Wilson and Douglas Graham, *Saudi Arabia: The Coming Storm*, New York: M. E. Sharpe, 1994, pp. 81 and 185. The term 'Saudi welfare state' has even been employed and emphasised by the Saudis themselves: Royal Embassy of Saudi Arabia, London, *The Kingdom of Saudi Arabia: A Welfare State*, London: Royal Embassy of Saudi Arabia, 1997.

In the view of Sharaf Sabri, the fact that Saudi Arabia is a family- or kinship-based society complicates the effects of unemployment in a poor economic environment. Despite the 'welfare state', the rate of unemployment is high. On the one hand, the poor and disadvantaged who are likely to be increasing in number, are benefiting from the corporatist social networks of the family-based society. On the other, because the concept of a greater society has not become embedded, those (arguably also increasing in number) who somehow fall outside the corporatist networks are left exposed. For more details on kinship and corporatist politics see Sharaf Sabri, *The House of Saud in Commerce: A Study of Royal Entrepreneurship in Saudi Arabia*, New Delhi: IS Publications, 2001, p. 92; Gary Samore, 'Royal Family Politics in Saudi Arabia 1953–1982', PhD thesis, Harvard University, 1983, p. 199; and Kiren Aziz Chaudhry, *The Price of Wealth: Economies and Institutions in the Middle East*, Ithaca, NY: Cornell University Press 1997.

For some time now the Saudi authorities have waged a sustained campaign against anti-regime fundamentalists and opposition groups resorting to violent means of self-expression. The crackdown campaign was initially launched in the aftermath of the series of explosions that ripped through Saudi Arabia in the early 1990s and more noticeably in the more recent past.[15] Table 1 (see appendix) tracks a detailed timeline of the series of terrorist operations perpetrated on Saudi Arabian soil. Violent dissidence in Saudi Arabia has almost always been associated with the presence of US military troops on Saudi soil, as illustrated in Table 2 (see appendix). However, the ramifications, for the Saudi opposition, of the United States decision to pull its troops out of Saudi territory are yet to be seen.

Mapping Political Opposition in Saudi Arabia

Political opposition is not a new phenomenon in Saudi Arabia. For a long time individuals and groups, both within the ruling family and across wider society, have expressed their political discontent. Throughout the 1950s and 1960s political forces across a broad political spectrum carried banners as varied as Liberal, Nationalist, Ba'thist, or Nasserite. The political *Zeitgeist* of the Arab world at the time was markedly dominated by the confrontation between the nationalist and conservative camps. On the fringes of this ideological confrontation a few religious groups, both Sunni and Shi'i, intermittently manifested their own grievances.[16] Table 4 provides a categorisation of the main opposition groups and organisations in Saudi Arabia.[17]

[15] See also Gilles Kepel, *Jihad: The Trail of Political Islam*, London: I. B. Tauris, 2nd edn, 2002, p. 368.

[16] For a broad survey see Toby Jones, 'Seeking a "Social Contract" for Saudi Arabia', *Middle East Report*, 228 (fall 2003), pp. 42–8; and Bernard Lewis, 'Communism and Islam', *International Affairs*, 30, 1 (January 1954), London: Royal Institute of International Affairs, pp. 1–12.

[17] For a brief survey of the Saudi opposition see Gerd Nonneman, 'Terrorism, Gulf Security and Palestine: Key Issues for an EU-GCC Dialogue', *EUI Policy Paper*, no. 02/2, Florence: European University Institute, The Robert Schuman Centre for Advanced Studies, 2002, pp. 27–35. For an earlier more extended treatment see Fandy, *Saudi Arabia and the Politics of Dissent*. See also the chapter by Madawi Al-Rasheed in this volume. A recent profile of the Islamist opposition can be found also in International Crisis Group, *Saudi Arabia Backgrounder: Who are the Islamists?*, Amman/Riyadh/Brussels: ICG Middle East Report no. 31, 21 September 2004. Available on http://www.icg.org/home/index.cfm?id=1096&1=1.

As already pointed out, the non-Islamist opposition strands (from liberals to nationalists) represent a minority form of opposition. Among the Islamist opposition, the Shi'a variety can be distinguished from the much larger Sunni ones. Much of its rationale and support came from the specific grievances of the minority Shi'a community in the country, and for the most part these movements have not aimed at the overthrow of the Al Sa'ud. A 1993 understanding with the Saudi government on improving the community's status and condition, led to the dissolution of the main organisation (Organisation of the Islamic Revolution). Among the Sunni opposition, the 1990–1 Gulf War and its aftermath brought a resurgence of radical groups. However, these too must again be subdivided. The so-called *Sahwa* ('Awakening')—led by younger preachers—challenged the legitimacy of the regime and despite their lack of political organisation violence became an implicitly accepted means for some in the trend.[18] Even so, they cannot be considered 'revolutionaries' in the full sense of the word; the partial recanting of some of its leading figures in the wake of the surge in bombings in 2003, perhaps illustrates this. On the other hand, a number of other, *jihad*ist, groups—most prominently Al-Qa'ida in the Arabian Peninsula[19]—do aim squarely at bringing down the House of Sa'ud. As of 2004 Sunni Islamists in Saudi Arabia can be generally categorised into:

- A conservative, non-violent and not overtly political Wahhabism, firmly rooted in Saudi society and among the *ulama*;
- A violent *jihadi* trend with a following among radicalised youth and enjoying the (overt or covert) support of part of the ulama;
- the self-styled 'ulama of the centre', emerging from the *Sahwa*, such as Salman al-Awda and Ayed al-Qarni, who have recently sought to act as intermediaries between the young jihadis and the government, and whose main focus has turned to opposing social reform;

[18] The *Sahwa* or 'Awakening' Shaikhs are those who 'heard their voices' during and after the Second Gulf War; they are not politically organised but have many followers polarised from lecturing in the universities and mosques. The most prominent are Safar al-Hawali, Ayedh al-Qarni and Salman al-Awda. See the chapter by Stéphane Lacroix in this volume; Gwenn Okruhlik, 'Networks of Dissent: Islamism and Reform in Saudi Arabia', *Current History*, January 2002; and International Crisis Group, *Saudi Arabia Backgrounder: Who are the Islamists?*

[19] *Tanzim al-qa'ida fi jazirat al-'arab.* See the chapter by Roel Meijer in this volume.

- the 'liberal', or 'new' Islamists, themselves divided into those prioritising political reform and those prioritising social reform;[20]
- Sunni Islamists outside the country, such as the London-based Movement for Islamic Reform in Arabia (led by Sa'd al-Faqih), which claims to promote the non-violent removal of the House of Sa'ud;
- other trends, including the Muslim Brotherhood, which has a small but active following among urban, educated Saudis.

Far from being uniform, the face of political dissidence in Saudi Arabia historically is a mix of workers, university students, intellectuals, religious scholars and royal princes. Ideologically, political opposition in Saudi Arabia subsumes diametrically opposed currents. Liberals, Nationalists, radical Islamists and *Salafis* converge and coexist within the same dissident tableau. Still, and in spite of this broad diversity, dissidence in the Kingdom has so far failed to expand and numerous movements have simply evaporated.

While some Saudi opposition groups chose to make their voices heard inside the Kingdom, others have opted for exile. The Committee for the Defence of Legitimate Rights (CDLR)[21] and the Movement of Islamic Reform in Arabia (MIR), both based in London, are good instances of the latter. The two organisations are a good example of the long-established pattern of fragmentation among Saudi opposition forces—a pattern that is unlikely to change in the foreseeable future. The splitting of the CDLR in March 1996 is a classic case: they fell out over what the CDLR stood for and how its campaign should operate and be focused. Until its split the CDLR had been the most organised and professional Saudi political opposition group.

[20] See the chapter by Stéphane Lacroix in this volume, for a survey of new trends in 'Liberal' Islamism in Saudi Arabia, and International Crisis group, *Saudi Arabia Backgrounder: Who are the Islamists?*

[21] The CDLR's origins lay with the loosely-knit political reform groups that began expressing themselves after the 1991 Gulf War. The organisation was founded in Riyadh on 3 May 1993; on 11 May it was banned and, within days, many of its members were arrested. The CDLR was re-founded in London by exiled members and sympathisers in April 1994. The highest-profile CDLR member was its secretary-general, Muhammad al-Mas'ari, around whom several controversies raged in the UK from 1994 to 1996.

Moreover, most opposition groups remained for some time largely cut off from their popular bases and thus substantially enfeebled and marginalised (in a way reminiscent of the fate that befell Nationalist and Marxist movements). Since the early 1990s they have managed to capitalise on the ubiquitous use of IT, the media and communication tools such as the internet, fax-messaging, electronic mail and satellite television.[22] In addition, opponents in exile have enjoyed extensive freedom of action in the host countries. They have been able to secure funds to sustain their activities from a variety of sources (one channel has consisted of a number of legal suits against a number of parties, from which compensation was gained).[23]

While some dissident groups rely on peaceful means to voice publicly their critique of Saudi domestic governance and their dissatisfaction with the way foreign policy is conducted, others resort to violence, as was the case with the followers of Juhaiman al-Utaibi, who forcibly took over the Grand Mosque in Mecca in 1979. In 1995 and 1996 violent dissidents carried out bomb attacks against US military personnel stationed in Saudi Arabia. The series of blasts that has ripped through the Kingdom in recent years seemingly bears the seal of operatives and cells either directly associated with the Al-Qa'ida network or subscribing to its tactics.[24]

Yet perhaps the most striking observation is that most dissenting groups and movements, shown in Tables 4 and 5, have not survived for long. Generally opposition movements in Saudi Arabia have suffered from lack of funds and organisation, and in many cases from embracing a political course that failed to appeal broadly to the population—whether because of substance and discourse, or because of the tactics employed.

Religious creeds and politico-ideological discourse of the opposition

An examination of the manifestos of broad beliefs and politico-ideological tenets that animate dissident forces in Saudi Arabia[25] shows

[22] Mamoun Fandy, 'Cyber Resistance: Saudi Opposition Between Globalization and Localization', *Comparative Studies in Society and History*, 41, 1 (1999), p. 19.

[23] Interview with anonymous well-informed Saudi intelligence source.

[24] See the chapter by Roel Meijer in this volume.

[25] What follows is largely based on an on-going analysis of the various groups and

that they have revolved around a set menu of issues. The first—at least among the Sunni Islamists who form the majority, as well as some of the Shi'a—is the application of the *shari'a* law in the Kingdom.[26] Some dissident groups categorically reject the way Islamic law is currently applied in Saudi Arabia. They regard it as tainted by human reason and unfaithful to the Qur'anic text. For them a genuine exegesis of Islamic precepts and teachings should be rigorously and strictly tied to the letter of the text, irrespective of the passage of time and the ever-changing conditions of life. This method of interpreting the religious text is loyal to mainstream Wahhabism,[27] which strictly adheres to transcription of religious text and rejects reasoning. Accordingly, some opponent groups view the Saudi regime as having abandoned these tenets. However, the government finds itself increasingly under pressure to cope with modernity and non-Wahhabi sects, and obliged to relax the degree of strictness in implementing the Wahhabi method of religious enforcement.[28]

The second feature of the opposition creed questions the nature of Al Sa'ud governance. A number of dissidents question the performance legitimacy of the Saudi monarchy. They expose what they perceive as the untenable shortcomings in Saudi domestic- and foreign-policy-making. This aspect of opposition criticises the level of efficiency in making policy and denounces the contents, while questioning how the public wealth is generated and spent. Indeed, there is palpable popular frustration over the fact that the state, with its reputed wealth, is indebted by more than $150 billion (2003).

movements' statements, documents and websites, undertaken at the Gulf Research Centre, Dubai, in addition to the author's own observation in Saudi Arabia. See also International Crisis Group, *Saudi Arabia Backgrounder: Who are the Islamists?*, and Madawi Al-Rasheed's contribution to this volume.

26 L. Diamond, Marc F. Plattner and D. Brumberg, *Islam and Democracy in the Middle East*, Baltimore, MD: Johns Hopkins University Press, 2003, *passim*.

27 Wahhabism in this regard follows the Hanbali school of jurisdiction, in which transcription outweighs reasoning; therefore, at least the majority of its adherents believe that religious text should be interpreted lexically without imposing a reasoning explanation.

28 This divergence between the government and religious establishment is clear in the gradual stripping the Police of Virtue and Vice from its extensive authority over society. Ironically, this matter has been exploited by some of the royal factions in bidding against each other.

This links closely to the issues of corruption and mismanagement of the state's resources.

The third feature is the issue of Palestine and the conflict with Israel. Due to the boom in communications and media that show the daily suffering of Palestinians, people have increasingly become aware of the different political stances of different parties involved in this conflict. There is now a widespread sense in the country of international (and in particular US) policies being imposed that are unjustly biased against the Palestinians. The regime's own claim to being the guardian of Islam has meant that its failure to achieve any results over an issue that includes Islam's third-holiest place (Jerusalem) has left people distinctly dissatisfied—especially given the close links between the Al Sa'ud and the United States, which is universally considered Israel's staunchest supporter. Virtually all Saudis, it is safe to say, firmly believe that, were it not for America's uncritical support, Israel would not dare to adopt its hard-line policies and rob the Palestinians of their land, desecrating their religious shrines. The stationing of US troops in Saudi Arabia fuelled those feelings of resentment among much of the population, and became a catalyst for the violent subversive groups, while also combining with the economic situation to facilitate recruitment.

The relatively smaller, liberal end of the opposition spectrum also raises issues of corruption and mismanagement. But they focus also, in particular, on the themes of democracy, human rights and freedom of speech and assembly.

There is also a large passive opposition composed of the people who do not explicitly express their demands, grievances and dissatisfaction in any public or organised fashion: they nevertheless increasingly do so in closed circles and private gatherings. It is not fanciful to imagine that a significant segment of this strand of society might turn active once the performance/demands balance tips even further against the regime.

The petitioning phenomenon

After the 1990–1 Gulf War a new and unprecedented practice came to the fore on the Saudi socio-political stage. Groups demanding reform, drawn from both Islamist and Liberal camps and explicitly recognising the legitimacy of the House of Sa'ud, have tendered petitions to the ruling family. Several such petitions were submitted to the Saudi royals and almost all revolved around a list of demands encompassing a wide reform agenda calling for the need to set up a *shura* (consultative) council through free elections—a council that should be endowed with wider legislative and oversight leverage—together with the need to keep state powers separate. They also called for an independent judiciary, and the eradication of corruption and cronyism. Centrally, these petitions called for a more inclusive and representative form of governance that would ensure broader participation by Saudi citizens in the management of public affairs via legal and institutional channels and the necessity to implement viable economic, social, educational and administrative reform policies.[29]

In other words, what these reformists are demanding is nothing less than the construction of institutional pillars for the edifice of the Saudi state, to be supported and cemented by the principles of equal citizenship for all, the rule of law, respect for human rights, social justice and modern institutions capable of riding the globalisation wave with confidence. Educated Saudi women also joined the call for reform: more than 300 women, alongside a wide spectrum of male signatories, signed what might be called a 'consensus petition' in December 2003 urging the Saudi authorities to implement a raft of reforms including some specific to women. The very fact of a number of reformist trends coming together, as evidenced by this

[29] These petitions are displayed on various websites run by intellectuals and activists, such as on 29 September 2004, Memorandum of Advice, http://www.alhramain.com/text/payan/alnseha/1.htm; Shi'a Petition to the Crown Prince, http://www.alhramain.com/text/payan/mostqela/8.htm. There are three important reform petitions: In Defence of the Nation; A Vision for the Present and Future; and A National Call: Leadership and People Together…Constitutional Reform First, http://www.rasid.net/artc.php?id=2556. Most opposition groups have their own website: Islamic Movement: http://www.alhramain.com/text/payan/islamyh/islamyh.htm; Gathering of Hijaz Religious Scholars: http://www.alhramain.com/text/payan/tjmi/tjmi.htm; Hizbullah of Hijaz: http://www.alhramain.com/text/payan/hzb%20alah/fah.htm; Human Rights Defence Committee in the Arabian Peninsula: http://www.alhramain.com/text/payan/lijnadefa/defa.htm; Committee for Defence of Legitimate Rights: http://www.alhramain.com/text/payan/almsiry/masari.htm; Reform Islamic Movement: http://www.alhramain.com/text/payan/islah/islah.htm. See also the contribution by Stéphane Lacroix in this volume; and International Crisis group, *Can Saudi Arabia Reform Itself?*, ICG Middle East Report no. 28, 14 July 2004. Available on http://www.crisisweb.org/home/index.cfm?id=2864&1=1, pp. 13–15.

petition, may have been the cause of the more hard-line response of the authorities this time around: prominent signatories were arrested, and three remain in detention at the time of writing (October 2004).[30] Table 6 lists the major petitions and memoranda delivered to the Saudi authorities since the Second Gulf War.

Yet some observations on these petitions and the peaceful Saudi opposition in general need to be made. The project of reform has not yet transcended the élitist discourse and is confined to the intelligentsia. It has provided a general framework without presenting a comprehensive and precise reform agenda. As already indicated, the reformists have been drawn from a wide political spectrum; consequently, they still retain their suspicions towards each other and have not so far been able to form a solid front. Moreover, the post-9/11 environment significantly affected perceptions and calculations, which diverged widely between different groups. Many misinterpreted the consequences of acts of terror both for the US–Saudi relationship and for the government's position: the latter became clearly more defensive. Both jihadists and reformists misjudged the strength and position of the regime. The jihadists see the regime as highly vulnerable and ripe for collapse; while the reformists see it as essentially still strong but in need of rejuvenating its legitimacy. As a result the jihadists have adopted head-on confrontation as their tactic, while the reformists have adopted a position of compromise—producing disarray among opposition forces. This has also been reflected in a widening gap between the opposition's political discourse and presented programmes on the one hand and the society on the other.

More important, most of the opposition draws heavily on the same source of legitimacy that the regime adopts, namely religion. Consequently, they do not provide alternatives, but rather compete with the regime on the same source of legitimacy, only with much fewer resources. This partially explains why the regime responded by using the same tools and mobilised the official religious establishment to legitimise the regime and denounce the opposition regardless of the differences between different movements in ideology or the adopted means of political action. Different tactics may be deployed, with extremist factions facing violent crackdowns while other op-

[30] See the chapter by Stéphane Lacroix in this volume; and International Crisis Group, *Can Saudi Arabia Reform Itself?*, pp. 16–22.

position or critical voices receive less draconian treatment. But in some instances peaceful critics, including the liberals, who work to reform the system without ousting the royal family, have been arrested alongside those who explicitly call for deposing the regime. Ironically, in late 2004 a number of moderate reformists arrested earlier that year remained in detention, while at least some more radical elements, who had responded to the regime's call to 'come in from the cold', were released after their initial arrest.

Finally, apart from the small, if high-impact, minority of violent opposition groups, all opposition trends have confined themselves to petitions to decision-makers and the circulation of criticism via the web, cassette tapes and the foreign media, but they have stepped back from developing other non-violent means, such as demonstrations and sit-ins. Just as striking has been their failure to develop close working relationships with the institutions of civil society. Outside the country also, a number of research centres and institutes, managed by Saudi liberals, have sprouted up across Europe and the United States. These monitor domestic developments in the Kingdom, particularly in connection with human rights. Making use of the facilities readily available in Western countries, they put out magazines and statements and hold symposia during which Saudi policies come under intense attack.[31] Yet, based outside the country, these organisations too lack significant roots in Saudi society at large, and their discourse remains elitist.

Mounting Islamist Dissent in a Religious State

Some political analysts have hastily, almost mechanically, connected 'Wahhabism' with the phenomenon of violent extremism unfolding in Saudi Arabia.[32] As will already have become clear from much of

[31] For example, the London-based Saudi Human Rights Centre and the Washington-based Saudi Institute are among the most active of the Saudi centres, see, http://www.saudiinstitute.org/.

[32] For some of the better examples of analyses making a link with Wahhabism, see Eleanor Doumato, 'Manning the Barricades: Islam According to Saudi Arabia's School Texts', *Middle East Journal*, 57, 2 (spring 2003), p. 235; and Eleanor Doumato, 'Women and Work in Saudi Arabia: How Flexible are Islamic Margins?', *Middle East Journal*, 52, 2 (spring), p. 582. See also the chapter by Michaela Prokop in this volume (although neither of these two authors claim Wahhabism as the sole or even central cause of violent extremism).

the foregoing, any analysis using this as a stand-alone explanation fails to recognise the much wider dynamics at work. Indeed, the fallacy of arguments that put the blame squarely on 'Wahhabism' becomes obvious in the light of the evidence from other Arab countries, such as Egypt, Algeria and Yemen, which were or still are confronted by similarly violent groups, even though 'Wahhabism' as such has no more than a very limited foothold in their societies. Such interpretations also tend to overlook the more nuanced picture of 'Wahhabism' that recent scholarship is bringing to light.[33] Whether inspired by their particular interpretation of 'Wahhabism' or not, in essence the phenomenon is one of groups and movements that employ religion as a tool of, and justification for, political opposition. The most extreme and violent groups espouse extremist interpretations of some religious texts and shape their interpretations to fit their own points of view. In this, Saudi extremists are hardly exceptional, either in the Muslim world or outside it.[34]

In the case of Saudi Arabia there have certainly been a number of external developments with a religious 'flavour' that played a role in the emergence of various types of Islamist (including violent) opposition activity in the country. Yet these too should be seen in their political or socio-economic context. The Iranian revolution moved some Shi'a groups to violent outbursts for a limited time in 1979 and 1980 in both Bahrain and the Saudi city of al-Qateef. These incidents, apart from being connected to specific local Shi'a grievances as already discussed, were also stimulated by the activities of some in the leadership of Iran's Islamic Revolutionary regime in its most radical phase—driven by their ambition to export the Islamic revolution to neighbouring countries. Moreover, in the same period (1979–80) the Afghan episode of Jihad was declared against the then Soviet invaders, giving birth to the 'Afghan Saudi' militants who, subsequently, would bring their zeal and training back to Saudi Arabia (in a context where employment opportunities and welfarism were

33 See in particular Abdulaziz Al-Fahad, 'From Exclusivism to Accommodation: Doctrinal and Legal Evolution of Wahhabism', *New York University Law Review*, 2004, also available on-line at http://www.saudi-us-relations.org/history/saudi-history.html; and the chapters by Guido Steinberg and Stéphane Lacroix in the present volume.

34 An extensive survey of roots, nature and trends in Islamist opposition that does not fall into this trap, is Anthony Cordesman, *Saudi Arabia Enters the 21st Century: IV. Saudi Arabia: Opposition, Islamic Extremism, and Terrorism*.

shrinking, while US presence and Middle East policies provided a particular catalyst for opposition).

Moving to the early twenty-first century, the removal of Saddam Hussein opened the way for the Iraqi Shi'a to embrace a more influential role in politics—although this could have both moderate and more extreme versions. At the same time, the way in which the Iraq war was executed and the post-War phase mismanaged, has provided an ideal stage for Al-Qa'ida and associated extremist groups to operate from that country—a development which may well have far-ranging consequences throughout the region.[35]

But the key sources of grievances for opposition movements in Saudi Arabia remain socio-economic dissatisfaction and frustration, an increased questioning of the roles of rulers and ruled in a faltering rentier state, and an associated resentment of policies and behaviour seen as improper for an Islamic society and regime—not least a regime that bases its claim to legitimacy to a significant extent on its Islamic credentials. It is in the latter context also that grievances over foreign policy are brought into the equation. It is the chronological coincidence of worsening socio-economic stresses on the one hand and the foreign policy issues to have emerged since the 1990–1 Gulf War on the other that have given rise to the surge of radical and violent opposition activity in the country since the mid-1990s. However, while the underlying grievances are shared by significant portions of the population, it must be remembered that the most radical expressions remain confined to a very small fraction.

Containing the Opposition: the State's Approach to Political Opposition

The Saudi royal family exercises absolute power. Political participation has been very restricted in the past—mainly limited to traditional practices of tribal and elite representation and petition, which has often been labelled 'desert democracy'.[36] In practice, the oppor-

[35] For a challenging and informative paper on this, see Royal Institute of International Affairs, 'Vortex or Catalyst?', Middle East Programme, Briefing Paper 04/02, September 2004.

[36] Tim Niblock, 'Social Structure and the Development of the Saudi Arabian Political System' in Tim Niblock (ed.), *State, Society and Economy in Saudi Arabia*, New York: St Martin's Press, 1982, p. 89.

tunity to raise and discuss issues with the king was not the same as participation in the decision-making process: the historical *majlis* (sitting/gathering session) system may be interpreted as a traditional public relations exercise—but a generally accepted one in the Arabian context—on behalf of the king and, by extension, of the royal family. The exercise bolstered specific decisions, the general royal decision-making process, and overall Al Sa'ud legitimacy, by promoting the image of consultation, discussion and consensus, and for providing the king and senior royals with the opportunity to be benevolent patrons and patriarchs.[37]

The different types of opposition necessitated different containment policies. The regime moved to shore up religious support where it existed. Such moves signified the increasing importance attached to legitimation of the government by the religious establishment in the face of the radical fundamentalists' ongoing threat. The establishment ulama found it easiest to condemn the overseas-based CDLR rather than the 'Awakening' (*Sahwa*) shaikhs at home, while the government-controlled press initiated a smear campaign against the latter.

In spite of the government reliance on the official religious establishment for legitimising the regime, the growing assertiveness of the religious establishment worried the regime. Indeed, the radicals and the religious establishment increasingly seemed to share similar educational experiences and hold relatively similar views. Disappointed with the Council of Senior Ulama, King Fahd announced in October 1994 the creation of a Supreme Council of Islamic Affairs and a Council for Islamic Mission and Guidance, both of which were designed to marginalise and neutralise the traditional religious establishment.

In the 1990s the Saudi government also realised that accommodating the Shi'i opposition could easily temper a serious conflict. Both the government and the Shi'i opposition seemed to have greatly desired an arrangement, which resulted in many exiled Saudi Shi'is returned to the Eastern Province of the country, but both sides kept the news of the agreement fairly quiet for fear that too much publicity would draw fire from the Sunni radical fundamentalists.[38]

[37] *Ibid.*, pp. 88–91.

[38] The Sunni orthodox Wahhabis perceive the Shi'a as apostates and denounce dealing with them. This is in part legacy of early political Islam and in part fuelled by politics tailored to contain the Islamic revolution in Iran.

Saudi Arabia does not face major political challenges from the mix of progressives, democratic reformers, human rights advocates, Arab socialists, Marxists or other secular political movements that shape the political debate in many other Arab countries, though Saudi Arabia has political advocates in all of these areas, and some are quite active as individuals. Instead, as shown above, the real challenges to the Saudi regime come from an Islamic environment that the rulers themselves have created, shaped and maintained. Nonetheless, Saudi Arabia does have its modernisers.[39] Many Saudi princes, educators, technocrats, businessmen, Western-educated citizens and more progressive Islamists have favoured more rapid social change than has been possible in the face of Islamic extremists and conservatives, who influence large elements of Saudi society and have often delayed progress. Yet most Saudi modernisers recognise that Saudi socio-religious practices and traditions can only be changed slowly. In spite of their moderate political point of view, a few businessmen, technocrats, and western-educated professionals have been arrested, or have had difficulties with the authorities, for asking for systematic and time-scheduled reform. However, such incidents are relatively rare. Most modernisers understand that the Royal family and Saudi technocrats offer a far more practical evolutionary mechanism toward change than opposition to the regime and hence it is safer and more productive to work from within the system.

Understanding these interactions and realities, the Saudi authorities have employed manifold tools and instruments to deal with political opposition: tools of security, and tools of a legal and political nature.

State security authorities have resorted to straightforward security methods whenever they have had to deal with violent elements and groups. Security agents have aimed to dismantle underground cells, confiscate their ammunition and explosives, and apprehend and prosecute those implicated in subversive acts. Following 9/11 the security services interrogated more than 2000 former combatants who participated in the wars in Afghanistan, Bosnia and Chechnya, and in a step to target the reputation of the people involved, the government revealed the identity of members of dismantled underground cells and engaged in a dialogue with detainees, showing them leniency.

[39] Richard H. Dekmejian, 'The Liberal Impulse in Saudi Arabia', *Middle East Journal*, 75, 3 (summer 2003), pp. 400–13.

In addition, Saudi authorities have concluded extradition agreements with some countries, such as Iran and Yemen. An official request was made in 2002 to the International Police Organization (Interpol) to pursue 750 suspects. The government maintains a joint Saudi–US anti-terrorist commission. The commission holds regular meetings to exchange information and draw up plans to demolish terrorist networks. The government also encourages state departments to contribute to, and participate in, international conferences and symposia focusing on the issue of terrorism.

Especially from 2002 onwards the Saudi authorities have also adopted a strengthened set of financial and economic measures in a bid to cut off funds destined for extremist groups (in 1995 the government had already set up a special anti-laundering unit affiliated with both the Interior Ministry and the Saudi Arabian Monetary Agency). Serious attempts have been made to trace and dismantle funding networks, and the control exercised by the Saudi Arabian Monetary Agency over the movement of capital and bank accounts has been tightened.[40]

At the level of legal procedures, the government joined the UN Convention on Illegal Trade and Trade Fraud. It also issued legislation and codifications through the Saudi Arabian Monetary Agency empowering banks to investigate bank accounts, and created a financial intelligence unit within the Ministry of Interior. As part of the attempt to dry up all source of funding to terrorists, the Saudi authorities have, since 9/11, adopted tight measures against philanthropic organisations and charities. The bank accounts of the Somali and Bosnian satellite offices of the Al-Haramain Islamic Foundation in Saudi Arabia were frozen in March 2002 in the wake of evidence that the two branches were involved in supporting terrorist activities. The government also created a higher committee in charge of overseeing the fundraising activities of humanitarian organisations and stipulated the auditing of the account sheets of charity organisations.

At the political level, the government opened channels of political dialogue. The numerous meetings Crown Prince Abdullah held with

[40] The Saudi government broke up a network of fifty companies used by Usama bin Ladin as money laundering businesses for channelling funds around the world. Previously, the government had already frozen funds belonging to Usama bin Ladin in 1994.

delegations of intellectuals and opinion-leaders fall squarely under this heading. In this context, Prince Abdullah announced in August 2003 the establishment of the King Abd al-Aziz Center for National Dialogue in Riyadh.[41] The Center is to be entrusted with the task of sustaining and fostering the dialogue with Saudi intellectuals that the Prince launched some time ago. Three successive conferences for national dialogue had been held by the time of writing (autumn 2004), the first two in June and December 2003 and the third in June 2004, in which aspects of reform were debated and recommendations issued regarding future steps. Directives were given to hold a new session of debates every three months. While this was a striking initiative that allowed discussion of subjects long deemed too sensitive, and did so between interlocutors not previously willing to engage (e.g. bringing together Wahhabi and Shi'a scholars), some critics from the reformist side have argued that tangible effects remain extremely limited.[42]

In a step progressive by Saudi standards, it was announced that partial municipal elections would take place in February 2005, which, it was suggested, might lead at some point to an elected *Shura* Council.[43] The decision to move forward on the reform front was clearly in response to domestic and foreign factors. The fledgling reform programme itself could be seen as dating back to March 1992 when King Fahd announced the decision to create a Saudi Consultative Council (*Majlis al-Shura*) whose members are appointed. A number of additional amendments to the system of governance were also included as part of this reform package (in the process creating the first 'Basic Law' for the country other than the Qur'an, although the term 'constitution' was avoided). Today the ruling elite in Riyadh is sharply aware of the need to reform, as a pre-requisite to tackling the novel developments both at home and overseas.

[41] The King Abd al-Aziz Centre for National Dialogue can be viewed at http://www.national_dialogue.org.sa/prince.php.

[42] For a good, brief overview and assessment of the first three National Dialogue sessions, see International Crisis Group, *Can Saudi Arabia Reform Itself?*, pp. 16–18; and Toby Jones, 'Seeking a "Social Contract" for Saudi Arabia'.

[43] The municipal elections constitutes one of three phases for electoral reform: the first is to elect half of the 178 municipal councils and appoint the other half; the second phase is to elect the members of the provincial councils after two years and; finally, a year later, election of the members of the *Shura* Council is mooted.

In the same vein, the Middle East reform and democracy initiative, floated by US Secretary of State Colin Powell, was a preamble to the US-led Coalition's invasion of Iraq and an instigator of reform across the region. The initiative focused on the issues of democratic practices, education, women's rights and civil society. It is worth noting that the US initiative came a short time before the first missiles hit Baghdad in March 2003, apparently in an effort to send signals to those claiming that Washington supports dictators in the Arab world. Arab countries undeniably suffer from a deficit in democracy and a surfeit of corruption. Yet strong suspicion prevailed among Arab publics—including Saudis—about the apparent shift in the US stance towards democratic reform, given the history of support for dictatorial regimes, of past active involvement in masterminding *coups d'état* in Chile and elsewhere, and the perceived double standard employed in the case of the Palestinians' elected President, Yasir Arafat. As a result, neither the regime nor the various strands of the opposition in Saudi Arabia give more than limited credence to the United States over the issue of democratisation. The prevailing view (indeed, not only in the Arab world) remains that Washington would probably make use of this new pressure for democracy to subdue governments that oppose its policies in the region, while treading much more gingerly at best when dealing with those governments that are willing to serve and facilitate its interests. This perception has strengthened the regime and weakened the opposition.

The Future of Political Opposition

Apart from the Juhaiman al-Utaibi group that forcibly seized the Grand Mosque in 1979, and the current Al-Qa'ida-associated opponents of the regime, dissidents do not pose a threat as serious as that projected by opposition groups in countries such as Egypt and Algeria during the 1990s. Despite the severity of the crack-down on armed cells and the arrest of hundreds of radical Islamists, Al-Qa'ida and its affiliates still clearly enjoy the support of sections of Saudi society, including a number of radical clerics whose *fatawa* lend legitimacy to their actions. Although many religious conservatives have condemned the suicide bombings in Saudi Arabia, many of them feel threatened by the government's response, fearing that under the guise of fighting terror the government will deprive the

Wahhabi ulama of their traditional pre-eminence. Traditional ulama felt threatened when the authorities initiated a 'national dialogue' which for the first time brought together different religious currents within the Kingdom—Sunni, Shi'i, Sufi and Isma'ili.

In the final analysis this political opposition lived on as contained groups that had carried out some acts of violence but could not find themselves any resonance in Saudi society nor significantly penetrate its institutions and bodies of government.[44]

Nevertheless, the status quo now looks untenable. One reason is rapid social change. A youthful society, where three quarters of the population are under thirty, is becoming increasingly vocal about unemployment, corruption and the absence of free speech. The advent of the internet, satellite TV and the mobile phone means the population is far more connected to the outside world. The Kingdom is no longer an island. It has become far harder for the authorities to control the lives of their citizens, who are making much more pressing demands on their rulers.

A second and perhaps decisive factor is the Islamist campaign of violence, which has forced a painful reassessment of the role of Wahhabism in Saudi life. The authorities have done much more than crack-down on the militant groups. They have launched a concerted effort to draw Saudi hearts and minds away from extremism and intolerance towards a kinder, gentler Islam. This has involved an energetic media campaign, the removal or 're-education' of hard-line *imams*, the partial revision of school textbooks, the closure or tighter monitoring of Islamic charities, and a range of other measures. At the same time, officials are promoting economic reform (privatisation of state-run industries, Saudisation of the workforce, the encouragement of foreign investment) and, on the political front, a gradual process of enhanced participation.

The future of opposition trends depends mainly on the way some problems and social issues are tackled. These include the everyday hardships suffered by ordinary Saudis such as unemployment and deteriorating standards of living. Addressing these issues in an effective

44 There have been claims that some violent dissidents have had roots in some state agencies, such as the National Guard; yet no strong evidence has emerged to corroborate these claims. See also the argument put forward by Roel Meijer in this volume.

way may help facilitate the establishment of a new social contract between state and society. While helping to eliminate some of the main factors conducive to spawning violence and extremism, this could also forestall external forces from pressuring the Kingdom through its human rights record. The issues of renewing religious thought and introducing reforms into the educational curriculum are also on the reform agenda. Their critical importance points to the necessity of accelerating this process. The state has begun to move in the right direction by adopting the initiative to reform education as well as encouraging religious preachers to promote the values of forgiveness and tolerance, two central Islamic concepts.[45]

Yet until the reforms yield the expected results, Saudis must accept the fact that there is a price to be paid. Regardless of the accompanying uncertainties and short-term difficulties, the costs of reform are without doubt less than those of procrastination or dealing with reform in a piecemeal, arbitrary way. It goes without saying that the success of reform depends to a great extent on the ability of the Saudi state to contain the anti-reform forces who oppose it only to protect their own interests and maintain the status quo. The opponents of reform come from across the socio-political spectrum, and include some traditional clergy and influential merchants as well as tribal leaders and a good many royals who are concerned that any new arrangements might negatively affect their own privileges. It is also crucial to revisit the existing balance between the state and society, which is ill-defined but leans drastically in favour of the state. This imbalance needs to be addressed, and a new social contract developed, endorsing reforms in the Kingdom and establishing constitutional institutions protected by law. In such a context, all the factors that facilitate the emergence of extremism and violence could be mitigated, reduced, and eventually largely eradicated. Indeed, such a development would pave the way for all factions and groups in the Kingdom to have their say and express their demands and interests by peaceful means and through legitimate and legal channels. The royal family, of course, realises that serious reform, leading to more transparent and accountable government, would ultimately threaten their power and privileges. Yet sticking to the tried and trusted

[45] See the chapter by Michaela Prokop in this volume.

methods, co-opting or coercing opponents, using oil wealth to buy time, promising reform but delaying its implementation, can only lead to the gap between what their people want and what they are ready to deliver, growing dangerously wider.

APPENDIX

Table 1

Terrorist Bomb Attacks in Saudi Arabia, 18.03. 2003 to 3.11.2004

Incidents		*Casualties*								*Perpetrators*				
		Dead				*Injured*								
Site	*Total*	*Security officers*	*Civilian*		*Total*	*Security officers*	*Civilian*		*Total*	*Wanted*	*Dead*	*Injured*	*Apprehended*	*Total*
			Nationals	*Residents*			*Nationals*	*Residents*						
Inside the Kingdom	116	44	19	53	116	104	13	346	463	101*	72**	13***	312****	498

* Five non-Saudi nationals
** Five non-Saudi nationals
*** One non-Saudi national
**** Nineteen non-Saudi nationals, fourteen women, six children; ten surrendered themselves voluntarily to the authorities.

Table 2

US Troops in Saudi Arabia, 2005

Designation	*Date of establishment*	*Location*	*Personnel**	*Type of equipment**	*Date of withdrawal*
King Abd al-Aziz Air Base	1951	Dhahran		A fleet of fighter aircraft and Patriot missiles since 1990–91	
Prince Sultan Air Base	1990	80 kms south of Riyadh	4500 soldiers	Unknown number of fighter aircraft	September 2003; 500 personnel remain stationed at a residential compound
King Abd al-Aziz Brigade	1991	Hofouf		Providing training and consultancy	
US Military Training Mission		– Dammam Air Base – National Guard Eastern Command – Ta'if Base – Khamis Mushayt Base – Dhahran Base – Jeddah Base		Providing training, consultancy and logistic support for the operation of F16s at Ad-Dahran and Khamis Mushayt Bases, RF5s at al-Taef Base, and the C130s at Jeddah Base	
Duty Force 1–7	2001	Riyadh	500	Missile air defence	

* *Subject to periodic changes*

Table 3

Political & Administrative Reforms in the Gulf Cooperation Council (GCC) Countries

Country	*Constitution*	*Parliament*	*Last elections*	*Status of women*
Bahrain	2002	Elected	October 2002	Women have the right to vote and contest/some women hold executive positions
Kuwait	1962	Elected	July 2003	Women obtained the right to vote and contest in 2005/some women hold executive positions
Oman	1996	Elected	October 2003	Women have the right to vote and contest/some women hold executive positions
Qatar	2003	Two-thirds of the members are elected	Referendum on the constitution held April 2003	Women have the right to vote and contest/some women hold executive positions
UAE	1996	Appointed	–	Some voices call for women's right to vote and contest—but the UAE has no elections

Table 4

Main Opposition Movements, Groups and Organisations in Saudi Arabia
(italic indicates still active movements and organisations)

Movement	*Representative group*	*Date of emergence*	*Prominent figures*	*Membership*
Liberal organisations	Al-Hijazi Liberation Party	1927	Hassan ad-Dabagh	Hijazi merchants
	The Free Emirs [princes]	1960s	Tala bin Abd al-Aziz	A number of royal princess
	Najdo al-Fatat	1960s	Abdullah at-Tariqi, Abdullah bin ma'amr and Fayssal al-Hajelan	Some Saudi intellectuals abroad
	Saudi-Arab Liberation Commission	1969	–	Officers and intellectuals
Nationalist Organisations	Bin Rifada revolt	1932	Hamed bin Rafada	Tribesmen and merchants from al-Hijaz
	Association of Knowledge for Militancy	1949	Hassan al-Habshi and AbdRaouf al-Khanzi	Intellectuals and workers
	Arab Nationalists	1950s	–	Students and workers
	Peninsula Union (Nasserite)	1950s	Nasser Sa'id	Functionaries and workers
	Arab Socialist Ba'ath Party (Saudi)	1950s	Mohamed ar-Rabi'i and Ali Ghanam	Students
	Revolutionary Avant-garde Students (Ba'ath)	1962	–	Students

Table continued

Table continued

	Arab Liberation Front (Saudi)	1962	Hussein Nasseef and some tribal chiefs	Union of Young Nationalists
	Arab Avant-garde Youth (Saudi)	1964	–	Young nationalists
Islamist Organisations	Artawiya Conference	1926	Fayssal ad-Dawish, Sultan bin Bejjad and Dhaidan bin Hathleen	Al-Ikhwan Group
	First Riyadh Conference	1927	Imam abdul Aziz ibn Sa'ud	Al-Ikhwan
	Second Riyadh Conference	1928	Imam abdul Aziz ibn Sa'ud	Al-Ikhwan
	Al Kateef Secession Movement	1948	Mohamed Hussein al-Arraj	Al-Kateef Shi'ites
	At-Tabligh Group	1953	–	Scholars and students
	Al Kateef riots	1970	–	Al-Kateef Shi'ites
	Seizure of the Grand Mosque in Mekkah	1979	Juhaiman bin Seif al-Utaibi	Remnants of al-Ikhwan
	Saudi Hizbullah	1980	–	Shi'ites
	Reform Movement	1996	Dr Sa'ad al-Faqih	Religious scholars and university professors
	Committee for the Defence of Legitimate Rights	1993	Dr Mohamed al-Mas'ari	Religious scholars and university professors
	Al Qa'ida	1990s	Usama bin Ladin	Islamists

Table continued

Table continued

Marxist organisations	National Reform Front	1953	–	Members of the military, workers and civil servants
	National Liberation Front	1958	–	*Petite bourgeoisie*, intellectuals and workers
	Democratic Popular Front for the Liberation of the Arabian Peninsula	1960	–	Oil workers
	Saudi Communist Organization	1961	–	Oil workers
	Union of Democratic Forces in the Arabian Peninsula	1960s	–	Workers and civil servants
	Socialist Front for the Lib-eration for the Arabian Peninsula	1963	–	Oil workers in the Eastern province
	League of Arabian Descendants Abroad	1969	Saudi community overseas	Intellectuals and workers
	Popular Democratic Party in the Arabian Peninsula	1969	–	Functionaries and students
	Popular Militant Front	1970s	Saudi students in Europe and the United States	Students

Table 5

The Saudi Opposition Timeline
(italic indicates still active movements and organisations)

1912	Creation of the first Hijrah (Jihadists Settlement) in Artaweeah
1916	Widening the base of Ikhwan
1926	Artaweeah opposition conference
1927	First Riyadh conference announced Ibn Sa'ud an Islamic Imam
1928	The partially decisive second Riyadh conference in Riyadh for purging of extremists
1948	Haraj Movement in Qatif for secession
1949–50	Enlightenment Struggle Association
1950s	Union of Arabian Peninsula
1950s	Saudi Ba'th
1950s	Labour Committee
1953	National Reform Front
1953	Tableegh Group
1953	Taif Document for Political Reform
1955	Free Officers
1958	National Liberation Front
1960	Democratic Popular Front for Liberation of Arabian Peninsula
1960s	Najd al-Fatat
1960s	Union of Democratic Forces in the Arabian Peninsula
1961	Organization of Saudi Communists
1962	Movement of Free Princes
1962	Revolutionary Students Vanguard
1962	Saudi Liberation Front
1963	Socialist Front for Liberation the Arabia Peninsula
1964	Youth Vanguard
1969	The Saudi Liberation Committee
1969	League of Sons of the Arabian Peninsula
1969	Popular Democratic Party
1970	Shi'ite Uprising
1970s	Front of Public Struggle
1979	Juhaiman Rebellion and Seizure of Mecca Shrine
1980	*Saudi Hizbullah*
1990s	*The Saudi Institute in Washington*
1990	*Al-Qa'ida*
1991	Liberal and Orthodox Petitions of Naseeha

Table continued

Table continued

1993	*Committee for Defending Legitimate Rights CDLR*
1996	*Movement for Islamic Reform in Arabia*
2003	Petitions

- In Defence of our Nation.
- View for the Present and Future of our Homeland.
- National Appeal: Constitutional Reform First.
- Women rights document.
- London conference.

Table 6

Major Reform Petitions since the 1990s

Designation	*Date of presentation*	*No. of signatories*	*Political affiliation of signatories*	*Social background of signatories*	*Demands*
Reform petition	1990	43	Liberals	Academics	– Comprehensive political reforms
Moderates' petition	1991	40	Moderate Islamists	Functionaries and intellectuals	– Judicial and administrative reforms – Transparency and accountability – Eradication of corruption – Upgrading state departments
Memorandum of Advice	May 1992	107	Hard-core Salafists	Religious scholars, Ulamas, mosque speakers and some university professors	– Eradication of corruption – Application of *shari'a* law – Reduction of expatriate labour force
Fatwa by the International Islamic Front against Jews and Crusaders	February 1998	Statement	Hard-core fundamentalists	Usama bin Ladin	– Expelling Americans and their allies from the Arabian Peninsula

Table continued

Table continued

'A Vision for the Present and Future of the Nation'	January 2003	104	Liberals	Academics and intellectuals	– Upgrading the monarchy – Constitutional reforms – Independence of the judiciary – Protection of freedom – Improving women's status
Shi'a petition	April 2003	450	Moderate Shi'ites	Shi'ite leaders	– A larger role for the Shi'a in political life
'In Defence of the Nation'	September 2003	–	Liberals	Academics and intellectuals	– Wide-ranging reforms through peaceful means
'National Call; Leadership and People Together: Institutional Reform First'	December 2003	–	Liberals	Academics and intellectuals	– Changing the current monarchical system into a constitutional monarchy – The change needs to be finalised within three years – Protection of the right to assemble and demonstrate

Table continued

Table continued

Women's rights petition	December 2003	300	Liberals	Women liberal academics, intellectuals and functionaries	– Recognising women's rights as full citizens and discarding the need of a legal guardian – Civil rights – General education of both sexes – Launch new specialised university courses for women – Recruit women in all economic sectors following the establishment of trade unions

THE 'CYCLE OF CONTENTION' AND THE LIMITS OF TERRORISM IN SAUDI ARABIA

Roel Meijer

This chapter analyses the events and the men involved in the bomb attacks and shootouts that have taken place in Saudi Arabia since May 2003. It concentrates on the political, organisational and biographical background of those held responsible for the attacks, members of *Al-Qa'ida on the Arabian Peninsula* (QAP). Social movement theory (SMT), especially the notion of cycle of contention, has been used to analyse these events. First follows a brief overview of the main concepts of this theory, then an outline of the cycle of contention as it emerged in Saudi Arabia in the 1990s until the winter of 2004.

Social Movements, Cycles of Contention and Violence

In *Power in Movement: Social Movement and Contentious Politics*, Sidney Tarrow gives an outline of the results of research of contentious social movements during the previous two decades. A social movement is based on collective action and 'becomes contentious when it is used by people who lack regular access to institutions, who act in the name of new or unaccepted claims, and who behave in ways that fundamentally challenge others or the authorities.'[1] The central concepts of 'contentious action' would seem to be highly relevant to the Saudi case. One key concept is that of 'framing', because a movement must

[1] Sidney Tarrow, *Power in Movement: Social Movements and Contentious Politics*, Cambridge University Press, 1998, 2nd edn, p. 3.

create meaning and an identity, defining 'us' and 'them', based on a problem that it claims it can solve. Creating identities, furthermore, is a precondition for consensus building and 'frame resonance'.[2] Another concept is that of 'political opportunity structure', which is defined as 'dimensions of the political environment that provide incentives for people to undertake collective action [...]'. Political opportunities, such as the fall of the communist regimes in 1989, allow social movements and challengers to emerge and make their claims. To put the authorities under pressure, challengers adopt a 'repertoire of contention', which, depending on the political circumstances and the cultural background, can take the form of petitions, strikes, marches, disruption, or violence.[3] Depending on the opportunity structure, social movements can take advantage of the weakness of the authorities, gain access to political and participation power, achieve shifts in ruling alignments, and in extreme cases, split the ruling elite. Cycles of contention occur when opportunities widen and information spreads down and ordinary people 'begin to test the limits of social control'. During such periods of diffusion, characterised by heightened information flows and rapid mobilisation, the opportunities created by 'early risers' provide incentives for the formation of new alliances and the experimentation with new forms of contention.[4] As the cycle widens and becomes more powerful, movements create opportunities for elites to join or support the movement. The result of this phase of mobilisation, if it is successful, will be reform or a revolution.

Two additional remarks should be made. The first is related to the state, which in modern history has become the focus of contentious politics.[5] The state has three options in dealing with the contenders: facilitation, accommodation, or repression. The outcome of the conflict depends on the strength of the state. If a ruling elite is split and weak and the movement is strong, as was the case in Iran in 1979, the outcome will be the destruction of the former. On the other hand, if the state is strong, the ruling elite united, and the challengers divided and weak, as was the case in the struggle between the Syrian state and the Muslim Brotherhood in 1982, the contentious movement

[2] *Ibid.*, pp. 18–19.
[3] *Ibid.*, p. 20.
[4] *Ibid.*, p. 24.
[5] *Ibid.*, pp. 58–63.

will be destroyed. If the ruling elite is smart, it will opt for a combined policy of repression, accommodation and facilitation.[6] In this manner it will split the moderates from radicals and integrate the moderates into the system, or hold them at bay, while at the same time repressing the radicals. For, 'movements not only create opportunities for themselves and their allies; they also create opportunities for their opponents.'[7] For instance, this happened in Egypt in the 1990s when the state split the Islamist movement.[8] It also spelled the end of the phase of mobilisation and the beginning of the phase of demobilisation.

The second remark is related to the issue of violence. Tarrow and others, like Della Porta and Diani,[9] believe that the *threat* of violence can be effective, but that *actual* violence raises the 'costs' to the participants in collective action and eventually undermines the goals of the social movement. Violence is often used when the movement is either being repressed or has exhausted itself. In these situations, 'physical violence and exaggerated rhetoric are used to reinvigorate flagging militants, attract new supporters and retain the notice of the state.'[10] The result is mostly negative, unless the state has collapsed, or the struggle is an ethnic, religious or national conflict, as in the case of the Sunni resistance in Iraq.[11] Tarrow argues that '[violence] has a polarising effect on conflict and alliance systems, transforming relations between challengers and authorities from a confused, many sided game of allies, enemies, and bystanders into a bipolar one in which people are forced to choose sides, allies defect, and the state's repressive apparatus swings into gear.'[12] Thus, in general, radical contenders 'chill the blood of the bystanders, give pause to prospective allies and cause many who joined the movement in its enthusiastic early phase to defect.'[13] When that happens 'organisers are trapped in

6 *Ibid.*, pp. 147–50.

7 *Ibid.* (1994 edn), p. 97.

8 Gilles Kepel, *Jihad: The Trail of Political Islam*, London: I. B. Tauris, 2000, pp. 276–98.

9 Donatella Della Porta and Mario Diani, *Social Movements: An Introduction*, Oxford: Blackwell, 1999, pp. 188–90.

10 Tarrow, *The Power in Movement* (1994), p. 112.

11 Roel Meijer, '"Defending our Honor": Authenticity and the Framing of Resistance in the Iraqi Sunni Town of Falluja', *Etnofoor*, 2005 (forthcoming).

12 Tarrow, *The Power in Movement* (1994), p. 104.

13 *Ibid*, p. 112.

a military confrontation with the authorities that is virtually impossible for them to win.'[14] As Hafez and others point out, the exclusive organisations that emerge from this struggle lead to protracted violence, a development that took place in Algeria and Egypt in the 1990s.[15]

The Saudi Cycle of Contention

From non-violent to violent opposition

Many of the above-mentioned characteristics of social movements and the cycle of contention apply to Saudi Arabia since the 1990s. The first phase of mobilisation and diffusion of the cycle of contention dates from the Iraqi occupation of Kuwait in 1990. Allowing US troops to launch their attack on the Iraqi troops from Saudi Arabia, caused significant difficulty for the Kingdom's rulers. This decision in itself provided an important structure of opportunity for the opposition to launch its contentious politics. Having been based since its foundation on the coalition between the ruling House of Sa'ud and the *ulama*, who upheld the conservative (Salafi) Wahhabi doctrine of Islam, the monarchy was now arguably exposed as hypocritical as it was revealed to be highly dependent on the 'infidel' United States. What made matters worse, was that the state had for decades supported the most radical Jihadi Salafi groups as long as they exported the *jihad* to countries Saudi Arabia attempted to control.[16]

Initially, peaceful petition was the main repertoire of contention adopted by the non-violent opposition. Saudi liberal businessmen and intellectuals were the first to submit a petition calling for greater

[14] *Ibid.*, p. 105. Aside from the many studies on the role of violence in social movements, Tarrow and Della Porta draw their conclusions from their own work on the radicalisation of the Italian Left in the 1970s.

[15] Mohammed M. Hafez, *Why Muslims Rebel: Repression and Resistance in the Islamic World*, Boulder, CO: Lynne Rienner, 2003, pp. 109–13; Mohammed H. Hafez, 'From Marginalization to Massacres: A Political Process Explanation of GIA Violence in Algeria' in Quintan Wiktorowicz (ed.), *Islamic Activism: A Social Movement Theory Approach*, Bloomington, IN: Indiana University Press, 2003, pp. 37–60; and Mohammed H. Hafez and Quintan Wictorowicz, 'Violence as Contention in the Egyptian Islamic Movement' in Wictorowicz, *Islamic Activism*, pp. 61–88.

[16] Kepel, *The Trail of Political Islam*, pp. 61–80.

democratic openness in 1990,[17] but this form of contention of the 'early risers' was quickly defused, and petitions were drawn up by the religious radical opposition that were far more important and threatening. In May 1991 the 'Letter of Demands' (*khitab al-matalib*), signed by 400 ulama, judges, university professors and other leading scholars, was submitted to the King. It was followed a year later by a clarification that was harsher in tone, the Memorandum of Advice (*mudhakkirat al-nasiha*). In contrast to the liberal petition, these two petitions demanded a more rigorous application of religious norms (council for the conformity of *shari'a*) and the building up of a strong army that would guarantee Saudi Arabia's independence and its championing of Muslim causes. They also accused the royal family of nepotism, corruption and moral decadence.[18] Formulated in a master frame, the radical opposition stated their grievance in general terms that citizens of the state should withdraw their allegiance from rulers as long as they did not abide by the *shari'a*. For the first time the theme of *takfir*, the proclamation of unbelief of one's opponent, was used as a means of de-legitimating the ruling family of Sa'ud. The second theme, which was to become part and parcel of oppositional rhetoric, was the condemnation of the United States as the embodiment of evil, decadence, and the spearhead of the Western, Christian 'war on Islam'.[19]

Relations with the state entered the second phase of the cycle of contention—that of demobilisation—when the state temporarily arrested the signatories of the petitions.[20] Having recovered from the initial shock of the Iraqi invasion of Kuwait and the boldness of the internal opposition, the ruling family announced that it would not accept criticism outside the limited boundaries of 'consultation'

[17] Joshua Teitelbaum, *Holier than Thou: Saudi Arabia's Islamic Opposition*, Washington, DC: The Washington Institute for Near East Policy, 2000, p. 31.

[18] Daryl Champion, *The Paradoxical Kingdom: Saudi Arabia and the Momentum of Reform*, London: Hurst Company, pp. 219–29; Teitelbaum, *Holier than Thou*, pp. 25–47; Mamoun Fandy, *Saudi Arabia and the Politics of Dissent*, New York: Palgrave, 1999, pp. 48–60; International Crisis Group, *Saudi Arabia Backgrounder: Who are the Islamists*?, Amman/Riyadh/Brussels: ICG, Middle East Report, no. 31, 21 September 2004.

[19] Teitelbaum, *Holier than Thou*, pp. 35–8.

[20] Madawi al-Rasheed, *A History of Saudi Arabia*, Cambridge University Press, 2002, p. 175.

(*shura*). In the words of King Fahd, 'I hope that efforts will be confined to giving advice for the sake of God. If, however, someone has things to say, then he can always come to those in charge and speak to them in any region, in any place. As advice, this is wanted and desired.'[21] During the subsequent years the regime opted for a combination of accommodation and repression, with the emphasis on repression. For instance, the leaders of the Committee for Defence of Legitimate Rights (CDLR), an Islamic human rights organisation that had sprung up during the phase of mobilisation and hoped to mobilise Western support for democratic reform in Saudi Arabia, were forced to flee the country and establish themselves in London in 1994, from where they launched their attacks on the royal family. (Note that the word 'legitimate' in the English name for the organisation is in fact used to represent the Arabic *shar'i*, strictly meaning 'according to the *shari'a*').[22] Those that remained had the option of spending their lives in jail or cooperating with the authorities. Two of the most forceful members of a new generation of radical opposition shaikhs, Safar al-Hawali and Salman al-Awda, called the 'shaikhs of the Awakening' (*shuyukh al-sahwa*), who had signed the Memorandum of Advice, chose the second option. They were arrested in 1994 but later succumbed to pressure from the state and toned down their radical rhetoric.[23] As a result, by the second half of the 1990s the non-violent opposition was either suppressed, exiled, incorporated, or allowed to voice their ideas as long as they remained within the strict limits the state had laid down.

The repression and control of the non-violent opposition opened the way for a violent phase of the cycle contention, which was launched by a bomb attack on an American building in Riyadh on 13 November 1995, killing five Americans and two Indians. In the declarations of the three Salafi Jihadi organisations that claimed responsibility for the attack the familiar threats and arguments of the master frame of contention were repeated. One stated that unless the 'Crusader forces' leave Saudi Arabia, foreigners as well as Saudi forces and members of the royal family would become 'legitimate targets'. They regarded the bomb attack as part of a jihad against both

21 Teitelbaum, *Holier than Thou*, p. 40.

22 *Ibid.*, p. 49–71; Fandy, *The Politics of Dissent*, pp. 115–47.

23 ICG, *Saudi Arabia Backgrounder*, p. 7.

the rulers and the Americans. Three of the four men arrested for their role in the bomb attack were 'Saudi Afghans', veterans of the Afghan war against the Soviet Union.[24] Their ideas coincided with the non-violent opposition: the ruling family was *kufr* (infidel) because it did not apply the *shari'a* and was aligned with non-Muslim countries.[25] The violent phase was underscored by an attack on the American Khobar Towers complex in Dhahran on 25 June 1996, although the Shi'ite opposition seems to have been responsible for this attack.[26] After 2000 violence in Saudi Arabia was for a while characterised by a series of minor attacks on individual foreigners in which six persons were killed.

That it would take until after 9/11 for the violent phase of the cycle of contention to reach a new height was due to the tactics of the man who would become if not the actual at least the symbolic leader of the terrorist phase of the struggle, Usama bin Ladin. Usama bin Ladin shared many of the ideas of the 'shaikhs of the Awakening', establishing an oppositional organisation in London in 1994, the Advice and Reformation Committee (ARC).[27] Their arrest in that year further deepened his dislike of the regime.[28] Nevertheless, his innovative tactical step was to focus first on defeating the 'greater' or 'external enemy' (the United States) and then the 'lesser' or 'internal enemy' (the Saudi monarchy). His arrival in Afghanistan in 1996, where he was welcomed by the Taliban regime and could benefit from the training camps that had been operative after the defeat of the Soviets, allowed him to wage this war first against the external enemy.[29]

However, even during this phase of waging jihad against the external enemy and the 'Crusader-Zionist' alliance, Usama bin Ladin constantly castigated the Saudi regime. His first communiqué, issued in Afghanistan on 23 August 1996, entitled 'A Declaration of War Against the Americans Occupying the Land of Two Holy Places', was characteristically also directed against the ruling Saudi family, which

[24] Jason Burke, *Al-Qaeda: Casting a Shadow of Terror*, London: I. B. Tauris, 2003, p. 140.

[25] Teitelbaum, *Holier than Thou*, p. 76.

[26] Burke, *Al-Qaeda*, p. 140.

[27] Fandy, *The Politics of Dissent*, pp. 177–94.

[28] Burke, *Al-Qaeda*, p. 126.

[29] *Ibid.*, p. 151.

was accused of tyranny (*zulm*), imposing unjust rule and deviating from the true Islamic path. As the government had not implemented the *shari'a*, resistance against it was regarded as an individual duty (*fard 'ayn*) on every Muslim: 'It is the duty of every tribe in the Arab peninsula to fight the jihad and cleanse the land from these occupiers.'[30] Foreshadowing the later terrorist attacks in Saudi Arabia, Usama bin Ladin in subsequent announcements called for 'fast-moving light forces that work under complete secrecy' and will 'hit the aggressor with an iron fist.' The youth of Saudi Arabia would constitute the 'vanguard' of this movement that would martyr itself for the cause.[31]

Whether it was Usama bin Ladin's decision to target Saudi Arabia in May 2003, and refocus the jihad from the 'external enemy' to the 'internal enemy', remains unclear.[32] However, given the virulent verbal attacks on the regime voiced during the previous decade by the non-violent Salafi opposition and the way this was moulded into its master frame of contention, it cannot have been a difficult step. The real difficulty with this new tactic is that it encounters all the problems that a social movement faces once it needs to build and mobilise a following. Whereas Al-Qa'ida could suffice by playing on the worldwide resentment against the last world power during its transnational jihad against the United States, once the struggle became localised, its branch, Al-Qa'ida on the Arabian Peninsula (QAP), had to take into consideration a novel type of logistics necessary to topple a regime. This is a much more complex operation.

Mobilisation and destabilising the state

The vicious war between QAP and the state that ravaged Saudi Arabia from May 2003 should be regarded as part of the violent phase within the larger cycle of contention that began in 1990.

[30] *Ibid.*, p. 147.

[31] *Ibid.*, pp. 147–8.

[32] Only on 17 December 2004, after the attack on the American Consulate in Jeddah on 6 December, did Usama bin Ladin announce his support for the jihad in Saudi Arabia. Although it is not certain that the voice on the audio tape is that of Bin Ladin, most experts agree this is the case. The accusations against the Saudi royal family were the usual: 'violating God's rules' and alignment with the 'infidel' United States. Sources: *CBC News*, 19 December 2004 and *Dar al-Hayat*, 16 December 2004.

In line with Tarrow's cycle of violent contention, both sides had to do their utmost to win the struggle. It was a matter of life or death. From its side, QAP had to destabilise the political system, gain access to the authorities, split the elite, and succeed in mobilising and recruiting a larger following of sympathisers and allies by maintaining the credibility of the Salafi movement's master frame that held that its opponents were unbelievers (*kuffar*). The US-led Coalition's invasion of Iraq in March 2003 and the Saudi support must have convinced QAP that the time to launch its campaign was ripe. Damaging the vulnerable oil economy of the country by targeting foreigners or its infrastructure would be one of QAP's most effective weapons to bring down the regime.[33] In its defence, the state had to appeal to the rationality and trust of the population, demonstrate its efficacy by destroying QAP as quickly as possible, and isolate and marginalise the radicals from the moderates by demonstrating that they were un-Islamic and therefore 'deviants from Islam', 'fanatics' and 'terrorists'. Symbolically, the struggle between the two sides was represented by the capacity of the authorities to arrest or kill the members of the two lists of 'terrorists' it published during the year 2003, whereas the contenders had to remain at large. As in the larger cycle of contention, the violent sub-cycle consists of two phases: one of upswing and potential mass mobilisation and severe shock to the state, and one of downturn, of the phase of demobilisation and the crushing of violent contention.

The clash began when on 18 March 2003 a bomb accidentally exploded in an apartment in al-Jazira, a neighbourhood of Riyadh, killing one of the members of what later appeared to be a cell of QAP. During the following month the police were able to trace the group to an apartment in another neighbourhood of Riyadh, Ishbiliya, where it found considerable stockpiles of weapons and explosives. Although here and in other safe houses the militants had escaped by the time the police arrived, the police found enough evidence to identify the members of the 'Ishbiliya cell'. On 7 May the Minister of Interior made the unprecedented step to publish the by now famous list of nineteen names and photographs of the most wanted

[33] Anthony Cordesman and Nawaf Obaid, *Saudi Petroleum Security: Energy Infrastructure Security Improving. Threats Loom from al-Qaeda, Shiite Population*, Washington, DC: Center for Strategic and International Studies, 2004.

'terrorists' for which a reward had been set (Appendix I).[34] By taking this step the state had for the first time declared war on the Salafi Jihadi movement.

That its members were indeed dangerous, was underlined on May 12 when virtually simultaneous bomb explosions went off at three different suburban compounds in Riyadh, one of them belonging to the US military subcontractor Vinnell. The explosions killed thirty-five people, among them seven Americans, in addition to sixteen members of the suicide commando. In June a list of twelve of the suicide bombers in the Riyadh 'operation' (*'amaliyya*) was published (Appendix II).[35] The high number of 'martyrs' in this operation and its subsequent wide publicity in videos indicates that the bomb explosions were not just a means of targeting both the American and Saudi enemy and undermining the economy and the legitimacy of the state, but were also part of a repertoire of contention that is typical of Al-Qa'ida's cosmic struggle between the forces of good and evil.[36]

However, it is doubtful whether the action succeeded in attracting wide support. The shock to the Saudi public concerning the high level of violence would not be confined to the Riyadh bombing. With growing concern, Saudis discovered that during the next months, with two exceptions, none of the members of the Ishbiliya cell were willing to allow themselves to be arrested. In most of the cases they fought themselves to death, an action called 'indirect suicide' (*intihar ghayr mubashir*) or 'the method of suicidal resistance' (*uslub al-muqawama al-intihari*) by one commentator.[37] Although, for instance, Yusuf al-Ayiri (no. 10), the leader of QAP at the time, was killed near the town of Turba in the province of Ha'il when he resisted his arrest on 31 May 2003 while his companion survived,[38] the raid on the group of Turki al-Dandani (no. 1) was more typical. Despite several attempts

[34] *Al-Sharq al-Awsat*, 6 May 2004. The following abbreviations will be used hereafter: *al-Sharq al-Awsat*—SA; *al-Hayat*—HA; *Jaridat al-Riyadh al-Yawmiyya*—JRY; *Islam Today* (website)—IT; *al-'Arabiyya* website—A; *Sawt al-Jihad*—SJ; *IslamOnline*—IO; and sahat.fares.net—SF.

[35] In October another two of the Riyadh suicide bombers were identified when a video of the testaments was released by their own group (*SA*, 17 November 2003). The identities of the last two remain unknown.

[36] Burke, *Al-Qaeda*, pp. 26, 37, 87.

[37] *SA*, 5 and 10 July 2003.

[38] *SA*, 4 June and 30 July 2003.

by the security police to persuade him to hand himself over, he detonated a bomb on 3 July 2003 in a mosque in the town of Suwayr in the province of Jawf, ending his own life and that of three of his companions—among them Abd al-Rahman Jabara (no. 18).[39] Similar violent clashes occurred in July at a date farm in the province of Qasim, where two members of the List of 19 (no. 14 and no. 13) died.[40] A month earlier, they had managed to escape from an apartment in Mecca, Khalidiyya (hence, the 'Khalidiyya cell'), during which five members died and twelve were arrested (Appendix IV).[41]

Finally, the violent, suicidal character of the movement was confirmed when in September another member of the List of 19 (no. 16) was killed together with two other members of his group, during a shoot out with security forces in a building adjacent to the hospital in the town of Jazan.[42] Other violent confrontations took place in November with a group that had taken refuge in a flat in the neighbourhood of Shara'i' in Mecca, subsequently called the 'al-Shara'i' cell' (Appendix VIII)[43] and in al-Suwaidi, a neighbourhood in Riyadh.[44] As usual, in all these cases the quantity of weaponry and explosives found by the police and subsequently put on display for the press was impressive.

However, measuring the impact of the 'operations' and subsequent suicide actions should not be confined to their effect on the general public: just as important is the effect of the violence on 'sympathisers'. These fall into three broad categories. First, the larger list of 'wanted persons' (*matlubin*), who form the inner circle around QAP, and whose names are only very rarely disclosed by the authorities. They are part of its network, some of them in sleeper cells. These *matlubin* must primarily be sought among the 5,000 to 15,000 'Arab-Afghans', mostly of Saudi nationality. A second group consists of members of some of the NGOs supporting the jihad in Chechnya, Tajikistan, or before in Algeria and Bosnia. Together, these first two groups make up the main sympathizers of QAP.[45] Between

[39] *SA*, 7–10 July 2004.
[40] *SA*, 29–30 July 2003 and 3–8 August 2003.
[41] *IT*, 15 June 2003.
[42] *SA*, 29–30 July 2003 and 25 September 2003.
[43] *IT*, 3 November 2003; *SA*, 10 November 2003.
[44] *IT*, 6 November 2003.
[45] Speculation on the number of 'Saudi Afghans' differs from one author to another.

the two, a division of labour exists. While the *matlubin*, who were less conspicuous than the hardcore QAP members, organised safe houses, rented cars, provided other logistics such as opening bank accounts, and formed a potential reservoir of fighters, the more distant sympathisers followed closely the websites of QAP and spread its ideas. The third group of potential supporters consists of the reformists, the followers of the 'shaikhs of the Awakening', who dominated the first, non-violent cycle of contention, and whose ideas hardly differ from the Jihadi Salafi movement. That the sympathisers were indeed active can be gleaned from the clashes with the security forces. The months after the Riyadh bombing were marked by numerous announcements about shoot-outs and arrests in Riyadh and the provinces of Qasim, Sharqiyya and Jazan between security forces and members of radical groups whose identity remained unclear, but who probably belonged to the *matlubin* or the larger group of sympathisers and potential supporters.[46] Nowhere, however, does the opposition appear to have been coordinated or strong.

One of the reasons for the limited response of the sympathisers of QAP was the success of the security police in hunting down the members of the original group of the List of 19 and the *matlubin* during the first months after the Riyadh bombing.[47] By September five of the List of 19 had died in the bomb attack on Riyadh, six had died in shoot outs, and only six would survive the year 2003. The remaining two (no. 2 and no. 12) would be taken into custody; one of them, Ali al-Faq'asi al-Ghamidi, handed himself over through the

---

According to Champion there are 15,000 'Saudi Afghans' (Champion, *The Paradoxical Kingdom*, p. 217); according to Teitelbaum around 5,000 (Teitelbaum, *Holier than Thou*, p. 75). The difference can be solved. According to Gwen Okruhlik 12,000 Saudi men went to Afghanistan, but actually only 5,000 were trained and saw combat ('Understanding Political Dissent in Saudi Arabia', *Middle East Report Online*, 24 October 2001, www.merip.org). The issue of numbers is debatable for other reasons of interest. For instance, Burke makes a distinction between: a 'hard core', a small group willing to die for Bin Ladin's cause; the 'Saudi Afghans', which constitute the 'network of networks'; and finally those who were not close to him but regarded him an inspirational force and a 'godfather'. The first and second group partially overlap, as by definition members of the 'hard core' are 'Afghan Arabs'. The third group would form a broad movement (Burke, *Al-Qaeda*, pp. 127, 155, 194).

[46] *JRY*, 14 July 2003, 8 December 2003, 9 December 2003 and 21 May 2004.

[47] *JRY*, 2 October 2003.

mediation of the 'awakening shaikh', Safar al-Hawali—an indication of how the non-violent and violent opposition were connected.[48] This high rate of success convinced the Saudi security forces that they had disabled the 'Ishbiliya cell' (or the List of 19). Their optimism was reflected in the appeals by family members of the activists to hand themselves over to the authorities in the newspaper *Jaridat Riyadh al-Yawmiyya*. The amnesty announced in October was intended to stimulate them to take this step.[49]

Demobilisation and hunting down the terrorists

Official optimism vanished temporarily with the bomb explosion on 8 November 2003 at the Muhaya residence compound in Riyadh. In the blast eighteen people were killed while more than 122 people were wounded, but only two suicide bombers died in the operation (two survived and managed to escape). Yet, although the operation jolted the authorities, it was not a success for QAP in terms of enhancing the organisation's reputation. Its major flaw was that all the victims were Arabs and most of them were Muslims. To underline its determination to stamp out QAP, the Ministry of Interior reacted swiftly by publishing on 6 December a new list of twenty-six of the most wanted terrorists. This list was much more accurate and therefore more intimidating than the previous one—and therefore discouraging to potential supporters—ranking those listed according to their hierarchy within QAP. Six of the List of 26 had also appeared on the List of 19; these appeared to be the oldest, the most experienced, and by far the most dangerous: Khalid Hajj (no. 3/26), had become leader of QAP after the death of Yusuf al-Ayiri (no. 10/19) in May 2003; Abd al-Aziz al-Muqrin (no. 1/26) would succeed Khalid Hajj after his death in March 2004, while Salih al-Awfi (no. 5/26) would succeed Abd al-Aziz al-Muqrin when the latter was killed on 18 June 2004[50]. Although by June 2004 the authorities would be successful in hunting down most of the members of the List of 26, in the meantime tremendous damage was done to the reputation of the government and its national credibility and international standing.[51] The

[48] *SA*, 26–8 June 2003 and IT, 26–9 June 2003.

[49] *SA*, 2 October 2003.

[50] This succession remains unclear: it later appeared that al-Muqrin had in fact designated Sa'ud al-Utaibi as his successor.

[51] According to Faris bin Hazzam, the Saudi journalist who provided most of the

violent onslaught the regime was confronted with led some commentators to believe its fate hung in the balance and that it might succumb to internal divisions.[52]

The first success for the authorities came on 8 December when the security police killed one of the members of the List of 26 (no. 6) on the streets in al-Suwaidi in Riyadh; on 30 December another member (no. 14) handed himself over to the authorities, and subsequently probably informed on his comrades. Some success also came in the ideological battle. To the dismay of the radicals, in December 2003, during interviews with A'idh al-Qarni on Saudi state television, the Jihadi Salafi shaikhs, Ali al-Khudair and his two colleagues, who had been arrested in June, recanted their own former *takfiri* ideas and the whole Jihadi Salafi master frame in public. In the course of the following year the state would succeed in co-opting and mobilising to its side many other former oppositional shaikhs, including Muhsin al-Awja and Safar al-Hawali, thereby weakening the force of the *takfiri* oppositional frame of contention.

In hindsight the biggest logistical success was achieved on the morning of 29 January 2004, when Khalid Hamud al-Farraj was arrested. Although he was not on the List of 26 (but probably a *matlub*, and in any case an Arab-Afghan), Khalid al-Farraj was close to the core of the cell of Abd al-Aziz al-Muqrin and Faisal al-Dakhil (no. 11), the two most dangerous members of the List of 26. Their hide-out was located in his house in al-Fayha', a neighbourhood of Riyadh. When he and his father were led there by the police they were attacked by his own group, who were probably informed by Farraj's wife. Among the six killed was Khalid al-Farraj's father, who was mistaken for a member of the security police. Called the 'treasure chest of information' (*khazinat al-ma'lumat*), Khalid al-Farraj seems subsequently to have cooperated with the police out of anger of the killing of his father, representing a major breach in security of the organisation. The incident is also interesting for the insight it provides into the *jihadi* culture of the group Kahlid al-Farraj was

---

information on the lists for *al-Sharq al-Awsat*, the list of (remaining) '*matlubin*' in June 2004 was around a hundred names, most of whom were not involved in operations, but provided facilities for those who were (*al-'Arabiyya* website, 24 June 2004).

52 Michael Scott Doran, 'The Saudi Paradox', *Foreign Affairs*, January/February 2004, http:www.foreignaffairs.org.

part of. It appears that he was married to a sister of one of the two *matlubin* who were killed by the police on Id al-Fitr (25 November 2003) in Riyadh. Moreover, the other three brothers of his wife had died in the jihad outside Saudi Arabia, while Khalid al-Farraj himself was a cousin of an important *matlub*.[53]

Another success for the authorities was announced at the beginning of February, when the police were informed that two members of the group had died as a result of the wounds they had received during the shoot out on 6 November in al-Suwaidi.[54] On 15 March the security police were able to track down the leader of QAP, Khalid Hajj, who was killed in Riyadh. At the end of April the police surprised five members of the List of 26 in Jeddah, all of whom were killed. It now seemed clear that the police was on the heels of the main leaders of the group of Abd al-Aziz al-Muqrin.

Yet the police proved unable to hunt down the rest of the QAP members in time to prevent further damage being done to its own prestige and the national economy. On 12 April the security police surrounded one of the main hide-outs in Riyadh of the group of Abd al-Aziz al-Muqrin which included Faisal al-Dakhil, Rakan al-Sikhan (no. 2/26) and Nasir al-Rashid (no. 19/26). One of the group, the *matlub* Khalid al-Subait, was able to hold off the police, allowing his companions to escape[55] and kill four highway patrolmen the next day during the escape to Buraida.[56] These escapes—besides discrediting the regime's claim to efficiency and providing security, an important factor in upholding its legitimacy—formed the background for a series of setbacks that would dominate the attention of the Saudi and international public over the following months. On 21 April 2004 Abd al-Aziz al-Madihish drove a car full of explosives to the traffic police/security police building in Riyadh in a suicide mission. The attack, claimed by the Battalions of the Two Holy Places, one of the cells of QAP, killed six and wounded 144, leaving the security building in shambles (earlier the group had

53 See the following articles: *SA*, 30–1 January 2004 and 10–15 February 2004; and *SJ*, 16, p. 10 and 23, p. 20. Much confusion surrounds the incident, but the full story was revealed by Saudi journalist Faris bin Hazzam in *al-Sharq al-Awsat* on 10 and 15 February 2004. He has subsequently been arrested.

54 *SA*, 23 February 2004 and 7 June 2004.

55 *SA*, 12 May 2004; *HA*, 3 July 2004.

56 *SA*, 14 April 2004 and 21 May 2004.

tried to assassinate the third most important police authority in Riyadh, Abd al-Aziz al-Huwairina).[57]

If this attack, for the first time directly targeting state institutions, was an attempt to compensate for the backlash from the Muhaya complex operation, subsequent attacks on foreigners resumed the tactic of targeting one of the main sources of 'corruption' in society and the economic props to the regime. On 30 April four men from the al-Ansari clan went on a rampage for four hours through the streets of the important oil town of Yanbu on the Red Sea coast killing five foreign engineers and one Saudi and wounding another twenty Saudis in the Swiss-Swedish company office of ABB.[58] The leader of the group, Mustafa Abd al-Qadir al-Ansari, had been an internationally wanted *mujahid*.[59] Even more damaging for the authorities was the attack on Khobar on 29 May. For more than 24 hours a group of terrorists was not only able to kill any foreigner it found in its way and take a number of foreigners hostage (twenty-two people were killed in all), three of its members, among them the leader, Turki bin Fahid al-Mutairi, were able to escape and later tell their full story in their bi-weekly, *Sawt al-Jihad*.[60] In the following weeks the reputation of the Saudi government was further damaged as several foreigners were killed in Riyadh, most notoriously the beheading of the American military technician Paul Johnson. As a result of these actions many expatriates who had their families in Saudi Arabia announced that they would leave.

It was not until June 2004 that the authorities definitively turned the tables on QAP and caught up with those responsible for the assaults of the previous months. A crippling blow was dealt to the Salafi Jihadi opposition when Abd al-Aziz al-Muqrin and Faisal al-Dakhil were killed on 18 June.[61] Turki bin Fahid al-Mutairi, the leader of the so-called al-Quds Squadron (*al-Sarriya al-Quds*), who had led the Khobar massacre three weeks earlier, was also killed. During the next few weeks the police were able to mop up most of the rest of the group during raids in the Malik Fahd and al-Wurud neighbour-

[57] *IO*, 22 April 2004.

[58] *SA*, 1 and 4 May 2004.

[59] *SA*, 5 May 2004.

[60] 'Commander of the Khobar Terrorist Squad Tells the Story of the Operation', MEMRI Special Dispatches Series, no. 731, 15 June 2004.

[61] *SA*, 19 June 2004.

hoods in Riyadh, killing a number of *matlubin* or others thought responsible for some of the killings of foreigners, although Salih al-Awfi, leaving his wife and children in the hands of the security forces, escaped.[62] On 2 July the authorities announced that Rakan al-Sikhan (no. 2) and Nasir al-Rashid (no. 19) had probably both died of their wounds after the assault on the safe house in April.[63] On 22 July Isa Awshan (no. 15) was killed together with another member of his group,[64] while on 5 August one of the most important of the 'theoreticians' of the List of 26, Faris al-Zahrani (no. 12), was arrested while he was preparing a bomb attack on a cultural centre in the town of Abha, in the south of the Kingdom.[65]

Nevertheless, the last stretch of tracing the members of the List of 26 would prove difficult, even if it was clear that most QAP actions were now desperate counter-attacks in retaliation for crippling government raids. Throughout the next half year, until April 2005, when Salih al-Awfi was one of the two last members of the List of 26 at large, heavy fighting was regularly reported throughout the whole country, but mostly in Jeddah, Riyadh and in the conservative region of Qasim, one of the main bases of QAP, where it made its last stand. In Jeddah, the base of Salih al-Awfi, three major clashes took place in November and December 2004 and March 2005. In retaliation, on 6 December the American consulate was attacked during which all four fighters and a number of Saudi guards died, but no American personnel was injured. In Riyadh several shoot-outs occurred at the end of December 2004 in which Sultan bin Jad al-Utaibi (no. 9) and Bandar al-Dakhil (no. 20) died, among several '*matlubin*'. This clash was followed by a bomb attack on the Ministry of Interior and an office of the Security Forces on 29 December. On 6 April 2005 Abd al-Rahman al-Yaziji (no. 25) was killed during a raid of his house in the neighbourhood of Khalidiyya in Riyadh.[66] Finally, heavy fighting occurred in the region of Qasim. The clash in Buraida and Aniza on 3 November lasted eighteen hours, while that clash in Ras, the third-largest town of Qasim, lasted sixty hours from

62 *SA*, 2 July 2004; *HA*, 3 July 2004; *SA*, 18 March 2005.
63 *SA*, 3 July 2004; *SJ*, 20, 7 July 2004.
64 *SA*, 25 August 2004; *SJ*, 22, 2004.
65 *SA*, 7 August 2004.
66 *SA*, 7 April 2005.

April 3 to 5. During the latter, between an unprecedented large concentration of QAP members (twenty) and security forces, fifteen members of the group died, among them one of the most sought after international terrorists, the Moroccan Karim al-Tuhami al-Majati (no. 4) and the probable leader of QAP, and one of its ideologues, Sa'ud al-Utaibi (no. 7).[67] Other members of the List of 26, Abd al-Majid al-Muni' (no. 18), had died on 12 October in a security raid,[68] while the Moroccan Husayn al-Hasaki was arrested in Belgium in July 2004.[69] In March 2005 *al-Sharq al-Awsat* announced that the last leading ideologue of QAP, Abdullah al-Rashud (no. 24) had probably been liquidated in June by Abd al-Aziz al-Muqrin and his assistant Faisal al-Dakhil because he had questioned the legitimacy of attacking Saudi targets under the leadership of al-Muqrin, especially the attack on the Muhaya compound.[70] These last clashes made clear that besides the members of QAP on the List of 26, many '*matlubin*' were also active in the fighting. Around fifty of them died in the period between 18 June and the end of April 2005 alone. Many of them were as prominent as those on the List of 26: one of those killed on 28 December 2004, Ibrahim Ahmad al-Rimi, was a Yemeni believed to have been one of the leaders of QAP.[71] The state announced on March 7 that it had 700 '*matlubin*' in detention.[72]

Although at the time of writing QAP had not been completely destroyed, it was clear that it had not succeeded in any of its goals: It had not vitally damaged the economy, destabilised the regime, split its elite or made inroads into its security forces; and it had proved unable to mobilise its sympathisers or the following of the *Sahwa* shaikhs, let alone the larger public. As Prince Turki al-Faisal, the former intelligence chief and present ambassador to Great Britain, pointed out, the group did not succeed in expanding its following and therefore the security forces could concentrate on eliminating the members of the two lists one by one.[73] Symbolically, this slow but systematic elimination of QAP members from the List of 26,

[67] *SA*, 7–10 April 2005.
[68] *SA*, 13 and 14 October 2004.
[69] *SA*, 27 October 2004.
[70] *SA*, 15 March 2005.
[71] *SA*, 30 and 31 December 2004.
[72] *SA*, 8 March 2005.
[73] *SA*, 9 September 2004.

splashed over the front pages of the newspapers, was a dramatic counter-propagandistic move by the state. Although QAP tried to present its casualties, especially the death of Abd al-Aziz al-Muqrin, as martyrs for the cause against the *kuffar,* the death cult of QAP did not mobilise concrete support. Later attacks, like the one on the American consulate on 6 December 2004, have not turned this situation around.[74]

Members and Structure of QAP

There were additional factors that undermined QAP's means of breaking through its isolation and aligning itself with the larger social movement of Salafi contention. These relate to the geographical origins, age, career patterns, type and level of education of the members of QAP. Their experience in the Jihadi Salafi movement, especially Afghanistan, and the organisational structure of QAP, are also relevant.

The available biographical information for the most important individuals concerned—sixty-four in all—is analysed below. The data include: the members of the List of 19 (Appendix I); the List of the 16 suicide bombers (Appendix II) (only nine additional individuals: 14 who have been identified, minus five who are already included in the List of 19); and the List of 26 (Appendix III) (six of whom are already on the List of 19). In addition, the twelve members of the 'Khalidiyya cell' are included, as well as four of the most important individual leaders not included in the lists, but who belonged to the *matlubin* (the information on the forty-eight persons on the three official lists, plus the suicide bombers, is more extensive than that for the others, and is represented more fully in the appendixes).

Location and urbanisation

One of the strong points of QAP is the geographical, tribal, social and locational diversity of its members. Of the members of the List of 19, six originally came from the south, three from the Hijaz, three from the east and two from Riyadh (the regional origin of five is

[74] *The Economist*, 11–17 December 2004, p. 37.

unknown). Although determining their residence before the 'operations' is difficult—as most of them moved around constantly—four of them had lived in Riyadh prior to the May 2003 bomb attack there.

The social background of the List of 19 is harder to trace. We only know for certain that the fathers of nos 6, 7 and 9 were, respectively, a dentist,[75] a high police officer in the Ministry of Interior,[76] and a high civil servant in the Ministry of Commerce in the province of Sharqiyya.[77] Information on the others is inconclusive. Remarkably for the activist profession they chose, at least four were married, but it is quite possible that the number is higher.

Of the additional nine identified individuals from the List of 16, five had lived in Riyadh, one in Medina and one in Jazan. Very little is known of their social background. The fathers of nos 3 and 8 were low-ranking police officers.[78] Four of the suicide bombers were married.

More is known about the members of the List of 26. We know for sure that five of the group were born in Riyadh and that twelve lived in Riyadh at the time of the bombings, nine of them in the neighbourhood of al-Suwaidi alone, including the leader of QAP, Abd al-Aziz al-Muqrin. It is this densely populated neighbourhood and other sha'bi neighbourhoods in southern Riyadh (such as Khalidiyya) with a strong conservative religious character, where a host of militant preachers preach in local mosques, that is the hotbed of Jihadi Salafi resistance in Saudi Arabia.[79] This neighbourhood is probably also linked to the Imam Muhammad Sa'ud Islamic University, where seven of the List of 26 studied. Other populous neighbourhoods in Mecca (*Khalidiyya*), Medina and Jedda (the Univeristy district), and the region of Qasim with the towns of Buraida, Aniza and Ras, were also centres for resistance, although quite a number of the List of 26 also come from the south.[80]

[75] *SA*, 28 May 2003.

[76] *SA*, 17 November 2003.

[77] *SA*, 8 December 2003.

[78] *SA*, 17 November 2003.

[79] For more information on this social and urban environment of the militant groups, see *SA*, 9 December 2003 and 7 June 2004; also *HA*, 5 July 2004. See *SA*, 31 December 2004 for an overview of the different neighbourhoods in Riyadh where attacks took place.

[80] *SA*, 21 May 2004, 10 November 2004, 18 November 2004, 5 April 2005.

Age

An important indicator of the nature of the movement and its more sectarian character is the age of its members. The information on the members of QAP confirms the trend that the average age of Al-Qa'ida members and members of other radical movements had declined in the 1980s and 1990s to become the 'young urban poor' who form the dynamite of the Islamist movement.[81] The average age of the List of 19 (for whom we have all the data) is 28; that of the additional known nine on the List of 16 is 26; and the average age of those 19 on the List of 26 for whom the information is available is 27. Yet the average age is deceptive as it is pushed up by older members such as Uthman al-Umari (no. 21), an arms dealer who had been caught up in the events, who was 35. Three of the List of 19 were only 23 years old, and two of the List of 26 were 22 years old, while one was 23 years old. With an average of 19 years, the members of the 'Khalidiyya cell' were even younger. Five out of the twelve arrested were 17 and younger.

The leadership of both the Lists of 19 and 26 (plus the List of 16) belonged to the oldest members. The first three leaders, Yusuf al-Ayiri, Abd al-Aziz al-Muqrin, Khalid Hajj, were 30 years old, while the fourth, Salih al-Awfi, was 38. Other potential leaders who died in shoot-outs or the blast in Riyadh in May 2003, like Turki al-Dandani (no. 1) and Khalid al-Jahani (no. 5), were 29 years old. For the four other *matlubin* we have no precise age, but they must have been around 30 and belonged to the same generation as they were well-acquainted with the leaders and had the same biographical itinerary.

Education and careers

If the youthful character of the movement is not exceptional for Al-Qa'ida and other violent Islamist networks and movements, the

[81] Saad Eddin Ibrahim, 'Anatomy of Egypt's Militant Groups: Methodological Notes and Preliminary Findings' in Saad Eddin Ibrahim, *Egypt, Islam and Democracy: Twelve Critical Essays*, Cairo: The American University in Cairo Press, 1996, pp. 1–33; Saad Eddin Ibrahim, 'The Changing Face of Egypt's Islamic Activism' in Ibrahim, *Egypt, Islam and Democracy*, pp. 69–79; Luis Martinez, *La guerre civile en Algérie*, Paris: Karthala, 1998; Séverine Labat, *Les islamistes algériens. Entre les urnes et le maquis*, Paris: Éditions du Seuil, 1995; Kepel, *The Trail of Political Islam*; Hafez, *Why Muslims Rebel*; Burke, *Al-Qaeda*, pp. 71, 155. Most of the information on the age of members of the lists is obtained from *al-Sharq al-Awsat*, 13 November 2003 and *al-'Arabiyya* (website), 22 July 2004.

educational background of the Saudi Al-Qa'ida group is.[82] While one often finds that members of radical Islamist movements have a background in technical and natural sciences or medicine,[83] and almost none of them are specialised in religious studies, in Saudi Arabia it is quite the opposite. Only one member of the List of 19, Turki al-Dandani (no. 1), attended the Faculty of Science. He had intended to become a doctor, but had broken off his studies to go to Afghanistan. Hamad al-Shamari (no. 14/19), who worked for Aramco for a while, probably had a technical background as well.[84] Two of the List of 19 (nos 13 and 2) had a religious higher education and had studied at the Faculty of Shari'a of the Imam Muhammad bin Sa'ud Islamic University in Riyadh. Of the List of 16, two (nos 5 and 7) had studied for some time at a university, although it is not known in which field and where; three (nos 2, 3 and 8) had graduated (they are also on the List of 19).

The specialisation in religious studies is more pronounced with the List of 26. Nine of the list studied at the Imam Muhammad bin Sa'ud Islamic University. In fact, a distinction is made between 'intellectuals', called '*shari'a* theoreticians' (*munazzarin shari'iyyin*) and the rest, who are called 'foot soldiers' (*muqatilin maydaniyyin*).[85] In contrast to the foot soldiers, the intellectuals also seemed to be more integrated into society, although due to their alliance to their Salafi ideas they did get into trouble with the authorities. At the peak of the intellectual hierarchy in religious knowledge are the five graduates who were also members of the *shari'a* committee of the organisation: Abdullah al-Rashud (no. 24), followed by Faris al-Zahrani (no. 12), Sultan al-Utaibi (no. 9), Isa al-Awshan (no. 15) and Abd al-Majid al-Muni (no. 18). The role of these 'theoreticians' has been

[82] Most of the information on the education of the members of the lists is obtained from *al-Sharq al-Awsat*, 17 November 2003, *al-'Arabiyya* (website), 22 July 2004, and *Jaridat al-Riyadh al-Yawmiyya*, 8 December 2003, unless otherwise indicated. The preponderance of ulama in the Saudi opposition, in contrast to the usual make-up of the Islamic movement has been noticed by Teitelbaum (*Holier than Thou*, p. 3).

[83] Ibrahim, 'Anatomy of Egypt's Militant Groups'; Valerie Hoffman, 'Muslim Fundamentalists: Psychosocial Profiles' in Martin E. Marty and R. Scott Appleby (eds), *Fundamentalisms Comprehended*, University of Chicago Press, 1995, pp. 199–230.

[84] *SA*, 8 December 2003.

[85] *HA*, 5 July 2004.

important for the rest of the members, for their stature in giving religious opinions has provided legitimacy for the actions of the movement. It is here that their organ *Sawt al-Jihad* has played a crucial role. Not only did it inform its sympathisers, but it also provided them with information and held their own group together. Without this QAP would have been much less successful in projecting their ideas to a general public, although its message of jihad, both as a means to an end and as a goal in itself, does not seem to have attracted a substantial number of followers. One explanation for the difference between the 'theoreticians' and the 'foot soldiers' is that QAP is a coalition between Arab Afghans and a new generation of local radical Salafi 'intellectuals', although the two categories overlap.[86]

On the whole, the Saudi movement also differs from other movements in its *level* of education.[87] While in most countries, the Islamist movement is a typical student movement,[88] this is not the case in Saudi Arabia. Of those forty-eight members for whom detailed information could be obtained, only nineteen attended university courses for a certain period and only eleven actually obtained a degree. Remarkably, none of the four leaders of the movement had finished their secondary school, most of them having gone off to Afghanistan during their teens. This does not of course mean they were 'illiterate'; yet it does indicate that many obtained much of their intellectual baggage from informal religious and highly ideological and narrow education on the spot, enhancing their isolation from society. Yusuf al-Ayiri, for instance, serviced his own website and publication, *al-Bitar*, and had published several books, all of them available on the internet.[89] Nevertheless, a lack of formal education does seem a common phenomenon. Aside from the four who had a higher education, four of the List of 19 (nos 5, 6, 10 and 19) had only a pri-

86 For an interesting analysis of QAP along these lines, see *SA*, 6 April 2005. Faris al-Zahrani is also known under his pen-name Abu Jind al-Azdi. Many of his works are available on the main Jihadi Salafi website, www.tawhed.ws.

87 The low level of education of the Afghan-Arabs in the 1990s has been noticed by Burke, *Al-Qaeda*, p. 155. My information largely corroborates his. This would contrast with the largely middle-class background of the followers of the non-violent Islamic opposition (Teitelbaum, *Holier than Thou*, pp. 3, 7).

88 Ibrahim, 'Anatomy of Egypt's Militant Groups'; Martinez, *La guerre civile en Algérie*; Labat, *Les islamistes algériens. Entre les urnes et le maquis.*

89 See www.tawhed.ws.

mary school certificate, four had only obtained a secondary degree (nos 3, 4, 11 and 16) and two had acquired a degree as secondary teachers (nos 9 and 17). The level of education of the five others is unknown. The List of 16 suicide bombers (minus those on the List of 19) confirms the information of the List of 19. Three had not finished secondary school (nos 10, 11 and 14), two had left university early (nos 5 and 7), and only one had graduated from university (no. 3), although it is not known what field he was specialised in. Unfortunately, we do not know what schooling the four others had.

The List of 26 is a bit of an exception. As mentioned, nine of its members had attended university courses, five actually graduated. Three of the List of 26 (nos 8, 14 and 22) did not obtain a secondary school degree, one of them (no. 22) leaving school early and joining a radical group in Mecca after his brother was killed in Afghanistan in 1998. Another member (no. 20) had only had a secondary school education. For six members we do not know their educational background, but it is unlikely that it is high (except for the two Moroccans), otherwise they would have been included with the intellectuals who wrote in *Sawt al-Jihad*. Remarkable are the professional connections with the security police. For instance, Ahmad Saqr al-Fadli (no. 8), who did not finish his secondary education, attended technical training, after which he first joined the army and then the police. Al-Salih Awfi (no. 4/19) also had connections with the security police.

Not surprisingly, the group had erratic careers. With the exception of the fourth leader, Salih al-Awfi (no. 4/19), who had a long if undistinguished career as a policeman and security officer, most of the members of the List of 19 had become professional insurgents at an early age, most of them breaking off their education and their relations with their families or leaving their jobs to join the jihad. The older members of the List of 16 had working experience, such as Muhammad al-Shahri (no. 7), who had worked in a grocery shop. Of the List of 26, Ahmad al-Fadli (no. 8) was a policeman in Mecca, Faris al-Zahrani (no. 12) was a judge, Khalid al-Qurashi (no. 13) was in the army, Isa Awshan (no. 15) was a judge/*imam*, as was Amir al-Shahri (no. 23), while Abdullah al-Rashud (no. 24) was a teacher. Several were still students, as was the case with Mansur Faqih (no. 14). Some were unemployed, like Abd al-Majid al-Muni (no. 18). Most had become professional terrorists.

Afghanistan and the international jihad

Undoubtedly the most decisive common feature of these members is their experience in Afghanistan and their connection with Al-Qa'ida. While this is not unusual for radical Islamist movements,[90] the fact that, for the QAP members, Afghanistan has remained important even after 9/11, does stand out. In total at least half of the forty-eight persons of the three lists researched had been to Afghanistan, many of them even having participated in the war of the Taliban against the Americans. Some had also been to Bosnia (3), Chechnya (4), Tajikistan (1), Somalia (1), Algeria (1) and Kashmir (2). These figures are on the conservative side as we do not have the relevant information on four members of the List of 19 and thirteen of the List of 26, while there are only eight for whom we know for certain that they did *not* go. It seems likely, therefore, that many more than half of the forty-eight went to Afghanistan and to other jihadi theatres of war.

The three original leaders had been there when they were extremely young and subsequently became professional *mujahids.* Abd al-Aziz al-Muqrin, 'Abu Hajir', had gone to Afghanistan when he was seventeen, subsequently going back and forth in the period 1990–4, being trained in the al-Wal camp. He took part in the battle of Khost with other Arab-Afghans. Later he became a trainer himself and left Afghanistan to fight in Algeria, Bosnia and Somalia. On returning to Saudi Arabia he was arrested and detained for two and half years before going again to Afghanistan. During this period, just before the American invasion of Afghanistan in October 2001, he met the younger generation of the List of 19. When he returned to Saudi Arabia, he visited his family and disappeared again, training the group in the hills around Mecca and Medina.[91] Yusuf al-Ayiri had the same experience. At an early age he went to Afghanistan, where he was trained in 1992 in al-Faruq camp, later himself becoming a trainer. He was for a while the personal guard of Bin Ladin after he had left Afghanistan.[92] Khalid Hajj, Abu Hazim al-Sha'ir', had probably been to Afghanistan at a later date, and trained there. He too

[90] Barnett R. Rubin, 'Arab Islamists in Afghanistan' in John L. Esposito (ed.), *Political Islam: Revolution, Radicalism or Reform?*, Boulder, CO: Lynne Rienner, 1997, pp. 179–206; Kepel, *The Trail of Political Islam*, pp. 136–58.

[91] *SA*, 10 December 2003.

[92] *SA*, 4 June 2003 and 30 July 2003.

had been a personal guard of Bin Ladin, probably at a later date than Yusuf al-Ayiri.[93]

Of the independent individuals we know that Khalid al-Subayt, who provided the safe house in Riyadh for Abd al-Aziz al-Muqrin, had a similar experience to that of the leaders. Like Abd al-Aziz al-Muqrin, he had left for Afghanistan when he was seventeen years old. After he was severely wounded in his foot, he returned to Saudi Arabia for treatment, later joining the jihad in Tajikistan and Chechnya, where he married a Chechnyan woman. When he was wounded again and returned, unable to participate in the jihad, he set up a NGO to support the war in the Caucasus.[94] The leader of the Yanbu operation, Mustafa Abd al-Qadir Abid al-Ansari, also had extensive experience in international jihad. He fought in Bosnia and the Ogaden, before staying in London for two and half years, where he worked with the Sa'd al-Faqih of the Movement for Islamic Reform in Arabia (MIRA), a split-off from CDRL. After leaving London in 1997, he travelled to Afghanistan—where he fought in 2001 in Tora Bora—and Yemen where he was arrested and released before returning to Saudi Arabia.[95] The same applies to Turki al-Mutairi, the leader of the Khobar operation, who went to Afghanistan a year before 9/11 and was almost on one of the planes that flew into the World Trade Center. Having missed his opportunity for martyrdom, he was able to celebrate the event with Usama bin Ladin. Like the others, he fought the Americans with the Taliban.[96] The same applies to Khalid al-Farraj.[97]

Remarkably, the younger members of the three Lists had had their Afghan experience at the end of the 1990s and even right up till the American battle against the Taliban. Among those on the List of 19, Turki al-Dandani (no. 1) had gone to Afghanistan six months before 9/11, where he visited al-Faruq camp, and participated in the war against the Americans. Ali Abd al-Rahman al-Faq'asi al-Ghamidi (no. 2) had stayed five years in Afghanistan, before fighting side by side with Usama bin Ladin in the caves of Tora Bora. This also applies to Khalid al-Jahani (no. 3), who the Americans believe had

[93] *SA*, 23 February 2003.
[94] *SA*, 12 May 2004; *SJ*, 16, 2004.
[95] *SA*, 5 May 2004.
[96] *SJ*, 22, 2004.
[97] *JRY*, 22 September 2004.

been assigned to lead Al-Qa'ida in Saudi-Arabia with Abd al-Aziz al-Muqrin and Ali Hajj. Also Salih al-Awfi (no. 4) was in Afghanistan for the first time in 1993–4 and is believed to have met both Bin Ladin and Mullah Omar before returning to Saudi Arabia with Khalid al-Jahani after the Taliban had been defeated. The recent connection with Afghanistan is confirmed by itineraries of the other five members of the List of 19 (nos 8, 9, 13, 14 and 15), all of whom had fought with the Taliban regime against the Americans. Even members as young as Hani Abd al-Karim al-Ghamidi (no. 7), who was 23 years old, had been to Afghanistan.

The pattern is much the same with the other lists. Nine of the List of 16 (five when the members of the List of 19 are subtracted) had direct Afghan experience, while six of the suicide bombers had not been to Afghanistan. The List of 26 is less conclusive. We know that at least four members of the twenty not appearing on the List of 19 (nine if one counts all 26) did go to Afghanistan. For only six members can we be certain that they did not; on ten we have no information one way or the other, but there seems no reason to assume that the pattern would have deviated much from the other lists.

Although most of the members of the lists were Saudis, this gives the wrong impression of QAP. Given the transnational character of the movement and the strong links with Afghanistan and Chechnya, it is not surprising to find many other nationalities among the group. Among the seven who were killed or arrested together with Turki al-Dandani, one of the leaders of the List of 19, in May 2003, one was Syrian and two were from Kuwait.[98] Al-Faq'asi was married to a Moroccan woman, Khalid al-Subayt to a woman from Chechnya. The leadership of the lists was disproportionately represented by non-Saudis, which even gave rise to some problems as it is thought that some within Al-Qa'ida believed that foreign leadership in the Arabian Peninsula would not be acceptable with the population. The best example is Khalid Hajj, a Yemeni who was the *de facto* leader for a while until he was killed on 15 March 2004, while Abd al-Aziz al-Muqrin was presented as the real leader even at that time.[99] The suspicion that Yemenis were in fact running QAP was renewed after the shoot outs in Riyadh on 28–9 December 2004, when the

[98] *SA*, 7–10 July 2004.
[99] *SA*, 23 February 2004.

Yemeni Ibrahim Ahmad al-Rimi was killed. According to some insiders it was he instead of Abd al-Aziz al-Muqrin who had succeeded Khalid Hajj after his death, because Usama bin Ladin trusted the Yemenis more than the Saudis.[100]

Organisation and tactics

One of the most difficult aspects to unravel is the actual organisation of QAP. Although it is quite possible that on the international level Al-Qa'ida works like a 'loose network of networks',[101] forming a 'loose coalition',[102] and must be considered 'less an organisation than an ideology',[103] evidence in the Saudi Arabian case forces one to conclude that QAP was a structured and hierarchical organisation. It had a permanent leadership, which, when one of its leaders was killed, was replaced. In addition, there was a council of advisers with several committees, for Islamic law, military affairs, propaganda and finance. Under command of the military committee was the section of 'operations', which controlled the cells. Among these were probably the 'al-Quds Squadron', 'the Battalions of the Two Holy Places'. How tight this organisation was, is not clear. For instance, the Yanbu 'operation' was probably an independent initiative. But its secret, exclusive form indicates that it was well-organised and maintained strict discipline. QAP only began to crack and break into separate parts after the List of 19 was published and the security forces began their hunt. This is confirmed by the information that is available on recruitment and discipline. Characteristically, members of a cell were recruited when they were young, were held in complete isolation from society and were forbidden to read newspapers.[104]

It is against the background of this constant crisis that the change of tactics must be analysed. As part of a larger social movement whose goal is to mobilise the population against a regime it regarded

[100] *SA*, 31 December 2004.

[101] Burke, *Al-Qaeda*, p. 16.

[102] Rohan Gunaratna, *Inside Al Qaeda: Global Network of Terror*, New York: Berkley, 2002, p. 76.

[103] Jason Burke, 'Think Again: Al Qaeda', *Foreign Policy*, May/June 2004, www.foreignpolicy.com.

[104] Interview with Khalid al-Farraj and Abd al-Rahman al-Rashud on Saudi Television Channel 1 on 21 September 2004, published the next day in *Jaridat al-Riyadh al-Yawmiyya*.

as un-Islamic, QAP tried constantly to adapt its tactics to public opinion. It started out with the tactic of massive suicide attacks against foreign residential compounds in the hope of mobilising public opinion against foreigners just after the invasion of Iraq. The number of casualties—including important figures (e.g. Khalid al-Jahani)—however, must have been considerable. The second attack on the Muhaya compound was a propaganda disaster, as the only casualties were Muslims or other Arabs. Afterwards QAP tried to regain sympathy by attacking government buildings in Riyadh for the first time, in April 2004. But the explosion did not seriously affect the government's infrastructure; by then QAP's resources and stockpiles of weapons were quite probably being discovered so it was no longer able to launch spectacular attacks. Therefore the attacks with automatic weapons on foreigners in Yanbu and Khobar were probably the result of weakness rather than strength. The death of al-Muqrin and most of his consorts confirms this picture.

Conclusion: The Limits of QAP

After two years of upheaval, QAP proved unable to break through its isolation and take the cycle of contention with the state to a new level. Although it did thoroughly jolt the ruling family and the foreign community, as well as the countries aligned with Saudi Arabia, it did not succeed in destabilising the regime or crippling its economy, nor in mobilising the population. One of the main reasons lies in the weakness of terrorism in general, as a tool. As Tarrow concluded, terrorist violence will 'chill the blood of the bystanders, give pause to prospective allies and cause many who joined the movement in its enthusiastic early phase to defect.'[105] Once state repression swung into gear the risks became too high for others to join, although martyrdom was adopted as part of the repertoire of contention of QAP. Violence and repression were able to prevent QAP from finding allies among the groups that formed part of the larger reformist cycle of contention that had emerged in the 1990s. Insofar as they did find allies among the *matlubin*, and sympathisers, many of these were arrested, killed or were intimidated enough to prevent them from actively supporting QAP. To make matters worse for

[105] Tarrow, *The Power in Movement* (1994), p. 104.

QAP, the regime regained some of its previous resources as the economy boomed on the back of high oil prices. Indeed, the state appeared to feel emboldened to retreat somewhat from its promises on reform, and resort to its traditional politics of repression and co-opting of the reformists.[106]

Besides the larger strategic weakness of violence when applied in a specific country, which has been demonstrated in the case of Egypt during the failed struggle of the *Gama'at al-Islamiyya* in the 1990s and the GIA in Algeria, QAP suffered from a specific weakness, which lay in the background of its members, and its organisation isolated them further from the larger Salafi social reform movement. It is true that the diversity of their location, social background and tribal affiliation should be regarded as important potential assets, and that their publication *Sawt al-Jihad* allowed them to retain contact with their 'sympathisers' and even beyond with the curious public. But the isolation they found themselves in once they had decided to use violence against the state, was only further enhanced by the youthful age of its members, their even earlier recruitment into the movement, the low level of their education (religious or otherwise), their early, often traumatic and decisive experience in Afghanistan (no doubt partly responsible for the turn to violence), in addition to the hierarchical and closed-cell structure of the movement.

[106] *The Economist*, 12–19 December 2004; Faiza Saleh Ambah, 'Moves Toward Reform Wane in Saudi Arabia', *The Christian Science Monitor*, 4 October 2004, www.csmonitor.com.

APPENDIX I

LIST OF 19, ISSUED 7 MAY 2003

		Age	*Nat.*	*Afg.*	*List of 26*	*Died**	*Edu.*	*Born*	*Profession***
1	Turki Nasir Mish'al al-Dandani	29	Saudi	yes	----	3-7-03 Suwair/ Jawf	univ. grad.	Skakaka/ Jawf	student
2	Ali Abd al-Rahman Sa'id al-Faq'asi al-Ghamidi	27	Saudi	yes	----	26-6-03 arrested	univ. grad.°°	Raghban/ al-Baha	student
3	Khalid Muhammad bin Muslim al-Arwi al-Jahani	28	Saudi	yes	----	12-5-03 Riyadh	sec. school	?	
4	Salih Muhammad Awadallah al-Awfi	38	Saudi	yes	no. 5	----	sec. school	Medina	security/ merchant
5	Abd al-Aziz al-Muqrin	30	Saudi	yes	no. 1	18-6-04 Riyadh	prim. school	Riyadh	
6	Abd al-Karim Muh. Jabran al-Yaziji	35	Saudi	yes	----	12-5-03 Riyadh	prim. school	?	NGO worker
7	Hani Sa'id Ahmad Abd al-Karim al-Ghamidi	26	Saudi	yes	----	12-5-03 Riyadh	univ. grad.	?	teacher
8	Muhammad Uthman Abdallah al-Walidi al-Shahri	25	Saudi	yes	----	12-5-03 Riyadh	univ. grad.	Nimas/ Asir	

Table continued

Table continued

9	Rakan Muhsin Muhammad al-Sikhan	26	Saudi	yes	no. 2	29-1-04 Riyadh	univ. left	Riyadh	teacher
10	Yusuf Salih Fahd al-Ayiri°	30	Saudi	?	----	31-5-03 Turba/ Ha'il	prim. school	Damam	
11	Uthman Hadi Maqbul Al Mardi al-Umari	36	Saudi	no	no. 21	26-6-04 gave up	sec. school	Shabariq/ Nimas	weapons merchant
12	Bandar Abd al-Rahman al-Ghamidi	28	Saudi	?	----	4-9-03 arrested	?	?	
13	Ahmad Nasir Abdallah al-Dakhil°	26	Saudi	yes	----	28-7-03 Qasim	univ. grad.°°	Dir'iyya	
14	Hamad Fahd Abdullah al-Aslami al-Shamari	26	Saudi	yes	----	28-7-03 Qasim	?	al-Khafigi	
15	Faisal Abd al-Rahman Abdallah al-Dakhil	25	Saudi	yes	no. 11	18-6-04 Riyadh	?	?	
16	Sultan Jabran Sultan al-Qahtani	27	Saudi	?	----	23-9-03 Jazan	sec. school	Asir	
17	Jabran Ali Hakami Khibrani	27	Saudi	?	----	12-5-03 Riyadh	teach. college	?	teacher
18	Abd al-Rahman Mansur Jabara	30	Kuw. Can.	?	----	3-7-03 Suwair/ Jawf	?	Kuwait	
19	Khalid Ali bin Ali Hajj	30	Yem.	yes	no. 3	15-3-03 Riyadh	prim. school	Jeddah	

* unless otherwise stated

** where known and where the individual did not become a full-time mujahid directly after his education

° ideologue

°° religious studies

APPENDIX II

LIST OF 12 (14) SUICIDE BOMBERS KILLED IN RIYADH ON 12 MAY 2003

List of twelve of the suicide bombers of Riyadh bombing of May 12 (issued on 7 June 2003). Added to the list are two names identified in October (*SA*, 17 November 2003). In total sixteen persons participated in the attack, but two remain unidentified.

Note: not all the middle names have been found.

		Age	*Afg.*	*List of 19*	*Edu.*	*Born*	*Profession*
1	Khalid Muhammad bin Muslim al-Arwi al-Jahani	28	yes	no. 3	sec. school	?	
2	Muhammad Uthman Abdullah al-Walidi al-Shahri	25	yes	no. 8	univ. grad.	Nimas	
3	Hani Sa'id Ahmad Al Abd Karim al-Ghamidi	23	yes	no. 7	univ. grad.	?	teacher
4	Jibran Ali Ahmad Hakami Khibrani	27	?	no. 17	teach. college	?	
5	Khalid bin Ibrahim Mahmud Baghdadi	29	yes	----	univ. left	?	
6	Mihmas bin Muhammad Mahmas al-Hawashla al-Dawsari	26	yes	----	?	?	
7	Muhammad bin Shazaf Ali Al Mahzum al-Shahri	25	?	----	univ. left	Nimas (province)	employee
8	Jazim Muhammad Sa'id Kashmiri	35	yes	----	univ. grad.	?	NGO worker
9	Majid Abdullah Sa'd bin Akil	27	no	----	?	?	
10	Bandar bin Abd al-Rahman Manawwar al-Rahimi al-Mutairi	23	?	----	prim. school	?	
11	Abd al-Karim Muhammad Jabran Yaziji	35	yes	no. 6	prim. school	?	
12	Abdallah Faris bin Jafin al-Rahim al-Mutairi	23	?	----	?	?	mosque employee
13	Muhammad Abd al-Wahhab al-Muqit	28	yes	----	?	?	
14	Ashraf al-Sayyid	23	yes	----	prim. school	Medina	

APPENDIX III

LIST OF 26, ISSUED ON 6 DECEMBER 2003

	Age	Nat.	Afg.	List of 19	Died*	Edu.	Born	Profession
1 Abd al-Aziz Isa Abd al-Muhsin al-Muqrin	30	Saudi	yes	no. 5	18-6-04 Riyadh	prim. school	Riyadh	
2 Rakan Muhsan Muhammad al-Sikhan	26	Saudi	yes	no. 9	12-4-04 Riyadh	univ. left	Riyadh	teacher
3 Khalid Ali bin Ali Hajj	30	Yem.	yes	no. 19	15-3-04 Riyadh	prim. school	Jeddah	
4 Karim al-Tuhami al-Majiti	?	Mor.	yes	----	5-4-05 Qasim	sec. school	Morocco	
5 Salih Muhammad Awwadallah al-Alawi al-Awfi	38	Saudi	yes	no. 4	----	sec. school	Medina	security/ merchant
6 Ibrahim Muhammad Abdallah al-Rayyis	?	Saudi	?	----	8-12-03 Riyadh	?	?	
7 Sa'ud Hamud Abdilahi-Qataimi al-Utaibi°	33	Saudi	yes	----	5-4-05 Qasim	?	?	
8 Ahmad Abd al-Rahman Saqr al-Fadli	27	Saudi	?	----	23-4-04 Jeddah	prim. school	Mecca	police
9 Sultan Bijad Sa'dun al-Utaibi	?	Saudi	no	----	28-12-04 Riyadh	univ. grad.**	?	
10 Abdullah Sa'ud Abuniyan al-Siba'i°	22	Saudi	no	----	----	univ. left**	?	

Table continued

Table continued

11	Faisal Abd al-Rahman Abdallah al-Dakhil	25	Saudi	yes	no. 15	18-6-04 Riyadh	?	Buraida	
12	Faris Amad Jama'an Al Shuwail al-Zahrani	27	Saudi	yes	----	5-8-04 arrested	univ. grad.**	Jawfa' (Zahran)	judge
13	Khalid Mubarak Habiballah al-Qurashi	27	Saudi	no	----	22-4-04 Jeddah	sec. school	Mecca Utaibiya	student
14	Mansur Muhammad Ahmad Faqih	22	Saudi	no	----	30-12-03 gave up	prim. school	Mecca	
15	Isa Sa'd bin Muhammad bin Awshan°	26	Saudi	?	----	22-7-04 Riyadh	univ. grad.**	?	judge/imam
16	Talib Sa'ud Abdullah Al Talib	26	Saudi	no	----	22-4-04 Jeddah	univ. left**	Buraida/ Qasim	
17	Mustafa Ibrahim Muhammad Mubaraki	25	Saudi	?	----	22-4-04 Jeddah	?	?	
18	Abd al-Majid Muhammad Abdallah al-Muni'°	25	Saudi	yes	----	12-10-04 Riyadh	univ. grad.**	Riyadh	
19	Nasir Rashid Nasir al-Rashid	?	Saudi	?	----	12-4-04 Riyadh	univ. left**	Riyadh	
20	Bandar Abd al-Rahman Abdallah al-Dakhil	23	Saudi	?	----	29-12-04 Riyadh	sec. school	Buraida	
21	Uthman Hadi Al Maqbul al-Umari	36	Saudi	no	no. 11	26-6-04 arrested	sec. school	Shabariq	
22	Talal Anbar Ahmad Anbari	?	Saudi	?	----	22-4-04 Jeddah	prim. school	?	

Table continued

Table continued

23	Amir Mushin Maryaf Al Zaidan al-Shahri	22	Saudi	yes	----	23-12-03 Riyadh	univ. left**	Riyadh	–
24	Abdallah Muhammad Rashid al-Rushud°	30	Saudi	no	----	June 04? Riyadh?	univ. grad.**	Aflakh/ province?	–
25	Abd al-Rahman Muhammad Muhammad Yaziji	26	Saudi	?	----	6-4-05 Riyadh	?	Jazan/ Jazan	–
26	Husayn Muhammad al-Hasaki	?	Mor.	?	----	July 04 Belgium	?	Morocco	–

* unless stated otherwise
** religious study
° ideologue

APPENDIX IV

NAMES OF THE 'KHALIDIYYA CELL' IN MECCA ASSAULTED ON 14 JUNE 2003

Those who died

1. Ibrahim Abdullah al-Fanisa (Saudi)
2. Abd al-Hamid Tarawari (Mali)
3. Adnan
4. Khalid
5. unknown

source: al-shaha.fares.net/shahat/, June 2004

Those arrested

1. Ahmad Abd al-Rahman Harun (Chaadi). 15 years.
2. Ahmad Khalid Muhammad al-Hisan (Saudi). 17 years.
3. Musa'id Abd al-Rahman al-Kharisi (Saudi). 17 years.
4. Khalid Ali Tahir Muhammad Ali (Chaadi). 17 years.
5. Amin Muhammad Abdullah Al Uqqal? al-Ghamidi (Saudi). 18 years.
6. Bashir Muhammad Harun (Chaadi). 18 years.
7. 'Isam Khilf Muhammad al-Ghamidi (Saudi). 19 years.
8. Muhammad Fathi Abd al-Ati al-Sayyid (Egyptian). 20 years.
9. Rashid Abdullah Rashid al-Khithlan (no nationality given). 21 years.
10. Amir Abd al-Hamid Sa'ud al-Sa'adi (Saudi?). 24 years.
11. Majid Ibrahim al-Mughaynim? (Saudi). 25 years.
12. Abi Dhar' 'Ibrahim' (nationality unknown). 25 years.

Average age of this group of twelve is nineteen years. (*SA*, 13 November 2003). 17 June, Ministry announces the names of twelve terrorists, and of the five killed in al-Khalidiyya, seven of them were younger than eighteen years old, among them three from Chad, one from Egypt and one from Mali.

Additional information from al-saha.fares.net/shahat/, documents begin March.

APPENDIX V

GROUP OF AL-DANDANI AT AL-JAWF, 3 JULY 2003

Arrested

1. Muhammad Sulayman al-Sab'abi (Saudi)
2. Nasir Farhan al-Ruwaili? (Saudi)
3. Muhammad Badr Hazbar (Syrian)

Those who died

1. Turki Nasir Mish'al al-Dandani (Saudi)
2. Rajih Hasan al-bin Hasan al-Ajami (Kuwaiti)
3. Abd al-Rahman Jabara (Kuwaiti)
4. Umash? al-Siba'i (Saudi)

Source: fares.net (it is not totally clear whether the people were arrested there; said that five had been arrested).

APPENDIX VI

GROUP OF AHMAD AL-DAKHIL IN QASIM, 28 JULY 2003

This group had fled from Mecca and were living in the Khalidiyya appartment. It is the most multi-national group.

Those killed:

1. Ahmad bin Nasir Abdullah al-Dakhil (Saudi)
2. al-Farid al-Harbi (Saudi)
3. Sa' ud Amir Sulayman al-Qurshi (Saudi)
4. Muhammad Ghazi Salim al-Wafi (Saudi, but according to *SA*, 6 May 2004 he is Chaadi.)
5. Isa Kamal Yusuf Tahir/Khatir (Chaadi)
6. Isa Salih Ali Ahmad (Chaadi)

One member was arrested: Ali Ibrahim bin Abdullah khilf al-Harbi
Source: fares.net and *SA*, 6 May 2004 and 21 May 2004.

APPENDIX VII

GROUP OF SULTAN AL-QAHTANI AT AL-JAZAN, 23 SEPTEMBER 2003

Two (unknown members) handed themselves over, three were killed

1. Sultan Jabran bin Muhammad Al Isman al-Qahtani
2. Turki bin Sa'id bin Muhammad Al Thiqfan? al-Qahtani
3. Khalid bin Muhammad bin Ali Al Isa al-Shahri

APPENDIX VIII

LIST OF NAMES OF THE SHARA'I' CELL IN MECCA, 3 NOVEMBER 2003

1. Muhammad al-Harqan. 25 years
2. Ta' 'Ayn 'Ayn. [letter abbreviation only identification] 25 years
3. Muhammad Sulayman al-Jahani. 25 years.
4. Hamid al-Sa'adi. 25 years
5. Mut'ab al-Muhyani. 26 years
6. Sami al-Lahibi al-Harbi. 27 years
7. S.Q. 27 years.
8. Muqayyim Tshadi. 33 years.

Of this group two were killed and two committed suicide, but just who is unknown (*SA*, 13 November 2003).

Part IV. EXTERNAL RELATIONS

DETERMINANTS AND PATTERNS OF SAUDI FOREIGN POLICY: 'OMNIBALANCING' AND 'RELATIVE AUTONOMY' IN MULTIPLE ENVIRONMENTS

Gerd Nonneman

The aftermath of 11 September 2001 brought into sharper focus areas of friction between the United States and its long-standing ally (or, as some critics would have it, 'dependency' on) Saudi Arabia—over the latter's level of cooperation in the 'War of Terror' and the related question of Saudi policy stances within the Middle East. Although many of these differences were not really new, a good many US observers in particular reacted with surprise, irritation, or even anger. Some of this reaction, of course, was inspired by an exaggerated view of the extent of Saudi 'disobedience'. But a somewhat more explicitly 'polygamous' Saudi policy was nevertheless evident.[1] On the face of it, this suggests that Saudi Arabia may offer an interesting case study of the question of dependence versus autonomy in 'centre-periphery' relations, and more broadly about the foreign policies of 'developing' or 'small' states. More immediately, the evidence also shows that, contrary to most interpretations, Saudi Arabia and the other monarchical Gulf states have been pursuing 'polygamous' relations for much longer, and more consistently, than they are often given credit for.[2]

1 The term is used by Fareed Mohamedi and Yahya Sadowski to describe the apparent new Saudi policy line, in 'The Decline (But Not Fall) of US Hegemony in the Middle East', *Middle East Report*, 220 (fall 2001), pp. 12–22.

2 Mohamedi and Sadowski, for instance, paint the policy as a new phenomenon that started after the end of the Cold War, and especially from 1995: *ibid.*, p. 21. While

Approach

The assumption underlying this chapter is that the best way to analyse the foreign policies of states, especially those outside the West, is to use a 'theoretically pluralist'[3] approach that, while taking on board many of the insights of the Realist school of thought in International Relations (IR), goes beyond this by delving into factors and dynamics internal to the state, and examining how these may or may not intertwine with transnational 'values'. Indeed, while the Realist focus on the pursuit of the 'national interest' defined in terms of 'power' does remain one useful angle, this needs to be qualified by the following realisations: (1) the interests being pursued by decision-makers are multiple, aimed at domestic and sometimes narrow elite-based aims, as well as at security from external threats; (2) the label 'state' covers a multiplicity of groups, interests and intertwining dynamics; and (3) domestic, regional and global factors are often inextricably intertwined. Thus, outside the realist mainstream some approaches have focused on decision-making, or the elites and personalities making policy. Others, from a structuralist viewpoint, have interpreted states' interaction and foreign policy as determined largely by 'structures' beyond the state level. Such structuralism can come in a 'neorealist' shape (e.g. Waltz), which sees a global system of anarchy determining not only what the component units do but even what they become. At the other end of the ideological spectrum are a number of approaches (often though not always Marxian in inspiration) that assume there are some states that are dominant, others dominated or 'dependent'—the '*dependencia*' school making the latter view explicit in its very name. Approaches that in this way distinguish between states of the 'centre' or the 'core', and states of the 'periphery', tend to grant the latter little significant autonomy—whether they are powerless to obstruct the interests of the core, or because the local elite's interests are seen (contrary to the population's as a whole) as coinciding with those of the centre.

The intention in this chapter is not only to view Saudi foreign policy through a lens that lets through a wider spectrum than the

---

some shift was certainly noticeable, I argue this does not represent a break with long-established patterns.

[3] Barry Buzan and Richard Little, *International Systems in World History*, Oxford University Press, 2000, p. 35.

classical realist one, but also to challenge the '*dependencia*' assumption that has spread well beyond the practitioners of the school of that name—in other words, to suggest that 'weak', or 'small', or so-called dependent states (categories that overlap and blur into each other even if they are not synonymous) have been able to carve out a significant degree of relative autonomy. The Saudi case, indeed, is a particularly useful example. The approach not only helps us to understand the past century of Saudi foreign policy, but also makes the developments since the start of the twenty-first century less of a surprise than some observers have seemed to think.

In other words, there is a place for what has been called 'agency'—as opposed to 'structure'. That is not to say that such 'agency' operates in a vacuum. But an excessive focus on a country's 'structural' position obscures variations in foreign policy that may result from particular domestic configurations and policy choices. By the same token, of course, an over-emphasis on, say, the role of a leader's personality and idiosyncratic choices can obscure the external and other internal environmental determinants without which the foreign policy pattern cannot be properly interpreted.[4]

The case of Saudi foreign policy provides a good illustration that, at least when it comes to states of the 'global south', it is most useful (1) to start one's analysis from the domestic environment and the survival imperative of regime and (related but quite different) state; (2) to view this in the context of the regional environment and transnational ideological and identity factors; (3) to pay close atten-

[4] The best existing volumes avoiding these pitfalls in analysing the foreign policies of the Middle East, are Bahgat Korany and Ali Dessouki (eds), *The Foreign Policies of Arab States*, Boulder, CO: Westview Press, 1991, 2nd edn; C. Clapham (ed.), *Foreign Policy Making in Developing Countries*, Farnborough: Saxon House, 1977; and Raymond Hinnebusch and Anoushiravan Ehteshami (eds), *The Foreign Policies of Middle East States*, Boulder, CO: Lynne Rienner, 2002. A further attempt has been made in another collective project of systematic analysis: Gerd Nonneman (ed.), *Analyzing Middle East Foreign Policies*, London: Routledge, 2005; published in an early version, with an additional book reviews section, as a special issue of *Review of International Affairs*, winter 2003/4. Excellent analyses on Saudi foreign policy in particular—even if under-emphasising the long history of actively-pursued 'managed multi-dependence'—can be found in William Quandt, *Saudi Arabia in the 1980s: Foreign Policy, Security and Oil*, Washington, DC: Brookings Institution, 1981; and Gregory Gause, 'The Foreign Policy of Saudi Arabia' in Hinnebusch & Ehteshami, *The Foreign Policies of Middle Eastern States.*

tion—as, indeed, do policy-makers themselves—to the threats and opportunities, the constraining and enabling effects, of the international environment; and (4) to take into account decision-making structures and decision-makers' perceptions and role conceptions.

The two key aims which Saudi Arabia's rulers have pursued and continue to pursue in their foreign policy are: (1) domestic security; (2) external security. Moreover, the way in which the second is pursued is to a large degree determined by the first. Hence, apart from any questions about potential external threats, the key question must be: what does domestic security rest on? As in other states, the answer will be a combination of three factors: control; acquiescence; and support—the latter being translated as 'legitimacy'. Since the first of these is by itself unlikely to be a viable long-term means, maintenance of at least acquiescence, and where possible positive legitimacy, is crucial. By the same token, the greater the established level of legitimacy for state and regime, the greater may be the room for manoeuvre and autonomy that the leadership has in foreign policy, vis-à-vis its society.

Because of the above it makes sense to begin one's analysis of the determinants of Saudi foreign policy (as also for other 'developing' states) by looking at the *domestic environment* and the levels and bases of support and legitimacy which foreign policy can serve, damage, or, indeed, draw strength from. This will be surveyed briefly in the following section.

The chapter then turns to the *regional environment*. This is both (a) a source of threats and opportunities concerning external security; and (b) a source of transnational factors affecting *domestic* legitimacy.

Thirdly, the chapter turns to the wider *global environment*. This represents: (a) a source of resources—both protection and other; and (b) a realm to be dealt with in a way that demonstrates effectiveness in one of the traditional criteria for legitimacy in Arabian society: dealing effectively with the outside world and forming a 'buffer' between it and domestic society, drawing the necessary resources from it, while safeguarding that domestic society from being penetrated too much by external control, meddling or influences.

On this basis we can then turn to the question of Saudi foreign policy 'role conception', and to the decision-making system through which all of these determinants and role conception are distilled into policy and action. It will be argued that the way in which this is done, and the pattern which emerges, is one of 'omnibalancing'[5] between a shifting constellation of both internal and external challenges and resources; and that the Saudi regime is continuing a century-old pattern of 'managed multi-dependence'[6] by which it aims, and in part succeeds, to carve out and maintain a measure of relative autonomy.

The Domestic Environment

The key elements in the domestic environment are:

(1) the rentier nature of the state;
(2) the shifting balance of demands and resources;
(3) the main interest groups and 'stakeholders', their conceptions of their own and Saudi Arabia's role, and the ways in which they can make their voices heard (these are: various factions within the royal family; the Al ash-Shaikh[7] and the mainstream *ulama*; notable families; and, increasingly, voices of discontent among radical ulama and the disaffected young);
(4) above all, of course, the way in which the Al Sa'ud decision-makers perceive the effects these factors have on regime security.

This latter point returns us to the question of what the basis for the Al Sa'ud's legitimacy has been. Notwithstanding the huge advances and changes that have taken place in Saudi society and economy since the middle of the twentieth century, traditional themes in Arabian politics and ethos retain some influence—both *de facto* and because the Al Sa'ud have consciously attempted to make it so. It may be suggested that, in traditional Arabian society, a leader's legitimacy depended on five elements: (1) personal reputation and charisma; (2) success in battle; (3) ability to raise armed men; (4) generosity; (5) ability to deal with the outside world, to which Abd al-

[5] A term coined by Steven David in 'Explaining Third World Alignment', *World Politics*, 43, 2 (1991), pp. 233–56.

[6] A term I first introduced in 'Saudi-European Relations, 1902–2001: A Pragmatic Quest for Relative Autonomy', *International Affairs*, 77, 3 (July 2001), pp. 631–61.

[7] Literally: 'the Family of the Shaikh'—the name referring to the descendants of Shaikh Muhammad bin Abd al-Wahhab, the eighteenth-century religious reformer who began the 'Wahhabi' alliance with the Al Sa'ud.

Aziz 'ibn Sa'ud' added the specific element of religious legitimacy, as the one who revived the old alliance between the Al Sa'ud and the descendants of Muhammad ibn Abd al-Wahhab, and who thus became the protector of 'pure' Islam and, after the conquest of Hijaz, of the Holy Places.[8]

To a large extent these same criteria remain central in modern Saudi Arabia, even if their particular form may have evolved. Indeed, the key available bases of regime legitimacy for any Gulf ruler today may be summed up as the following: (1) personal charisma; (2) tradition and maintenance of values; (3) patronage and delivering quality of life; (4) effective dealing with the outside world. In the case of Saudi Arabia in particular one must add: (5) performance as the protector of the Holy Places and of Islam in the Kingdom.

These factors are, of course, often tightly intertwined. Foreign policy can serve or damage all of them. Moreover, the stronger its legitimacy, the greater the autonomy the regime is likely to have from society in the pursuit of foreign policy. In turn, regime legitimacy is connected to and intertwined with what Hinnebusch and Ehteshami have called the 'level of state formation'[9]—i.e. the legitimacy (society's acceptance) of the state and its structures.

Difficulties in a single one of these five factors can usually be absorbed by performance on the others; by the same token, *the greater weaknesses there are across different factors, the more of a potential threat to regime stability each one becomes.* At the start of the twenty-first century, performance on any of the five cannot be taken for granted—indeed there are problems with several. The severe negative shift in the economic demands/resources ratio since the mid-1980s has been perhaps the most important factor, together with the effects of the 1990–1 Gulf crisis.

The rentier state under strain

Saudi Arabia has, at least since the onset of the oil age, become one of the prime examples of a 'rentier state'—highly dependent on the revenue generated by the sale of hydrocarbons. Control over these

[8] See Gerd Nonneman, 'Governance, Human Rights and the Case for Political Adaptation in the Gulf', *EUI Policy Paper*, no. 01/3, Florence: European University Institute, Robert Schuman Centre, 2001 (available on www.ieu.it/RSCAS), pp. 13–16.

[9] Hinnebusch & Ehteshami, *The Foreign Policies of Middle Eastern States*, p. 10.

resources has given the state (and those controlling it) a measure of leverage and influence on the world stage, and the ability to buy large amounts of weaponry. By the same token, especially after the oil boom of the 1970s which further increased such influence and resources, it can be argued that its *dependence* increased as well: dependence on the revenues themselves, on the consuming markets, and on the suppliers of goods and technology for the spending plans that this wealth made possible.

Indeed, internally, the rentier element of the social contract meant that the regime remained highly dependent on government largesse for political survival: it has become a new expression of some of the traditional bases for legitimacy.

Inevitably this also influenced foreign policy, as the regime in this rentier context could hardly opt for autarky. Since the market effects of the double oil shock in the 1970s became clear, no-one in the leadership wished to risk endangering continued oil revenue or disrupting industrialised economies. Together with the historical pro-Western orientation (itself the consequence of the story of state formation), this helps explain the consistent Saudi policy of aiming for moderate prices in coordination with the main consumer countries. Equally important was the economic fact that Saudi Arabia is a relatively low-population, large-reserves producer, which means policymakers need to secure long-term prospects for oil markets, but can afford to forego immediate price maximisation.

Yet the part of the 'social contract' that relied on extensive use of oil wealth for patronage and general welfare, in return for support, or at least acquiescence in the autonomy the Al Sa'ud enjoyed in running the state, and that helped shore up the regime's legitimacy also in traditional terms, has come under tremendous strain since the collapse of oil prices in the 1980s and amidst the population boom. Even following the resurgence of oil prices from 2003, these strains will not disappear altogether. Indeed, the challenges of economic globalisation and the march of information technology will only further exacerbate this.

The drastic reduction of Saudi Arabia's GNP per capita to half the $18,000 level obtaining in 1981 (fluctuating in the $7–9,000 range in the late 1990s and early 2000s) is an illustration of the shift that happened (even if 2003 saw a surge in GDP of over 7 per cent). Saudi

Arabia's population has undergone a huge change in size and composition, as its infant mortality dropped and life expectancy rose to developed-world levels. The country's population, which doubled in just fifteen years (1980–95), could in 2005 be estimated at around 24 million, although only about 17 million are native Saudis. Well over 40 per cent of the population was younger than 15 in 2005, and over 60 per cent was 25 or younger. This has two obvious implications: a continuation of the high rate of population growth even if the birth rate drops, and a demand for jobs, services and welfare proportionately even larger than today.[10]

The era of the oil boom came to an end with the slide in prices (and in the Saudi share of the oil market) from the early 1980s. The temporary switch away from the country's traditional role of swing producer, to recover market share helped bring about the further price collapse to below $10 per barrel in 1986. Notwithstanding a few subsequent spikes, by 1998 prices had again fallen to the same level. Subsequently, new OPEC production discipline succeeded in restoring prices to a price band of $22–28 per barrel. 2003 and 2004 saw a surge in prices, hitting $50 per barrel, as a result of the unsettled situation in Iraq coinciding with production cuts and uncertainties in Russia, Nigeria, Venezuela and Mexico, and larger-than-expected growth in demand. The new consensus, as of 2005, appears to be that prices will settle at around $32–35 per barrel, bringing a significant windfall for the main producers. The price surge in 2004 brought a tripling of revenues compared to 1998. Yet in real terms the drop in the value of oil revenues has been even more pronounced, and the 2004 spike loses its record status.[11] Even while such circumstances may bring budgetary relief, they may also weaken the impetus for the necessary reforms, thereby potentially worsening the longer-term difficulty.

[10] Growth appears to have begun slowing, but remains around 3 per cent. Official Saudi projections have it fall to 2.6 per cent by 2005. This may be somewhat optimistic. As of 2000 the rate was still around 3.5 per cent (and even higher according to some estimates). Data and estimates from Ministry of Economy and Planning, Saudi Arabia, World Bank, *World Development Indicators, 2000*; and US Census Bureau, 'IDB Summary Geographic data for Saudi Arabia', http://www.census.gov./ipc/www/idbsum/html. World Bank projections are somewhat more conservative, expecting average annual growth of 2.9 per cent in the period to 2015.

[11] See *The Economist*, 25 September 2004, p. 85.

Equally important is the changing composition of oil supply to the world's markets. By 2020 OPEC's share is expected to rise again to about 50 per cent of world supply, from some 40 per cent today. OPEC output in absolute terms is likely to double to some 60 million barrels per day (mbd). The largest share of this production expansion will be from the Gulf. Saudi Arabia may aim to double its exports by 2020. Increased gas production will also contribute. But the development of capacity in oil and gas will itself require major investment, and puts in the spotlight the question of attracting foreign investment in this area—an issue where domestic and foreign policy intertwine and one that has significant non-economic implications for regime legitimacy.

Problems will continue to be caused by the sharp fluctuations in prices and revenues that have buffeted the economy. Admittedly budget balances prior to 2003 only looked tight because of huge defence outlays of up to 40 per cent of revenues, and the large, usually unaccounted for, slice of national revenue going into the maintenance of the extensive royal family. But a reallocation of resources in those fields will not be easy. The royal family has been experiencing an annual growth rate at least as high as the population overall.[12] Even with a cutback in the royal subsidy regime—difficult enough to achieve—outlays will still rise. Defence will remain a sensitive and important area, given the uncertainties in the regional environment. Weapons purchases may be slowly reduced, but a drastic reallocation from defence to other areas seems unlikely. While it is true that much of the high-tech hardware being purchased is less than fully effectively deployed, part of the function of these purchases is as 'insurance', making it more likely that the supplying countries will come to Saudi Arabia's aid in a crisis.

In short, the squeeze on resources experienced since the 1980s is not quite past history, especially given increased domestic energy consumption, and the 'youth bulge' in the population statistics.

Since the mid-1980s, therefore, the Saudi regime has been in a position where it has been less and less able to rely on the rentier dynamic to assure its legitimacy, and thus has begun to lose some of

[12] Royal males under eighteen are already thought to be some 70 per cent more numerous than those over that age. Anthony Cordesman, *Saudi Arabia: Guarding the Desert Kingdom*, Boulder, CO: Westview Press, 1997, p. 27.

the room for manoeuvre in foreign policy that stems from state and regime legitimacy. *The reduced ability to perform on the criteria of welfare and patronage has increased the relative importance (and vulnerability) of the other legitimacy resources.* This has reinforced the need to take account of the effect of certain foreign and security policies on domestic legitimacy, with particular reference to the themes of Islamic probity and the Arab cause—themes that will be picked up below. The threat to legitimacy from perceived failures to live up to the criteria of 'protecting Islam' and personal reputation of the rulers, emerges not just from the obvious domestic issues; foreign policy, too—always a potentially treacherous field—has increasingly begun to bring problems in this regard, quite apart from the direct effects on the criterion of effective dealing with, and buffering from, the external environment.

Interest groups and stakeholders

The extent to which, and the ways in which, different groups and interests feed into the process that produces policy is intimately connected to the nature of the state, in combination with the changing economic climate and regional events. The Saudi state, in essence, is a family oligarchy using:

(1) 'dynastic rule'[13]—relying on family personnel to man key posts of administration, control and information gathering, and to ensure system cohesion;
(2) traditional values and custom;
(3) legitimation of temporal power by the alliance with the religious guidance of the ulama and of the Al ash-Shaikh in particular, and the protection of the Islamic values propagated by the *Muwahhidun*;
(4) understandings and alliances with key notable clans and families—from kinship and status to material patronage;
(5) the rent from oil, to construct a 'rentier state' as discussed earlier;
(6) traditional and modern means of dispensing patronage (largely derived from this rent) throughout society, turning the state into the 'provider'.

[13] Michael Herb, *All in the Family: Absolutism, Revolution and Democracy in the Middle Eastern Monarchies*, Albany, NY: State University of New York Press, 1999.

In this context the importance of the following groups can be understood, both as actively nudging policy in a certain direction, and as constraining what policies are possible:

(1) *Various factions and individuals within the royal family.* These may divide along several axes: more or less Arab nationalist; more or less Islamist; more or less pro-Western. To this must be added the individual and sectional interests—political and economic—that different princes aim to safeguard.[14] The senior foreign policy makers inevitably find themselves pushed and constrained by these forces; given the importance of 'dynastic rule'—as opposed to simply monarchical rule—intra-family politics and interests need to be managed in ways that do not threaten the effectiveness of the family's exercise of power.

(2) *The Al ash-Shaikh and the mainstream ulama.* These have an interest in ensuring the survival of the system with which they have become so tightly intertwined, but at the same time they see themselves as the guardians of Islamic propriety. To an extent they are a resource that can be used by the Al Sa'ud to legitimise policies, but only to a degree: some lines are too risky to cross. Even so, they are not in a position to overrule the senior decision-makers on policy decisions the latter deem essential.[15] Elmadani concludes:

> the interest and the influence of the Ulama and their associated government-funded institutions .... evolve around three major factors: 1) their duty to advocate ... the teaching of Wahhabi Islam in foreign countries through building schools and mosques and arranging social aid programmes; 2) their power to issue Fatawa crucial to justify .... Saudi foreign policy actions; and 3) their ability to lobby the government to back Muslim countries and groups with political and financial assistance .... or to hinder such aid to regimes that violate Islamic teaching.[16]

[14] Compare the chapter by Madawi Al-Rasheed in this volume.

[15] See Quandt, *Saudi Arabia in the 1980s*, p. 89; Bahgat Korany, 'Defending the Faith amid Change: the Foreign policy of Saudi Arabia' in B. Korany and A. Dessouki (eds), *The Foreign Policies of Arab States*, pp. 310–53, 325; Gause, 'The Foreign Policy of Saudi Arabia'.

[16] Abdullah Elmadani, *Indo-Saudi Relations 1947–1997: Domestic Concerns and Foreign Relations*, PhD thesis, Exeter University, 2004, p. 99.

(3) *Notable, often merchant, families.* A lesser but not insignificant role is played by well-placed and wealthy families, who derive their wealth and position from early support for or association with Abd al-Aziz's rule, incorporation into the kinship group by intermarriage, or their fortunes acquired as merchants (often helped along by their association with, or patronage by, the Al Sa'ud). As Elmadani observes, 'the strong link between the regime and merchant houses due to the valuable support extended by the latter to Al-Saud throughout the years of [state] formation, [explains why] the commercial elite has a role in influencing the decision-makers, at least in those areas related to the Kingdom's economy and its foreign economic relations.' He points to the 'fact that the prominent merchant houses have always been represented in the cabinet' as evidence of this role.[17]

(4) *Tribal notables and forces.* Similar factors of long-standing association with Al Sa'ud rule as those listed above for the merchant elite, explain why these forces retain importance. Additionally, the traditional support for and alliance with the Al Sa'ud in this case extends beyond the elites into the tribes at large, as many of them were part and parcel of Abd al-Aziz's state-building exercise between 1902 and 1932 (even if this is not true for all tribes alike). This is reflected amongst other things in the National Guard. These forces have generally been supportive and do not have a direct voice in foreign policy issues. By the same token, there appears to be some evidence that, since the 1990s, strains within the ruling family may have brought 'a resurgence in tribal power as princes and factions have sought allies'.[18]

(5) Increasingly, *the voices of discontent among radical ulama and the disaffected young* can be seen to play a role, as a consequence of the worsening resources/demands ratio and the strains on the rentier state discussed earlier. Combined with events in the region (Palestine, Iraq) and the role of the United States, this has resulted in strident demands also with regard to foreign policy, and domestic demands which affect, or may affect, foreign relations. Their importance derives

[17] *Ibid.*, p. 100.

[18] Peter Wilson and Douglas Graham, *Saudi Arabia: the Coming Storm*, New York: M. E. Sharpe, 1994, p. 20.

from the link to some of the legitimacy resources of the Saudi state. Saudi policy must therefore 'omnibalance'—which means that even in the absence of any formal input into policy from these groups, the challenge they pose needs to be factored into foreign as well as domestic policy.

Policy emerges, in part, from the *combined* effect of the different pushes, pulls and constraints emanating from the varying groups and 'factions'—something that can be observed in the decision-making system (see below).

Capabilities

Saudi Arabia, while large and wealthy, and flush with military equipment, has nevertheless remained vulnerable. This is in part a function of its huge territory, long coastlines, porous borders, and exposed oil facilities; in part, of potential threats located on all sides in its immediate neighbourhood (see the following section). In part, the vulnerability is a function also of the limited capability of its armed personnel fully to operate the military hardware available. The dynamics of the rentier state have also meant a reluctance on the part of the state to ask its citizens to take on the full rigours of military training and duty—a situation naturally reflected in the citizenry's own attitudes. Finally, there has been some concern that the military might be a source of armed revolt. The sense of vulnerability that has resulted from all this has in turn brought a need for external protection. But that in turn has the potential to conflict with some of the domestic legitimacy needs listed earlier; hence there has always been, and will increasingly be, a need to tread carefully in obtaining and clothing such protection.[19]

Saudi Arabia also has at its disposal financial means which can be deployed in support of foreign policy aims—whether in direct aid to governments or as assistance to activities by Saudi or foreign organisations—not least on Islamic themes. Direct financial hand-outs apart, leverage may be derived from the country's control of economic assets other than the hydrocarbons themselves. As the world's

[19] See Anthony Cordesman, *Saudi Arabia Enters the 21st Century: Military and Internal Security Issues*, Washington, DC: CSIS, 2002: see especially the conclusions at http://www.csis.org/burke/saudi21/SaudiMilBook_11.pdf.

most significant swing producer and one of the two top exporters, Saudi Arabia wields enormous influence over the oil market and among other producers. The extent to which this influence can be wielded without damaging the state's own interests is of course constrained, but is nevertheless significant and brings with it, at the very least, the attention of other states. Other economic assets too, even if not actively deployed in pursuit of foreign policy goals, may feed Saudi Arabia's 'structural power' since other powers are likely to take heed of them, and of Saudi interests, in their own calculations. These include the investments which Saudi Arabia has in the international financial markets and in international companies. Again, decision-makers need to be extremely cautious in how such assets are employed in foreign policy strategies, as the economic (let alone foreign political) backlash of mishandling them could be serious (sudden withdrawals or sales of stock on a large scale would damage the direct revenue stream these assets bring, and may cause wider damage to the international economy, which would affect the country's other revenue streams, including those from oil).

Dramatic acts of defiance against the West, for instance, are therefore out of the question: they would severely affect the country's domestic economy, its longer-term foreign revenues, and the assurance of protection. Nevertheless, the extent of 'structural power' which such assets afford is significant even without active deployment, and their subtle management whether declaratory or actual is a useful toolbox for policy-makers. While in many areas and ways Saudi dependence on world powers and the world economy has increased dramatically over the past fifty years, so have the elements of dependence of the latter on the former: the relationship is one of interdependence, albeit a decidedly asymmetrical interdependence in favour of the industrialised West.

The Regional Environment

As stated earlier, the regional environment is (a) a source of threats and opportunities regarding external security; and (b) a source of transnational factors that affect domestic legitimacy (while also to some extent linking to decision-makers' identities and role conceptions). The first derives from potential threats located on all sides in its immediate neighbourhood: from Iran and Iraq (as illustrated by the concern over a possible Iraqi invasion in 1990); from potential instabilities in Yemen and the Horn of Africa; and from conflagrations in the Arab-Israeli theatre (which is, after all, only separated from the Kingdom by a tiny sliver of Jordanian land), along with the difficult-to-gauge potential threat from Israel itself. The second derives both from direct state-inspired ideological threats (such as erstwhile republican Iraq, or revolutionary Iran), and from the wider currency of Arab and Islamic themes in regional politics.

The regional environment, of course, has changed and continues to evolve. Important changes from the Saudi point of view have been, for instance, the political and foreign policy moderation in Iraq from the mid-1970s; the Iranian revolution and the implicit and explicit threats emanating from it; the Soviet invasion of Afghanistan; the outbreak of the Iraq-Iran war and its subsequent evolution; the evolution of Iranian attitudes; and Iraq's invasion of Kuwait. Clearly the removal of Saddam Hussein has once again changed the environment and Saudi calculations. The impact of wider transnational values and themes has also evolved.

The Arab World/The Middle East

In Arab foreign policies generally, the 'Arab system' has become gradually less dominant as a determinant since the 1970s. Arab themes in general, and certainly Pan-Arabism in particular, no longer have the force they had from the 1940s until the use of the oil weapon in 1973. State and regime interests have become predominant, in a context of international (asymmetrical) interdependence. Yet an Arab dimension persists. This is no doubt in part because of residual convictions among ruling elites, and the strongly varying extent to which this element remains one part of their identities. But probably more important is the rulers' and policy-makers' perception of the danger of ignoring what remains a potent, albeit no longer dominant, value among their populations.[20] The Palestine question is still

[20] There is still some considerable debate about this issue. See for instance views of Michael Barnett, *Dialogues in Arab Politics*, New York: Columbia University Press, 1998; compared to Stephen M. Walt, *The Origin of Alliances*, Ithaca, NY: Cornell University Press, 1987; and the useful conceptual article by F. Gregory Gause III, 'Systemic Approaches to Middle East International Relations', *International Studies Review*, 1, 1 (spring 1999), pp. 11–31. The most recent incisive contribution is Raymond Hinnebusch, 'Explaining International Politics in the

an issue to be reckoned with in this respect. Consequently, close collaboration with the United States retains elements of political risk.

The Palestine issue also has its Islamic resonance, of course, focusing in particular on Jerusalem. Indeed, it is perhaps the Islamic factor that has begun to impose increasing constraints on the room for manoeuvre of the foreign policy elites in Middle Eastern states, both because of popular pressures and because rival regimes may be able to utilise this theme. Arguably such themes are achieving increasing resonance as a result of the twin pressures of economic pain (itself resulting from the combination of external pressure to liberalise, domestic population growth and government ineptitude and corruption) and popular resistance against the perceived impact of US/Western hegemony and regimes' perceived 'collusion' (whether cultural, political or military).

These transnational values apart, the Middle East system also contains a number of strategic features that impact on Saudi foreign policies. The key elements can be grouped in three categories. First, Israel's regional superpower status and nuclear capability remain a central concern alongside the destabilising potential of the Palestine conflict itself. The close geographical proximity of the Arab-Israeli theatre heightens the conflict's potential impact on Saudi security. These factors help explain feelings of insecurity and attempts to ameliorate this both by traditional security means and by a moderating diplomacy. By the same token, Israeli objections to Saudi Arabia's acquisitions of sophisticated weaponry have long bedevilled US–Saudi relations (providing opportunities to Britain and other competitors). Second, are the implications of the rich-poor divide in the region—with the Gulf Cooperation Council (GCC) states in particular falling in the rich camp. This has long been a source of potential insecurity for the latter, feeding into their foreign policies both towards the Middle East and potential protectors elsewhere. Third, there are the strategic realities of the 'wider Middle East', or indeed beyond the region proper, that affect the fears and calculations of regional states such as Iran, which in turn affect those of Saudi Arabia. This brings us to the sub-system of the Gulf itself.

Middle East: The Struggle of Regional Identity and Systemic Structure' in Nonneman, *Analyzing Middle East Foreign Policies*, pp. 243–256.

The Gulf

As with general foreign policy, the two key driving concerns in the Gulf policy of Saudi Arabia's rulers have been external security and domestic security. For the former, four means have been pursued: (1) external protectors; (2) collective security within the GCC; (3) the 'management' of regional relations through cautious diplomacy (including 'riyal-politik') and the pursuit of a regional balance of power; and (4) the purchase of arms, which has been aimed as much at gaining prestige and a tying-in of Western interest and commitment, as it has been at deterrence and defence. An additional feature of policy is that Saudi Arabia has also seen itself as rightfully dominant on the Arabian peninsula. The maintenance of *domestic* security has meant the need to keep revenues flowing; to avoid being seen as totally dependent; and to collaborate in the GCC.

The Gulf sub-system has featured several types of clashes or tensions. Most prominent for a long time were the ideological ones between Arab-nationalist, secular republican Iraq, revolutionary-Islamic republican Iran, and the neo-traditionalist conservative pro-Western GCC monarchies. Clearly this forms a large part of the explanation for the monarchies' continued desire for outside protection. But the nature of the ideological question has been changing. By the turn of the millennium Iran had matured into essentially a status-quo power and was increasingly being seen as such.[21] Instead, Iran and the GCC states now shared a concern about Iraq. Riyadh's own relationship with Tehran, while still wary, has definitively left behind the blockages of the late 1980s.[22]

[21] This was illustrated by Iran's posture during the 2003 Iraq war, and earlier in the Kuwait crisis and the 2001 campaign against Al-Qa'ida and the Taliban in Afghanistan. For analysis underpinning this assessment, see also Anoushiravan Ehteshami and Raymond Hinnebusch, *Syria and Iran: Middle Powers in a Penetrated Regional System*, London: Routledge, 1997, pp. 43–6. Iran's position and trajectory remains complicated, of course, by its complex internal politics; see Ziba Moshaver, 'Revolution, Theocratic Leadership and Iran's Foreign Policy' in Nonneman, *Analyzing Middle East Foreign Policies*, pp. 174–196.

[22] For an examination of Saudi (and other GCC) relations with Iran and Iraq since the 1970s, see Gerd Nonneman, 'The Gulf States and the Iran-Iraq War: Pattern Shifts and Continuities' in L. Potter and G. Sick (eds), *Iran, Iraq and the Legacies*, New York: Palgrave, 2004, pp. 167–92.

While ideological threats from the immediate region have subsided, there remains nevertheless the 'realist' perception that both Iran and Iraq continue to form a potential strategic challenge, given their larger populations and the outlook for their medium- and longer-term capabilities (including the possibility that Iran might aspire to nuclear weapons).

A third type of clash has been that based on differential economic needs. Iran has relatively lower oil reserves and a very large population, and will therefore be relatively less interested in the very-long-term future of the oil market: it faces higher immediate needs than Saudi Arabia, Kuwait and the UAE, where the opposite applies. Iraq falls between these two ends of the spectrum, although its reconstruction and eventual rearmament needs will, for the foreseeable future, nudge it towards a higher-price stance. Saudi Arabian decision-makers will therefore, in oil policy, always need to manoeuvre between their own domestic politico-economic needs, and the need to manage regional sensibilities in this regard. At the same time, they also need to balance this with the wider interests of the world economy (on which a healthy oil demand depends) and the blandishments from their Western allies.

The traditional Saudi aspiration to hegemony on the Arabian peninsula remains a cause of fluctuating levels of friction with its GCC neighbours and Yemen—whether because they resent Riyadh's actual or perceived attempts to dominate them, or because of the Saudi leadership's irritation with such attempts as they make to resist or escape Saudi dominance—Qatar being a case in point, and the areas in which it is played out being both regional and international (e.g. over trade agreements with the United States). This is combined also with inter-personal dynamics between the leading figures among the ruling families. Yet the GCC has nevertheless provided a useful organisation and framework. Apart from its function as a means to contain, circumvent or resolve tensions between the member states, it has also proved an excellent means for all GCC states, and for Saudi Arabia in particular, to allow the adoption of varying policy stances simultaneously, where such ambiguity could be useful. Thus GCC declarations could be used to send one message to one audience, while bilateral policy, declaratory or otherwise, could be used to send a different message to a different audience. Examples of this abound, not least from the years of the Iran-Iraq war.[23]

The Global Environment

As argued earlier, the global environment represents (1) a source of resources—both protection and otherwise; and (2) a realm to be dealt with in a way that demonstrates effectiveness in one of the traditional criteria for legitimacy: dealing effectively with the outside world and forming a 'buffer' between it and domestic society, and drawing the necessary resources from it, while safeguarding that domestic society from being penetrated too much by external influence. Given the need for external protection, the march of the communications and internet revolution, and globalisation in economic and other matters, the second task has become a huge challenge.

The domestic challenge presented by the global environment comes in three parts: (1) the dangerous perception of political dependence on the United States; (2) the perceived damage to local interests from economic globalisation; (3) the cultural penetration that many feel accompanies the Kingdom's insertion in the global economy and the presence of foreign workers. A further challenge comes in the form of the demands made by the West, and the United States in particular, on anything from oil policy to education and foreign policy. Arguably, also, Saudi Arabia's place in the international political economy constrains its options: even if the relationship is one of interdependence, it still remains asymmetrical. By the same token, as already suggested, this environment also offers resources. Its oil revenues derive from the country's insertion in the international economy; much of its non-oil revenue derives from its financial, stock market, or industrial investments in the world economy; and the rest from non-oil exports such as petrochemicals, to world markets. Its control of a quarter of the world's oil reserves (and most of the spare production capacity) mean that outside powers take note of what Saudi leaders say and of what they need to assure stability in the oil market. Technology, consumer goods and arms are also sourced from this same international environment, and feed into efforts at state building and 'delivering the goods'. And outside powers

[23] *Ibid.*

can be used to balance the threat from regional powers. Moreover, there has always been some room for exploiting divisions among those outside powers themselves. Of particular significance has been the growing importance of Asian energy consumption as the Chinese and other regional economies surge ahead—indeed their demand is in part responsible for the oil price surge since 2003. Hence the sharp rise in Saudi attention for—and investment in—Asian economies is no coincidence.

Arguably the change in the international system represented by the end of the Cold War and the disappearance of the Soviet Union was always likely to increase pragmatic policies towards Britain and the West, by taking away a key option for playing off East against West. It is true that in 1990 Saudi Arabia moved closer to an explicit reliance on Washington and other Western protectors, but this was mainly the result of the Kuwait crisis, and the direct implications of that crisis for Saudi security. Still, the resolution of the crisis could also be seen as demonstrating just how unipolar the new world disposition had become. If one adds the effect of 9/11 in the context of a George W. Bush administration, and the consequent shift in US foreign and security policy towards the neoconservative agenda and a more unilateralist, pre-emptive agenda that distinguished increasingly sharply between those 'with us' and 'against us', the room for manoeuvre that states such as Saudi Arabia have was arguably doomed to shrink further.

However, there are a number of factors that must qualify such a conclusion. First, the difficulties experienced in Iraq since the removal of Saddam Hussein and the reverberations this has had within the US political scene have already put pressure on the 'neo-con' camp and its interpretation of US interests and policy. Second, other smaller powers—including aspirant great powers such as China—have challenged US policy stances, or at least have offered states such as Saudi Arabia a partial alternative source of diplomatic, economic and military support (without pretending that any power but the United States could give the ultimate military assurance that regimes may want). Third, the need to *omnibalance* may mean that states make quite different, complex, calculations not solely based on an appreciation of the overwhelming power of the United States: domestic threats and opportunities need to be factored in. This, of course, is precisely what has been happening in the Saudi case since 2002, and has only been reinforced further by domestic reactions to the juxtaposed US policies on Iraq and Palestine in 2003. In turn, an outside 'hegemon' such as the United States may well recognise this reality, and agree to reduce its demands in line with the domestic stability requirements of the regime. That, too, has at least in part been happening in the Saudi case.

This context means that states—such as, again, Saudi Arabia—may still find both a need and the room for manoeuvre in the post-Cold-War system. Indeed, Bronson has argued that the Cold War acted as a glue in US–Saudi relations that has now disappeared.[24] This theme will be returned to in more depth in the section 'Policy Output' below.

Decision-making

A focus on the decision-making, or policy-making, system is needed to understand how the various inputs surveyed above are turned into policy. We do not need to replicate here the existing analyses of the shifting nature of the decision-making process in Saudi Arabia;[25] but it is worth restating the key features relevant to foreign policy-making:

(1) the supreme dominance of the royal family and, within it, of the senior princes, whose opinions may differ;
(2) the fluctuating importance of the King—with strong figures like Abd al-Aziz and Faisal stamping their authority on policy, and policy-making becoming more diffuse under Khaled and Fahd; Crown Prince Abdullah, the *de facto* ruler since Fahd became incapacitated by a stroke in 1996, has not been able to impose full control;
(3) a measure of 'division of labour', or a degree of personal 'ownership' by certain princes over certain aspects of foreign relations, such as Crown Prince Abdullah regarding relations with Syria, and Prince Sultan with respect to relations with Yemen;

[24] See her chapter in this volume.

[25] Especially Quandt, *Saudi Arabia in the 1980s*; the brief but good overview in Gause, 'The Foreign Policy of Saudi Arabia', pp. 204–6; and the most recent brief survey by Elmadani, *Indo-Saudi Relations*, pp. 93–101.

but this has been cut across by factors 2, 4 and 5 (as illustrated in the sea-change in relations with Yemen under the Crown Prince's impetus);

(4) the very gradual professionalisation of the policy-making bureaucracy;[26]

(5) the consensus-seeking principle, both within the royal family and between it and other important constituencies—including the religious establishment and the other key groups and interests listed in 'The Domestic Environment' above.

As Gause has observed, while the religious establishment does to varying degrees influence foreign policy, it does not have a decisive voice: its support may be sought, as was indeed the case when King Fahd invited foreign troops to help in the defence of Saudi Arabia, but that is quite different from asking permission. 'There is no case in recorded Saudi history where a foreign-policy decision … was … dropped because of publicly expressed disapproval by the ulama.'[27] Indeed, King Fahd's ability to push seven of his most senior ulama into retirement in 1992, when they refused to rescind their signature of a petition critical of the government, shows where ultimate power lies.[28] Even so, they do have an advisory role, and in some areas of policy they have a special influence, as outlined earlier.

The Consultative Council, which has a Foreign Affairs committee, may act as a sounding board and formulate suggestions, but clearly has an even less decisive impact. Significant further reforms will be needed before it can become a significant player in foreign policy formulation.[29]

The Council of Ministers and the government bureaucracy have gradually become more important in administering the country, as their tasks grow more complex along with the increasing complex-

[26] Author's interviews with Saudi academic observers and members of the *Majlis al-Shura*, 1997–2003; Elmadani, *Indo-Saudi Relations*, pp. 95–7, 100. See also, specifically on the oil sector, Nawaf Obaid, *The Oil Kingdom at 100: Petroleum Policymaking in Saudi Arabia*, Washington, DC: The Washington Institute for Near East Policy, 2000.

[27] Gause, 'The Foreign Policy of Saudi Arabia', p. 205.

[28] Elmadani, *Indo-Saudi Relations*, p. 99.

[29] This impression is confirmed by discussions with members of the *Majlis*, 1997–2003; see also Gause, 'The Foreign Policy of Saudi Arabia', p. 205; Elmadani, *Indo-Saudi Relations*, pp. 97–8.

ity of society, the economy and foreign relations. Yet even in the Council of Ministers, real power lies with the royal ministers. The Foreign Minister's clout derives in large part from his status as King Faisal's son and one of the most senior among the grandsons of Abd al-Aziz. Even so, the increasing presence of technocrats both in the Council and the rest of the bureaucracy, have brought an increased influence. Non-royal ministers, for instance, may attempt to follow their own agenda 'through the process of implementation and control of the budget ... They may also influence the King's perception of particular issues by approaching him or the senior princes in private, depending on these ministers' talent, diplomacy, and social standing.'[30] The implementation stage is also where technocrats throughout the rest of the bureaucracy may make their impact felt.

A special case is that of the 'royal technocrats': 'junior' princes with skills and ambition, who occupy increasingly senior positions in the state bureaucracy. Often their position in sensitive posts—e.g. in key embassies, or in key military or economic appointments—may mean they are able to exert a direct or indirect influence on the formulation and implementation of policy.[31]

Even so, most of the real decision-making power lies with the senior royal princes. Nevertheless, there are sufficient countervailing interests and forces at work, both in society at large and in the key decision-making structures themselves, to complicate the process considerably. William Quandt has observed that the effect of these factors has been that the Saudi leadership, 'pushed and pulled in various directions, will try to find a middle ground, a consensus position that will minimise pressures and risks.' This tendency has often been exacerbated by the nature of the foreign policy decision-making process, which, after King Faisal's death, became more diffuse—with several senior princes' voices being heard, each expressing views reflecting their somewhat differing backgrounds, views and sympathies. In this context, 'decisions may be postponed or compromises forged to preserve the façade of consensus.'[32]

Nevertheless, in moments of crisis, the Al Sa'ud leadership have shown that they will indeed come off the fence and take some quite

[30] Elmadani, *Indo-Saudi Relations*, p. 96.

[31] Quandt, *Saudi Arabia in the 1980s*, pp. 83–6.

[32] *Ibid*. Two decades on this assessment has remained pertinent.

radical decisions if the alternative is thought worse. Examples prior to the 2003 Iraq war would be the decisions to back Iraq in the Iran-Iraq war, and to invite foreign troops in 1990.

Role Conception

The foreign policy 'role'[33] of a state, or the 'role conception' of a decision-making elite, sums up the longer-term 'belief system' underlying foreign policy thinking. In part these decision-makers' role conceptions are likely to be built on domestic political history and culture, but as Hill has pointed out, they can, over time, in turn 'become a more pervasive part of the political culture of a nation [and thus become] more likely to set limits on perceived or politically feasible policy alternatives.'[34] Contrary to the implied assumption often found in country case studies, foreign policy 'roles' are plural, depending on the issue and the arena in question.[35] They are also changeable: 'The "belief system" of the practitioner is a deep-rooted legacy of experience and political culture, but it is also an organic set of attitudes which is capable, within limits, of self-transformation.'[36] The Saudi foreign policy 'role', or 'roles', must be seen as defined through the lens of Al Sa'ud perceptions about the security of their regime; about the opportunities and challenges presented by both their domestic and their external environments; and about the family's own history and its place in Arabian, Arab and Muslim society and politics.

[33] This term has been defined in a number of ways. I use it here to refer to a state's characteristic patterns of behaviour—patterns which themselves result both from the 'objective' position the state occupies in its regional and international environment, and from policy makers' own perceptions and definitions (see e.g. K. Holsti, 'National Role Conceptions in the Study of Foreign Policy' in Stephen Walker (ed.), *Role Theory and Foreign Policy Analysis*, Durham, NC: Duke University Press, 1987, pp. 5–43.; Lisbeth Aggestam, 'Role Conceptions and the politics of Identity in Foreign Policy', *ARENA Working Papers*, 99/8, available on http://www.arena.uio.no/publications/wp99_8.htm).

[34] Holsti, 'National Role Conceptions…', pp. 38–9.

[35] For a European case study of the simultaneous existence of multiple roles, see Aggestam, 'Role Conceptions…'.

[36] Christopher Hill, 'The Historical Background: Past and Present in British Foreign Policy' in Michael Smith *et al.* (eds), *British Foreign Policy: Tradition, Change and Transformation*, London: Unwin Hyman, 1988, pp. 25–49: p. 30.

The key historical factors that shaped the Al Sa'ud's foreign policy role conception, would, together with the three environments described earlier, seem to be:

(1) local/regional political culture involving tribal values and custom, and the 'rules of shaikhly exchange';[37]
(2) the history of, albeit fluctuating, Al Sa'ud predominance on the Arabian peninsula;
(3) the linkage with 'Islam', both because of the established values of local society and the presence of the two Holy Places, and because of the 260-years-old alliance with the Al ash-Shaikh;
(4) the fate of the first and second Saudi states as compared to Abd al-Aziz's success: the collective memory of the collapse of those states has remained potent. Both collapsed due on the one hand to the combined pressures from regional challengers and external powers, but on the other also to the leadership's lack of pragmatic adaptation and its failure to build bridges to possible allies. The third key factor was intra-family conflict. Abd al-Aziz's success was built on a conscious avoiding of these pitfalls—and his successors have clearly borne them in mind. His success at playing off Britain against the Ottomans, the United States against Britain, and European and other actors against the United States, became part of the Al Sa'ud's foreign policy heritage.

These factors have meant that the Saudi foreign policy 'role conception' has included (1) an absolute focus on state and dynastic survival; (2) an awareness of the need for pragmatic adaptation to the presence of external (regional and global) threats and resources; (3) a view of non-regional powers as potentially useful resources, and as amenable to a degree of 'management'; (4) a sense of the 'natural' dominance of the Al Sa'ud and its domains on the Arabian peninsula; (5) a sense of the Saudi role as a central Muslim power with a responsibility for the well-being of Islam and Muslims elsewhere; and (6) within the Peninsula and the Arab Mashreq, a sense that international relations are (to a perhaps lessening degree) a matter of interpersonal relations and 'shaikhly exchange'.

[37] This refers to the personal nature of much of diplomatic exchange on the Arab side of the Gulf (and to an extent in the Arab world as a whole), along with the assumptions of what is right and proper in the conduct of such relations. I owe the term to a fellow scholar of the region.

Policy Output: 'Omnibalancing' and 'Managed Multi-dependence'

Actual Saudi foreign policy output, then, filtered through the decision-making context described earlier, has been determined by the needs of the regime at home, the changing availability of resources, and the international strategic and economic framework within which the country always took a subordinate, but not powerless, role. It was also influenced and circumscribed by the regional ideological and political context (with especially the themes of Islam and Arabism) both because this links into the domestic security imperative, and because it has been a genuine element among the various role conceptions of the Al Sa'ud leadership.

Throughout the twentieth century and into the twenty-first, the resulting policy output has essentially been pragmatic, in pursuit of regime and state security; of acquiring outside protectors while maintaining relative autonomy; of securing economic resources at home and in the world economy; and of regional and Islamic status. Policy has exhibited a concern for Islamic causes and the cause of Palestine—although not to the extent of damaging the other aims. Indeed, the Saudi sense of vulnerability to both 'hard' and 'soft' spill-over from the close-by Arab-Israeli theatre has helped produce a policy of seeking to help resolve the conflict while maintaining Arab consensus. In these pursuits, the inherent complexity of omnibalancing, together with the characteristics of royal family decision-making, have generated a tendency to postpone or fudge difficult decisions and avoid conflict; but this did not always prove an obstacle to decisive action at times of acute regional crisis.

Exporting the Islamist threat?

The above analysis sits somewhat awkwardly with the accusations of, in particular, US commentators since 9/11, that Saudi Arabia and the Al Sa'ud were responsible for fostering Islamist radicalism throughout the world, through their domestic education policies but also by conscious support for Islamist organisations and 'supporters of terror' in the Middle East and elsewhere, whether from conviction or to divert the attention of domestic Islamist critics.[38]

[38] See for instance Khaled Dawoud, 'Squeezing Saudi Arabia', *Al Ahram Weekly*, 18 December 2003 (http://weekly.ahram.org.eg/2003/669/re4.htm). Saudi anger

Undeniably aspects of Islamist thought, education and organisation in the country have been part of an environment that inspired radicalism among some groups[39]—although, as suggested in 'The Domestic Environment' above, grievances over aspects of domestic and foreign policy have probably been a more important part of the explanation. Equally, it is clear that Saudi Arabia (along with the UAE) was in a special position by virtue of having for some time had diplomatic relations with the Taliban; also, Usama bin Ladin himself had originally been in contact with some members of the royal family, and had in effect functioned as a representative of Saudi Arabia in the Mujahidin's struggle against the Soviet occupation of Afghanistan. Yet that episode was wholly in line with US policy: even the take-over by the Taliban was not seen as a particular problem by US policy-makers at the time. However, what this situation did bring about was the growth of an organic link between groups in Afghanistan on the one hand and Saudi Arabia (and the UAE) on the other, as contact, travel and financial flows between them did not encounter the problems faced elsewhere.

The Saudi government has certainly funded Islamic missionary activity and other Islamic charitable work. In part, this has been aimed at shoring up their legitimacy on the domestic and wider Islamic stages. Clearly, some of the groups and individuals benefiting have engaged in, or given support to, militant activities involving violence, or channelled funding to others who did. In a few cases this violence included terrorist tactics. However, there is no case of the latter being condoned by the government, nor is there any evidence that they did in fact know about the terrorist end-use of specific funds. In addition, many private individuals, including royals, have long contributed to similar causes. Such money flows—often outside the formal banking system—were extremely difficult to trace effectively.[40] Again, some such funds did find their way to groups

over such accusations has been palpable. See for instance Karen De Young, 'Saudis Seethe Over Media Reports on Anti-Terror Effort', *Washington Post*, 6 November 2001, p. A01; and the chapter by Rachel Bronson in this volume.

39 See the chapter by Michaela Prokop in this volume.

40 See also Anthony Cordesman, *Saudi Arabia Enters the 21st Century*, Washington, DC: CSIS, 2002, part IV: 'Opposition and Islamic Extremism' (available on http://www.csis.org/burke/saudi21/S21_04.pdf), pp. 6–7, 61–7.

engaged in violence, including at times terrorist tactics. The Al-Qa'ida network does appear to have obtained some of its resources this way. Yet here too, the vast majority of donors would appear to have been unaware of specific funds' end-uses of a terrorist nature. Nevertheless, there was certainly a more general awareness, both at the governmental level and beyond, that some funds did end up being used for terrorist and related purposes; however, this was mostly felt to be beyond the donors' control. Moreover, in the absence of clear and indisputable trails, the government was constrained in any attempts to contain or proscribe private charitable funding to Islamic organisations abroad, since this would go directly against its self-proclaimed mission of defending and propagating Islam—and thus undercut its claim to legitimacy. It should be stressed also, that (especially private) aid to organisations such as Hamas in Palestine, would be considered perfectly legitimate as these are seen as movements resisting foreign occupation and looking after the social welfare of Palestinian Muslims. In the latter respect, as also in the friction occasionally in evidence over the extent of the Saudi responsiveness to US demands for intelligence and law enforcement cooperation,[41] Saudi decision-makers were clearly not prepared simply to accede to any US demands except on terms that were deemed balanced, compatible with their role conception and in keeping with their domestic standing and interests.

Yet, given that the threat from Al-Qa'ida and like-minded groups within Saudi Arabia has been perceived, at least since the Al-Khobar bombing in 1996,[42] as directed squarely at the Al Sa'ud themselves, active collusion between the regime and such organisations since then is implausible, even if that has not excluded attempts to co-opt and thus contain those within the country receptive to such an approach. As attacks within the country increased in 2003, the realisation of the extent of the threat of violent Islamism did give a serious jolt to the policy establishment, leading to a crackdown on extremist actors within the Kingdom and increasingly effective coop-

[41] See e.g. the case study on the Al-Haramain charity, attached to the US 9/11 Commission report, on http://www.9-11commission.gov/staff_statements/911_TerrFin_Ch7.pdf.

[42] The attack killed nineteen US servicemen and injured 373 others at the US military housing complex in Khobar Towers. Not long after, the Taliban made major advances in Afghanistan, where bin Ladin had sought refuge.

eration with foreign intelligence agencies, as well as a severe tightening of the controls on financial flows through charitable institutions and the informal sector—as demanded by the United States and other international actors concerned with terrorist finance. It also sparked a new (albeit still strictly circumscribed) debate in wider Saudi society and media, and brought forward gradual reforms in the education sector.[43] At the same time, Saudi public diplomacy was stepped up in an attempt to counter both a range of specific accusations especially in the United States, and the longer-term difficulty of the country's image problem that gave such accusations greater purchase.[44]

Policy patterns

Returning to the wider patterns of policy, it is important to note that for much of the time, the main focus of Saudi policy-makers (as indeed has been the case for the other GCC states, and a majority of developing states) has been on their immediate domestic and regional environment, rather than on global issues. Indeed, to the extent that their gaze was directed at the wider world, it was usually in order to serve their aims in this more immediate environment. Beyond global issues with direct local relevance, such as the state of the energy markets, international trade negotiations (whether with the European Union or over accession to the World Trade Organisation), or, indeed, increasingly Saudi Arabia's international image, they have had relatively few ambitions at that level. Even so, the global scene was always closely observed in order to underpin the policy of managed multi-dependence within the broader context of the Al Sa'ud's omnibalancing strategy. In this sense, Europe, China, Japan and Russia have in recent years been viewed and used in the

[43] See International Crisis Group, *Can Saudi Arabia reform itself?*, Cairo/Brussels: ICG, 14 July 2004; and the chapter by Michaela Prokop in this volume.

[44] This included, among other things, increased appearances in the US broadcast and print media; interviews in the British media by the Ambassador to the UK, Prince Turki bin Faisal, and a high-profile Saudi cultural festival in London in the summer of 2004. Specific accusations aired in the United States in 2004 (including in Michael Moore's film *Fahrenheit 9/11*) were countered with highly professional radio spots quoting the findings of the official 9/11 Commission report (see http://www.saudi-us-relations.org/newsletter2004/saudi-relations-NID-08-27.htm. The 9/11 report is available on http://www.9-11commission.gov/). See also the chapter by Rachel Bronson in this volume.

same way as was the United States in the days of British hegemony, and just as Britain and others were once seen, the United States has itself become the new hegemon: making the most of these powers' own perceived interests to help maintain the 'wriggle room' for Saudi Arabia in the international system—without really endangering the relationship with the main hegemon. This policy has been shaped not only by geopolitical calculation, but equally, especially recently, by the pragmatic calculation of economic interest: the striking expansion of relations with Asia (not least China and India in recent years) and, tentatively, Russia, can be seen in this light.

Perhaps the first internationally-noted controversial breakthrough in Chinese-Saudi relations came with the supply of 36 CSS-2 missiles (theoretically nuclear-capable but heavily modified for non-nuclear use only) delivered between 1987–9, at about $3 billion. Much recent commentary about a surge in Chinese-Saudi nuclear cooperation and weapons supplies notwithstanding, there is precious little reliable evidence of this.[45] If anything, China's arms supplies to the Kingdom appear to have dwindled over the past decade. That is not to say Saudi decision-makers have not considered the possible usefulness of keeping their nuclear options open given regional uncertainties. But apart from the country's technological limitations the most likely conclusion to have been reached for the time being is that even the perception of such capacity being acquired from abroad would do more harm than good to the country's overall position. More recent, tangible and important were Chinese President Jiang Zemin's 1999 state visit to Saudi Arabia and the pronouncement of a 'strategic oil partnership' between the two countries; China's increasing importance both as an imports (5th-largest in 2003) and exports partner (4th) since then; the Saudi acquisition of a stake in a refinery in Fujian province and negotiations for a stake in a chemical factory in Quangzou and a refinery in Shandong; and the participation in

[45] Such sources generally make assertions that are either unsupported, rest on claims by opposition figures with a political agenda, or draw current conclusions from out-of-date evidence (such as the CSS-2 missile deal), in addition to speculating about future possibilities (e.g. Dan Blumenthal, 'Providing Arms: China and the Middle East', in *The Middle East Quarterly*, Vol. 12, no. 2 (Spring 2005), on www.meforum.org/article/695). See also NTA, 'China's missile exports and assistance to Saudi Arabia', on www.nti.org/db/china/msarpos.htm.

2004 of Sinopec in two major new gas exploration/development deals in the Rub' al-Khali.[46]

Even so, Saudi Arabia's arms imports since the 1980s illustrate well the pattern noted above. Military limitations on US arms supplies to Saudi Arabia, induced by the pro-Israeli lobby, led Riyadh to look elsewhere.[47] From the 1980s European arms suppliers (British and French in particular) challenged the pre-eminence of the United States, together easily outstripping it over the period 1979–94. The most striking European contract was the giant al-Yamamah deal, concluded in 1985 after five years of Saudi attempts to buy F-15 fighter-bombers were defeated by effective opposition from the pro-Israeli lobby in the United States: this would become the world's largest-ever oil-for-arms deal, and shifted the structure of the Saudi air force from dependence on the United States towards Britain.[48]

Western Europe (and Britain in particular) remains a very important source for Saudi defence imports, even if the first decade of the twenty-first century may well see a reassertion of the United States' pre-eminent position. Since the 1991 Gulf War Washington has been able to waive previous objections from Congress, becoming once again a much more formidable competitor, and capturing twice the share of European suppliers in the new orders placed in

[46] As a partner in a consortium with Lukoil and ChevronTexaco for bloc A (together 80 per cent), and as lead partner in a consortium with ChevronTexaco (also 80 per cent) in bloc B. See Economist Intelligence Unit, *Country Profile: Saudi Arabia*, 2004–5, pp. 47–50.

[47] The instances over several years of Saudi requests for arms being blocked as a result of pressure from Israel and/or the Jewish lobby, are detailed in Cordesman, *Saudi Arabia: Guarding the Desert Kingdom*, Boulder, CO: Westview Press, 1997, pp. 155–8; and Cordesman, *The Gulf and the West*, Boulder, CO: Westview Press, 1988, pp. 283–95, 361, 419.

[48] Originally estimated at £20 bn, the second phase signed in 1993 brought this to an estimated £35 bn. See Anthony Cordesman, *Saudi Arabia*, pp. 155–8; and Nawaf Obaid, *The Oil Kingdom at 100*, pp. 105–6. Of a total of over $73 bn-worth of arms supplied to Saudi Arabia over the period 1979–94, the share of the United States can be estimated at up to $27 bn, the UK's at up to $22 bn, France's at $12 bn, and other European suppliers' at up to $4 bn (based on Arms Control and Disarmament Agency, *World Military Expenditures and Arms Transfers*, issues for 1985–95, Washington, DC: Government Printing Office, 1985–96; and Richard Grimmet, *Conventional Arms Transfers to Developing Nations*, various issues, Washington, DC: Congressional Research Service, 1987–2000. Compare B. Korany, 'Defending the Faith amid Change', p. 337).

the four years after the invasion of Kuwait. Nevertheless, in 1995–9 equilibrium was restored.[49] It is possible that with the dwindling of Britain's military projection capability relative to the United States, the latter will henceforth retain the upper hand. At the same time, however, the concerns over the de-legitimising effect of overly visible security dependence on the United States may have a mitigating effect.[50]

However prominent the United States, then, the Saudi leadership still values the benefits of 'multi-dependence' in maintaining its relative autonomy. This was also illustrated in the 2003 decision to conclude the country's first deals opening up the gas sector to foreign companies, with European firms alone (Royal Dutch/Shell and Total)—followed by further contracts in 2004 with Russian, Chinese, Spanish and Italian firms—leaving the United States strikingly absent.[51] At the same time the strain in relations with the United States formed the backdrop for a Saudi diplomatic offensive to reinvigorate ties with Europe.[52]

Saudi Arabia's regional policy has been marked throughout by the pursuit of *raison d'état*, 'omnibalancing' between the various threats the regime has perceived, trying to forge or maintain consensus in the region even to the extent of a willingness to cooperate with the

[49] Of the $22 bn in new orders which Saudi Arabia placed in 1991–4, the United States captured some $16 bn and Europe $7 bn. In 1995–9, both won some $17 bn in new orders. Based on Arms Control and Disarmament Agency, *World Military Expenditures and Arms Transfers*; and Richard Grimmet, *Conventional Arms Transfers to Developing Nations.*

[50] As one further illustration, it may be worth noting that the head of Russia's main arms export agency was quoted by ITAR-TASS in February 2005 as saying that Russia's first major arms contract with Saudi Arabia was being prepared. (ITAR-TASS dispatch, 10 February 2005).

[51] This followed a breakdown of negotiations with US firms earlier in 2003. The fact that no US firms at all were involved in this initial opening of the Saudi gas sector to foreign investment, was widely remarked upon, and raised some hackles in the United States—even if it was thought likely that US firms would at some later point get another chance. See also Gawdat Bahgat, 'Foreign Investment in Saudi Arabia's Energy Sector', *Middle East Economic Survey*, 23 August 2004 (also available on http://www.mees.com/postedarticles/oped/a47n34d01.htm).

[52] Discussions with EU and Gulf diplomats and observers in Doha, Dubai, Muscat, Brussels, January–May 2003. An EU-Saudi agreement was also reached in 2003 on the Kingdom's accession to the WTO.

Arab 'radicals' (especially once the latter's radicalism was waning, from the mid-1970s), using its wealth to smooth relations, and attempting to maintain reasonable relations even with revolutionary Iran, as an Islamic country (as well as a potential threat). Nevertheless, neither these consensus-seeking, conflict-avoiding instincts, nor the domestic decision-making factors referred to above, have meant that Saudi Arabia avoided more drastic policy choices in the few but momentous instances where the alternative appeared worse. Thus, after initial attempts to appease the young revolution in Iran, the conclusion that the Iranian regime had become a real threat to the region that would not be subdued by conciliatory gestures led the Saudi leadership to react assertively by extending strong support to Iraq in the war against Iran. Within the Gulf, this has been combined with a determination to achieve a power balance concerning Iraq and Iran, and to maintain a degree of hegemony on the Arabian peninsula. In the latter respect, the global environment has made itself felt in combination with the determination of the smaller GCC states to limit that very hegemony: for instance, since 2004 the United States has found one after another of these states willing partners for its invitation to establish far reaching bilateral free trade agreements, thus sabotaging the Saudi-led attempt to make the agreed GCC-wide customs union a reality (while continuing to block Saudi WTO accession). It was particularly galling for Riyadh that it was Bahrain, long a close (and subsidised) ally, that signed a deal first.[53]

In the Arab world more widely, a tentative leadership role has on occasion been adopted on selected issues, such as the Arab-Israeli dispute. This flows from a combination of the Saudi role conception and considerations of regime status and legitimacy, but also concerns for regional stability and for the defusion of the tension between Saudi economic and security links to the United States and the West on the one hand, and the perceived US role in the conflict on the other.[54]

[53] Saudi irritation was expressed not only in Crown Prince Abdullah's staying away from the December 2004 GCC summit in Bahrain, but apparently also by reducing the crucial Saudi oil subsidy to the country by one-third, from 150,000 b/d to 100,000 b/d (Economist Intelligence Unit, *Country Report Bahrain*, 4 March 2005).

[54] I would not, in other words, go as far as Kostiner, who argues in his chapter in this volume that the Saudi peace initiatives were largely a matter of posturing rather than substantial concern to help settle the conflict.

Policy, then, has been driven essentially by pragmatic considerations of political and economic advantage, even if other aspects of the Al Sa'ud's role conception have helped shape it. This is not to say there have not been issues where deep conviction (whether religious or political), matters of pride, or questions of inter-cultural communication have come very much to the fore. Examples would include the decision by King Faisal in 1973 to impose an oil embargo in response to Western support for Israel; the debate in the late 1990s over policy towards Iraq; or the friction with the United States over Palestine, and over what was seen as undue US criticism and pressure in 2002–3. Yet such issues usually become especially important when they link in with the key considerations listed above (for instance, when they are seen to impact on the legitimacy of the Saudi regime, or on the security of mutual economic interests). On their own, and away from those linkages, they tend not to reorient policy very significantly or for very long.[55]

In sum, the Al Sa'ud has managed its external relations adroitly. That is not to deny the continuing existence of difficult dilemmas which need at the very least to be contained if not solved. These difficulties have been largely inherent in Saudi Arabia's geographical position, the pressures and expectations associated with being a central member of the Muslim and Arab world, and its exposed, vulnerable wealth—in juxtaposition with the domestic requirements for regime legitimacy. Yet given these stresses, the success in coping with those inherent foreign policy limitations—demonstrated in the very fact that both state and regime continue after more than a century—is remarkable.

Some of the credit must clearly go to Abd al-Aziz and the way in which he wove state-building and foreign policy together. The process by which he welded the country into existence was not merely a feat of territorial conquest, but at least as much one of constructing a viable polity on political, ideological, traditional-tribal and personal foundations.

[55] For a good concise survey of the patterns of Saudi 'Arab' and 'Islamic' policies, see Gause, 'The Foreign Policy of Saudi Arabia'. On the 'Islamic' content of policy in particular see also the incisive analysis by Piscatori, 'Islamic Values and National Interest: the Foreign Policy of Saudi Arabia' in Adeed Dawisha (ed.), *Islam in Foreign Policy*, London: Cambridge University Press, 1983, pp. 33–53.

> [The] growing domestic strength [under Abdul-Aziz] is part of the *explanation* for the success in managing relations with the outside world. At the same time, however, it was also in part the *result* of this foreign policy success. On the one hand, Abdul-Aziz *needed* to handle his external relations carefully in order to secure the success of this new state-building exercise. On the other hand, part of the reason why he was *able* increasingly to extract the necessary assistance and/or tolerance from the external powers he was dealing with, was that those powers recognised that he, and the fledgling Saudi state, were indeed growing into a local power to be reckoned with. In other words, domestic success at state building increased his bargaining power with actors such as Great Britain, while the successful management of relations with those powers at the same time helped the state-building exercise succeed and thereby helped secure the rule of the Al Saud. It is only from this already more secure basis that the arrival of the oil age would bring additional internal resources and more extensive external interest, both of which would again be harnessed by King Abdul-Aziz and his successors to the project of consolidating the state and the rule of the Al Saud.[56]

By the time of Abd al-Aziz's death a measure of continuity had already been assured by the creation of a foreign ministry, and by the long apprenticeship of Prince Faisal at the head of the fledgling foreign policy apparatus.

Lessons from the Saudi case for the question of relative autonomy of 'small' states

The case of Saudi Arabia contradicts the assumption that 'small,' 'developing', or 'weak' states must lack autonomy.[57] The country's foreign relations exemplify this throughout its existence, following a pattern set by Abd al-Aziz from the start of his state-building project in 1902. With a pragmatic awareness of limitations and opportunities, it proved possible simultaneously to obtain great power pro-

[56] Nonneman, 'Saudi-European Relations, 1902–2001', p. 637.

[57] For an overview of the quantitative and case-study research done in this regard since the 1980s, see Jeanne Hey, 'Foreign Policy in Dependent States' in Laura Neack *et al.* (eds), *Foreign Policy Analysis: Continuity and Change in its Second Generation*, Englewood Cliffs, NJ: Prentice Hall, 1995, pp. 201–13. The empirical record shows 'there is no unidimensional relationship that expresses itself constantly over time. Instead, the association between [economic dependence and foreign policy behaviour] is complex and subject to influences at the individual, domestic and international levels of analysis.' (*Ibid.*, p. 212).

tection (and sources of technology, arms and other imports), and balance such dependence by keeping options, and channels towards alternative sources, open.

The sources of the ability to carve out such relative autonomy are both domestic and external. A more extensive elaboration of the argument can be found elsewhere, but for current purposes a summary may suffice:

> The external circumstances include limitations on, and competition between, great powers. … [T]hey also include the global scattering of great power interests, as opposed to local actors' ability and propensity to concentrate on their immediate region. … Moreover, some states' possession of a valued resource, whether in strategic position, in oil, in wealth, or otherwise, may afford it some leverage with greater powers. By contrast, the very insignificance of a state may mean that it does not [attract] the level of external powers' attention and resources needed to constrain its autonomy. Indeed, the question of the relative power and influence of 'developed' and 'developing' states needs to be considered not in overall absolute terms, but by considering what, for the supposedly weaker party, is most relevant in terms of its foreign policy aims. For most developing states, this is unlikely to be the battle with the great powers. …. Rather, they are likely to direct their attention and energy towards the regional arena …. [where] there are many dynamics over which outside powers have little or no control. …. [This] international-level constellation of factors …. provides the fluctuating room for maneuver within which the pragmatic multi-level balancing game becomes possible. The long-term foreign policy patterns of *managed multi-dependence* and pragmatism which …. can be observed …. are a crucial part of this.[58]

Indeed, the pragmatism displayed by the Al Sa'ud in playing off outside powers against each other and avoiding 'mono-dependence' is necessary to take advantage of this constellation of factors. Yet this in turn will at times require a degree of regime autonomy from *domestic* and *regional* ideological pressures or constraints—an autonomy that 'can be acquired through the judicious use of resources available from outside powers and at home'. This can involve a positive feedback loop: 'On the one hand, …. a key domestic resource in this game is domestic legitimacy; the further advanced

[58] Gerd Nonneman, 'Analyzing the Foreign Policies of the Middle East and North Africa: a Conceptual Framework' in Nonneman (ed.), *Analyzing Middle East Foreign Policies*, pp. 6–18: at pp. 15–16.

the level of state formation, the easier it will be to transcend regional [ideational] constraints. On the other, successful deployment of the omni-balancing strategy may ultimately help the process of state formation and increase regime legitimacy.'[59]

Like the other conservative Gulf states, then, Saudi Arabia is an *'omni-balancer'*, balancing between threats and resources within and between the domestic, regional and global levels simultaneously. This explains the more reserved Saudi position vis-à-vis the military role of the United States in the Kingdom and the region, and vis-à-vis the Bush administration's new global and regional policy positions that emerged around the beginning of 2002. Coincidentally, trans-Atlantic differences, both in the analysis of Middle Eastern politics and over the best way to respond to regional developments, fit in well with the policy preference of *managed multidependence* that states such as Saudi Arabia have shown. While the particular situation in evidence since early 2002, with its modest 'polygamous' tendencies on the part of the Saudi leadership, appears at first sight a shift away from 'business as usual', and a result of 11 September 2001, it is in fact merely one more application of the pattern that has been established for more than a century.

[59] *Ibid.*, p. 16.

COPING WITH REGIONAL CHALLENGES: A CASE STUDY OF CROWN PRINCE ABDULLAH'S PEACE INITIATIVE

Joseph Kostiner

Among the more striking developments in Saudi Arabia's policy in the Middle East in the wake of 9/11 was Crown Prince Abdullah's peace initiative in the Arab-Israeli conflict, announced in February 2002. A most noteworthy feature of this was its detachment from the specific actors and events in the Palestinian-Israeli theatre itself. Thus the initiative was announced without coordination with the Israeli or the Palestinian parties and without immediate reference to the escalating low-intensity warfare that was spreading in Israel and the occupied territories. The Saudi initiative was in fact addressing other issues, which directly challenged the security of the Saudi Kingdom. Indeed, the Saudis chose to come up with a peace initiative in the Arab-Israeli arena in order to respond to challenges that arose in their more immediate spheres of activity.

The most acute challenge emanated from the sphere of Saudi relations with the United States. This relationship, which had been based on the stable flow Saudi oil to the West, and on the US role as a supreme strategic defender of the Kingdom, deteriorated in the months preceding Abdullah's Initiative. The events of September 11, 2001 were definitely a turning point in Saudi–US relations. Although paramount officials and spokesmen of the Bush administration did not direct any major criticism against Riyadh, voices originating in the US Department of Defense found their way to the media and were highly critical of the Kingdom. Fifteen of the nineteen perpetrators of the 9/11 attacks, members of Al Qa'ida, were Saudi citizens. Their leader, Usama bin Ladin was born, raised and educated in Saudi Arabia and he had had Saudi citizenship, of which he was stripped in 1994 due to dissident activities. The US media carried numerous reports about thousands of Saudi youth who had become *Mujahidin*, or holy warriors in Afghanistan (and about smaller numbers in Chechnya and Bosnia), who were encouraged by Saudi clerics to act against any US interest. Many members of the Saudi younger generation bore anti-US opinions and were potential enemies of the United States.[1] Other US media articles claimed that the Saudi state's official religious doctrine was 'Wahhabism' which espoused fanatic-fundamentalist ideas, among which the Americans featured as the leaders of the infidel world. The Saudi regime itself, it was argued, was therefore a bastion of anti-US propaganda, cultivated by the official Wahhabi school system. Moreover, the official Saudi system also encouraged the channelling of financial charity to Islamic foundations active in Western as well as in other Arab and African states. Some Western reports claimed these foundations were actually used to finance terrorist activities in these states, including the preparation of the 9/11 attacks. Saudi authorities, it was alleged, were hoping to pacify the radical elements among their inhabitants and therefore connived at the contacts between Saudi financiers and terrorist movements.[2]

From a Saudi viewpoint, the growing tension in its relations with the United States brought several potential damages. One was the problem of a compounded negative image in US public opinion. The country, its leaders and its religious educational and financial systems were portrayed as conducive to the growth of anti-US terrorism, hence the possibility emerged that Washington would view the Kingdom with hostility.[3] Second, US policy in the region might assume aspects that were damaging to Saudi security interests. Thus the US pursuit of terrorists in Afghanistan, Washington's intention

1 See for example, *Washington Post*, 11 November 2001; 11 February 2002; and 9 April 2002; Also see J. E. Peterson, *Saudi Arabia and the Illusion of Security*, Adelphi Paper 348, London: The International Institute of Strategic Studies, 2002, pp. 60–70.

2 *New York Times*, 17 February 2002; and *Washington Post*, 9 April 2002. For an authoritative alternative viewpoint, see F. Gregory Gause, 'Saudi Arabia Challenged', *Current History*, 103 (2004), pp. 21–7.

3 See the interview with Prince Al-Walid Bin Talal, *Middle East Insight*, January–February 2002.

to destroy Saddam Hussein's regime, and its support of Israel against the Palestinian *Intifada*, were viewed in Riyadh as dangerously inflaming the opinion of Muslims everywhere and thus also likely to drive its own population to become increasingly anti-US. US policies could also damage Saudi interests by demanding the use of Saudi facilities for an attack against Iraq. This, apart from adding fuel to the fire of domestic anger, could also curdle Saudi relations with Iran, Syria and Iraq itself, all of which opposed US military initiatives in the Gulf and strongly criticised any attempt by any Arab Gulf state to aid the United States in such ventures. Saudi leaders therefore sought to craft a policy that would restore cooperative relations with the United States.

The inter-Arab arena was another challenge. The pro-Western Arab governments, notably Egypt, Jordan and Morocco, were facing daily large-scale demonstrations launched in support of the Palestinian *Intifada*, which often turned into riots. While demonstrations were forbidden in Saudi Arabia, large segments of the Saudi population held similar opinions and were critical of their government's failure to assist the Palestinians more forcefully. Abdullah therefore sought an initiative that would demonstrate how useful his Kingdom could be for the Palestinians and thereby help the pro-Western states in the Middle-East.[4] Moreover, to avoid alienating the more radical Arab states, such as Syria, the Saudi initiative should also take into account Syria's interests, namely, the requirement that Israel should withdraw from all the land it had occupied (including territories claimed by Syria and Lebanon) in 1967 and embark on a comprehensive peace initiative that would include all the relevant parties in the region.[5]

Components of the Initiative

The eight-point proposal had three main components:

- A complete Israeli withdrawal from all the territories that had been occupied by Israel in 1967 including the Golan Heights, the Gaza Strip and the West Bank including East Jerusalem. In proposing this step the Saudi leaders sought to appeal to the Syrian

[4] See *al-Dustur* (Amman), 20 February 2001.
[5] *Al-Zaman* (London), 19 February 2002; *Monday Morning* (Beirut), April 2002.

and Palestinian parties (after Egypt and Jordan had already concluded peace treaties with Israel in 1979 and 1994 respectively, and had retrieved land from Israel), so as to establish a symmetry among all the Arab parties who were entitled, in Arab perception, to the return of territories from Israel.

- The initiative also required a complete withdrawal of Israeli forces from the areas in the occupied territories they had re-entered, in order to suppress the Palestinian uprising, in the months preceding the announcement of the Saudi initiative. This would enhance the independence and safety of the Palestinian Authority in the occupied territories and facilitate the emergence of a Palestinian state. Crown Prince Abdullah thereby wanted to allay the pro-Palestinian Saudi public opinion as well as the public voices coming from different Arab states, especially from the pro-Western ones. Abdullah was interested in turning Saudi Arabia into an instrument that would help to mend fences between the Arab street and the Arab governments and among the latter, around a popular and much-needed step to improve the position of the Palestinians.[6]
- The third main issue of the peace initiative included a '*quid pro quo*' to Israel and the United States: in return for withdrawal, peace and normalisation with Arab states were promised. This was the main card played toward Washington. The peace plan was thought out by Adil al-Jubair, a former diplomat in Washington and presently an adviser to Crown Prince Abdullah, who utilised his expertise in US politics. First publicised on 13 February 2002 by Thomas Friedman of the *New York Times*, the initiative was included in a personal interview with Crown Prince Abdullah. This step was aimed to give the initiative broad credibility. 'Normalisation' was the initiative's jewel: for Israel this meant peace in political terms as well as trade and business relations with all Arab states. In the Saudi perception this was a goal Israel had been seeking since the 1973 war, which would satisfy the Israeli consumer society's interests to purchase oil and find new markets. The United States should therefore wish to coax Israel to accept the initiative. Moreover, Saudi leaders also believed they could add to

[6] See Shibley Telhami's argument in *Peace Watch*, 372: 'Special Policy Forum Report on the Arab Israeli Peace Process', The Washington Institute for Near East Policy, 8 April 2002.

> the existing US peace initiatives for a cease-fire in the Intifada. The latter drew on ideas raised earlier by the US senator Mitchell and the CIA director Tenet, who had led earlier missions to that effect, but failed to force the Israeli and Palestinian parties to moderate their positions. The Saudi initiative was supposed to 'deliver' the broader Arab world as a driving force to peace, by harnessing an Arab majority that would turn peace into a regional all-embracing project.[7] Thereby the initiative would show the suspicious US public that the Saudis were seeking peace, and that it was up to Israel's government, led by its hard-line Likud Prime Minister Ariel Sharon, to prove their good will.[8]

The initiative received initial praise and encouragement from Arab quarters (notably Egypt and Jordan), the European Union and Washington. Crown Prince Abdullah therefore felt sufficiently encouraged to raise the plan in the forthcoming inter-Arab conference, in order to turn it into an all-Arab plan for peace. In preparing for the Beirut conference at the end of March 2002 several adjustments were made to the original plan. Under Syrian pressure, the Beirut resolutions stressed that Israel's withdrawal from the 1967 occupied territories should also include territories of South Lebanon (which according to the Lebanese and Syrian interpretation, Israel should have returned to Lebanon upon its with withdrawal from South Lebanon in 2000). Another matter (also raised under Syrian pressure), which had not appeared in Abdullah's original text, was the resolution of the Palestinian refugee problem, based on a consensus that would rest on UN Security Council Resolution 194. While the intention to reach a consensus amongst the parties was supposed to make room for an open discussion that would include the Israeli viewpoint, the actual 194 Resolution focused on the right of Palestinian refugees to resettle in the homes they had left in 1948–9, which was a non-starter for Israel.

The second accommodation stressed that future negotiations would be among the parties directly concerned (Syria, the Palestinians and Israel), and thereby prevent Washington from playing the role of the main adjudicator, dictating the Arabs their positions. Thus, while

7 *New York Times*, 24 March 2002; *al-Nahar* (Beirut), 29 March 2002.

8 See Henry Siegman, 'Will Israel Take a Chance?', *New York Times*, 21 February 2002.

Saudi Arabia had to endorse certain positions excluded from Abdullah's original peace initiative, it managed to turn the main principles of the initiative, i.e. Israeli withdrawal from the territories occupied in 1967, in return for Arab states' acceptance of 'normal relations' (a different term, instead of 'normalisation' with Israel) into principles accepted by all Arab states. Saudi Arabia thereby emerged as the key player in this inter-Arab initiative.[9]

Abdullah entered another process of mediation, by helping improve relations, at least on the surface of it, between Iraq and Kuwait. During the Beirut Conference Abdullah persuaded Iraqi Vice-President Izzat Ibrahim to state that Iraq would honour 'Kuwait's sovereignty and territorial integrity', meaning that Iraq would not again invade Kuwait. Kuwait was ready to view this declaration as a step of reconciliation and announced it would not demand any additional and special guarantees to prevent an Iraqi invasion. The collective security pact of the Arab League that was based on mutual non-aggression would be a sufficient guarantee. Thus under the presumption of a peace initiative, the Saudis managed to improve somewhat the relations between Iraq and its main adversaries, and in so doing, helped Iraq re-enter Arab ranks. An appeased Iraq meant a more stable Gulf region, which surely helped Saudi security. This move was sealed with a televised hug between Abdullah and Izzat Ibrahim. The purpose of this initiative may have been more far-reaching. Since a pacified Iraq, which had undertaken to abstain from attacking its neighbour, should be regarded as cooperative and peaceful, Washington might avoid attacking Iraq. Such a step would be welcomed by most Arab states and by the European Union. It would surely reward Riyadh with prestige and appreciation.

The Rationale Behind the Initiative

Saudi spokesmen often pointed out that US–Saudi relations, while resting on a sound exchange of economic and strategic interests, are nevertheless differentiated by some major disagreements. These revolve around the United States' firm (and in Saudi eyes over-extended)

[9] *Al-Usbu' al-'Arabi* (Beirut), 1 April 2002; www.aljazeera.net/cases-analyses, 4 April 2002.

support of Israel, and around the Saudi promotion of Islamic causes,[10] which had led both the Saudi government and individuals to support the Taliban regime in Afghanistan, to improve relations with Iran (notably after 1997 when Muhammad Khatami had become president in Iran), and finance mosques, Islamic charities and movements, to Washington's obvious dismay.

These disagreements in fact attest to a deeply-rooted sense of limitation, which the Saudis attribute to US policies in the region. From a Saudi viewpoint, the US defence proved effective only in the supreme strategic sphere against an actual attack of Iraqi or Iranian forces against Saudi Arabia (or another smaller Gulf state), against the use of ballistic missiles as part of such an attack, and as the Kingdom's main source of heavy arms purchases. However, the United States proved unable to act as a defender against terrorism: indeed the attacks on US army personnel compounds in November 1995 and in June 1996 demonstrated that the US military bases became a liability, as targets for terrorists attacks (a conclusion that became more evident during the terrorist wave that beset Saudi Arabia in 2003–4). The challenges of an internal uprising, or mutiny, if at all likely, would have probably been fashioned in an anti-US mode and atmosphere, which would have captured the Saudi public. Reliance on US forces to quell an internal Saudi uprising was therefore not a valid option for Saudi leaders. Another challenge, often directed at Riyadh, came in the form of sharp de-legitimising criticism—portraying the Kingdom as a corrupt regime, in breach of its Islamic and Arab commitments and subservient to the United States—which Iraq and Iran (before the thaw between the two states) sometimes voiced. The danger of such criticism was the emergence of a broadly-based campaign, which would relentlessly smear Saudi Arabia in the Arab media and erode its position in the region. Washington was viewed in such criticism as the usurper of the Arab world and Islam. The United States clearly could not usefully help the regime in its defence against such criticism.

Saudi leaders' calculations focused on establishing an additional source of defence for their Kingdom: reliance on Arab states and

[10] See for example an interview with a Saudi member of the advisory (*shura*) council, Uthman al-Rawwaf, *al-Sharq al-Awsat* (London), 15 January 2002; see also *Washington Post*, 11 February 2002.

parties, sometimes engaging in direct cooperation with Arab radical parties. Thus in March 1979, against the backdrop of the signing of the Egyptian-Israeli peace treaty, Riyadh joined the Arab initiative ('the Baghdad decisions') to boycott Egypt and reject the peace process. The partnership with at least some Arab parties helped block the criticism against the Kingdom from other regional forces. To put it simply, reliance on cooperation with Arab states was a strategy that could add the portion of legitimacy, coined in Arab and Islamic terms, that the Kingdom lacked due to its contacts with the United States. In Saudi eyes, playing the 'Arab card', in the Palestinian, Iraqi or Islamic contexts, was a means to prove that Riyadh was loyal to Arab and Islamic causes and not worthy of being a target of either terrorism or criticism. Saudi Arabia continuously sought contacts with states such as Syria and Egypt, which enjoyed credibility in the Arab world as true Arab nationalist and historical-cultural centres, to provide political legitimacy to Saudi policies.[11] They also tried, notably since 1997, to mend fences with Iran in order to stabilise the Gulf basin and prevent Tehran from launching insurgency operations against the Kingdom.

However, the Saudi leaders did not seek to abandon US protection: Washington's commitment and military abilities were demonstrated during the 're-flagging' campaign in 1987–9, when the United States and other European fleets successfully defended Gulf states' oil tankers; in 1990–1, by restoring Kuwait's liberation from Iraqi occupation; and thereafter in the 1990s by implementing the 'dual containment' of both Iraq and Iran, limiting their ability to threaten Saudi Arabia. The optimal arrangement, from a Saudi viewpoint, was to integrate the two policies, namely, reliance on US protection and cooperation with the Arab states, into one embracing strategy. Saudi Arabia regarded itself the central leaning post for these two policies, the only regional actor who could exercise both policies in an integrated and balanced manner, so the policies would complement

[11] *Al-Safir* (Beirut), 28 February 2002. The analysis of the limitations of US credibility and other security options in the Gulf derives from several writings, in particular Michael Collins Dunn, 'Five Years After Desert Storm: Gulf Security, Stability and the US Presence', *Middle East Policy*, IV, 3 (March 1996), pp. 30–8; Rolin G. Mainuddin, Joseph R. Archer Jr and Jeoffery M. Elliot, 'From Alliance to Collective Security: Rethinking the GCC', *Ibid.*, pp. 39–49; Alon Ben-Meir, 'The Dual Containment Strategy Is No Longer Viable', *Ibid.*, pp. 50–72.

rather than conflict with each other. Thus this position was meant to place the Kingdom as a supreme coordinator, or mediator in the Middle East.

Saudi leaders had attempted to obtain such a supreme-mediator's position before, in spring 1977, when they had sought to coordinate a broadly-based inter-Arab policy to advance an Arab-Israeli peace accord, by enlisting Egypt and Syria and striving to obtain Washington's support. This initiative was overtaken by the Begin-Sadat agreement. Again in 1982 the Saudis tried to link the principles embodied in the Arab League Fez Conference's resolutions (based on the 'Fahd Plan' for peace of August 1981) to the 'Reagan Initiative' for a settlement of the Palestinian issue,[12] which did not materialise either. The Saudi drive to position their Kingdom to gain benefit from both US and broad Arab support was again manifested during the Kuwait-Iraq war in 1990–1. Saudi Arabia led a coalition against Iraq consisting of US and other Western forces, in alignment with Egyptian and Syrian forces. The US forces were supposed to provide Saudi Arabia the military edge, while the Arab coalition members were supposed to guarantee the legitimacy, in Arab and Islamic eyes, for the readiness to wage a war against Iraq. Clearly Riyadh was repeatedly seeking to establish itself, in the eyes of other players in the region, as the coordinator of US-Arab policies, resting its security on both fundamentals.

Yet the calculations of the Saudi leaders did not rely on this coordination of strategies necessarily becoming an effective and successful reality. Merely the *posture* sufficed, giving them credit for playing the mediating role, and gaining them the trust of the parties who were coordinated. It therefore elevated the Saudi regional position thereby helping to improve the country's security.

However, there were occasions when the Saudi leaders could not uphold the optimal position of coordinating, or resting on, both US and Arab strategies, and were forced to cooperate with Arab parties against US interests. Thus after the signing of the 1979 Camp David accords Riyadh joined the more radical Arab states ostracising Egypt. In the 1990s Saudi leaders chose to mend fences with Iran while the

[12] David E. Long, 'Saudi Foreign Policy and the Arab-Israeli Peace Process: The Fahd (Arab) Peace Plan' in W. A. Beling (ed.), *Middle East Peace Plans*, London: Croom Helm, 1986.

United States upheld the policy of 'dual containment', which espoused political isolation and pressure on Tehran to abandon its revolutionary policies. In 2000 they chose to aid the Palestinian al-Aqsa Intifada financially and permit, on a continuous basis, financial assistance from the Kingdom to reach the activities of Hamas.[13] This policy too was exercised to Washington's obvious displeasure.

However, even when Saudi Arabia did not act as supreme coordinator, strategically linking Arab and US policies, its leaders tried to exercise mediation policies at a lower level, among Arab states, by bridging their disputes. They initiated the Ta'if agreement of 1989 that legitimised, in Arab eyes, Syrian intervention in Lebanon, and engineered the consent of the various Lebanese factions to accept that reality. In late July 1990, prior to the Iraqi invasion of Kuwait, the Saudis hosted a mediation meeting in Jeddah between the two countries, albeit to no avail.[14] The Arab League summit in 2000 was also the outcome of a Saudi initiative, to coordinate the Arab states in a uniform pro-Palestinian direction.[15] All these instances indicate that Saudi leaders view the inter-Arab arena as their mediating ground. There they can demonstrate to all parties their special skills and irreplacability as a regional pacifier and policy coordinator, their friendship, and their solidarity with all Arab causes, thereby obtaining 'immunity' from all Arab corners. As they exercised their mediation with financial assistance offered to one or both parties in dispute, the image of a 'donor-mediator' (to use Abdul-Reda Assiri's phrase[16]) was meant to add to the Kingdom's prestige and bestow on it the unique and essential role of an effective and benevolent mediator.[17] Moreover, assuming the role of a supreme mediator by linking US and Arab strategies was a major step upwards, placing Saudi mediation in a global context.

13 *Mideast Mirror*, 23 October 2000.

14 Bruce Maddy-Weizman and Joseph Kostiner, 'From Jidda to Cairo: The Failure of Arab Mediations in the Gulf Crisis', *Diplomacy and Statecraft*, 7 (1996), pp. 466–92.

15 *Mideast Mirror*, 23 October 2000.

16 Abdul-Reda Assiri, *Kuwait's Foreign Policy: City-State in World Politics*, Boulder, CO: Westview Press, 1990, chapters 3, 4, 5 and the conclusion.

17 On roles and patterns in inter-Arab relations, see Michael N. Barnett, *Dialogues in Arab Politics*, New York: Columbia University Press, 1998.

Hence, the value of acting as a regional mediator was evident. By utilising its obvious advantages (not least financial) and compensating for its relative weaknesses, Saudi Arabia could acquire an influential role in regional and international contexts. Although they lacked the military or Arab nationalist pedigree of states such as Egypt and Syria, the Saudis were content with a secondary, consensus-building or regional pacifying role.

However, playing the role of a regional mediator means accepting some anomalies in Saudi Arabia's performance. One such anomaly concerns the need to balance its own initiatives to suit a broad inter-Arab denominator. Thus to craft the inter-Arab agreement of the Beirut conference in 2001, Riyadh was ready to compromise its original peace plan by incorporating Syria's caveats, mainly about UNSC resolution 194 concerning the Palestinian refugees' right of return. In Israeli eyes these changes turned the Saudi initiative into a useless tool.[18]

A second anomaly concerns the scope of the actual mediation activity. The Saudi leaders view their role in terms of a posture. They do not necessarily strive to engage in the actual process of mediation and activate strategies therein. In the case of Abdullah's initiative, Saudi leaders sought to attract the attention of the United States, Syria and Egypt, Iraq and Iran, but avoid direct negotiations with the Palestinians and Israel. This left Saudi Arabia as an initiator of the process, without involvement in its later intricate procession.

This argument differs from Gawdat Bahgat's view that Saudi Arabia considered the Arab-Israeli arena a major concern directly affecting its security.[19] Palestinian grievances certainly stirred-up internal public opinion in the Kingdom against what could be regarded as the two passive roles the Kingdom (and other states) played in favour of the Palestinians. And the Saudis also feared the ripples of radicalism which the Palestinian problem occasionally kindled in other Arab capitals. However, Palestinian-Israeli problems did not belong to its sphere of immediate security. Moreover, it was not an arena in

[18] See the analysis of a former Israeli Ambassador to the United States and an expert on Syrian affairs, Itamar Rabinovich, in *Ha'aretz*, 7 April 2002; also *al-Safir*, 28 February 2002.

[19] Gawdat Bahgat, 'The New Middle East: The Gulf Monarchies and Israel', *Journal of Social Political and Economic Studies*, 28 (2003).

which the Saudi leaders sought to interfere directly. Other than the very general destination of 'achieving peace' in this arena, the Kingdom did not develop a practical strategic agenda for the Arab-Israeli sphere. It exploited mediation as a means to improve Saudi standing with Washington, the main Arab parties and Iran, rather than to pacify the Israeli-Palestinian dispute for its own sake.

The Impact of Abdullah's Initiative on Saudi Arabia's International Standing

Relations with the United States

As mentioned earlier, Abdullah's initiative was aimed mainly at improving Saudi relations with the United States. Certainly there were already several overriding interests which bonded the two states and guaranteed the continuity of cooperative relations between them: Primarily the consistent flow of oil to the West, and the provision of weapons and security guarantees for Saudi Arabia. The initial effect of the Beirut resolutions seemed to improve the US attitude towards the Kingdom, and weakened the offending image of the Saudi link to perpetrators of the 9/11 attacks. Thus in late April Crown Prince Abdullah visited President Bush at the latter's ranch in Crawford, Texas. At this summit the two leaders made some moves towards implementing the Beirut resolution, and agreed to start an orchestrated effort to bring peace to Arab-Israeli relations. The summit was widely televised and reported, portraying Saudi Arabia as a catalyst for peace rather than an instigator of terrorism.[20] This impression was strengthened in June 2002 when President Bush declared his support for the establishment of a Palestinian state. The Saudi initiative became a fundamental component in the launching of the 'Road Map', which then became the accepted peace plan for the Middle East, with the United States, Russia, the European Union and the United Nations the partnership behind it. In August 2002 the Saudi Ambassador to Washington, Prince Bandar ibn Sultan, sealed the process with a visit of his own to President Bush's ranch.

Nevertheless, the Saudi initiative had its shortcomings. Strategically the United States was developing a new policy concerning

[20] *New York Times*, 28 April 2002 and 7 May 2002.

the Middle East, focusing on a pursuit of terrorism and on fighting parties which, to Washington's eyes, were members of the pro-terrorist 'Axis of Evil', notably Iraq and Iran. As a consequence the pacification of the Palestinian-Israeli dispute was relegated to secondary place. Although Washington welcomed the Saudi plan as an initiative to help quieten the conflict, it did not become a priority. This became more evident in the ensuing months. In January 2004, in his 'State of the Union' address, President Bush did not even mention Palestine, to the Saudis' (and other Arabs') dismay.[21] Washington was more interested in the wider regional picture: the elimination of hostile regimes, linked, in US eyes, to terrorism; the encouragement of pro-Western and democratic values in Middle Eastern states; and the suppression of terrorist groups in the region.[22] In this context, Saudi Arabia's entire strategy lost its supremacy. In 2004 President Bush announced the Greater Middle East Initiative (GMEI), aimed at fostering democracy in the Middle East. This had a direct abrasive effect on Saudi Arabia, which came under pressure to change its school curriculum and to adopt democratic values, notably elections, and the right to openly criticise the regime. The Saudis regarded this an unwanted intervention of Western influence in its internal affairs. They rejected succumbing to any external pressure.

Moreover, Saudi leaders could hardly be comfortable with the trends in US public opinion. Although the Bush administration itself—several of whom had established business and personal links with the Kingdom—maintained a friendly position toward Riyadh, other quarters were less sympathetic. In July 2002 a research fellow of the Rand Corporation, Laurent Murawiec, argued to the Defense Policy Board that Saudi Arabia was an 'enemy' of the United States, which deserved a strong American reaction.[23] His supporters included a number of important neo-conservative officials in the Department of Defense.

Summer 2002 also marked the publication of the Congressional report on the events of 11 September 2001, of which, on the administration's orders, twenty-eight pages were kept secret to protect Saudi Arabia from public suspicion of indirect financing of the attackers. Moreover, some of the 9/11 victims' relatives contemplated law-

[21] Economist Intelligence Unit, *Viewswire*, 30 January 2004.

[22] *New York Times*, 28 April 2002; *Ha'aretz*, 22 May 2002.

[23] *Washington Post*, 6 August 2002.

suits against the Saudi Minister of Defense, Prince Sultan, and other top Saudi functionaries, for aiding the perpetrators.[24]

Furthermore, signs of anti-Americanism were widely evident in the Kingdom and reported in the United States. There was even evidence that the Saudi high-school curriculum carried anti-Western messages, and that some of the Saudi popular clerics (Ali al-Khudair, Humud al-Shu'aibi) issued religious opinions (*fatwa*) encouraging anti-US violence. There was also the continued channelling of funds to Islamic religious causes, which at times found their way to terrorist groups. While the Saudi authorities announced in 2003 that they had closed down the main Islamic aid foundation (the Haramain Foundation), which allegedly aided terrorist activities abroad, Saudi money was still flowing to Hamas, and volunteers were found in Iraq and Chechnya.[25]

It can be argued that the Saudi leaders themselves were not sure how far they should improve relations with the United States, and what price they should pay for this. Although they were ready to play their role as peace makers in the Palestinian-Israeli conflict and reap the fruit of improving relations with Washington, given the context of the US's new anti-terrorist policy in the Middle East, Saudi leaders could not ignore that there was a genuine anti-US trend in the Kingdom among certain clerics and their following. Having had to crack down on terrorist activities that had spread in the Kingdom between May 2003 and June 2004 (see the chapter by Meijer), Saudi leaders did find a common interest with the United States.[26] The Saudi leadership also tacitly allowed US forces to make use of some of the Kingdom's air and ground facilities in the American-led coalition attack on Iraq in April 2003—albeit under strict limitations. However, while suppressing the terrorists, Saudi leaders also tried to establish a rapprochement with some of the radical groups. In doing so they also had to take account of public opinion,

[24] *Gulf States Newsletter*, 693, September 2002.

[25] *National Interest*, summer 2004; *Gulf States Newsletter*, 730, 19 March 2004.

[26] Gawdat Bahgat, 'Saudi Arabia and the War on Terrorism', *Arab Studies Quarterly*, 26 (2004) pp. 51–63; Martin Sieff, 'Sand in Our Eyes: US–Saudi Relations After Iraq', *National Interest*, summer 2004, pp. 93–100; see also the analysis of Gregory Gause, 'Be Careful What You Wish For: The Future of US–Saudi Relations', *World Policy Journal*, 19, 1 (2002), pp. 37–50.

by allowing criticism of US policies on Iraq, the Palestinian issue and the pressures put on Saudi Arabia 'to democratise'. Hence, they responded by tolerating the preaching of extremist, anti-US clerics, something that Washington found problematic. Thus to pre-empt the indigenous criticism of the US military presence in the Kingdom, Washington in August 2003 moved its military headquarters from Dhahran to Qatar. By mutual agreement this was considered the best way to resolve the problem of the American presence in the Kingdom. However, it also reflected the tensions and difficulties affecting US–Saudi relations.[27] In sum, therefore, the policy of mediation was only partially effective in obtaining the Saudi leadership the results they aimed for in Washington.

The Arab-Israeli and inter-Arab arenas

Soon after the declaration of the Beirut summit resolutions, it became evident that the Saudis—and for that matter other Arab parties—did not have a clear strategy for how to advance the peace initiative. Prince Abdullah's summit with president Bush at Crawford in Texas was supposed to produce a division of labour: the United States would put pressure on Israel to make territorial concessions and Saudi Arabia would 'deliver' the Palestinians and other Arab parties. Yet under the new anti-terrorist US policy, Washington hardly put any pressure on Israel, whose 'anti-terrorist' activities were understood and appreciated in the US capital. Moreover, there was hardly any planning on how to coordinate policies among the Arab states themselves. Egypt, apparently, undertook to mediate between Hamas and the Palestinian Authority, in order to establish cooperation between them, which was supposed to lead the entire Palestinian side to accept the ceasefire and a truce with Israel.

Typically, the Saudis did not assign themselves the role of direct negotiator with the Palestinians, let alone Israel, and even denied rumours that the Saudi authorities were involved in tacit negotiations for that purpose. At most, their officials planned to meet Egyptian counterparts for debriefing and reports.[28] Thus, while Crown

[27] Economist Intelligence Unit, *Saudi Arabia: Country Report*, May and August 2003, February 2004; see also *Gulf States Newsletter*, 2 May 2003; 25 July 2003.

[28] *Middle East International*, 16 May 2003 and 5 November 2003; *Gulf States Newsletter*, 709, 2 May 2003.

Prince Abdullah took the credit for the initiative, the Saudis had neither the authority nor the experience required to influence the Palestinians and in effect left the nitty-gritty to the Egyptians. To be sure, most Arab states, notably the pro-Western ones like Egypt and Jordan, viewed Abdullah's initiative as a means to demonstrate that they had a way to offer the Palestinians (and the masses who demonstrated in their favour all over the Arab World) a diplomatic outlet for a settlement. However, the Saudis' aloof position, of mediator disconnected from the theatre, was viewed critically among the Palestinians themselves. Indeed, the Palestinian media stressed the initiative was only a means to silence US criticism of the Saudi Kingdom. Palestinians also emphasised that the initiative did not establish a practical apparatus to carry out its decisions, expressing the fear that it would become a long, protracted process that would allow Israel to avoid carrying out its commitments.[29] Furthermore, Hamas spokesmen denied rumours that the Saudi authorities were involved in secret negotiations with their leaders to achieve a ceasefire with Israel.[30]

In any case, the positions of the Palestinian Authority and Hamas remained uncoordinated. As Palestinian violence against Israel did not subside and as Israel did not withdraw from the main Palestinian cities it had re-taken during the Intifada, the 'peace process' was a non-starter. However, Saudi Arabia did not conclude from these events that there was any need to change its tactics and involve itself more directly in the negotiations. Its leaders rather sought to resume their former 'from-a-distance' tactics. In July 2003 Abdullah visited a number of Arab states, notably Syria, to 'reactivate' his initiative, stating the need for a Palestinian state. In the wake of the US-led intervention in Iraq, and the possibility of a US attack on Syria, the foreign ministers of the Arab states followed suit, visiting Syria and discussing a 'joint Arab action', including Iran, on the questions of Iraq, Syria and the Palestinian-Israeli peace initiative. In early August the Palestinian leader Mahmud Abbas (Abu Mazen) visited Saudi Arabia to update the Saudis on the state of negotiations with Israel.[31]

However, none of this carried the Saudis very far beyond declarations. Saudi leaders, notably Crown Prince Abdullah himself, were

[29] *Al-Quds* (Jerusalem), 4 December 2003.
[30] *Middle East*, April 2002.
[31] Radio Kuwait, 30 July 2003; *Middle East News Agency* (Cairo), 1 August (via Foreign Broadcasting Information Service, 1 August 2003).

certainly concerned about the viability of their initiative, but did not try to transform it into an active platform in which they would be directly involved. A case in point was the summit in early June 2003 when Arab leaders met President Bush at the Egyptian resort of Sharm al-Shaikh. Despite the resemblance of the final Sharm al-Shaikh resolutions to Abdullah's initiative, he objected to a paragraph saying that the participants agree to normalise relations with Israel as part of the introduction of 'confidence-building measures' between the Palestinians and Israelis. The Saudis prevailed and the paragraph was excluded from the final communiqué. Ostensibly, this was an active Saudi involvement in the Arab-Israeli arena. However, the Saudi intervention concerned only inter-Arab relations, rather than Arab-Israeli affairs. The Saudis explained that according to the Beirut resolutions, 'full normalisation' with Israel was due only after the end of Israeli occupation and not as an intermediary stage in the process. It should therefore be delayed. The Saudi Crown Prince preferred to maintain the widely accepted Beirut resolutions, which represented the manifestation of a successfully achieved Saudi mediation, rather than to seek implementation of these resolutions as a practical and immediate means of encouraging peace.[32] The risk of losing broad Arab support and of curdling Saudi Arabia's relations with states such as Syria and Iran, which would reject the proposed Sharm al-Shaikh resolutions, was most undesirable to Riyadh.

Abdullah, it would seem, preferred to keep the plan as an inter-Arab initiative, a cause for Arab summits, for declarations of joint Arab action (in linking the issues of Iraq, Syria and Palestine). The Saudis were able once again to array most Arab states behind their initiative and thereby obtained the legitimacy and security offered by the mediating posture. However, they remained largely disconnected from the Palestinian-Israeli arena, leaving the action to Egypt and to the Palestinians themselves. The latter were sufficiently attentive to grasp and criticise this aloofness.

The Gulf

Saudi Arabia's relations with other Gulf states in the period under discussion remained pretty much the same. In this respect, Abdullah's initiative contributed to maintaining the *status quo*.

[32] Economist Intelligence Unit, *Country Report: Saudi Arabia*, August 2003, p. 21.

Saudi leaders can be satisfied that the other members of the Arab Gulf states—Kuwait, Bahrain, Qatar, the United Arab Emirates (UAE) and Oman, incorporated within the Gulf Cooperation Council (GCC)—stood behind Saudi Arabia in supporting the initiative. This in itself was a reassertion of Riyadh's ability to coordinate the policies of the other Gulf states. The Saudi ambition to gain hegemony over the GCC has been opposed by the smaller states: the UAE, which lost its partial authority over the Abu Musa island in the Gulf to an Iranian forceful takeover in 1992, have ever since resisted the Saudi rapprochement with Iran; Oman too had intensive diplomatic contacts with Saddam's Iraq as well as diplomatic and economic contacts with Iran that were frowned on in Riyadh;[33] and Qatar's independent policy line, since Shaikh Hamad came to power, had been a serious irritant to Saudi Arabia, and there remained issues over the border between the two states. However, Abdullah's initiative was supported by all GCC states and permitted Saudi Arabia to act as their coordinator. The Saudis used this improved atmosphere to further mend fences with Qatar. Diplomatic exchanges and Saudi pressures on Qatar which took place during summer 2003, led to growing cooperation between the two states—even if the open discussions and criticism voiced by the al-Jazeera television channel from Doha kept overshadowing the relations between the two states.[34]

As for the US-led Coalition's war on Iraq, the GCC states accepted it along with Saudi Arabia. Some of them, such as Kuwait and Bahrain, were more openly supportive of the attack than Riyadh. The war, in any case, did not cause new friction between Saudi Arabia and the GCC members.[35]

Saudi Arabia's relations with Iran also remained relatively stable. The improved relations that Crown Prince Abdullah and Iran's President Khatami had engineered since 1997, were maintained in 2002–4, illustrating a significant thaw between the Iranian Shi'i and Saudi-Wahhabi denominations—at least as seen at the government level. Saudi Arabia had also agreed that Iran should play a role in Gulf security, but there was no official document to that effect, and Iran's

[33] See Simon Henderson, *The New Pillar: Conservative Arab Gulf States and US Strategy*, Policy Paper 58, Washington, DC: The Washington Institute for Middle East Policy, 2003, pp. 20–33.

[34] *Gulf States Newsletter*, 689, 26 June 2002; and 736, 11 June 2004.

[35] Henderson, *The New Pillar*, pp. 85–7.

role was not defined. The Saudi acceptance of an Iranian role was arguably left unspecified on purpose, as the United States would reject any recognised role given to Iranian forces in the Gulf, and Saudi Arabia still had to rely on US defence against a possible foreign attack. Indeed, Saudi Arabia remained suspicious of some of Tehran's interests and intentions. These included possible aspirations to develop nuclear capability, supported by ballistic weapons, intervention in Afghanistan and Iraq (where Iran was competing with Saudi interests), and a large army prepared for outside intervention. These suspicions notwithstanding, Saudi leaders avoided provoking Iran. Although Abdullah's initiative was initially criticised and rejected by Iran as being too favourable to Israel, in time it became evident that Saudi Arabia was not really involved in Israel's appeasement, and Tehran dropped the criticism.[36] Thus the initiative did not really affect Saudi relations in the Gulf area.

Conclusion: Posture over Engagement

Assuming the posture of a mediator or coordinator of different regional policies exercised by different parties, was a logical pursuit for Saudi Arabia, reflecting the Kingdom's need to balance various regional security options, as well as its leaders' wish to resolve such problems through diplomatic means. Moreover, it demonstrated the leadership's determination to earn legitimacy and influence through this means, rather than through aspiring to be an activist 'ring leader' in the Arab nationalist mould.

As such, Crown Prince Abdullah's peace initiative succeeded in improving the Kingdom's regional standing, and had some effect on its standing in the United States. Saudi Arabia's initiative was regarded in Washington as useful in advancing a Palestinian-Israeli peace—although it did not achieve the profile or the results the Saudis had hoped. The Arab states viewed the initiative as the only diplomatic move that could help the Palestinians. The Saudis were credited with these achievements, for their ability to set the tone and for obtaining regional and international support.

[36] Gwenn Okruhlik, 'Saudi-Iranian Relations: External Rapprochement and Internal Consolidation', *Middle East Policy*, 10 (2003), p. 113; Henner Fuertig, *Iran's Rivalry with Saudi Arabia between the Gulf Wars*, Reading, PA: Ithaca Press, 2002.

Yet Saudi leaders did not develop a mechanism to lead or actively participate in such mediation. This arguably was at least part of the explanation for their failure to make a success of their peace initiative in terms of its ostensible aims. Moreover, they were unable to transform the initiative into a means to deflect the United States from its 'terrorist-chasing' strategy. Despite Washington's appreciation of Abdullah's initiative, the United States confronted Saudi Arabia over its link with terrorism. While Abdullah's initiative, therefore, had an easing and improving effect on Saudi Arabia's regional position, it ultimately left the Kingdom facing the full force of regional challenges and international pressures.

UNDERSTANDING US–SAUDI RELATIONS

Rachel Bronson

A Puzzle

No sooner did the dust settle over the rubble of the September 11th attacks than the international spotlight shifted on to the US–Saudi relationship. Fifteen of the nineteen hijackers who perpetrated the gravest terrorist attack in American history came from the Kingdom of Saudi Arabia, one of America's closest and longest standing Middle Eastern partners. Across the globe, many began asking a very basic and very appropriate question: why had American and Saudi Arabian decision-makers built such close ties in the first place? The two countries after all seem to have very little in common. One is a long-standing democratic secular state, the other a young monarchy that cloaks itself in religion. As a senior Saudi representative asked me: What does the United States share with a state 'where women can't drive, the Koran is the constitution and beheadings are commonplace?'

The obvious answer to why the two states have over time developed a close and binding relationship comes down to a basic bargain of oil for security. Saudi Arabia ensures a steady flow of oil at reasonable prices. In return, the United States provides Saudi Arabia an overarching security umbrella.[1]

But the 'oil for defence' caricature, like most caricatures, is simplistic and problematic. It leads to a profound misunderstanding of the relationship's underpinnings and obscures the reasons why the relationship deteriorated so quickly after September 11th. It has also

[1] See Nonneman, 'Determinants and Patterns of Saudi Foreign Policy' (pp. 333–335) and Aarts, 'Events and Trends', in this volume.

made it difficult to move beyond mutual recriminations over whether American policies or Saudi Arabia's domestic environment explains the terror attacks.

Oil has, of course, been an important factor in every country's relationship with the Kingdom of Saudi Arabia. It can hardly be otherwise for a country that sits astride one quarter of the world's proven oil resources and relies on its export of 'black gold' for 90 to 95 per cent of its total export earnings.[2] And Saudi Arabia's ability to put oil onto the market in times of crisis gives it a unique standing among all oil producers.

As the world's 'swing producer' it has enormous influence over global oil prices. Saudi Arabia holds about 70 per cent of OPEC's spare capacity, which, given current problems in Venezuela, Nigeria and elsewhere, has come to mean about 70 per cent of the world's spare capacity.[3] If any single problem hits another big producer (e.g., Nigeria's political situation devolves, Venezuelan oil workers strike, hurricanes damage US oil refineries) only Saudi Arabia can quickly make up the volume.

But oil alone does not explain why the United States and Saudi Arabia forged such an intimate partnership. After all, America's relationships with other major oil producing states have proven exceedingly troubled. For the entire Cold War period the United States was in conflict with the Soviet Union, a major oil producing state. For 30 of the 36 years between 1967 and 2003 the United States had no official political relations with Iraq, a country whose oil holdings are estimated at 115 billion barrels of proven reserves, second only to Saudi Arabia. Iran, with 10 per cent of the world's oil, has lived under US sanctions for 25 years. Libya experienced 19 years of American-led sanctions. In 2002 the Bush administration quietly encouraged an unsuccessful extra-legal effort to remove Venezuela's President Hugo Chavez. In the fall of 2004 the United States actively encouraged international sanctions against Sudan's oil exports, in response

[2] Energy Information Administration, *Country Analysis Briefs: Saudi Arabia*, Washington, DC: Department of Energy, June 2004. According to The Economist Intelligence Unit, since the 1990 Gulf war the oil sector has accounted for 85 per cent of Saudi Arabia's export receipts. The Economist Intelligence Unit, *Country Profile: Saudi Arabia*, 2004–5.

[3] In the 4th quarter of 2004, OPEC's spare capacity was estimated at 1.78 million b/d and Saudi Arabia's at 1.22 million b/d.

to egregious human rights abuses taking place in that country. Successive US administrations have shown a clear willingness to bear the costs of poor relations with oil-exporting states. Having a lot of oil does not neatly translate into close relations with the United States.

For much of the Cold War many of these countries were simply not 'available' to the United States as allies or clients as they explicitly positioned themselves *against* them. But this only underscores the importance of understanding what makes one state 'available' to another in the first place. Saudi Arabia, a wealthy, religiously motivated monarchy was attractive to the United States in its heated global contest with the atheist Communists. The United States, for its part helped Saudi Arabia beat back regional and international rivals, while tacitly accepting (and sometimes overtly encouraging) its proselytising tendencies. Together their relationship helped draw the battle lines for the Cold War.

America's close relations with the Kingdom has made it easier for Washington to sanction the oil exports of states it defines as threatening. This in turn has made Saudi Arabia's position ever stronger and more valuable. The importance of Saudi Arabia's oil holding is, in part, politically constructed, rather than pre-ordained.

To understand the long-standing US–Saudi relationship more attention must be given to the global political environment in which oil was needed and its profits employed. As with all other relationships, the US–Saudi partnership operated within a Cold War context and was useful for managing certain political realities. Tensions that emerged within the relationship, including differences over Israel, were compartmentalised because of larger shared interests in combating the Soviet Union. The Cold War's strategic environment is as important to explaining close bilateral relations as Saudi Arabia's sub-soil holdings and the Kingdom's defensive needs. It is at least part of the reason why America could not depend on the oil resources of Iraq and Libya to help diversify away from Saudi Arabia. It also explains why the Saudi Arabian monarchy forged ties with the United States, rather than the anti-monarchical, officially atheist Soviet Union. As history evolved past the Cold War the US–Saudi relationship began fraying in ways not dissimilar to a number of other global partnerships that the United States has long valued. The end of the Cold War explains why the relationship deteriorated so quickly after September 2001. Left unattended by policy makers on both sides, the foundation of the relationship had been deteriorating for over a decade.

The Birth of the Relationship

Although the US–Saudi relationship came of age during the Cold War, it was born prior to World War II. In 1932 the US based Standard Oil of California (SOCAL) struck oil in Bahrain, a small island shaikhdom just off the eastern coast of Saudi Arabia. Prospectors quickly turned their attention toward the Kingdom, which shared similar geological features with Bahrain. The British backed Iraq Petroleum Company (IPC), a consortium that at the time dominated Persian Gulf oil, and SOCAL both approached Saudi Arabia's King Abd al-Aziz ibn Abd al-Rahman al Faisal Al Sa'ud (known in the West colloquially as Ibn Sa'ud) for the now more promising Saudi Arabian concession.

Strategically there was good reason for the King to choose IPC. The British crown had for years quietly supported King Abd al-Aziz both monetarily and militarily.[4] Giving IPC the concession would have bought the Saudi monarchy smoother working relations with the region's power broker.

But the benefits of choosing IPC were overshadowed by real economic and political risks. As a new monarch, the King worried about British colonial designs. One of the benefits of signing up with the American company was that Americans, in the King's eyes, were first and foremost businessmen and did not share the British inclination for altering local political arrangements. In addition SOCAL had a proven track record of finding oil in places where others doubted its existence.

What ultimately convinced the King to choose the American company was the advice he received from his British confidante, H. St John Philby who warned that IPC's primary interest in acquiring the Saudi concession was to keep the oil in the ground and off the market. One IPC official told Philby that his company 'did not need any more oil, as they already had more in prospect than they

[4] See for example Gerd Nonneman, 'Saudi-European Relations 1902–2001: A Pragmatic Quest for Relative Autonomy', *International Affairs*, 77, 3 (July 2001), pp. 631–61, at p. 643.

knew what to do with, at the same time they were vitally interested to keep out all competitors.'[5] For 30,000 pounds of gold, which Saudi Arabia agreed to pay back in future oil revenue if it ever materialised, and an annual payment of 5,000 pounds, the King awarded SOCAL the Saudi concession.[6] IPC offered five times less.[7] The agreement gave birth to the Saudi–US business relationship. In 1938 the company struck oil at Saudi Arabia's Dammam-7 field. Within months it was producing 11,000 barrels per day. Ten years and several oil finds later that number hovered around 477,000 barrels per day and the company now called the Arab American Company (Aramco) accounted for slightly more than five per cent of world production and about 35 per cent of all Middle Eastern output.[8]

In February 1945, King Abd al-Aziz and President Roosevelt met for the first and only time at the Great Bitter Lake aboard the *USS Quincy.* The meeting was not prompted by Saudi Arabia's oil holdings alone. Both President and King shared a profound curiosity about the other: one the leader of one of the world's most powerful countries, the other a charismatic desert potentate whose territory included Islam's most important shrines. President Roosevelt was also eager to meet the leader of the country that in 1943 the United States made eligible for Lend Lease assistance, one of only four Arab states so designated. This recognised that during the war King Abd al-Aziz, although officially neutral, had leaned toward the Allies. He

[5] IPC representative Stephen Longrigg, as quoted in Daniel Yergin, *The Prize*, New York: Free Press, 1993, p. 291.

[6] Technically, the concession was assigned to California Arabian Standard Oil Company (CASOC), a company owned and formed by Standard Oil of California (SOCAL).

[7] See H. St John Philby, *Arabian Jubilee*, New York: The John Day Company, 1953, p. 178. IPC's low bid may have been a result of some double dealing by Philby, who did not tell the IPC representative that Abd al-Aziz was about to accept SOCAL's offer of payment in gold. 'Thereby Philby ensured that the representatives of Iraq Petroleum Company would not raise the stakes, which they might have done if they had realised how close Standard Oil was to closing the deal.' Anthony Cave Brown, *Oil, God and Gold*, New York: Houghton Mifflin, 1999, p. 55.

[8] 'The International Petroleum Cartel: Staff Report to the Federal Trade Commission', released through the Subcommittee on Monopoly of Select Committee on Small Business, US Senate, 83rd Cong., 2nd sess., Washington, DC, 1952, chapter 5, 'Other Common Ownerships in the Middle East', pp. 113–36.

allowed Britain and the United States to over-fly Saudi territory, which significantly shortened the routes Allied aircraft had been taking. Saudi support also facilitated the major Soviet re-supply effort that the Allies were running up the Persian Gulf. According to James Byrnes, Franklin D. Roosevelt's Secretary of State, the President 'determined that in view of the strategic location of Saudi Arabia, the important oil resources of that country and the prestige of King Ibn Sa'ud throughout the Arab world, the defense of Saudi Arabia was vital to the defense of the United States.'[9] As would be true for the next fifty years, Saudi Arabia's oil, its geographic location and political leanings all argued for significant US support.

Six months later the two sides agreed to build an air field at Dhahran, on the eastern coast of Saudi Arabia. The original intent of building the air field was to help the United States deploy its troops to the Pacific theatre of WWII. The war, however, ended before the air field was finished. As the Cold War dawned, the Dhahran air field became a potentially useful second strike air field from which the United States could contain the Soviet Union. Economically, politically and militarily the United States was eclipsing Britain's traditionally powerful role in the Gulf and deepening its relationship with Saudi Arabia.

The Cold War

Throughout the Cold War American and Saudi leaders had many reasons to work together. Saudi oil holdings were important to the United States in the early days of the Cold War, although not for its own consumption, as the United States still relied on its own indigenous production. American leaders relied on a cheap regular supply of Middle Eastern oil to fuel Europe's post-WWII reconstruction. Had America been indifferent to the fate of Europe, Saudi Arabia would have been a less important partner. During the Cold War, however, American security was inextricably tied to Europe and therefore Middle Eastern oil. Later, as American demand outstrip-

9 'Hearings on Petroleum Arrangements with Saudi Arabia', *Mulligan Papers*, box 8, folder 27.14, 16 February 1948. This testimony was in response to Congress arguing that war time decisions were made at the behest of, and for the benefit of oil executives at Aramco, and that they had overcharged the US Navy for oil.

ped indigenous supply, access to Saudi oil became an ever more pressing strategic interest.

Saudi Arabia's geographic location was also prized. At the end of WWII the United States valued access to Saudi territory in order to contain Soviet adventurism. As the Cold War heated up, the State Department worried that 'the area is highly attractive to the USSR because of oil, its strategic location at the air, land and sea crossroads of Eurasia and its vulnerability to attack from without and within.'[10] The US Defense Department increasingly valued the air field at Dhahran. US Ambassador Raymond Hare spent most of his time negotiating American access to the air base. It was in fact the main reason he had been sent to Saudi Arabia. As he recalled,

> The Russians were acting in a very alarming manner. Dhahran airfield was particularly important as a staging point in the event there was trouble with the Russians. We did have an agreement with the Saudis regarding that airfield, but it was imprecise and we wanted to put in some installations—no guns or that sort of thing, but facilities.[11]

In those days, Ambassador Hare remembered, 'you could practically hear the Russian boots clumping down over those desert sands.'[12]

Saudi Arabia's ideological leanings were also compatible with US interests. For Saudi leaders Communism had become an existential threat. The House of Sa'ud, after all, drew much of its legitimacy from the original bargain it struck with the religious leader Muhammad ibn Abd al-Wahhab, back in 1744. It also took seriously its role of speaking for Islam's holiest sites. For the Al Sa'ud there was little appealing, and much threatening, in Soviet inspired atheism. Unlike in Egypt, Syria or Iraq, the United States rarely had to warn Saudi Arabian leaders of the Soviet Union's threatening nature. Soviet support, after all, bolstered many of the monarchy's regional antagonists, such as Egypt and later Yemen. This ideological antagonism toward Communism prevented Saudi Arabia from playing the Soviet Union off against the United States, as Iraq, Egypt and so many other Third

10 'Memorandum of Conversation', *Foreign Relations of the United States* (FRUS), V, 19 March 1950, p. 1134.

11 'Recollections of Raymond Hare', *Frontline Diplomacy: The US Foreign Affairs Oral History Collection*, 2000, Association for Diplomatic Studies and Training.

12 *Raymond Hare*, Eisenhower Library Oral History Collection, p. 56.

World countries did at the time. The Soviet Union was simply not a viable alternative for the Saudi leadership.[13] When Brigadier General Day, the US commander of the Dhahran airfield met with King Abd al-Aziz in 1951, the King assured him, 'if you could find a Communist in Saudi Arabia, I will hand you his head.'[14]

Over the course of the first half of the Cold War different US administrations looked to the Kingdom to counter growing Soviet influence in Egypt. Under President Gamal Abd al-Nasir (Nasser), Egypt was the major Arab power and was fostering pro-Egyptian, Arab nationalist and, in effect, pro-Soviet ferment in countries throughout the area. At different times both the United States and Saudi Arabia tried to co-opt or challenge Nasser. For example, after the Eisenhower administration realised that Nasser could not be brought into America's camp, Secretary of State John Foster Dulles began looking to support potential regional rivals. Dulles hoped that Saudi Arabia's King Sa'ud could lead a religiously motivated bloc against Nasser's nationalism. Washington insiders began referring hopefully to King Sa'ud as the 'Islamic Pope'. The effort failed when it became clear that Sa'ud was not up to the task.

A few years later the tables were turned when US President John F. Kennedy tried drawing Nasser closer to the United States at the same time the Saudi leadership defined him as their primary regional threat. During a meeting with Kennedy in February 1962, King Sa'ud expressed considerable concern that Washington's new policy of accommodation with Egypt served only to 'aid states which have pronounced leftist tendencies and sympathise more with the Soviet Union than with the US.' US Assistant Secretary of State for

13 It is true, as has been pointed out (Nonneman, 'Saudi-European Relations 1902–2001', note 41), that this was not always so. Yet the Soviets were by and large seen by the Al Sa'ud as an existential threat from the early days of the Cold War, especially under King Faisal, through to the end of the 1980s. The fact that they turned down Russian debt relief in 1932 may still have been a case of pragmatic balancing of interest, but the dynamic changed as the Cold War heated up, and ideological differences became sharply, and dangerously, defined. A fear of Communism became a shared US–Saudi interest. It was most pronounced under Faisal, who dominated policy-making almost continuously from 1958 to 1975. His sons were very influential after his death in keeping the eyes of Kings Khalid and Fahd on the Soviets.

14 'Memorandum of Conversation Prepared in the Department of Defense', *FRUS*, V, 17 December 1951, p. 1072.

Near Eastern and South Asian Affairs Phillips Talbott recounted a conversation that he had with Crown Prince Faisal in which Faisal warned, 'Nasser is either a Commie or is afflicted with something hard to identify but which he could only describe as a rabid madness or schizophrenia.'[15] However, Both King Sa'ud and Crown Prince Faisal were unsuccessful in moving American policy away from its newly adopted pro-Egypt policy.[16]

Three changes occurred in the early 1970s that dramatically strengthened the US–Saudi relationship. First, the United States for the first time reached full capacity in its own oil production. For the first half of the Cold War the Unites States had produced oil below full capacity. Yet from 1972 on local demand required full production. Excess supply was no longer available to ease politically motivated or naturally occurring shortages. For example, when Arab exporters boycotted their European costumers in 1956 and 1967, the United States had put extra oil onto the market to alleviate the crisis. After 1972 the United States could no longer play the role of 'swing producer'.

Consequently, when Arab oil exporters including Saudi Arabia agreed to cut production and then to embargo the United States during the 1973 war, the United States could not make up the difference as it had during the two earlier embargos. OPEC countries were, for the first time, in a strong position vis-à-vis the United

[15] Memo 'To Secretary of State, from Talbott', 13 February 1962, JFK library, Country File: Saudi Arabia, 1–19 February 1962, 2.

[16] See Warren Bass, *Support Any Friend: Kennedy's Middle East and the Making of the US-Israel Alliance*, New York: Oxford University Press, 2003; and John S. Badeau, *The American Approach to the Arab World*, New York: Harper Row, 1968. What finally did move the Kennedy Administration towards a more pro-Saudi position was the war in Yemen. US Ambassador to Egypt, John Badeau, was instructed to urge Nasser to stop attacking the Kingdom and argue that Egyptian 'bombings of Saudi Arabia and airdrops of weapons… are forcing US close to [a] point where we will have no alternative but to make good our obligation to Saudis… we wish [to] avoid [a] rancorous dispute with UAR if possible but unless UAR stops overt attacks on Saudi Arabia USG will be forced to review its policy toward UAR.' His efforts were to no avail. See 'Telegram from the Department of State to the Embassy in the United Arab Republic', 2 March 1963, *FRUS*, XVIII, 1961–3, p. 391. Eventually, as Badeau warned, the United States sent a squadron of fighters to help defend Saudi Arabia. See Parker T. Hart, *Saudi Arabia and the United States: Birth of a Security Partnership*, Bloomington, IN: Indiana University Press, 1998, chapters 5 and 8.

States. Against the backdrop of surging demand and changing distribution of supply, the production cuts and embargo resulted in the quadrupling of oil prices and the greatest transfer of wealth in world history.

The second important change of the 1970s was Saudi Arabia's transformation into a very wealthy country. As a result of the embargo and subsequent price hikes, billions of 'petrodollars' flowed into the Kingdom. For the Kingdom this provided welcome relief as it desperately needed hospitals, schools, roads and modern services. The government set aside large numbers of scholarships to send citizens to the United States for the most up-to-date training in all fields.[17] Saudi Arabia's ports were so clogged with ships that cargo often perished on board before receiving entry clearance.

Enormous sums of Saudi cash were invested in the United States. US Secretary of State Henry Kissinger, Secretary of the Treasury William Simon and Saudi Arabia's Crown Prince Fahd constructed a Joint Economic Commission to encourage Saudi investment in the United States. Through new rules and incentives, Saudi investors received preferential rates on US-based investments. In the mid-1970s Saudi Arabia held at least $35 billion in fixed treasury bonds.[18] One of the most stunning statistics regarding US–Saudi collaborations is the $1.7 billion the United States paid out for Saudi oil in 1974. That same year $8.5 billion of Saudi funds flowed into the United States.[19] Saudi money also poured into the American arms industry. Billions of dollars were spent in a buying spree that began in 1967 but accelerated after 1973.

[17] In 2002, due to decreasing fortunes, a greater number of local options and a more hostile US environment, that number decreased 6,000. Saudi attendance in US schools tracks remarkably well with oil revenue. In 1976 there were 3,000 students, 1980: 10,000; 1985: 8,000; 2002: 6,000. In 2004 the number dropped to closer to 4,000. See, 'Foreign (Non-immigrant) Student Enrolment in College: 1976–2002', *Statistical Abstract of the United States*, US Census Bureau: NTIS, 2003, p. 183. The numbers posted by the Royal Embassy of Saudi Arabia show a greater disparity between the early 1980s and today. The King Faisal Specialist Hospital and Research Centre, relying on the KSA Royal Embassy, states that in the early 1980s, the Kingdom sent more than 15,000 students per year to the United States for undergraduate and post-graduate studies. Today they consider that number closer to 3,000 per year. See: http://www.kfshrc.edu.sa/arabian/html/faq_schooling.html.

[18] 'Saudi Power', *Newsweek*, 6 March 1978.

[19] Joe Stork, 'Saudi Arabia and the US', *MERIP Report*, October 1980, p. 26.

The third, and most overlooked, change of the 1970s came from Saudi Arabia's decision to use its new found money to heavily invest in international causes, many of which the United States welcomed. With revenues reaching tens of billions of dollars, there was more than enough left to finance a fair number of foreign operations. Saudi Arabia put its money into two main baskets, Islamic organisations and anti-Soviet operations. The two were often complimentary. As Jim Hoagland deftly put it in a 1977 *Washington Post* article, 'the Saudis are spending billions of dollars in an arc of influence that extends from Morocco eastward across Africa and the Middle East and deep into Asia. It is an arc that, by design or by accident, could easily have been traced by an American administration eager to help [overcome] new difficulties in persuading Congress to appropriate money for such causes.'[20]

Saudi money helped Egypt's new President Anwar Sadat extricate Egypt from Soviet influence. Riyadh's aid helped roll back Communist rebels in the Congo.[21] Saudi support was instrumental to Jonas Savimbi's early successes in Angola.[22] In an attempt to counter Soviet and Cuban support for Marxist Ethiopia, the Saudis sent up to $250 million in cash and military equipment to Somalia and

[20] Jim Hoagland, 'Practicing Checkbook Diplomacy', *Washington Post*, 21 December 1977, p. A1.

[21] For the fullest discussion of coordinated Saudi Arabian, Egyptian, Iranian, Moroccan and French anti-Communist activities in Africa, see Mohamed Heikal, *Iran: The Untold Story*, New York: Pantheon Books, 1982, pp. 112–16. Heikal sifted through the Shah's papers and discovered documents of the close coordination with the Saudis and others in Africa. Author's interview with Prince Turki al-Faisal, Saudi Arabia's Minister of Intelligence (1978–2001), April 2004, also highlighted the coordinated efforts in Africa. See also Mahmood Mamdani, *Good Muslim, Bad Muslim: America, the Cold War, and the Roots of Terror*, New York: Pantheon Books, 2004.

[22] Saudi Arabia assisted Angola's rebel leader, Jonas Savimbi, by providing Morocco with financial assistance to set up a training camp for UNITA forces. In 1981 Savimbi told *Business Week* correspondent Steve Mufson that UNITA's 'biggest aid donors were Morocco and Saudi Arabia' and that Morocco housed 'a key training base' for UNITA. See Steven Mufson 'Some Familiar Echoes in Financing of Angola Rebels', *Los Angeles Times*, 26 July 1987, p. 2. To *Le Figaro*, Savimbi admitted that 'some 80 per cent of our officers were trained in Morocco.' See 'Hearing before the Subcommittee on Africa of the Committee on Foreign Affairs House of Representatives, 1 July 1987, Possible Violation or Circumvention of the Clark Amendment', p. 115.

Djibouti. Aid to the Sudan was aimed at preventing Libyan or Ethiopian expansion. Saudi Arabia granted $100 million to neighbouring South Yemen, but failed to wean that country's Marxist government away from its close bond with the Soviet Union.[23]

Such anti-Soviet and pro-Islamic assistance was a boon to American foreign policy.[24] In Washington, Saudi Arabia's investment in Islamic organisations like the Muslim World League, and the World Association of Muslim Youth and other international Islamic organisations was non-controversial. During the Cold War religious giving was deemed a useful bulwark against atheistic Communism. Saudi Arabia's investment in mosques and religious schools that either accompanied or was a by-product of its foreign aid was overlooked and went under reported.

Throughout the 1970s and 1980s American decision makers relied on Saudi Arabia to fund a vast number of American overseas operations. Saudi Arabia was particularly valuable in areas where Congress was hesitant to fund. During the Iran-Contra scandal in the 1980s, for example, it was revealed that the Kingdom had provided up to $32 million to the Contras fighting in Nicaragua at the White House's behest. The US–Saudi partnership reached its pinnacle in the 1980s in Afghanistan when the United States and Saudi Arabia undertook a massive effort to defeat the Soviet Union matching each other's investment dollar for dollar. The two states ultimately put more than $3 billion each into that broken country.

During the Cold War the United States and Saudi Arabia shared a set of foreign policy interests. This is not to say that problems did not arise. Differences, like those revolving around how to deal with

[23] Reliable figures on actual amounts of Saudi aid are very difficult to come by, as they are carefully guarded by the Saudi government, and often given in cash instalments. These figures, and the ones above echo more qualitative accounts from 'Saudi Power', *Newsweek*, 6 March 1978.

[24] The United States, however, did not welcome all of Saudi Arabia's international giving. Some went to causes that greatly troubled Washington. The Government of Saudi Arabia, for example, gave significant support to Palestinian groups at a time when the United States still considered the Palestine Liberation Organisation (PLO) a terrorist organisation. Many of the states Saudi Arabia provided with foreign aid, particularly in Africa, also cut official relations with Israel. But the difficulties were overwhelmed by the other, more helpful, anti-Soviet activity. Differences over Israel, while deep and severe, were only one set of problems in an otherwise productive relationship.

Nasser's power, were very real and hard to manage.[25] Saudi Arabia's decision to cancel America's lease to the Dhahran air base in 1962, and the 1973 oil embargo were significant crises. The US Congress routinely criticised the Kingdom's restrictions on religious practices inside its borders. The Saudi leadership never understood America's policy of détente and worried America had dropped the ball in holding back Soviet influence, particularly in Africa. They were insulted by constant American limitations posed on arms sales. Differences regarding Israel always posed challenges. On numerous occasions, anti-American and anti-Israel protests erupted inside Saudi Arabia, especially in Eastern province, around Aramco's offices. But such problems were overshadowed by larger global interests. In the end, foreign policy elites on both sides wanted to reduce opportunities for Soviet penetration and to stabilise the region. The two countries often differed on the means to achieve these goals, but not on the ends themselves.

When the Soviets presented a real and present danger, American and Saudi policies were by and large mutually supportive. When the Cold War ended, so did some of the justification for the US–Saudi 'special relationship'.

From Desert Storm to 9/11

The end of the Cold War marked a turning point in US–Saudi relations. The problems that shared threat perceptions once helped mitigate now bubbled on the surface. In addition, during the 1990s a host of new challenges arose with no mutually understood strategic context to place them in. Iraq invaded Kuwait, domestic dissent permeated Saudi society, a political vacuum developed in Afghanistan

[25] Robert Vitalis' paper to the ISIM workshop that started the project underlying the present volume, ('The Origins of the Crisis Narrative in US–Saudi Relations: The Year Bin Ladin Was Born', presented to the conference on *Saudi Futures: Trends and Challenges in the Post 9/11, Post-Iraq War World*, Institute for the Study of Islam in the Modern World, University of Amsterdam and Lancaster University, 19–21 February 2004, Leiden, the Netherlands), detailed those difficulties; it is being developed into two chapters of his forthcoming book, *America's Kingdom* (Robert Vitalis, *America's Kingdom*, pre-publication version, 2005, posted on http://cas.uchicago.edu/workshops/cpolit/papers/vitalis.doc). For comparison with the post-9/11 era, see also Martin Sieff, 'Sand in Our Eyes: US–Saudi Relations After Iraq', *National Interest*, summer 2004, pp. 93–100.

and in 2000 the second Intifada broke out in the Palestinian territories. Each strained the US–Saudi relationship further.

Across the globe, many saw the end of the Cold War as an opportunity to re-orient their governments' international and domestic policies. In Eastern Europe, South America and elsewhere, democratic movements gathered steam, causing Samuel Huntington to describe a 'Third Wave' of democratisation.[26] Francis Fukayama crowed about the 'End of History', and President Bush pointed to 'a thousand points of light'.[27]

But Middle Easterners barely had time to absorb the new post-Cold War realities when on 2 August 1990 700 Iraqi tanks and 100,000 Iraqi soldiers swept across the Iraq-Kuwait border. The Iraqi government suddenly controlled 19 per cent of the world's oil. Iraq now sat poised to challenge Saudi Arabia and its oil fields. The President submitted to Congress a case for military action.

Iraq's invasion of Kuwait once again threw the United States and Saudi Arabia into each others' arms. US Secretary of State James A. Baker III hop-scotched the globe to forge an international coalition to oust Saddam Hussein from Iraq. On 7 August 1990 King Fahd met with US Secretary of Defense Dick Cheney. Impressed by America's resolve to reverse Iraqi aggression, King Fahd unabashedly welcomed into the Kingdom a half million members of the American armed forces who fell-in on massive state-of-the-art military installations. American and Saudi military officers operated through a joint command structure and closely coordinated their activity. They were helped by nearly a decade of joint efforts to improve access and interoperability.

The 1990 invasion, and the ensuing massive American military build up inside Saudi Arabia, corresponded with battle hardened Saudi fighters like Usama bin Ladin returning home from Afghanistan. They were embittered by the Saudi government's decision to rely on foreign fighters rather than their own citizens and soldiers, especially those returning from Afghanistan. Many were also disillusioned that the ideal Islamic state that they fought so hard to create

[26] Samuel P. Huntington, *The Third Wave: Democratization in the Late Twentieth Century*, Norman, OK: University of Oklahoma Press, 1993.

[27] Francis Fukuyama, *The End of History and The Last Man*, New York: Avon Books, 1992. Inaugural Address of George Bush, 20 January 1989, Washington, DC.

in Afghanistan was not better represented in the Kingdom. This anger led to roiling domestic dissent inside Saudi Arabia, which targeted both the Saudi royal family and their American supporters.[28]

In the pre-war August meeting Secretary Cheney assured King Fahd that American troops would depart the Kingdom immediately after the war. He was true to his word. After Iraq's withdrawal the United States significantly reduced (although never pulled all) its forces in Saudi Arabia and throughout the region.[29]

But in 1994, in an oft-forgotten incident, Saddam Hussein again threatened Kuwait's northern border. In early October a division of Republic Guard troops began marching south and joined up with two other Guard divisions shifting toward the border with Kuwait. 70,000 Iraqi military personnel, an increase of over 20,000 regularly situated forces, were moving toward the Kuwaiti border. Iraqi civilians demonstrated alongside the Kuwaiti border. The United States and its coalition partners rushed troops to the region. The Pentagon dispatched 36,000 ground troops to the Gulf. France and Britain also sent forces to what would come to be known as 'Operation Vigilant Warrior'. Kuwait, Saudi Arabia and Qatar pledged over $370 million in direct and in kind support. This time, however, troop levels did not come down. Indeed, after 1994 American force levels inside and around Saudi Arabia rose steadily.

Simultaneous to rising troop levels and Saudi internal problems in justifying the American presence, the political consensus on how to deal with Saddam Hussein's Iraq began to break down. Rising numbers of American troops in the region were met with mounting Saudi restrictions on American military activity. Trying to balance domestic dissent and national security requirements, Saudi Arabia withheld support for American operations inside Iraq for the first time in 1996. In 1998 the United States launched 'Operation Desert Fox', a four day campaign to set back Iraq's 'weapons of mass destruction' programme and leadership capabilities. Saudi Arabia again withheld

[28] See the chapters by Abdulaziz Sager, Stéphane Lacroix and Roel Meijer in this volume. Also Mamoun Fandy, *Saudi Arabia and the Politics of Dissent*, New York: St Martin's Press, 1999; Joshua Teitelbaum, *Holier than Thou: Saudi Arabia's Islamic Opposition*, Washington, DC: The Washington Institute for Near East Policy, 2000.

[29] See Rachel Bronson, 'Beyond Containment in the Persian Gulf', *Orbis*, 45, 2 (spring 2001), p. 196.

support. After the United States failed to significantly reduce Saddam's power, Saudi leaders, and many others, lost all confidence in America's ability to successfully resolve the situation. As Kenneth Pollack, President Clinton's Director for Gulf Affairs at the National Security Council remembers, 'by any measure, the Saudis ha[d] become less supportive of limited US military operations against Iraq.'[30]

By the end of the 1990s there was no agreement on how to manage the Iraqi threat. Tensions mounted as the United States viewed its role in Saudi Arabia as one of protector, while Saudi Arabia no longer warmly welcomed the form American presence had taken. Secretary of Defense William Cohen made regular trips to the Kingdom but Secretary of State Madeline Albright focused her attention elsewhere. American lawmakers called for regime change in Iraq, Saudi leaders saw it as only antagonising a wounded but still dangerous neighbour. Absent the ferocity of the Cold War, even a threatening regional actor could not refocus the US–Saudi partnership.

The failed state of Afghanistan was another area of policy divergence between the two countries. During the 1980s Afghanistan represented the height of American-Saudi cooperation and shared interests. Together the two states helped Afghanistan's Islamic fighters reverse Soviet aggression. Within Saudi Arabia the call to war in Afghanistan permeated nearly all aspects of society. Mosques, schools, Islamic centres, and news broadcasts urged fighting in, or at least support of, the ongoing war.

The Soviets left Afghanistan in 1989, and in 1992 the United States and Russia agreed to end all support to their allies there. But with victory and the end of the Cold War, there was no agreement on how to manage the post-conflict environment. There was never any real discussion about an endgame for Afghanistan. The United States simply packed up and departed—its political agenda already crammed full with the reunification of Germany, domestic calls for a peace dividend, Desert Storm and starvation in Somalia. Saudi Arabia, on the other hand, remained involved, trying somehow to fashion a post-war order, which eventually led it to support the zealously fundamentalist Taliban.

[30] Kenneth M. Pollack, *The Threatening Storm: The Case for Invading Iraq*, New York: Random House, 2002, p. 188.

Bin Ladin and the Taliban turned Afghanistan into a nationwide terrorist recruitment and training camp. Reports of severe restrictions on women, beheadings in public arenas and the wanton disregard of cultural symbols galvanised international attention.[31] Considerable amounts of money from Saudi citizens found its way into Afghanistan. The Saudi government, at best, turned a blind eye.[32]

Saudi influence began shaping other conflicts as well. As Gilles Kepel observed, 'the transnational Saudi system insinuated itself into the relationship between state and society in the majority of Muslim countries.'[33] In Bosnia, Chechnya and elsewhere, evidence of Saudi influence emerged. During the Cold War Saudi fighter and charitable giving were viewed as part of a larger global political struggle, fighting against the Soviet Union. Certainly few in the West would have objected to Saudis and other Arabs linking up with Chechen dissidents to shoot at Soviet soldiers. After 1990, however, these same men were now fighting against US friends and partners. They were working at cross-purposes with US interests.

In a 1999 White House visit Vice President Al Gore raised the issue of stemming Bin Ladin's fundraising efforts with Saudi Arabia's Crown Prince Abdullah. It was the first time the topic of Saudi Arabia's financial support for religious fighters had been defined as a problem, at such a high level. The State Department formally designated Al Qa'ida a 'foreign terrorist organisation' that same year. When the Administration of George W. Bush came to office, the Office of Policy Planning at the US Department of State was tasked to prepare a new 'white paper' on how to manage growing problems in Afghanistan. Although it took a back seat to what was going on in Iraq, Afghanistan was another area in which the United States and Saudi Arabia no longer shared political interests.

[31] In 1998 Iran and Afghanistan went to the brink of war after two Iranian diplomats were seized and executed.

[32] Maurice Greenberg (Chairman), 'Terrorist Financing: An Independent Task Force', New York: Council on Foreign Relations, 2002. A Saudi with close contacts with Intelligence told me that support was easy as the fighters were viewed 'like Wahhabis'. See also Steve Coll, *Ghost Wars: The Secret History of the CIA, Afghanistan, and Bin Laden, from the Soviet Invasion to September 10, 2001*, New York: The Penguin Press, 2004, which attributes a similar outlook to others in the Saudi intelligence arena.

[33] Gilles Kepel, *Jihad: The Trail of Political Islam*, Cambridge, MA: Harvard University Press, 2002, p. 70.

To add to the strain, in September 2000 fighting erupted between the Israelis and Palestinians, in what became known as the al-Aqsa Intifada. For the in-coming Bush Administration events there, while violent, were a secondary concern. There was a general belief that if President Clinton, with all his area-specific knowledge and with all the time he devoted to resolving that conflict, could not reconcile the two parties, there was little reason to believe that the new team could do any better.[34] In addition, the fighting was defined as a regional problem, one that regional actors should solve. The United States' main focus was on major powers like China and Russia. President Bush did not assign a special envoy to the region for a full ten months after assuming office.

But for Saudi Arabia, the al-Aqsa Intifada was closely followed and monopolised the airwaves of the relatively new satellite stations. It heightened the already significant anti-American and anti-regime sentiment.

Relations between the United States and Saudi Arabia deteriorated so badly around the fighting in Palestine that in August 2001 Saudi Arabia's Crown Prince Abdullah warned that because of the on-going fighting and lack of a serious American initiative, Saudi Arabia was prepared to go its own separate way from the United States. It was one of the most direct threats ever issued by a Saudi leader to the United States, and runs counter to the claims made in a number of recent books and other media (including Michael Moore's *Fahrenheit 9/11*) about the closeness between the Bush family and the Al Sa'ud.[35] President Bush immediately responded with a letter stating that he believed the Palestinians deserved their own state, something he later repeated more publicly in June 2002. A meeting was set for 13 September to develop a response to the Intifada and to try to salvage what was left of the US–Saudi relationship. Two days prior to the meeting the hijacked planes smashed into the Pentagon and the World Trade Center.

Not withstanding the growing problems, Washington continued throughout the 1990s its habit of asking Saudi Arabia to fund many of its international pet projects, an exercise referred to internally as

34 Rachel Bronson, 'The Reluctant Mediator', *Washington Quarterly*, autumn 2002.

35 Apart from Moore's film, see Craig Unger, *House of Bush, House of Saud*, New York: Scribner, 2004.

'tin-cupping'. At one point in the early 1990s the US ambassador to Saudi Arabia was asked to persuade the Saudis to buy surplus Polish ham to help the starving—now defined as friendly—Russians through that year's harsh winter and at the same time provide foreign exchange to the hard-pressed Poles. Exasperated by the constant and unfocused requests from Washington, he replied that this would be 'a bit like asking the Pope to buy condoms from the Lutherans for distribution to Muslims in Bangladesh' and he wasn't about to attempt it.[36] Unlike during the Cold War, when Saudi assistance went to a mutually agreed upon goal of fighting Communism, now the requests were *ad hoc*. Anger mounted inside the Kingdom especially as Saudi Arabia underwrote a considerable portion of the costs of Desert Storm, which put enormous strain on the state's coffers.

Anti-Americanism in Saudi Arabia, and elsewhere, increased throughout the 1990s. In a prescient article written in summer 2000 entitled 'The World's Resentment' Peter Rodman, now Assistant Secretary of Defense for International Security Affairs, pointed to rising levels of dissatisfaction with the United States.[37] To some extent, he correctly argued, the anger was inevitable—a result of the shift from a bipolar international structure.[38]

What is striking about the history of the 1990s is not that the United States built a global coalition to defend Saudi Arabia's oil and territorial integrity, but rather, how quickly the US–Saudi consensus deteriorated afterwards. Without a shared vision of the threats and the means to protect against them, oil interests alone could not return the relationship to its former closeness. Saudi leaders lost confidence in America's regional policy and tight US–Saudi relations

[36] Author's interview, Ambassador Chas. Freeman, September 2004.

[37] Peter Rodman, 'The World's Resentment', *National Interest*, summer 2000.

[38] The changing global structure does not of course explain the whole situation. Saudis and their neighbours in the Gulf questioned the value of US presence, especially as oil prices fell in the late 1990s and economic conditions deteriorated. Responsibility for Iraqi suffering was pinned on both Saddam Hussein and US policy. While Saddam Hussein was clearly to blame for the misery of his own people, many in the region believed that the leading proponent of sanctions was also guilty of expecting a vicious megalomaniac to protect the welfare of his own people. In the face of such challenges, the Saudi leadership did not publicly defend its own choice to rely on US power. Still, had the Cold War been raging, the Soviets would have likely restrained Iraq in the first place, and, if not, the Saudis would have probably more overtly defended their foreign policy choices.

were becoming increasingly unpopular at home. The United States chafed under increasingly restrictive 'rules of engagement' in its operations against Iraq and President Clinton was reportedly irate that Saudi Arabia had not been more influential during his attempts to mediate between Israelis and Palestinians.[39] The helpfulness of Saudi Arabia's role in regional politics was no longer as clear to American decision makers as had been assumed. Saudi Arabia, as the world's only swing-producer in the oil market, was still an important global actor and Saudi leaders still viewed the United States as an important protector of last resort.[40] Yet bereft of its erstwhile Cold-War-era strategic underpinning, the partnership devolved into crisis. As one astute Saudi businessman correctly concluded, the deterioration in US–Saudi relations after the September 11th attacks was 'an accident waiting to happen'.[41]

9/11 and The War on Terror

Continuing the relationship's downward spiral, the first 18 months after the September 11th attacks marked one of the lowest points in US–Saudi relations, certainly the lowest in a quarter century. In early 2001, according to a Zogby International poll, 56 per cent of Americans gave Saudi Arabia a favourable rating. By December 2001 that number had fallen to 24 per cent.[42] A July 2002 briefing to the Defense Policy Board, an advisory committee of American strategic luminaries devoted to assisting the Secretary of Defense, defined Saudi Arabia as 'the kernel of evil, the prime mover, the most dangerous opponent' in the Middle East and advised US forces to target Saudi Arabia's oil fields and seize its assets. A 2004 political campaign advertisement that linked Saudi Arabia to the administration of George W. Bush, increased support for Presidential contender John Kerry by eight percentage points.[43] Saudi citizens, once accorded

[39] To be fair, the Saudis were explicitly kept at arms length during negotiations at Camp David, and then were blamed when negotiations collapsed.

[40] As suggested in Nonneman, 'Determinants and Patterns' and in the next chapter by Paul Aarts.

[41] Author interview, 2002.

[42] http://www.cfr.org/background/saudiarabia_usforces.php.

[43] Thomas Richs, 'Briefing Depicted Saudis as Enemies: Ultimatum Urged to Pentagon Board', *Washington Post*, 6 August 2002. For the PowerPoint slides see

special status, were confronted with lengthy holds and often outright denials on visa requests. 29 per cent of US universities polled in an Institute of International Education survey recorded a sharp drop in newly admitted Saudi Arabian citizens between autumn 2002 and 2003.[44] This was particularly uncomfortable for a population that often considered themselves 'adjunct' American citizens.[45] Saudi money became suspect at major banking institutions worldwide. Saudis populated Guantánamo Bay, the prison where American officials brought dangerous fighters picked up in Afghanistan.

In Saudi Arabia anger increased against the United States. Saudi citizens began a grass-roots boycott of American goods and companies. Across the world, particularly in Muslim countries, anti-Americanism sky-rocketed. A 2003 PEW report came to the ominous conclusion, 'the bottom has fallen out of support for America in most of the Muslim world.'[46] American-Saudi relations had deteriorated far from the day in 1962 when Crown Prince (later King) Faisal told President Kennedy, 'after Allah, we trust the United States'.[47]

Although exceedingly tense, US–Saudi relations began to improve when the Kingdom itself dramatically changed its approach toward fighting terrorism in May 2003, after suicide bombers simultaneously struck three housing complexes in Riyadh. The Saudi leadership defined the attacks as a 'wake-up call' and 'our September 11th' and began undertaking drastic security, political and economic measures against the foundations of terrorism. Saudi commitment was doubled in November 2003 when terrorists attacked a residential compound and killed mostly Arab Muslims.

Jack Schafer, 'The PowerPoint that Rocked the Pentagon', *Slate Magazine*, 7 August 2002, http://slate.msn.com/id/2069119/.Jim Rutenberg, 'Kerry Ads Draw on Saudis for new Attack on Bush', *New York Times*, 5 October 2004, p. 16.

[44] Institute of International Education, 'Fall 2003 Survey: The State of International Educational Exchange—International Students', 3 November 2003.

[45] 'Crisis and Opportunities in US–Saudi Relations: Ambassador Robert Jordan Interview', *Saudi–US Relations Information Service*, 7 September 2004.

[46] The PEW Research Center, *Views of a Changing World 2003*, 3 June 2003, http://people-press.org/reports/display.php3?ReportID=185.

[47] Parker Hart, *Saudi Arabia and the United States: Birth of a Security Partnership*, Bloomington, IN: Indiana University Press, 1998, p. 236. See also sources in Robert Vitalis, *America's Kingdom*, chapter 10, note 54 (pre-publication version, 2005, posted on http://cas.uchicago.edu/workshops/cpolit/papers/vitalis.doc).

Ironically the 'War on Terror' may help salvage parts of the US–Saudi relationship. Fighting terror is now an interest both Washington and Riyadh share. Since the May attacks there have been regular reports of Saudi security forces hunting down militants, disbanding Al Qa'ida cells and seizing weapon caches. By late summer 2004 security forces had successfully foiled a number of potential attacks, rounded up hundreds of suspects and killed dozens of militants, including more than half of their twenty-six most-wanted list.[48] Radical clerics were warned to tone down their fiery sermons and many found themselves undergoing 're-education'.[49]

The Saudi government also became more serious about cutting the flow of funds to terrorists. In July 2004 the Financial Action Task Force, a multilateral organisation devoted to combating money laundering and terrorist financing, judged that the Kingdom was 'compliant or largely compliant' with international standards in almost every indicator of effectiveness.[50]

Saudi officials announced they intended to freeze the assets of al-Haramain, a charitable organisation responsible for dispersing $40 to $50 million per year and associated with the Saudi Arabian government. The Saudi government instituted a series of laws that made it much harder for its citizens to move money. It has put all charities, especially ones with an international mandate, under the watchful eye of state regulators. The Crown Prince urged Saudis to keep charitable support at home. Accordingly, Saudi citizens are now giving more money to local causes than to ones farther afield. In 2004, since new legislation was put in place and Crown Prince Abdullah urged Saudi citizens to give locally, Saudi domestic giving is up approximately 300 per cent.[51]

[48] See the chapter by Roel Meijer in this volume.

[49] Disturbingly, some reformists pressing for human rights and calling for a constitutional monarchy were also imprisoned. As of March 2005 three were still in jail, as was their chief lawyer.

[50] Financial Action Task Force on Money Laundering, 'Annual Report 2003–4', 2 July 2004, Annex C. The report also laid out three areas that Saudi Arabia were out of compliance. Ambassador J. Cofer Black, Coordinator for Counterterrorism, US Department of State, mentioned this in his 'Saudi Arabia and the Firght Against Terrorist Financing', testimony before the House Committee on International Relations Subcommittee on the Middle East and Central Asia, 24 March 2004, four months before the report was issued.

[51] Author's interview, State Department official, September 2004.

In other efforts to combat terrorism, the Kingdom has undertaken a series of meetings with local leaders from various segments of society to address domestic problems that nurture such activity. The attention of Saudi citizens was particularly drawn because the participants included prominent women and Shi'a clerics—an often reviled group in the predominantly Sunni society. The result is an unprecedented society-wide discussion on the role of women, education and ethnic and sectarian diversity within society. Municipal elections, after an initial delay, were finally held in three tranches starting in February 2005.

Most notable, Saudi Arabia is now actively and publicly cooperating with the United States and others in the fight against terrorism. In the past it was exceedingly difficult for the FBI to gain access to and information on terrorist suspects. Now there is open cooperation between the FBI and Saudi intelligence forces. Prince Nayif, Saudi Arabia's Interior Minister and one who for a long time publicly denied Saudi involvement in the September 11th attacks, announced the Kingdom's active cooperation with the United States, albeit in a roundabout manner. Prince Nayif stated, 'we want other countries to help us outside the Kingdom. We want to work jointly with them. We need help in the areas of intelligence, especially from the most powerful countries (operating) in Afghanistan and in Iraq.'[52] The FBI now has teams located inside the Kingdom and the two sides are cooperating through a joint task force on terrorist financing in which American law enforcement officials are working alongside Saudi security personnel. Such bilateral cooperation is unprecedented.

Such changes have prompted positive statements from the Bush Administration. As National Security Advisor in the first G. W. Bush administration, Condoleezza Rice regularly asserted that Saudi Arabia is a key partner in the fight against terrorism. In Congressional testimony, Ambassador Cofer Black, the State Department's Coordinator for Combating Terrorism, concluded Saudi Arabia was showing 'clear evidence of the seriousness of purpose and the commitment of the leadership of the kingdom to this fight [against terror].'[53] Most

[52] 'Riyadh-West Rift is Over Palestine: Naif', *Arab News*, 19 June 2004.

[53] Hearing of the Subcommittee on the Middle East and Central Asia of the House Committee on Internationals Relations, 'Saudi Arabia and the Fight Against Terrorism Financing', 24 March 2004.

important, in his acceptance speech at the Republican National Convention in August 2004, President George W. Bush mentioned Saudi Arabia explicitly, stating, 'four years ago … Saudi Arabia was fertile ground for terrorist fundraising,' but now 'Saudi Arabia is making raids and arrests.'[54] Given a political climate in the United States in which any statement construed as positive toward the Kingdom can bring instant public condemnation, this was particularly noteworthy.

New Saudi approaches and US responses were not the only instances of change: Washington's own approach toward the Kingdom also underwent transformation.[55] When, a year after 9/11, voices in Washington were expressing frustration at a perceived lack of Saudi cooperation on combating terrorism, Saudi officials angrily responded that the information the United States provided to Saudi Arabia was too vague and limited to act upon. In December 2002 key members of the US administration met to overhaul America's efforts toward Saudi Arabia.[56] They agreed on the need to coordinate US messages to Saudi Arabia by appointing a high-level official with strong ties to the President to take responsibility for handling the US–Saudi bilateral effort to shut down terrorist activity.[57] The United States also recognised that too often they had failed to give the Saudi authorities accurate and actionable intelligence, while still demanding immediate action. The Administration now decided not only to trust the Saudis with highly sensitive information (in turn made easier after May 2003 when Saudi Arabia became more demonstrably pro-active in its counter-terrorism strategy), but also to demand of itself a higher burden of proof that the information passed on to Riyadh was accurate. Finally, the Administration also came to realise that many of Saudi Arabia's problems resulted from poorly-

[54] George W. Bush, 'Speech to the 2004 Republican National Convention', New York, 2 September 2004.

[55] Interview, State Department official, September 2004.

[56] John Roth, Douglas Greenburg, Serena Wile, 'Monograph on Terrorist Financing', The National Commission on Terrorist Attacks Upon the United States, Staff Report to the Commission, 2004, p. 120, http://www.9-11commission.gov/staff_statements/911_TerrFin_Monograph.pdf.

[57] The first official to take this position became Frances Townsend, Deputy National Security Adviser for combating terrorism.

trained operatives and began providing it with advanced training programmes. This new approach had already shown considerable success at the time of writing.

Into the future

While all this is good news for the US–Saudi relationship, there remain reasons for concern. While the War on Terror provides an interest the United States and Saudi Arabia can engage on, whether it can replace the Cold War and the ideological threat of the Soviet Union is not yet clear. The ideological glue of US–Saudi relations is no longer self-evident.

American and Saudi leaders are thus confronting a new and dangerous moment. The novelty of the situation has been underappreciated by those who disregard the ideological compatibility that the two states shared over the past six decades, almost the entire history of the modern Saudi state. Focusing only on the basic bargain of oil for security misses how fundamentally different today's political context is from what came before. The geo-strategic importance of Washington and Riyadh's shared willingness to use religion to fight communism vanished as soon as the Cold War ended in 1989.

Especially in light of the September 11th attacks, this new situation is highly problematic. Saudi Arabia has considerable cash at its disposal, as well as the religious bully pulpit of Mecca and Medina. In many ways it will dictate the future of Islam. Unless the United States and Saudi Arabia can find a way to work together, to rein in violent religious groups that they helped create, the political climate will only grow more anti-American, anti-modern, violent and dangerous.

But can the United States and Saudi Arabia work together? For those who understand Saudi Arabia's past foreign policy decisions as nothing more than a natural outgrowth of long standing religious bargains and compromises, the answer is clearly no.[58] However, the above history shows that over the past half century there has been a

[58] See for instance Dore Gold, *Hatred's Kingdom: How Saudi Arabia Supports the New Global Terrorism*, New York: Regnery Publishing, 2003; Stephen Schwartz, *The Two Faces of Islam: Saudi Fundamentalism and its Role in Terrorism*, New York: Alfred A. Knopf, 2003.

strong element of pragmatism to Saudi foreign policy making.[59] An austere and often violent strand of Islam was indeed encouraged, but often this was in order to achieve particular political ends. Over the course of its history, the Saudi royal family and the religious establishment harboured radical religious groups and promoted a very particular kind of religious interpretation in order to defend against regional and international threats. Now those threats have eased, there is reason to believe those very same leaders can reshape their religious message and support.

Saudi decisions over the last two years show that a group of pragmatists exists and is trying to shift course. Not only is charitable giving better controlled and monitored, but there is clear evidence of elements in society trying to reintroduce tolerance, diversity and a less violent interpretation of religion.[60] In fact a battle is currently occurring inside Saudi Arabia for how to interpret religion and the role of religion in politics. Whether the pragmatists have the upper hand is unclear, but it is a battle which reverberates far beyond Saudi Arabia's boundaries.

Both American and Saudi leaders should take something away from the above discussion. For Americans the message is one of timing. Until recently Saudi Arabia's religiosity has been viewed in Washington as a political asset, not a liability. Washington tacitly, and often overtly, supported Saudi proselytising. Even if the Saudi leadership makes a concerted effort to pursue a less violent interpretation of religion, a course correction will not happen overnight. Institutions have been created to promote a very particular kind of ideology abroad. Weak oversight mechanisms monitor curricula and foreign assistance. Reorienting long established proselytising institutions and norms will take time, even under the best of circumstances.

Saudi leaders, for their part, must recognise that notwithstanding the many issues that the United States cares about—including domestic reform, moderate oil prices and the peace process—the criteria along which they are judged is now the men and money that leave Saudi Arabia. The kind of people Saudi Arabia exports and the destination of its religious assistance will determine whether the United

[59] See also the chapter by Nonneman in this volume.
[60] See Lacroix's chapter in this volume.

States views it as a friend or foe. Expectations of warm relations with the United States will be dashed unless there is clear progress on the 'export' of terrorist activity and its support structures.

In sum, while there is good reason to believe the two states *can* work together, it is up to the respective leaders to decide how hard they want to work to make it happen.

EVENTS VERSUS TRENDS: THE ROLE OF ENERGY AND SECURITY IN SUSTAINING THE US–SAUDI RELATIONSHIP

Paul Aarts

The fact that fifteen of the nineteen 9/11 hijackers carried Saudi passports weighed heavily on Riyadh. It took the Saudi authorities a long time to accept publicly the fact that the country had at least been an indirect source of terrorism. Simultaneously, for many in the United States, including in the halls of government, patience with the Saudis started to run thin, questioning whether the US–Saudi relationship was sustainable.

As 2002 progressed, voices from the American neo-conservative establishment increasingly called the trustworthiness of the Al Sa'ud into question. The climate was most audibly pronounced by a Rand Corporation employee, Laurent Murawiec, in July of the same year, during his presentation before the Defense Policy Board. He branded Saudi Arabia the 'kernel of evil, the prime mover, the most dangerous opponent' in the Middle East. He presented a slide show with titles that included 'taking the "Saudi" out of Arabia'. Although government spokespersons dissociated themselves from these ideas, they could nevertheless be interpreted as a sign of Washington's changing attitude towards Saudi Arabia and, more important, the House of Sa'ud. In the same presentation, Murawiec went beyond a call for regime change in Riyadh. In words no less clear, he advocated taking over the rich oilfields in Saudi Arabia's eastern provinces (and, in passing, freezing all Saudi bank holdings in the United States).

Max Singer, of the Hudson Institute, had an idea of his own: why not make the eastern province, where Shi'ites are the majority, a new 'Muslim Republic of East Arabia'? This would take the area—and its oil—out of Saudi hands.[1] Although such 'Saudi bashing' was initially mainly a media pastime, similar views were increasingly expressed in a number of more heavy-weight publications and in Congress.[2] In November 2003, a group of senators presented the 'Saudi Arabia Accountability Act'. The Act entails imposing military and diplomatic sanctions on Saudi Arabia for allegedly failing 'to halt Saudi support for institutions that fund, train, incite, encourage, or in any way aid and abet terrorism.'[3]

The heated debate has led some—not seldom Likud sympathisers—to conclude that the American government seems to be under some kind of Saudi spell and that whenever Riyadh speaks Washington is all ears.[4] In *Sleeping with the Devil*, Robert Baer presents a good example of these sentiments. The conclusion is not surprising: 'At the very least, we will have to consider seizing the oil fields.'[5] In addition, he rightly points out that this line of thought was not

1 For a recent overview, see Joshua Teitelbaum, 'The "Desert Democracy"', *Jerusalem Report*, 15 December 2003; and Gary Leupp, 'On Terrorism, Methodism, Saudi "Wahhabism" and the Censored 9/11 Report', *Saudi-American Forum*, 12 August 2003, http://www.saudi-american-forum.org/.

2 The best survey so far is given by Max Rodenbeck, 'Unloved in Arabia', *New York Review of Books*, 21 October 2004, pp. 22–5. He deals with several publications, among which some figure prominently: Craig Unger, *House of Bush, House of Saud: The Secret Relationship Between the World's Two Most Powerful Dynasties*, New York: Scribner, 2004; and Robert Baer, *Sleeping with the Devil: How Washington Sold Our Soul for Saudi Crude*, New York: Crown Publishers, 2003. Also included, though certainly belonging to a less serious category, was Dore Gold, *Hatred's Kingdom: How Saudi Arabia Supports the New Global Terrorism*, Washington: Regnery, 2003.

3 Khaled Dawoud, 'Squeezing Saudi Arabia', *Al-Ahram Weekly*, 18–24 December 2003. The 'Saudi-American Forum' launched an 'action alert' to oppose the act. See *Saudi-American Forum*, http://www.saudi-american-forum.org/.

4 Under the title 'Who Has Bought the US Government?', Mamoun Fandy presents a survey of this kind of doubtful analysis. Apart from the claim that the US government is fully at the service of the Saudis, there is another 'theory'—with quite a few adherents in some Arab circles—that 'the Jews' were responsible for 'September 11' (because 'they told some other Jews' in the Twin Towers not to go to work on that fateful day…). In *Al-Sharq al-Awsat*, 5 September 2003, available from: http://www1.columbia.edu/sec/bboard/gulf2000/gulf2000–9/msg02132html.

5 Baer, *Sleeping with the Devil*, p. xviii.

pulled from the air. In August 1975 the Congressional Research Service presented a document titled 'Oil Fields as Military Objectives: A Feasibility Study' to the Special Subcommittee on Investigations of the House Committee on International Relations. At that time both Gerald Ford and Henry Kissinger spoke openly about a possible occupation of Saudi oil fields, should the oil embargo escalate into a strangulation of American industrial capacity.[6]

Baer and his 'partners in mind' agree that an American invasion should not be Washington's first option. A different, but difficult, option is available: 'Counterintuitive as it might seem, Syria offers one way out,'[7] suggesting the uncompromising way the former Syrian president Hafez al-Asad stopped the Islamic opposition dead in its tracks looks very appealing and should be tried in Saudi Arabia as well. At the same time, Baer *cum suis* consider the Saudi tendency to waver in the face of opposition a liability. They do not have confidence in Riyadh's capacity to take a firm position on this subject: 'Failing that, there's always the 82nd Airborne,' he concludes.[8] Analysing the regime's weakness thus, Baer positions himself in the camp of those that think the House of Sa'ud will soon come to an end.[9] The 2003–4 sequence of terrorist attacks within the country, aimed both at Saudi and Western (in particular American) targets, is considered a portent of the Al Sa'ud's bleak future.

Should we conclude from the above that we are witnessing the end of the 'special relationship' between Saudi Arabia and the United States?[10] Indeed, following the successful military campaign against Saddam Hussein's regime, to some the relationship between Washington and Riyadh no longer appears worth pursuing. After all, or so the plea goes, the United States have already withdrawn US troops

[6] The idea of an American intervention to 'protect' the oil fields was also brought up in Robert Tucker, 'Oil: The Issue of American Intervention', *Commentary*, January 1995.

[7] Baer, *Sleeping with the Devil*, p. 207.

[8] *Ibid.*, p. 208.

[9] The sequence of publications predicting the 'end of the House of Sa'ud' started with Said K. Aburish, *The Rise, Corruption and Coming Fall of the House of Saud*, London: Bloomsbury, 1994. Baer added some work of his own in 'The Fall of the House of Saud', *The Atlantic Monthly*, May 2003, pp. 53–62. It is worth remembering that predictions of the fall of the House of Sa'ud go back to Nuri al-Said in the late 1940s (thanks to Robert Vitalis for pointing this out).

[10] Cf. Rachel Bronson's contribution in this volume.

from Saudi soil and have alternatives in the region. Furthermore, dependence on Saudi oil is likely to diminish drastically once the full potential of Iraqi oil is realised. So why bother anymore with the House of Sa'ud?

At the same time the Saudis themselves may appear increasingly to be keeping the United States at arm's length. Some Saudi-watchers claim the regime in Riyadh no longer cares about the United States providing security and are consequently running down the special relationship: 'They feel that they can handle their own security themselves better, thank you very much.'[11]

This chapter scrutinises these claims, arriving at the conclusion that enough common interests remain to sustain the US–Saudi relationship—including, ironically, the 'war on terror'. Saudi–US relations date back to the 1930s—first mainly through oil firms, later also on a governmental level—and have remained pretty robust throughout, occasional sharp tensions notwithstanding.[12] Just as those earlier

[11] 'Crossroads in US–Saudi Relations: interview with Jean-François Seznec', *Saudi–US Relations Information Service*, 8 October 2004, http://www.SaudiUS-Relations.org.

[12] The US–Saudi relationship turned sour during the oil embargo of 1973–4, but even this has to be qualified: Obaid has shown that King Faisal resorted to the 'oil weapon' only after enormous domestic pressure (mainly from the religious establishment) and 'even then took steps to mitigate the negative impact he knew this policy would have on the United States.' See Nawaf Obaid, *The Oil Kingdom at 100: Petroleum Policymaking in Saudi Arabia*, The Washington Institute for Near East Policy, 2000, p. 99. Richard W. Murphy suggests that 'Many Americans would be surprised to learn that, over the decades, our bilateral relationship has not always been smooth sailing. [...] However, the strength and importance of the US–Saudi relationship during the Cold War was beyond dispute' (Richard W. Murphy, 'Why We Still Need Saudi Arabia', *bitterlemons*, 10, 2, 11 March 2004, http://bitterlemons-international.org/previous.php?opt=1&id=31. For a thorough historical exposé, see Robert Vitalis, 'The Closing of the Arabian Oil Frontier and the Future of Saudi-American Relations', *Middle East Report*, 204 (July–September 1997), pp. 15–21; and his 'Black Gold, White Crude: An Essay on American Exceptionalism, Hierarchy, and Hegemony in the Gulf', *Diplomatic History*, 26, 2 (spring 2002), pp. 185–213. In a recent essay, Vitalis argues that the past is very similar to the present, i.e. that there is nothing 'unique' in the annals of the 'special relationship' ('The Origins of the Crisis Narrative in US–Saudi Relations: The Year Bin Ladin Was Born', paper for the conference on *Saudi Futures: Trends and Challenges in the Post 9/11, Post-Iraq War World*, Institute for the Study of Islam in the Modern World, University of Amsterdam and Lancaster University, 19–21 February 2004, Leiden, the Netherlands).

moments of tension failed to undermine the underlying strength of the relationship, so it can be surmised this pattern will not be radically altered in the years to come. This does not mean that nothing has changed since the events of 11 September 2001. What certainly has changed is the deepening animosity of both the US and the Saudi public—once again clearly showing that the relationship has never relied on a broad-based public support on either side of the partnership. In effect, it always has been an elite bargain.

Certainly the artificial honeymoon is over. But while there is arguably some kind of separation or at least a parting of the minds, it would be wrong to conclude that we are heading for a complete divorce. The most likely scenario is that the United States and Saudi Arabia are entering a more 'normal' relationship, which is nonetheless still very much dictated by the logic of energy and security. Indeed, these form two of the four pillars upon which the 'special relationship' was built—the other two being Saudi Arabia's role as the moderate power in the Arab-Israeli conflict, and its prominent place within the Arab and Islamic world.[13] This chapter will limit itself to a discussion of the first two pillars: energy and security. Obviously the two are strongly interlinked, with energy relations to an extent 'dictating' security ties.

The Security Factor

It is striking that the American government went to considerable lengths to maintain good relations with Saudi Arabia in the immediate aftermath of 9/11—mirroring similar attempts by Saudi Arabia in 1973–4. Energy Secretary Spencer Abraham continued to cultivate relations with Saudi Arabia and Washington was at pains to stub out any suggestion that the Saudi regime could be even remotely implicated in the events. A number of incidents showcase this commitment. A number of incidents showcase this commitment,

[13] Concerning the fourth pillar, reference can be made here to the role pro-American Saudi Arabia played after the Islamic revolution took place in Iran, and to Saudi support in the fight against the Soviet occupation of Afghanistan. The pillars mentioned above also feature, though in a different shape, in the excellent survey of Saudi-European relations by Gerd Nonneman, 'Saudi-European Relations 1902–2001: A Pragmatic Quest for Relative Autonomy', *International Affairs*, 77, 3 (2001), pp. 631–61.

in particular the 28 pages that were blacked out in a 900-page document put together by Congress and Bush's ensuing declaration that 'security issues' demanded this level of secrecy. Despite this, Craig Unger's allegations that a number of Saudi royals, as well as members of the Bin Ladin family, were flown out of the United States in private jets shortly after 9/11, added fuel to the controversy—even if the subsequent 9/11 report disproved the claim that they had been let go before air space closures had been lifted.[14]

Security is a key issue of common interest for the two countries, dating back to early 1945 when Ibn Sa'ud received a pledge from Franklin Roosevelt that the United States would at all times guarantee Saudi territorial integrity. Throughout the Cold War period there were many reasons for the Saudi and American leaders to work together. In addition to oil, the Kingdom's geographic location and ideological leanings underpinned the 'special relationship'.[15] In the following decades, the agreement developed *de facto* into a *quid pro quo*: The United States guaranteed protection from external threats and favourable trading terms, while Saudi Arabia committed itself to producing sufficient oil at reasonable prices, and 'recycled' a significant portion of its oil income through the economies and banks of the developed world (prominently including the US). That such choices on the part of the Saudi leadership were arguably simply good economic sense given the country's low absorption capacity and its interest in long-term oil market stability, does not diminish the extent to which their consistent application helped consolidate the relationship with Washington.

Indeed, Saudi Arabia has been the destination of a great number of American arms exports, though it must be stressed that the Kingdom always has done its utmost to maintain the benefits of 'multi-dependence'.[16] Saudi Arabia spends more on defence per capita than

[14] Following his initial *Vanity Fair* article, Unger produced a book on the 'special relationship': *House of Saud, House of Bush*. It should be remarked that Unger's exposé is not always convincing, and, in places, factually inaccurate. For more on this, see the online discussion between the author and Rachel Bronson of the Council on Foreign Relations (and contributor to this volume) via http:://slate.msn.com/id/2103239 (between 6–8 July 2004). Also see Rodenbeck's critical review, 'Unloved in Arabia'.

[15] See Rachel Bronson's chapter in this volume.

[16] More data on this—including figures for European versus American arms

any other country in the world (more than one third of its budget). The total value of American arms sales to Saudi Arabia over the past half-century approaches $100 billion, with over a quarter of the contracts signed in the 1990s. These figures include weapons, support equipment, spare parts, support services, and construction.[17] The best known military facility in the country, built by the Americans, is the Prince Sultan air base ('PSAB', located south of Riyadh), home to some 4,500–5,000 American soldiers since 1991.[18]

The presence of these troops has always aggravated Bin Ladin and his followers, and he has never missed an opportunity to avow that he wanted to see an end to that presence.[19] To both Washington and Riyadh this constituted a devil's dilemma: how to remove the American presence without seeming to give in to Bin Ladin? Quicker than expected, the solution announced itself after the Iraq war, which did away with the need for a military presence on Saudi soil. Already in April 2003 the announcement had been made that most American troops would leave the country (evacuation had taken place by August that year). Thus the Gordian knot that had tied the two countries together since 1990 was cut.[20]

---

exports—are given by Nonneman, 'Saudi-European Relations 1902–2001', and in his contribution to this volume.

[17] Cordesman reports that Saudi Arabia bought $6.6 billion worth of new arms during 1995–8 ($4.9 billion from the US) and signed $4.1 billion worth of new arms agreements during 1999–2002 ($2.8 billion with the US); see Anthony H. Cordesman, 'The Prospects for Stability in Saudi Arabia in 2004', *Saudi–US Relations Information Service*, 23 February 2004. Cordesman confirms Nonneman's prediction that 'the first decade of the twenty-first century may well see a reassertion of the United States' pre-eminent position' (Nonneman, 'Saudi-European Relations 1902–2001', p. 650). Also see Josh Pollack, 'Saudi Arabia and the United States, 1931–2002', *MERIA Journal*, September 2002, http://meria.biu.ac.il/, pp. 35–9; J. E. Peterson, *Saudi Arabia and the Illusion of Security*, Oxford University Press, Adelphi Paper, no. 348); and James A. Russell, 'Deconstructing the US–Saudi Partnership?', *Strategic Insights: Middle East*, 3 September 2002.

[18] Before 1990–1 only a small number of American soldiers were present within Saudi borders, largely in training and support functions. The US protective umbrella was projected mainly from 'over the horizon'.

[19] See, for instance, his 'Declaration of War' (August 1996) in his call to establish the 'World Islamic Front for the Jihad Against the Jews and the Crusaders' (February 1998).

[20] Robert Vitalis points out, however, that the United States had given up bases under pressure before—at no cost. He argues that speaking in terms of 'dilemmas'

What is more, the Saudis had covertly supported the United States in the Iraq war.[21] As Guttman observed, 'Saudi Arabia [was] the hidden player in the American[-led Coalition's] war on Iraq.'[22] Even though American bombers were not allowed to take off from Prince Sultan air base, the PSAB command and control centre was used intensively. Virtually every request made by the Bush administration for military or logistical assistance was met positively. 'We would never have been able to conduct the war against Iraq as we did without Saudi assistance,' admitted an American diplomat in Riyadh.[23] Captivating detail is provided by Dobbs and Bradley.[24] The *Los Angeles Times* reported that even during the invasion of Iraq 10,000 troops were stationed at the PSAB.[25] It also quotes several Islamist websites that warn word of a troop withdrawal was a lie: 'The infidel soldiers weren't going anywhere... It was just government propaganda.'

The defeat of Saddam Hussein's regime has certainly helped to reduce some of the security risks in the Gulf, but not others. At the time of writing (October 2004), the condition in Iraq looked as if it might remain volatile for years. Hence, after the successful military campaign, the military bond between the United States and Saudi Arabia has not been cut off nor is it likely to be in the near future.

---

is merely part of a 'rhetorical strategy' (personal communication, February 2004). For a useful survey of US–Saudi relations, including the pre-9/11 strains, see Martin Sieff, 'Sand in Our Eyes: US–Saudi Relations After Iraq', *National Interest*, summer 2004, pp. 93–100. For more details on the relocated 'pre-positioning' of American military equipment in the Gulf, see Gregory Gause III, 'GCC-US Relations' in *Gulf in a Year: 2003*, Dubai: Gulf Research Center, January 2004, pp. 244–57.

[21] Alain Gresh, 'After the Winning of the War. Saudi Arabia: Radical Islam or Reform?', *Le Monde Diplomatique* [online, English edition], June 2003, http://mondediplo.com/; and Guy Dinmore and Roula Khalaf, 'Inside the Desert Kingdom: Part II', *Financial Times*, 19 November 2003.

[22] Nathan Guttman, 'Background: AIPAC and the Iraqi Opposition', *Haaretz*, 8 April 2003, http://www.haaretzdaily.com/.

[23] Gresh, 'After the Winning of the War'.

[24] Michael Dobbs, 'US–Saudi Ties Prove Crucial in War', *Saudi-American Forum*, 29 April 2003, http://www.saudi-american-forum.org/; and John R. Bradley, 'Saudi Islamists begin targeting the security forces', *Daily Star*, 7 January 2004, via http://www1.columbia.edu/sec/bboard/gulf2000/gulf2000-9/msg02427.html.

[25] Megan K. Stack, 'Jihad Hits Home in Saudi Arabia', *LA Times*, 25 April 2004, via http://www1.columbia.edu/sec/bboard/gulf2000/gulf2000–9/msg02637.html.

As a seasoned observer remarked, 'Saudi Arabia remains dependent on the United States for training and technical services. It cannot sustain independent combat without US support [...] and it cannot use many of its air control and warning assets without the US back up. [...] Any break with the United States would virtually derail its modernization efforts.'[26]

Still, both Riyadh and Washington are in high spirits over the almost total removal of any *visible* operational component on the Prince Sultan air base, and indeed the withdrawal marked the end of an extraordinary period of open military cooperation that started with the 1990–1 Gulf War.[27] The military relationship between the two countries has now clearly reverted to 'normal', i.e. to what it was before Iraq's invasion of Kuwait in 1990: cooperation on arms sales and military training, but without significant numbers of American troops on Saudi soil. Clearly a strong American involvement in the military infrastructure of the Kingdom of Saudi Arabia will, in a different, less visible way, remain.[28]

Elsewhere in this volume Nonneman points out 'The two key aims which Saudi Arabia's rulers have pursued and continue to pursue in their foreign policy are: (1) domestic security; (2) external

[26] Anthony H. Cordesman, 'Saudi Redeployment of the F-15 to Tabuk', *Saudi–US Relations Information Service*, 1 November 2003.

[27] For a plea as controversial as it is forceful, to come to a wholesale reduction of the American military's 'footprint' in the entire Gulf region, see Christopher Preble, 'After Victory: Towards a New Military Posture in the Persian Gulf', *Policy Analysis*, 477, 10 June 2003, pp. 1–15. Equally controversial is the view that the Saudis, after 'Iraq', completely lost confidence in the American military umbrella, seeing the Americans as 'a bull on its knees'. According to Youssef Ibrahim, former *New York Times* correspondent in the Middle East, the Saudis tend to see the United States more and more 'as a pussy they can fuck' (interview, Dubai, September 2004).

[28] Russell, 'Deconstructing the US–Saudi Partnership?'; Cordesman, 'Saudi Redeployment of the F-15 to Tabuk'; and Cordesman, 'Ten Reasons for Reforging the US and Saudi Relationship', *Saudi-American Forum*, 1 February 2004. Cordesman specifies to what extent the United States has *not* left Saudi Arabia in security terms. Also see Cordesman Nawaf Obaid, *Saudi National Security: Military and Security Services—Challenges Developments*, Washington, DC: Center for Strategic and International Studies, 30 May 2004, working draft. Kate Dourian, Middle East editor of Platts, confirms this by stating that the Saudis—notably Oil Minister Ali al-Naimi—still view the United States as 'the only superpower' (interview, Dubai, September 2004).

security.'[29] This is as true today as ever. Not only are they worried about persistent instability in Iraq[30] and about Iran's potential nuclear aspirations, but both Washington and Riyadh realise they have little option but to cooperate in the 'war on terror'. From a Saudi point of view the United States remains crucially the most powerful potential protector—even though the leadership is aware there is a trade-off with concerns over domestic legitimacy.[31]

The Energy Factor

The importance of Saudi oil for the American market seems self-evident, though in a different sense than some commentators have suggested. At face value the equation seems straightforward—the United States accounts for one fifth of the world oil consumption and Saudi Arabia is the world's largest oil exporter—but a closer look reveals a more complex situation. Even if the United States were to reduce its oil imports from Saudi Arabia or were to refrain from using Saudi oil altogether, it would still be in Washington's best interest to preserve a healthy relationship with Riyadh, for at least four reasons.

The short term: other sources, other problems

The short-term perspective is the closest to received wisdom that the 'United States cannot do without Saudi oil'. In the wake of 9/11 there has been an increasingly voiced demand in the United States, especially in neo-conservative circles, to minimise the Saudi relationship and import oil from elsewhere, including post-Saddam

[29] See Nonneman's chapter in this volume, p. 318.

[30] A recent Chatham House paper sketches several scenarios for Iraq in the 18-month transitional period which began with the handover of power on 28 June 2004. Of special interest is the survey of the implications for neighbouring countries. Concerning Saudi Arabia, the main conclusion is that 'Iraq is at best a competitor and at worst an enemy' (p. 16). Of even greater concern, although not perhaps very likely, would be the emergence of a powerful 'Commonwealth of Petrolistan', based on a 'significantly more assertive Shi'a power in Iraq and increased unity with their ideological brothers in the region' (idem). See Briefing Paper, *Iraq in Transition: Vortex or Catalyst?*, London: Chatham House, Middle East Programme BP 04/02, September 2004.

[31] On the 'omni-balancing' between these calculations in overall Saudi foreign policy, see the chapter by Nonneman in this volume.

Iraq.[32] In a similar vein, though with different accents, this trend was strengthened during the campaign for the American presidency when Senator John Kerry launched his ambitious 'Energy Independence Program' (EIP). At the Democratic Convention in July 2004 Kerry proclaimed, '(...) our energy plan for a stronger America will invest in new technologies and alternative fuels and the cars of the future—so that no young American in uniform will ever be held hostage to our dependence on oil from the Middle East.' He specified his wish to be no longer reliant on 'the Saudi royal family'.[33]

This echoes Richard Nixon's promise of energy 'independence'. However, the brutal fact is that this is no more feasible in the foreseeable future than it was then. Clearly, the biggest problem lies in developing a transport fuel that can compete with oil. But, as Cassidy has shown, concentrating on the demand side (without neglecting the supply side) would be more useful, thus getting serious about conservation would be a lot more practical than talking about the 'hydrogen economy'.[34] 'Sooner or later,' says Robert Mabro, 'we are going to have a lot of hybrid cars, electric cars, and, perhaps, at some time in the future, we are going to have a hydrogen economy. But, until we get there, to talk about energy independence is foolish. The

[32] An eloquent example of neo-conservative 'oil-thinking' is presented by Max Singer, 'Saudi Arabia's Overrated Oil Weapon', *Weekly Standard*, 18 August 2003, via http://www1.columbia.edu/sec/bboard/gulf2000/gulf2000-29/msg01389 html. Edward Morse gives an insightful analysis of the neo-con view of oil. High on this revisionist agenda are: lowering prices, undermining OPEC, using the oil weapon to isolate Libya and Iran, and fostering private ownership of oil resources; see his 'Is the Energy Map Next on the Neo-Conservative Cartography Agenda?', *Middle East Economic Digest*, XLVI, 33, 18 August 2003, via http://www1.columbia.edu/sec/bboard/gulf2000/gulf2000-29/msg01397.html. Also see John B. Judis, 'Who Will Control Iraq's Oil? Over a Barrel', *New Republic*, 20 January 2003, via http://www1.columbia.edu/sec-cgi-bin/gulf/dataplug.pl?dir=/www/data/cu/sipa/GULF2000. Interestingly, the role of Saudi Arabia as a target of the neo-conservatives' 'revisionist' agenda does not figure in Morse's overview, while it figures prominently in Judis's.

[33] John Cassidy, 'Pump Dreams: Is Energy Independence an Impossible Goal?', *New Yorker*, 11 October 2004, p. 1, via http://www1.columbia.edu/sec/bboard/gulf2000/gulf2000-29/msg01815.html. Also see Hisham Khatib, 'John Kerry: Energy Independence Program', *Middle East Economic Survey*, XLVII, 35, 30 August 2004, via http://www1.columbia.edu/sec/bboard/gulf2000/gulf2000-29/msg01780.html.

[34] *Ibid.*, p. 8.

two candidates, with due respect, are lying to the people, or they don't know what they are talking about.'[35]

Both John Kerry and the George W. Bush administration fantasise about America's 'energy independence', and although the Democratic and Republican energy plans differ, their underlying rationale is the same. The Bush administration apparently believes that there is still plenty of oil yet to be discovered beneath the North American continent, hence its proposal to expand tax breaks for drilling and exploration. The Arctic National Wildlife Refuge (ANWR), with possible reserves of 10 billion barrels, is Bush's new hope. In the optimistic scenario that this figure proves to be true, it might provide one million barrels a day, or five per cent of present US demand. But the practical effect would be to offset some drop in production elsewhere. American output peaked in 1970; since then it has declined some 34 per cent.[36] So one is tempted to conclude that both Bush's and Kerry's 'energy-independence' plans were no more than election gimmicks that would collapse when faced with US market and global energy realities.

What about non-Middle Eastern oil supplies? Russia (which in 2003 surpassed Saudi Arabia as the largest oil-producing county in the world) ranks high on the 'alternative list' and is followed, at a considerable distance, by Caspian Sea countries and some oil producers in Western Africa. All these alternative sources could supplement the imports already flowing from countries closer to home, such as Canada, Mexico and Venezuela. However, the short-term prospects for substantially increasing oil imports from Russia or the Caspian Sea countries are not very promising: oil found in these regions cannot easily find its way to the world market due to, among other factors, logistical problems.[37] Moreover, the oil reserves in these

35 As quoted in Cassidy, 'Pump Dreams', p. 9. Also see Robert J. Samuelson, 'Oil Fantasies', *Washington Post*, 6 October 2004. Interview with John Roberts, Senior Editor with Platts, Dubai, September 2004.

36 Samuelson, 'Oil Fantasies'.

37 More on this by Joe Barnes, Amy Jaffe and Edward L. Morse, 'The New Geopolitics of Oil', *National Interest*, Special Energy Supplement, winter 2003/4, via http://www.nationalinterest.org/ME2/Segments/Articles/Template1/Common/print.asp?m.... The message is simple: other sources, other problems. Also see Frank A. Verrastro's contribution to the panel discussion 'Securing US Energy in a Changing World', Washington, DC: Middle East Policy Council, 17 September 2004, http://www.mepc.org/public_asp/forums_chcs/37.html, p. 4.

countries are far less extensive than those in the Persian Gulf (Russia, for example, holds 4.6 per cent of proven world oil reserves whereas Saudi Arabia holds 25 per cent), while at the same time production costs are substantially higher than in the Middle East.[38] In short, there is little reason to conclude that Russia is likely to act as a ministering angel.

Will Iraq bring relief then? The country has proven oil reserves that amount to 115 billion barrels, second highest in the world after Saudi Arabia (and it is believed that the country's probable reserves are considerably greater). In the short term, however, Iraq will not be of great help to an oil-thirsty United States. Though regime change in Baghdad has definitely reshuffled the cards and has given American (and British) firms greater access to Iraq's oil sector, it will be many years before this materialises into substantially increased oil production (see below). Rehabilitating the existing infrastructure and regaining the pre-Gulf War capacity of around 3.5 million b/d might cost up to $5–6 billion.[39] Under present conditions, where such investment would come from is not clear. For the time being Iraq's oil industry will continue to be unreliable and erratic. Those

[38] Curiously, some recent sources name significantly higher estimates of Saudi oil production costs than the $1–2 per barrel usually quoted. See David Ignatius, 'Revising the Forecasts for Saudi Oil', *Daily Star*, 17 November 2003.

[39] Muhammad-Ali Zainy, 'Iraq's Oil Sector: Scenarios for the Future', presentation at the conference on 'The Gulf Oil and Gas Sector: Potential Constraints', Abu Dhabi: Emirates Center for Strategic Studies Research, 26–7 September 2004 and *Gulf News*, 2 October 2004. Also: Gal Luft, 'Iraq's Oil Sector One Year After Liberation', Washington, DC: Saban Center Middle East Memo no. 4, 17 June 2004, http://brookings.edu/fp/saban/luftmemo20040617.htm; and Kate Dourian, 'Sweet and Sour: Iraq May Need Time to Become a True Oil Power', *Gulf News*, 28 January 2004. In an optimistic scenario, one could speculate about the possible effects of Iraq's opening to the international oil companies through Production Sharing Agreements (PSA). These offer attractive conditions for prospective investors, certainly in comparison with the 'standard' contracts that are on offer in most Gulf states. In that case, private contractors or concessionaires would be encouraged to maximise output in order to reap maximum financial reward—and this would have an impact on Iraq's behaviour within OPEC and thus influence Saudi Arabia's own quotum policy within this organisation. For a succinct survey of different options for oil-field development (through national oil companies only, on service-contract basis, via PSAs, or licence-based), see John Roberts, 'Oil and the Iraq War of 2003', *Journal of Energy and Development*, 29, 1 (2003), pp. 1–24, pp. 9–10.

Washington hardliners who thought Iraq could easily emerge as a counterbalance to Saudi Arabia's power over the oil market will have to wait a while—and probably longer (see below).

Unintentionally, the American-led Coalition's invasion has even resulted in the loss of an average of 2 million b/d of Iraqi oil from the markets. Contrary to the rosy promises of some neo-conservatives, who had hoped Iraq would be turned into 'America's private gasoline pump', the world has lost much of Iraq's oil output.[40] Iraqi insurgents have designated the oil industry a prime target in their quest to incapacitate the Coalition's anointed government. First the attacks were largely against Iraq's northern pipelines that run to Turkey's Mediterranean terminal at Ceyhan. Later the southern network was also being hit.[41] Consequently, at the time of writing the country found itself in the humiliating position of having to import oil products such as gasoline, diesel and fuel oil. On good days, i.e. when one (or more) of the pipelines is not on fire, Iraqi oil exports amounted to just about 1.5 million b/d (and sometimes even less).[42]

Thus, at least in the short to medium term, it looks like the United States cannot do without oil supplies from the Middle East (and Saudi Arabia in particular), although the Kingdom's position has become a little less prominent since the end of 2002. This may have had to do with the fact that by that time the United States was getting ready for the invasion of Iraq, which obviously was not in tune with Saudi thinking.[43] For years on end Saudi Arabia has been the number one crude oil supplier to the US market. They managed to keep this position simply by the way they priced their oil. Although this is difficult to document, the Saudis up to late 2002 had been discounting their oil for the US market by around 30 cents a barrel—

[40] Youssef Ibrahim, 'An Oil Market Running on Empty', *Daily Star*, 2 October 2004; and interview with Kate Dourian.

[41] Ed Blanche, 'An Industry Under Fire', *Arabies Trends*, September 2004, pp. 40–3; also Justin Blum, 'Terrorists Have Oil Industry in Cross Hairs: Economic Disruption is a Key Goal', *Washington Post*, 27 September 2004; and Luft, 'Iraq's Oil Sector One Year After Liberation'.

[42] For more details, see Ibrahim, 'An Oil Market Running on Empty'; and in particular http://www.iraqrevenuewatch.org/.

[43] James Plancke in a panel discussion on 'How to Reform Saudi Arabia Without Handing It to Extremists', *Saudi–US Relations Information Service*, 19 September 2004, pp. 11–12.

some even speak of about $1 per barrel discount.[44] Since the 'special relationship' stopped being so special, the Saudis gradually have been going where the market takes them, i.e. to East Asia and China in particular. In recent years the United States has been increasing its oil imports from countries like Canada, Mexico, Venezuela and Nigeria. Even so, Saudi Arabia still figures among its top five suppliers. According to EIA figures, in 2003 Saudi Arabia ranked second (after Canada and just ahead of Mexico) as a source of total (crude plus refined products) US oil imports, and first for crude only (ahead of Mexico, Canada and Venezuela).[45] Both in 2003 and 2004, the United States imported over 2 million b/d from the Persian Gulf region, which is 12 per cent of its oil needs and 22 per cent of total net oil imports. The vast majority of its Gulf oil imports (over 70 per cent) came from Saudi Arabia.[46] It is by no means certain that the Saudis will drop out of the top-five exporters into the US market by 2010.

The longer term: growing imports

Related to the above trend is the second motive for the United States to preserve its good relations with the world's largest oil exporter. The Department of Energy's Energy Information Administration (EIA) projects the United States' import dependence will

[44] There is debate about whether this discount should be seen as a 'hidden subsidy' to the American consumer. Author's interviews with Kate Dourian and Ian Seymour, Editor Emeritus of *Middle East Economic Survey*, Dubai, September 2004. See also Abdullatif A. al-Othman, 'The Reliable Supplier' and Cyrus H. Tahmassebi, 'Refuting the Myths' (in 'Does Saudi Arabia Still Matter? Differing Perspectives on the Kingdom and Its Oil'), *Foreign Affairs*, November–December 2002, pp. 173–5, and 175–6. James Plancke holds the view that this 'discount' should be seen as nothing more than the difference in transportation costs that the Saudis had to absorb if they wanted to sell their oil in distant US markets rather than in nearby Europe or Asia. See Plancke, 'How to Reform Saudi Arabia' and his contribution to another panel discussion, 'Securing US Energy in a Changing World', Washington, DC: Middle East Policy Council, 17 September 2004, http://www.mepc.org/public_asp/forums_chcs/37.html, pp. 6–7.

[45] See Energy Information Administration, *Country Analysis Briefs: Saudi Arabia*, Washington, DC: Department of Energy, June 2004, http://www.eia.doe.gov/emeu/cabs/saudi.html, p. 6.

[46] See Energy Information Administration, *Country Analysis Briefs: Persian Gulf Oil and Gas Exports Fact Sheet*, Washington, DC: Department of Energy, September 2004, http://www.eia.doe.gov/emeu/cabs/pbgulf.html.

reach 67.9 per cent of its consumption in 2025 (compared to 54.9 per cent in 2001).[47] In this context, the EIA's most relevant forecast is that over the 24-year period 2001–25 not only is Middle East oil output to double, but also to grow three times faster than output in the whole of the rest of the world. Saudi production alone must increase from 10.2 million b/d to 23.8 million b/d—an increase of 133 per cent. Consequently, the United States will become increasingly dependent on oil supplies from the Middle East, and from Saudi Arabia in particular.

The United States' National Energy Policy Development Group (NEPDG), which had been charged with developing a long-range plan to meet US energy requirements, completed its report in early 2001. Bush subsequently anointed the report—also known as the Cheney report—the National Energy Policy (NEP). Close reading of this document shows that—apart from boosting production at home through the exploitation of untapped reserves in protected wilderness areas—its basic goal is less to focus on energy conservation than to find additional external sources of oil for the United States.

The report also calls for substantially expanding Saudi capacity, preferably through increased US oil company investments.[48] Naturally all successive American administrations will be concerned that US oil supplies come from a stable area. As John Roberts has remarked, 'The question is whether a natural concern for stability, coupled

[47] Energy Information Administration, *Annual Energy Outlook 2003, With Projections to 2025*, Washington, DC: Department of Energy, January 2003. The DOE estimates that Gulf OPEC states exported an average of 16.9 million b/d, or 30 per cent of the world total of 56.3 million b/d in 2002. It projects that Gulf exports will reach 35.8 million b/d by 2025 and then reach 37 per cent of the world total of 94.6 million b/d. Also see 'Why Reforge the US and Saudi Relationship?', an interview with Anthony Cordesman, *Saudi–US Relations Information Service*, 28 September 2004, and Cordesman, 'Ten Reasons for Reforging the US and Saudi Relationship', *Saudi-American Forum*, 1 February 2004.

[48] Michael Klare, 'Bush-Cheney Energy Strategy: Procuring the Rest of the World's Oil', *Foreign Policy in Focus*, 6 January 2004, via http://www.petropolitics.org. It is another matter, of course, whether the Saudis—as well as other OPEC members—are willing to increase production substantially, recalling the fateful decision to opt for its highest ever quota increase in 1997. It was a move that only months later helped bring about a collapse of oil prices as the Asian economy faltered and the West's dot-com bubble burst.

with an increased global reliance on oil from the Middle East and North Africa, needs to be transformed from an ability into an actual intention to secure greater physical control of the Middle East in order to ensure security of supply.'[49]

In this context, some have labelled the Iraq war 'a war for oil'.[50] That is misguided, as the third Gulf War is a prime example of how multifaceted and multicausal a war can be. There were a number of other core factors that drove the policy makers to march on Baghdad, even if oil did come into the equation (indeed, oil was one factor also in terms of conduct and consequences of the fighting).[51] Perhaps the key oil-related factor was a more global concern for longer-term security of predictably-priced energy sources to the world economy—with which the United States is so intricately connected (see the following section). Yet it would be wrong to view the Iraq war as a prelude to post-Saddam's Iraq as 'the linchpin of a new oil order'—in which a 'US dependent Iraq would supplant Saudi control of oil prices and marginalize the influence of the Saudi-led OPEC oil cartel'.[52] After all, while some may have fantasised about such outcomes, other factors and considerations were more important, and 'Big Oil' was by and large opposed to the idea of the war, which was considered destabilising and unpredictable in its consequences, contrary to the proven willingness of even Saddam himself to supply oil at acceptable prices.

[49] John Roberts, 'Oil and the Iraq War of 2003', p. 17.

[50] Roberts reminds us that five weeks before the war started, Robert Byrd, the former Democratic Senate leader asked: 'Will we seize Iraq's oil fields, becoming an occupying power which controls the price and supply of that nation's oil for the foreseeable future?'; see Roberts, 'Oil and the Iraq War of 2003', p. 18. The 'war for oil' argument is made by, for instance, Youssef Ibrahim, 'Oil and Politics Make for an Extremely Flammable Cocktail', *Gulf News*, 13 January 2004; Michael Klare, 'It's the Oil, Stupid', *Foreign Policy in Focus*, 2 May 2003, http://www.fpif.org; and Michael Renner. 'Oil Über Alles?', Washington, DC: World Watch Institute, 11 October 2002. Hardly anyone, however, claimed that the United States intended to take over Iraq's oil industry lock, stock and barrel.

[51] Roberts, 'Oil and the Iraq War of 2003', pp. 1–9.

[52] Isam Salim Shanti, 'Oil and the US War Against Iraq: A Strategic Goal' in *Gulf in a Year: 2003*, Dubai: Gulf Research Center, January 2004, pp. 106–17. For a critical analysis on this, see Edward L. Morse, 'Fighting for Oil?', *National Interest*, summer 2004, pp. 37–40; also Roberts, 'Oil and the Iraq War of 2003'.

In any case, the Iraqi oil industry will face substantial problems for a good many years to come, hence it is too soon to speak in grandiose terms about the future of 'Iraq's oil bonanza'.[53] On top of the roughly $5–6 billion needed to reach pre-war capacity, some $35–40 billion needs to be invested over the next ten years to boost production to 5–6 million b/d.[54] Suggestions that Iraq's output could rise to as much as 10 million b/d by 2020 are wide of the mark. All this underlines Saudi Arabia's continuous importance, hence Washington's unrelenting interest in stability in the Kingdom which in its turn influences American geostrategic thinking—as demonstrated in the Cheney report.

Anti-denial strategy

This geostrategic thinking dates back to January 1980, when president Carter decreed the doctrine, now named after him, which states that unrestricted access to the Persian Gulf is of vital interest to the United States and, in protection of that interest, the United States will employ 'any means necessary, including military force'.[55] As vital as ever, the Carter doctrine brings us to the third motivation, which is closely connected to the second. As already suggested, the United States is not only concerned about its 'own oil', but also (or even more so) about international supply through relations with pro-American regimes in the Middle East, thus making it possible to limit the autonomy of potential rivals like China, and at the same time 'servicing' partners like Europe and Japan (and asking favours in return).

[53] James A. Paul, 'The Iraq Oil Bonanza: Estimating Future Profits', *Global Policy Forum*, 28 January 2004, http://globalpolicy.org/security/oil/2004/0128oilprofit.htm; for a more nuanced treatment, see Michael Renner, 'Post-Saddam Iraq: Linchpin of a New Oil Order', *Foreign Policy in Focus*, January 2003; and idem, 'The Other Looting', *Foreign Policy in Focus*, July 2003.

[54] Luft, 'Iraq's Oil Sector One Year after Liberation', p. 3.

[55] Michael T. Klare, 'The Coming War With Iraq: Deciphering the Bush Administration's Motives', *Foreign Policy in Focus*, 16 January. For a more extensive treatment see his latest book, *Blood and Oil: The Dangers and Consequences of America's Growing Petroleum Dependency*, New York: Henry Holt, 2004. For a historical backgrounder, see the (edited version of the official) transcript of a speech by Secretary of Defense Harold Brown on 6 March 1980 in *MERIP Reports*, 90, September 1980, pp. 20–3.

In fact, even before the Carter presidency, the Truman administration had put in place a secret policy intended to deny the possibility of Soviet control of Middle East oil. Described in a National Security Council directive known as NCS 26/2, a plan was laid out to blow up the Persian Gulf oil fields to deny the Soviets the power that would come with their control. In the 1950s Eisenhower extended this 'oil-denial policy' to include 'hostile regimes' in the region, while president Reagan went a step further by establishing a US Central Command, based in Tampa, and charging it with defending US interests in the Middle East, East Africa and Central Asia. And despite the collapse of Soviet Russia, the US military did not withdraw from the Persian Gulf.[56]

In more recent years, both before and after the Iraq war, the Bush administration has not distanced itself from such thinking. As Dick Cheney once put it in his testimony before the Armed Services Committee: Whoever controls the flow of Persian Gulf oil has a 'stranglehold' not only on our own economy but also 'on that of most of the other nations of the world as well'.[57] 'The road to the entire Middle East goes through Baghdad,' said another Bush administration official in August 2002.[58] In line with these remarks, the administration's Quadrennial Defense Review stated: 'The United States must retain the capacity to send well-armed and logistically supported forces to critical points around the globe, even in the face of enemy opposition.'[59] In a press briefing in August 2001 Deputy Defense Secretary Paul Wolfowitz reiterated these words. Ironically, Wolfowitz formulated a kind of 'area-denial' and 'anti-access strategy', knowing that these words are usually used in military jargon for areas where the United States itself may be confronted with the anti-

[56] Cassidy, 'Pump Dreams: Is Energy Independence an Impossible Goal?', p. 6; Shibley Telhami and Fiona Hill, 'America's Vital Stakes in Saudi Arabia' (in 'Does Saudi Arabia Still Matter?), *Foreign Affairs*, November–December 2002, pp. 167–73; Telhami, 'The Persian Gulf: Understanding the American Oil Strategy', *Brookings Review*, 20, 2 (spring 2002), pp. 32–5, via http://www1.columbia.edu/sec/bboard/gulf2000/gulf2000-29/msg01058.html; idem, 'Are We Stuck in Iraq?', *San Jose Mercury*, 17 October 2004, via http://www1.columbia.edu/sec/bboard/gulf2000/gulf2000-14/msg08433.html; and Kenneth M. Pollack, 'Securing the Gulf', *Foreign Affairs*, 82, 4 (July–August 2003).

[57] Michael Klare, 'The Coming War With Iraq', p. 5.

[58] As quoted in Roberts, 'Oil and the Iraq War of 2003', p. 19.

[59] As quoted in Klare, 'Bush-Cheney Energy Strategy', p. 10.

access strategies of enemy powers.[60] One could argue about the real need for a physical (military) presence in vital regions to exercise control. Showing it has the capacity to intervene might be sufficient, just as the US nuclear umbrella shows the United States does not have to use its nuclear weapons to elicit a degree of compliance from other countries.[61]

In this respect the position of the People's Republic of China is paramount. It is a truism that the Chinese are not going to be content with long-term second-class status and, thus, will speed up their use of energy, primarily oil. China's imports of oil in 2004 were set to expand by some 40 per cent, giving Saudi Arabia the position of China's principal oil supplier. The country is already importing 60 per cent of its oil from the Gulf and this is likely to increase to 80 or 90 per cent in the coming two decades. By 2010 China is expected to have doubled its imports up to the amount of oil that the United States is importing today (and by 2030 its total energy consumption will equal that of the United States and Japan today). Already it has taken second place on the list of the world's largest oil importers, overtaking Japan.[62] In 2002 car sales increased by half, probably sig-

[60] See, for instance, Paul K. Davis, Jimmie McEver, and Barry Wilson, *Measuring Interdiction Capabilities in the Presence of Anti-Access Strategies: Exploratory Analysis to Inform Adaptive Strategy for the Persian Gulf*, Santa Monica, CA: Rand, 2002. Also see: 'From the Editors', *Middle East Report*, 225 (winter 2002), pp. 1, 55–6.

[61] Michael Klare, personal communication, February 2003.

[62] For more on China, see Nikolas K. Gvosdev, 'At the Intersection of Energy and Foreign Policies: Competing for Power', *National Interest* (Special Energy Supplement), p. 4; Ignacio Ramonet, 'China Wakes Up and Alarms the World', *Le Monde Diplomatique*, August 2004 (English internet edition); Philip S. Golub, 'All the Riches of the East Restored', *Le Monde Diplomatique*, October 2004 (English internet edition); Telhami and Hill, 'America's Vital Stakes in Saudi Arabia', p. 171; Andrew Thompson-Bush, 'Why Asia Means Business', *Arabies Trends*, September 2004, pp. 47–9. The most recent IEA figures confirm this trend, indicating an even larger dependence on Middle East oil for China, India and the United States; see *World Energy Outlook 2004*, Paris: International Energy Agency, October 2004.

Strikingly, Giacomo Luciani contests the conventional wisdom that East Asia is going to be the main importer of Gulf oil. 'By 2030 the US will [still] top the list of the oil-importing countries and its deficit will amount 16 million b/d'; see abstract of the workshop 'The External Factors and Political Stability in the GCC States', Dubai, Gulf Research Center, 8–9 January 2003. In a way, Kate Dourian concurs: 'It is all very well to look at demand growth in China and

nifying the start of the Chinese 'car wave', and it plans to complete a highway system more extensive than the US interstate network by 2015.

If China maintains its growth dynamic without major political and/or social disruptions, it will indisputably become a dominant player in the international economic and financial system. The country is already the world's number one importer of cement, coal, steel, nickel and aluminium.[63] Some Chinese economists believe that China's economy will catch up with the United States by 2030 or 2040. By then China's growing dependency on Persian Gulf oil may conflict with United States' 'vital' interests in the region.

Apart from intensifying commercial contacts,[64] there are thus far only limited indications that China is developing a very proactive diplomatic and strategic approach to the Middle East, but there can be no doubt that this will happen. There is a certain logic to the growing economic and political relationship between China and Saudi Arabia. From the Saudi side, 'they say: "wait a minute—we need a good relationship with a country that's a permanent member of the Security Council, is a strong and growing market for our oil, is a nuclear power, and, by the way, is untainted by having invaded any Arab country."'[65] The Chinese need large and increasing amounts of oil and its state-owned oil companies are eager to invest in Saudi Arabia (just like the Saudis are eager to get downstream access in the Chinese market). In early 2004 Sinopec signed its first major contract for exploring and producing Saudi gas (see below).

Economic interests and concerns over energy security could thus easily lead to increased Chinese political involvement in the region. As Michael Klare has forcefully argued, 'the name of the game is

---

India but the affluent American consumer is the prize customer rather than the Chinese buying his first car', *Gulf News*, 29 September 2004.

63 Ramonet, 'China Wakes Up and Alarms the World'; and Thompson-Bush, 'Why Asia Means Business'.

64 It could well be that by the end of this decade China will have displaced both the United States and Japan as Saudi Arabia's principal trading partners; see James A. Placke's contribution to the panel discussion 'Securing US Energy in a Changing World', p. 7.

65 Thomas Lippman, contribution to the panel discussion 'How to Reform Saudi Arabia Without Handing in to Extremists', *Saudi–US Relations Information Service*, 19 September 2004, p. 14.

reserves', the bulk of which lie in the Persian Gulf region. Whoever controls these reserves essentially controls the world economy—as Vice-President Dick Cheney acknowledged. Indeed, it has been suggested that the Bush administration 'has made the protection of global oil supplies an equal partner with the war on terrorism in guiding US foreign and defense policy.'[66] In the long term the possibility that the United States may one day consider using its power in the Middle East to frustrate oil supplies to a booming Chinese economy—or at least using a high-price strategy to contain China by putting pressure on its most vulnerable point, i.e. imported oil—cannot be excluded. Far-fetched as this may seem, president Bush hinted at such thinking in his June 2002 West Point speech, when he stated that the United States would not allow the development of any 'peer competitors' in the world.[67]

No one swings like the Saudis

A fourth, and certainly not the least important, motive for the United States to maintain relations with the Saudis is the unique position of Saudi Arabia as a 'swing producer': the country retains the single largest spare production capacity of any oil producers. Edward Morse terms this the 'energy equivalent of nuclear weapons'.[68] This means the world market—and the world's largest oil consumer in the first place—has a major interest in a cooperative Saudi government. The national spare capacity allows the Saudis to 'control' the

[66] Matthew Yeomans, *Oil: Anatomy of an Industry*, New York: The New Press, 2004, as quoted by Michael Klare, 'Crude Awakening', *Nation*, 21 October 2004 (a review article on five books dealing with 'peak oil').

[67] Conn Hallinan, 'Bush Sharon: The Oil Connection', *Foreign Policy in Focus*, 24 May 2004. It is true that high oil prices also hurt the United States, but compared to China it could sustain these much better because of its much lower use of energy per unit of GDP (five times less). 'Consider the old Russian farmer who plowed up a magic lamp and was granted a wish. One caveat, said the genie: Whatever you get, your neighbor gets double. Said the farmer: "Pluck out my right eye".' This high-price policy is the reverse of the low-price policy strategy in the 1980s to bankrupt the Soviet Union; see James R. Norman, 'Petrodollars', *Platts Oilgram News*, 81, 75 (21 April 2003) and 80, 172 (9 September 2002).

[68] Edward L. Morse and James Richard, 'The Battle for Energy Dominance', *Foreign Affairs*, March–April 2002, p. 4 (online edition). For a comparison of OPEC member states' spare production capacities, see Nawaf Obaid, *The Oil Kingdom at 100*, p. 133: appendix III, chart 1.

oil market to such an extent that they can fix or at least contain serious disturbances.

The United States, and the rest of the oil-consuming world, has, since the mid-1970s, depended on the Saudi capacity to 'manage' the oil market in this way—and not only under 'extreme' circumstances like in the aftermath of the Islamic Revolution, during the Iraq-Iran war, during the second Gulf War and, again, during the 2003 war against Iraq. Indeed, Saudi Arabia has fairly consistently performed this moderating role for the past quarter of a century (as have the other GCC states)—although there may have been moments when some particular country felt squeezed by the Saudis (such as the Soviet Union in the 1980s and Venezuela in the late 1990s).[69]

During 2004, when oil prices were starting to climb, it was rumoured that Saudi Arabia would soon face the challenge of tired oil fields. The most vocal recent sceptic was Matthew R. Simmons, chairman of a Texas-based investment bank specialising in energy. One of the strongest claims he made was that Ghawar, Saudi Arabia's largest field, producing about five million b/d, could be quickly running dry. Simmons expressed the fear that what he calls the Saudi miracle of abundant, cheap, easy-to-produce oil may be nearing its end.[70] Such scepticism was fiercely rejected from many sides and

69 Whether the Saudi motives are altruistic is subject to debate. See Abdullatif A. al-Othman, 'The Reliable Supplier,' pp. 173–5; Cyrus H. Tahmassebi, 'Refuting the Myths'; and Oystein Noreng, *Crude Power: Politics and the Oil Market*, London/New York: I. B. Tauris, 2002, p. 193. In theory at least, Saudi Arabia is in a position to drive prices sufficiently low to compel other (OPEC and non-OPEC) producers to production restraint. The pros and cons of this 'flood-the-market' strategy are clearly spelled out by Obaid, *The Oil Kingdom at 100, passim*. For different, outspoken views, see Simon Bromley, 'Global Petropolitics: US Grand Strategy, Iraq and Oil', Milton Keynes: Open University, June 2003, mimeo., p. 31; Fadhil J. Chalabi, 'What Future For OPEC?', *Middle East Economic Survey*, XLVI, 42, 20 October 2003; and Ådne Cappelen and Robin Choudhury, 'The Future of the Saudi Arabian Economy: Possible Effects on the World Oil Market' in Daniel Heradstveit and Helge Hveem (eds), *Oil in the Gulf: Obstacles to Democracy and Development*, Aldershot: Ashgate, 2004, pp. 41–62. A typical Saudi-bashing view is presented by Max Singer: 'Saudi Arabia's Overrated Oil Weapon', *Weekly Standard*, 18 August 2003.

70 Simmons gave speech after speech, using titles such as 'The Saudi Arabian Oil Miracle'; 'Saudi Arabian Oil: A Glass Half Full Or Half Empty?'; and most explicitly 'Twilight In The Desert: The Fading Of Saudi Arabia's Oil'; see http://www.simmonscointl.com/Search.aspx?Search=saudi%20arabia. Also see Jeff

market forces did not react to these gloomy predictions.[71] The fact that oil prices did not stop rising was clearly not to be blamed on Saudi Arabia, which raised its production as it was requested to do, but on other market conditions that the Saudis had little control over (such as surging demand in China and the United States, political instability in Venezuela and Nigeria, uncertainties in the Russian oil industry and of course 'energy terrorism' in Iraq). Most experts agreed that Saudi Aramco would be able to expand its production capacity to 12–15 million b/d.

'No one swings like the Saudis,' as *The Economist* rightly stated, and it is this that gives them many of the aces in the energy game.[72] It is hardly imaginable that a serious disruption of the Saudi oil supply (and its attendant rise in oil prices) would be without consequences to the American market—even if the Americans would stop using Saudi oil altogether.

The West needs to invest

The four motives outlined above show how the United States' position in regard to the world's largest 'swinging' oil exporter is constrained, but we should also consider the Saudi position in this constellation. Is it not, in turn, in their interest to accommodate the Americans and their oil companies? To answer this, we need only briefly examine the country's economic situation since the mid-1980s and relate this to developments on the oil (and gas) market.

Gerth, 'Forecast of Rising Oil Demand Challenges Tired Saudi Fields', *New York Times*, 24 February 2004. For more on this, from a Saudi point of view, see 'Saudi Arabian Oil Fields Brimming', *Saudi–US Relations Information Service*, 25 August 2004. For recent and sober evaluations, see Robert Bailey, 'Are We Running Out Of Oil?', *Gulf Business*, September 2004, pp. 58–62; and Kate Dourian, 'Saudi Arabia's Reserves: Is the Glass Half Empty?', *Gulf News*, 25 February 2004.

71 Some even surmised that this notion of Saudi oil fields going bust was politically inspired and smacked of 'revenge'. See, for instance, Youssef Ibrahim in a contribution to the GULF2000 list, where he argues that because of the fact that not a single gas contract had been given to an American company (in the 2003 and 2004 rounds), the US government and the American companies clearly had inspired the writers of these sceptic views (24 February 2004).

72 'Still Holding Customers Over a Barrel', *The Economist*, 23 October 2003.

Contrary to predictions, an oil shortage is nowhere near in sight.[73] There is, however, a shortage of oil revenues. Some oil-exporting countries lack sufficient means to finance further development of their production capacity—an urgently needed development on account of the anticipated rising demand for oil. The International Energy Agency recently predicted that a total investment in the Gulf states of $500 billion is required by the year 2030, which means an annual investment of some $18 billion a year. 'If there are problems relating to capital, these countries must open up their upstream sector to FDIs,' was the straightforward message of the Agency's chief economist, Fatih Birol.[74]

Although the higher oil prices of 2003 and 2004 have had a positive effect on Saudi Arabia's budgetary position, worries about the future, including about the required investments in its energy sector (not least in the gas sector—see below), have not been eliminated.[75]

73 For most recent estimates, see *World Energy Outlook 2004*, Paris: International Energy Agency, October 2004. For more on the debate between 'optimists' and 'pessimists' see Paul Roberts, *The End of Oil: On the Edge of a Perilous World*, New York: Houghton Mifflin, 2004; and Michael Klare's review article, 'Crude Awakening', *Nation*, 21 October 2004.

74 Fatih Birol, 'Investment Requirements and Capabilities in the Gulf', presentation at the conference on 'The Gulf Oil and Gas Sector: Potential Constraints', Abu Dhabi: Emirates Center for Strategic Studies Research, 26–7 September 2004 and *Gulf News*, 28 September 2004. Birol estimated $3 trillion needed for investments between 2003 and 2030. For a comparative viewpoint of the Saudi and other oil-exporting countries' situations, see Gawdat Bahgat, 'Foreign Investment in Saudi Arabia's Energy Sector', *Saudi–US Relations Information Service*, 2 September 2004.

If indeed there is a rise in demand this will have to be covered mainly by Middle Eastern countries. The non-OPEC countries will simply not have enough oil available for export in 10–25 years' time. The US Department of Energy and the International Energy Agency both project that global demand could grow from the current 80 plus million b/d to about 120 million b/d in 25 years, driven by the United States and the emerging markets of South and East Asia. The agencies assume that more and more oil will come from fewer and fewer countries, Saudi Arabia taking the number one position (also see note 47 above).

75 If prices stay in the range of $50 a barrel much longer, OPEC's earnings may be running at almost three times what they were in 1998, when a barrel fetched around only $10. Saudi Arabia alone seemed set to earn a whopping $100 billion from oil in 2004 (*The Economist*, 25 September 2004, p. 18). However, it should be noted that oil revenues in real terms are still far below their peak: in real 2003

Cutting expenditures to free the funds for such investments remains difficult because of the other expenditures the Saudi Arabian government has committed itself to—all of them hard to reduce—related to the huge public sector (providing employment), the welfare state, military expenditures, and the cost of the royal family.[76]

The conclusion is obvious: 'The real crisis is not one of supply but of revenue, and it is the security of the producers themselves that has been eroded.'[77] Certainly this is bound to increase their dependence on input from Western oil companies. Proof of this had already been given by major producers such as Algeria, Indonesia, Iran and Venezuela inviting back the international oil companies to their oil and gas industries. In July 2003 the Saudis followed suit. A consortium—led by Royal Dutch/Shell Group and including Total and the national oil company Saudi Aramco—was awarded a 200,000-square-kilometre area in the remote Empty Quarter to explore for gas.

Saudi Arabia has a total proven gas reserve of approximately 7 trillion cubic metres, placing the Kingdom fourth after Russia, Iran and Qatar. It has no immediate plans to export gas, but is mainly interested in generating jobs, expanding the petrochemical industry, satisfying a growing domestic demand, and more particularly freeing additional oil for export. The July 2003 accord—in operation since

---

dollar terms, crude oil prices in the 1979–81 period reached $103 barrel. For a more detailed treatment of Saudi Arabia's economy, see the contributions by Niblock and Malik, Giacomo Luciani and Steffen Hertog in this volume.

[76] One obvious solution would be to constrain military expenditure, given the disappearance of the direct Iraqi threat. However, this is harder than it seems: see also Nonneman's observations in his contribution to this volume. One complicating factor is the endemic corruption in military contracting. According to Kanovsky, 'Unofficial sources suggest that the "commission" on military contracts runs from 5 per cent to 40 per cent on the contract [...] A British source [*The Petroleum Economist*] quotes (unnamed) Middle East analysts who believe that $10 billion disappear annually in "kickbacks and skimming". If these figures are reasonably accurate, they imply that in 1995–2000 about *one-fifth* of Saudi oil export revenues ended up in the private pockets of some corrupt members of the royal family and their associates' (my italics); Eliyahu Kanovsky, 'Oil: Who's over a Barrel?', *Middle East Quarterly*, spring 2003, http://www.meforum.or/pf.php?id=527. The major study on the more general aspects of a 'petrolised' state, economy and society, is Jahangir Amuzegar, *Managing the Oil Wealth: OPEC's Windfalls and Pitfalls*, London/New York: I. B. Tauris, 1999.

[77] Kanovsky, 'Oil: Who's over a Barrel?', p. 9.

November of that year—was the first to allow foreign companies to explore and produce gas since the industry was nationalised in the mid-1970s. Later, in March 2004, similar deals were made with China Petroleum Chemical Corporation (Sinopec), Italy's Eni, Repsol of Spain and Russia's Lukoil.[78] The two programmes for gas exploration and development '(...) constitute the largest offering of new exploration territories the world has seen since the original Saudi concession was signed in May 1933.'[79] The companies have landed the kind of deal most non-OPEC countries normally offer, but which has not been available with some big Gulf producers.

The big American oil companies were not yet part of the deal, though some had been involved in the earlier mentioned gas initiative that failed in June 2003. One can speculate about the possible explanations for the absence of the US-based companies, but the most obvious reason is a disagreement over the rates of return (the companies wanting a significantly higher one than the Saudis were willing to accept). On the other hand, one cannot fully exclude Saudi frustration at the repeated accusations, made by some members in the US Congress, think-tanks and media outlets, that Saudi Arabia was not doing enough to combat terrorism.[80] By all odds, in future deals the American companies will have their share too.

Now the gas sector has been opened up, one can also speculate about the prospects for equity oil. Without doubt the companies involved in the gas deals hope they will eventually be able to produce and sell any oil they might find—something still taboo in Saudi Arabia. Realistically, however, this is not expected to happen soon. For the time being at least, Saudi oil development will most likely remain the prerogative of the state.[81] Of course, things may change if

[78] Stanley Reed, 'Suddenly, the Saudis Want To Play Ball', *Business Week*, 4 August 2003. For more on the gas deals, going back to the failure of the Saudi Gas Initiative (SGI) which was initiated by Crown Prince Abdullah in September 1998, see Bahgat, 'Foreign Investment in Saudi Arabia's Energy Sector'; and 'Saudi Gas: How Empty is the Empty Quarter?', *Middle East Economic Digest*, 5 March 2004.

[79] 'Saudi Gas: How Empty is the Empty Quarter?', *Middle East Economic Digest*.

[80] Bahgat, 'Foreign Investment in Saudi Arabia's Energy Sector', p. 4.

[81] For more on the sensitiveness of this issue, see Obaid, *The Oil Kingdom at 100*, pp. 53–60. Also see *Reopening of Upstream Oil Natural Gas to Foreign Investment: Views and Actions of Iran, Kuwait and Saudi Arabia*, McLean, VA: International Petroleum Enterprises, September 2004.

oil prices fall significantly or in the case of a major competition for market share—which might occur after the possible introduction of production sharing agreements in neighbouring Iraq. However, none of this is likely to happen soon.

Better The Devil You Know…

The downfall of the House of Sa'ud has been predicted countless times in the past. Against the backdrop of the terrorist attacks on Saudi (and Al Sa'ud) targets since 2002, such prediction has once again become a parlour game. At the same time, several journalists, commentators, scientists and some politicians have claimed to see—or argued for—the end of the 'special relationship' between Saudi Arabia and the United States. Their views are guided by the 9/11 attacks and the fall of the Saddam regime—among other things. Nonetheless, the House of Sa'ud is more resilient than some would like to see.[82] And Washington, it appears, is careful to preserve a good relationship with the government in Riyadh—even after 9/11 and the Iraq war. *Plus ça change, plus c'est la même chose.*

This is not to say that the Saudi system is not facing difficulties. The economic and security situations nurture plenty of worries, not to mention the uncertainties and possible problems over the succession (Abdullah and beyond). Nevertheless, the Al Sa'ud remains in control of plenty of 'capital'—economic, religious, political and symbolic.[83] Moreover, seeing that the current regime stays in power is in the best interests of the United States. Against the background of the factors highlighted earlier, Washington cannot afford to witness regime change in Riyadh (let alone contribute to it).[84]

[82] Paul Aarts, 'The Internal and the External: The House of Saud's Resilience Explained', *EUI Working Papers*, no. 2004/33, Florence: European University Institute, Robert Schuman Centre for Advanced Studies, Mediterranean Programme Series, 2004.

[83] This conception of 'capital' is taken from Ousmane Kane, *Muslim Modernity in Postcolonial Nigeria: A Study of the Society for the Removal of Innovation and Reinstatement of Tradition*, Leiden: Brill, 2003, with thanks to Joseph al-Agha, PhD student at the Institute for the Study of Islam in the Modern World (ISIM) in Leiden. For a different view, see Madawi Al-Rasheed's contribution to this volume.

[84] The nomination (in November 2003) of the new American ambassador to Riyadh, Jim Oberwetter, is the most recent indication of the renewed

As recent history has shown, radical domestic political changes in oil-producing countries often lead to suppressed output, whether the change is 'anti-American' (as in Iran) or 'pro-American' (as was the case after the collapse of communism in the Soviet Union).[85] Substantially higher prices would be the inevitable consequence, with concomitant effects on the global and US economies.[86] This is not to say that any reduction of Saudi oil production would automatically have deleterious consequences. The OECD countries have 90 days of oil reserves to guard against short-term shocks. But real problems would arise in the case of a more prolonged drop in

---

strengthening of relationships that were somewhat strained after the September 11 attacks. Oberwetter belongs to President Bush's Dallas friends and worked for Hunt Oil for the last 28 years. 'Although Oberwetter has no diplomatic experience, foreign policy veterans and supporters in Dallas said he would make a good choice, in part because the Saudis—a key allies [*sic*] in a tumultuous region—put a premium on emissaries who have the president's ear [...]The Saudi royal family prefers that US ambassadors be political appointees with close ties to the president, rather than career diplomats schooled in the complexities of the Middle East, analysts say,' *Dallas Morning News*, 17 November 2003, http://sunherald.com/mld/sunherald/news/politics/7286338.hnt?template=conte... Nicholas Confessore confirms: 'Oberwetter's nomination tells the Saudis that it's preservation of the status quo', *Los Angeles Times* ('Big Words and Big Oil Don't Mix'), 5 December 2003, via http://www1.columbia.edu/sec/bboard/gulf2000/gulf2000-14/msg06842.html.

85 Barnes, Jaffe and Morse, 'The New Geopolitics of Oil', p. 4. It is rather difficult to imagine a situation where a radically different Saudi regime willingly cuts *all* its oil exports and orders its citizens to tighten their belts for more than a month or so. 'Without air conditioners and desalination plants, the Kingdom would quickly look like Darfur. Not even religious fanatics are ready to go back to the sweaty business of raising goats and dates' (Rodenbeck, 'Unloved in Arabia', p. 24.) This is in line with the adage 'you cannot drink oil', but one can still question whether any US administration would welcome such a scenario with all its attendant instabilities. Washington will always prefer market stability, and thus tries to be on the safe side, keeping the reliable partners in power, or—if worst comes to worst—occupy the Eastern oil fields. Cf. Michael Mandelbaum, 'US Faces Dilemma on Saudi Policy', *Newsday*, New York: Council on Foreign Relations, http://www.cfr.org/pub6178/michael_mandelbaum/us_faces_dilemma_on_saudi_policy.php. Also interview with Abdulaziz Sager, chairman of the Gulf Research Center, Dubai, September 2004; and interviews with Kate Dourian and John Roberts. For a contrary view, see Preble, 'After Victory', pp. 3–5.

86 For a recent estimate about this (i.e. oil prices shooting up to $100 per barrel), see Afshin Molavi, 'Islamists Won't Blow Down the House of Saud', *Slate*, 18 June 2004, http://slate.msn.com/toolbar.aspx?action=print&id=2102644.

Saudi oil production, or in a tight market situation of ever growing demand without simultaneously increased production—in effect the situation both IEA and EIA were positing as potential scenarios in their 2004 reports.

A different scenario—with no less damaging effects—is also conceivable. Consider the possibility of a flood-the-market approach, which is not unimaginable under a radical Islamist regime that could impose on its people the hardships and privation of lower prices 'for the sake of a final victory over the enemies it deems unholy'.[87] This would not only have a devastating effect on US oil production, but also negatively impact on Russian oil production, endanger Caspian Basin prospects, and halt new exploration and technology development. Consequently, within five to seven years, the world would be far more dependent on the Persian Gulf than it is today, with no immediate way out—an outcome that would seem like a real victory for a radical Islamist regime.[88]

Both scenarios would have negative effects for the US economy, which raises the question of whether there is really any practical alternative to the present Saudi regime that would serve the interests of the United States. As Patrick Buchanan exclaimed:

> If the Saudi monarchy goes down, who and what do we think is going to replace it? [...] Can anyone believe that, should the 7000 princes go to the wall, 7000 liberal democrats will replace them? After Afghanistan and Iraq, do we still not know that when a state is destroyed, it requires years to rebuild, and the men with guns fill the vacuum? In the Middle East, Saudi Arabia is Big Casino. Lose that, and we have lost the game.[89]

Washington's conclusion looks obvious: it is better to deal with the devil you know.

Despite 9/11 and the rapid removal of Saddam Hussein, Riyadh and Washington are at least for the time being 'handcuffed' to one another.[90] The four pillars upon which the 'special relationship' has

[87] Leonardo Maugeri, 'Not in Oil's Name', *Foreign Affairs*, 82, 4 (July–August), http://www.foreignaffairs.org/20030701faessay15412/leonardo-maugeri/not-in-oil-s-name.html. Also see note 69.

[88] Maugeri, 'Not in Oil's Name'.

[89] Patrick J. Buchanan, 'Playing Into the Enemy's Hands', *Saudi-American Forum*, 1 July 2004, p. 2. For an opposite view, see interview with Jean-François Seznec.

[90] Gregory F. Gause, *The Approaching Turning Point: The Future of US Relations with*

been built—oil, security, Saudi Arabia's moderating power in the Arab-Israeli conflict, and its prominent place within the Arab and Islamic world—remain essentially intact, even if the last has become somewhat more controversial due to concerns over the perceived Saudi role in fostering Islamist sentiments and it having lost some of its importance with the end of the Cold War.[91] Paradoxically, one might add a fifth pillar, *viz.* the common interest in combating Islamic terrorism. Talk of divorce is therefore premature. Recent events have changed perceptions and stirred up strong feelings—both in Saudi Arabia and in the United States—and the visibility of the military component will be reduced. But this merely means one can expect the Saudi–US relationship to assume a more 'normal' character: these shifts will not have changed fundamentally the underlying realities of an interdependent relationship. In that sense, it does not really matter whether there is a Democrat or a Republican living in the White House.

---

the Gulf States, Brookings Project on US Policy Towards the Islamic World, Analysis Paper no. 2, May 2003.

[91] Indeed, the disappearance of the Cold War as a factor in undermining the special relationship is central in Rachel Bronson's argument in this volume—an argument that for precisely that reason presents a more negative prospect for the relationship than I am holding out in the present chapter.

CONCLUSIONS AND OUTLOOK

A TRIPLE NEXUS: IDEOLOGY, ECONOMY, FOREIGN POLICY AND THE OUTLOOK FOR THE SAUDI POLITY

Paul Aarts and Gerd Nonneman

Saudi Arabia is in flux—in domestic politics, society, the economy and foreign relations. That much is clear. The succession from the long-incapacitated King Fahd to Crown Prince Abdullah, expected any time after this book goes to press, will be only the most immediately visible instance of this, and indeed will be a transition around which many of the key questions of policy now being faced by the kingdom crystallise. Yet the preceding chapters make clear that in such flux a number of patterns and trends can be identified, which this final chapter attempts to draw together. It is immediately apparent that, although the book was divided into four parts, the contributions in each reached into parts other than the one where they were located. This reflects not only a conscious approach by the editors but an intrinsic intertwining of these different aspects. It is not just that the Saudi state is obviously not the 'billiard ball' of traditional realist assumptions (nor indeed is the House of Sa'ud). The many-faceted case study that this volume represents once again demonstrates the artificiality of the traditional distinction between domestic and external politics and policy: one is reminded here of Putnam's 'two-level game',[1] of David's 'omnibalancing' by regimes,[2]

1 For a discussion see e.g. Christopher Hill, *The Changing Politics of Foreign Policy* (Houndmills: Palgrave Macmillan, 2003).

2 Steven David, 'Explaining Third World Alignment', in *World Politics*, Vol. 43, no. 2 (1991), pp. 233–256.

and of the central role allocated to the domestic in the analysis of foreign policy by one of the present authors.[3] Not only do the domestic and the external turn out to be tightly linked, as is shown in almost all the chapters; the 'ideological/religious', 'social', 'economic' and 'political' are similarly intertwined. None of these can be quite understood without the others. Convenience dictates a practical division below into sections on religion and ideology, the economy, external relations, regime and opposition, and the politics of reform, but their mutual overlap and interaction will be readily apparent: there is a religious-political nexus as much as there is an economic-political one, and one between foreign relations and domestic politics, but the linkages spread right across the spectrum of factors, actors and dynamics discussed in the book.

A key question of policy interest addressed in this volume from various angles is whether the Al Sa'ud regime or the Saudi political economy more broadly can weather changing conditions at home and abroad—political, social and economic (and indeed within royal ranks). Oil apart, the most generally recognised pillar of the regime has been the alliance with the 'Wahhabi' creed and establishment. Wahhabism has at the same time also been at the centre of accusations concerning the Saudi role in fostering terrorism—while also apparently forming the soil within which the royal family's most virulent challengers have flourished. Let us start, then, with the religious-ideological dimension.

Religion and ideology: transformation and divisions of Wahhabism

As will be clear from the foregoing chapters—even those most critical of the regime—a consensus exists that the House of Sa'ud is not about to collapse. There is no question that the regime faces major challenges on almost all fronts, even if temporarily and partly relieved by the high oil prices of the 2000s, but none of the authors conclude that the system's days are numbered—for a range of reasons to which we return in the course of this chapter. One reason is that the relationship between Wahhabism's two premier families, the

[3] Gerd Nonneman, 'Analyzing the Foreign Policies of the Middle East and North Africa: a Conceptual Framework', in Nonneman (ed.), *Analyzing Middle East Foreign Policies, and the Relationship with Europe* (London: Routledge, 2005), pp. 6–18. See also his chapter in this volume.

Al Sa'ud and the Al ash-Shaikh, remains intact. Yet shifts in the relationship have occurred since the very early days. The Al ash-Shaikh has long since become the junior partner, and, just as important, has adopted a policy of pragmatism over ideological purity, firmly prioritising the joint survival of the Al Sa'ud, the Al ash-Sheikh and the rest of the religious establishment tied to Al Sa'ud rule. This has been clear for most of the existence of the third Saudi state, but it has if anything been further consolidated and, as it were, raised to an art form in the ensuing decades. This was strikingly illustrated in 1990 when the Council of Senior Ulama under Ibn Baz at the request of the royal family issued a fatwa in effect approving the presence of foreign troops on Saudi soil. It was again evident after 9/11 and especially after the wave of terrorist attacks in the kingdom from May 2003 onwards. Just as in earlier days, particularly in 1929 and 1979, the official religious establishment was once again challenged by more radical brethren who attacked both the royal family and its American allies, and, exactly as before, the establishment chose the side of the ruling power. This led to further disenchantment among large parts of the population and an equivalent reduction in the religious establishment's authority.

That establishment also saw its traditional role in the Saudi education system challenged in the wake of 9/11 and the combination of external pressure and internal reappraisal that took place in Saudi society and among the leadership: pressures to reform education at all levels, from primary to tertiary, accumulated fast. In this 'war of ideas' the House of Sa'ud faces the difficulty that significant interventions in the school curricula are all too easily interpreted as yielding to American pressure—something which in turn is grist to the mill of radical-salafi strands of opinion and activism (even as a string of bloody attacks within Saudi Arabia itself had undermined support for the most radical groups). As a consequence the government has moved cautiously. Educational reform is firmly on the agenda, but implementation proceeds tentatively, amid assertions that the bulk of the curriculum is unproblematic and that adjustments must be in the spirit of local culture and Islam. This is one example of the regime's (and liberal Saudi society's) wider dilemma: in countering the radical Islamist opposition they rely largely on the very same conservative religious establishment that presents the main hurdle in the way of introducing social, cultural and economic reforms.

Yet one of the more striking effects of 9/11 in this sphere has been the increased differentiation within Saudi religio-political thought, in particular with the emergence of what Lacroix calls an 'Islamo-liberal trend'. At the end of the 1990s and in the early years of the twenty-first century the 'established' Islamist opposition—the *sahwa*, or Islamic Awakening—was being challenged from two directions. On the one hand, the challenge came from a radical jihadi-salafi trend, supporting Usama bin Ladin and the 'global jihad'; on the other, a number of individuals from an Islamist background emerged who criticised the regime-allied Wahhabi establishment and called for political reform. This latter 'Islamo-liberal' trend stood out because of its willingness to form *de facto* coalitions with previously unimaginable partners such as liberals and Shi'ites. However, it is notable that this trend itself consists of two wings, one more concerned with social and religious criticism, the other more directly politically active. It is this latter wing that achieved the highest public profile through the initiation or support of a number of petitions to the regime. Although at least Crown Prince Abdullah was at first prepared to engage with some of these trends, by the end of 2003 the phenomenon took on such proportions—with coalitions straddling previously clear dividing lines—that key petitioners were arrested. At the time of this volume going to press three remained in custody, having received extended jail sentences in a trial verdict in May 2005 and declaring their intention to appeal. While the very fact that a trial was being held—with, for the first time ever, one open session, and extensive media coverage and discussion—was in itself an interesting departure, it nevertheless appeared that the 'Islamo-liberal trend' had become the victim of its own success, raising the question whether this kind of 'post-Islamism' really has a chance of succeeding in Saudi Arabia. Adding to a potential negative answer to this question is the finding that the movement also appeared to undergo a tentative reorientation back towards a more Islamist profile, thus perhaps losing its attraction to its more liberal adherents or sympathisers.

However, the evidence from Saudi Arabia does once again confirm the need to avoid 'essentialising' even supposedly rigid bodies of religious thought such as Wahhabism. Not only are the facts, on examination, likely to prove quite different, featuring far greater historical and current diversity than assumed, but fluctuations within and on the margins of such traditions are likely to remain significant, allowing for a range of religious, ideological and political interpretations and outcomes. In particular the Saudi case also confirms the evidence from other Muslim societies and movements that even varieties of 'strict' Islamism are not necessarily incompatible with a democratic impulse. We return to the implications for regime and opposition in a later section; first we need to consider the other two main areas of challenge and regime policy: the economy and foreign policy.

Changing political economy and the question of reform: beyond the rentier state?

High oil prices in the first years of the twenty-first century brought Saudi Arabia a major windfall, for a while reducing some of the pressures that had been building up. In 2003 GDP growth of 7.2% was achieved, and estimates for 2004 indicated a similar figure. Even so, the economy's structural problems are deeply rooted and require far-reaching reform. There remains a need to prepare for the return of periods when oil revenues will be less plentiful, especially given continued population growth. Most acutely, there is the challenge of providing jobs for young Saudis streaming on to the labour market—with possibly one in three of their number facing unemployment.

A number of partial reforms have gradually seen the light of day. Since 2000 some significant moves have been made with regard to privatisation and foreign direct investment. Yet such initiatives have not amounted to cross-sectoral reform: they remain incomplete, implementation has been slow and patchy, and the effect limited. Much more is needed, not least to make the economy compatible with WTO requirements, to control government expenditure (not least in the 40% still estimated to go to the military sector), and especially to raise the productivity and competitiveness of Saudi labour. Nor should the expectation be allowed to take hold that the execution of such measures would swiftly reduce unemployment—indeed in the short term the opposite could occur, which might be politically difficult.

Previous scholarship has suggested that the underlying problem has been the very nature of the Saudi political economy as a rentier state, with both the economy itself and the political system that relies on it being rooted in the distribution of the oil 'rent' and people's focus on accessing it. In this context, it was suggested, the pursuit of economic efficiency and competitiveness (as well as political participation) inevitably receives the least priority and indeed is largely incompatible with the central rationale and dynamic of the rentier political economy. In this schema the state has a large measure of autonomy in relation to the society. Despite some recent attempts to question this picture, it has remained perhaps the dominant analysis. The evidence and analysis put forward in this volume show that this can no longer be satisfactory. Not only have parts of the Saudi economy become significantly more productive and economically 'rational', as the chapters by Malik, Niblock and Luciani illustrate, but in the chapters by Hertog and Luciani the analysis is taken significantly further. Hertog provides an original and compelling explanation for the persistent difficulty of implementing cross-sectoral reforms, by complementing rentier state theory with the concept of 'segmented clientelism'; Luciani suggests that the Saudi economy has in fact to a significant extent moved beyond the pure rentier stage—something that has political as well as economic implications.

Hertog argues that both the resilience of the current set-up of institutions and political coalition, and their capacity to scupper wide-ranging reform projects, can be explained by the phenomenon of segmented clientelism. The 'state' in Saudi Arabia is not simply a unitary, autonomous actor separate from 'society'. State autonomy, in other words, is less than rentier state theory has assumed; rather, the state has co-opted chunks of society into itself, which has generated a rapidly growing state apparatus that is increasingly hard to control. As rentier state theory stipulates, distribution of revenue and the resulting intended formation of groups remain key features of the system, but the dynamics then quickly get complicated and entangling: 'state-society links and interaction have become much more complex than the original rentier state theory model allows.' We subscribe to Hertog's analysis that the Saudi polity came to be composed of 'a large number of parallel institutions which have grown on oil income, are suffused with informal networks, and coordinate and communicate little'. This is a process in which numerous factions have acquired stakes and effective veto power: the fiefs have become more than their holders. These 'fiefdoms' have emerged

both in state structures proper and in society, linking one to the other. The political corollary is that while clients in these 'segments' compete for top-level access, they remain fragmented and relatively easy to control. However, stability has thereby been purchased at the expense of reduced manoeuvrability for the Saudi state: Hertog suggests that even top-level willingness to reform is thus not sufficient to induce structural change.

The private sector in Saudi Arabia has clearly become more important and independent, often using the Majlis al-Shura, for instance, as a means to express views and pursue interests. Yet in the scheme proposed by Hertog, this does not make it a key opponent of the structures of segmented clientelism: given that private sector actors often boast personal links to key figures in various segments, 'the private sector is willing to speak, but not to openly confront the system which brought it into being.'

Luciani's analysis would seem to allow a somewhat more positive interpretation, at least in the longer term. In comparative context, the longer term is indeed the more relevant framework when examining processes of democratisation, absent sudden shocks: significant short-term democratisation is not a likely prospect in the Kingdom, nor should structural factors such as those examined in comparative democratisation studies be expected to yield short-term change. Luciani, too, develops and complements his own earlier rentier state theory, but does so by stressing the changing nature of the Saudi economy and political economy, and the emergence of what he terms a 'national bourgeoisie,' numbering at least half a million.

He shows that the activity, size and wealth of the private sector—even if originally rooted in rent circulation—has reached a level where it has meant the acquisition of a measure of genuine independence both in its economic activities and interests, and in its position vis-à-vis the state. He agrees with Hertog that these individuals remain close to the state and the ruling family, and cannot be construed as an 'opposition', nor do they have one single class interest or one single political position. Similarly, while he believes they are likely to favour greater transparency in (especially economic and commercial) decision-making, that does not necessarily translate into concerted support for democratisation—or a best in a very cautious gradualism. Yet, although this bourgeoisie remains attached to

Saudi Arabia—as also evidenced in the expansion of private investment within the Kingdom—they are not 'trapped' in the country: they have the demonstrated capability and willingness to invest elsewhere in the region and beyond, as shown in the spurt of investments in places such as Dubai: 'The game of competition in governance is very clearly on,' Luciani concludes. If the interests of this new national bourgeoisie were threatened by issues of Saudi governance, he suggests, it is at least conceivable that they might make more of their independence and economic wealth and clout.

Rentier state theory, then, clearly needs qualifying—and not just with regard to Saudi Arabia. The most obvious qualification is that where resources (rent) become limited—as they almost inevitably do, at least in relation to demands—some of the theory's ideal-type assumptions by definition no longer apply in quite the same way. Secondly, other social, cultural, political, and environmental factors are always likely to cut across, and interact with, the simple rentier dynamic, which means that 'rentierism' on its own can never provide a full explanation or description. Third, as it is in the GCC states that the most ideal-type confirmation of the theory's assumptions about the nature of economy and politics has been found, we must ask whether the model's view of state autonomy in the distribution of rent and in the formation of groups assumes not merely (1) exceptional wealth, but also (2) a small, homogeneous society, and (3) a unified elite. A useful contrast here would be Nigeria, where a vast, heterogeneous polity with a multiplicity of competing elite factions has given rise to quite different dynamics. The final qualification is to acknowledge a need to historicise the rentier state, showing that its nature and implications are path-dependent.

External Relations

In addition to the ideological/religious and the economic, the third area to form a nexus with the political is that of external relations. In this volume, the external factor was understood as a resource or a constraint for the regime, as a resource or perceived target for domestic audiences, and also as the wider context within which the Saudi political economy functions. Nonneman argues that 'what the regime has been, largely successfully, doing for many decades, is "omnibalancing" between different (and fluctuating) threats and needs located

in its multiple environments (domestic, regional and international), while attempting pragmatically to carve out a measure of autonomy from domestic, regional, and international structures and actors simultaneously.' This explains the instances of apparent 'polygamy' in its external relations, both today and in much of the twentieth century. In that light, neither the country's cautious and pragmatic regional policy, nor the apparent cooling in relations with the US in the first five years of the twenty-first century, balanced with efforts to strengthen relations elsewhere, should be particularly surprising—although Bronson makes the point that, contrary to previous moments of friction, the relationship faces a new context, where the 'glue' of the Cold War that gave the United States and Saudi Arabia an overarching set of compatible interests, is no longer present. Even so, Paul Aarts makes the case that, rather than heading for separation, the United States and Saudi Arabia are more likely entering a more 'normal' relationship, which is nonetheless still very much dictated by the logic of energy and security. Indeed, the new common interest in containing the threat from Islamist terror, together with the continued older shared interest of stabilization in the Middle East, mutual interests over oil and economic security, and the protection the US can still offer, increase the likelihood that the relationship will remain relatively close, albeit in need of some careful management. Aarts points to the possible future appearance of a 'China factor', where the aspirant superpower's thirst for energy might lead some US policy-makers to contemplate a 'denial strategy'—although the likelihood of such a scenario and the precise implications this would have for Saudi Arabia remain hard to gauge.

The Saudi case, both in its history of 'managed multi-dependence' and in the fact that the United States cannot rely on its presumed ally to do its bidding unquestioningly, illustrates the broader fact that states of the so-called 'periphery' (or 'developing states') not only *can* carve out a measure of relative autonomy in the international system, but that their regimes will in fact often *need* to maximise their room for manoeuvre at the international level if the challenges they face at the domestic level (and, especially in the Middle East, on the intimately related regional level) are to be faced successfully: that is precisely what omnibalancing is about. The available resources at the various levels will of course vary, as will the threats. Clearly the greater the resources available domestically—whether material or political—the greater will be the regime's room for manoeuvre regionally and internationally, while conversely adroit and pragmatic handling of the international and regional levels can further enhance domestic strength. Equally clearly, though, success at this omnibalancing act will in part be a matter of regime skill. None of this is to suggest that voluntarism is adequate to explain outcomes; the structural environments within which these regimes have to function—both ideational and material, and both domestic and external—determine the broad parameters within which they can operate. But in the crucial interaction between those different parts of the environment, the role of agency can be highly significant.[4]

Saudi Arabia itself, at the time of going to press in 2005, was facing particular challenges at all levels—challenges converging on a new King Abdullah following his expected succession. Precisely because he has been seen within the kingdom as somewhat more sensitive to local nationalist, Islamic and Arab concerns than Fahd, and somewhat less willing to follow Washington's lead unquestioningly (even if the difference is relative at best), he may be in a better position to deal with the tensions between the requirements of the domestic and regional scenes on the one hand, and the international on the other. It is worth stressing again, however, that *within* each of those levels there are conflicting demands and interests to be met, adding to the complexity of the regime's calculations. At least, however, Abdullah's accession is likely to reduce a little the diffuse nature of policy-making prevalent since King Fahd's stroke in 1995—although certainly it will not make him the sole arbiter. Together with his stronger legitimacy within the kingdom, that might make both for continued 'polygamy' in foreign policy and a better chance of success in reconciling the simultaneous demands of the different environments.

Domestically the demands of a burgeoning young population and a nationalist reflex will require a delicate balancing act when it comes to foreign policy and responses to external pressures over reform and the fight against terrorism. Regionally the environment is in a period of striking flux: first, the situation in Iraq poses challenges of violent

[4] See also Raymond Hinnebusch, 'Explaining International Politics in the Middle East', in Gerd Nonneman (ed.), *Analyzing Middle East Foreign Policies* (Routledge, 2005), pp. 243–256.

and jihadist spill-over at worst, and the novel possibility of boisterous if not wholly democratic politics being installed next-door at best; second, the Syrian regime is in a hard-to-predict period of transition and certainly weakness; third, Iran's regime may be pulling back from reforms and harbouring at least some who are considering the desirability of pursuing the nuclear option; fourth, Yemen suffers intermittent upheaval, acting as a reservoir and refuge for radical Islamist opponents of both regimes; and fifth, the kingdom's small neighbours show an increased determination to escape their neighbour's regional hegemony. Internationally, the combined pressures of the 'war on terror', the *Zeitgeist* regarding political reform, and the demands of economic globalisation, complete the circle of multiple challenges.

By the same token the opportunities for the pragmatic pursuit of multi-dependence persist even with the United States as sole superpower: other older as well as emerging powers offer complementary resources ('alternative' would be putting it too strongly, at least for the foreseeable future) politically and economically—something which Saudi Arabia under Abdullah, as indeed under his successors, will doubtless continue to make the most of.

Regime, opposition, and the question of political reform

Each of the three areas dealt with in the preceding sections has its own intrinsic demands and drivers; yet both individually and in mutual interaction they also form a nexus with domestic politics, including the questions of regime legitimacy and stability, and political reform. The political scene itself of course also features additional factors, including the nature and strength of the opposition; the performance, cohesion, and response of the regime; and the question of succession. The prospects for political stability, as for reform, depend on (1) the depth and breadth of the demands and pressures in each of the four areas dealt with in this book (both separately and in their cumulative interaction); (2) the strength and cohesion of organised opposition, in large part dependent on structural socio-economic factors; (3) external attitudes; and (4) the resources, skills and response of the regime, and its willingness to consider reform.

It will be clear from the chapters of this book and from the summing-up in the current chapter so far that the Saudi political system faces serious challenges in all the 'sectors' surveyed, and that a careful and precarious balancing act is required between the demands in these sectors (religious/cultural; economic; foreign relations; politics) and between the three levels (domestic, regional, international). We have seen also that against a proven record of pragmatism and adaptability, with skill at co-optation and an ability to mobilise legitimising resources while avoiding the coalescence of opposition strands, the regime faces several problems: (1) a population that has grown rapidly; (2) an apparently intractable youth unemployment problem; (3) the lack of manoeuvrability that has emerged as the price for the segmented clientelism that has characterised the Saudi polity; (4) the paradox that the reforms that are both needed and clamoured for from outside are opposed by the very actors in society and the polity (the non-radical Islamists and clerical establishment) whose help is needed in combating the appeal of the anti-regime extremists; and (5) the continued and arguably worsening puzzle of reconciling close relations with the United States (essential both for regime and more widely the economy) with the domestically delegitimising effects this has against the background of events in the Arab-Israeli and Iraqi theatres.

To this must be added longer-term *structural* changes in society and the economy, not least in the context of economic, technological and political globalisation; and a changing regional environment. The latter includes Iraq's democratic experiment, and the pattern of political reform in the neighbouring GCC states setting a standard to which the Saudi public are exposed daily, given the regional integration of personal, professional and media networks.

For the regime, then, a coherent policy response is essential in order to address these conflicting pressures, craft a sustainable omnibalancing act, and maintain or rebuild legitimacy. Policy coherence and regime cohesion are closely connected. Emerging from the analysis of Glosemeyer, Al-Rasheed and Hertog is a picture which suggests that such cohesion is often lacking when sustained, coherent policymaking in the domestic arena is called for. Al-Rasheed's 'headless tribe' simile, referring in particular to the period since 1995, expresses the phenomenon most starkly. Clearly there are positive aspects to a system that in effect produces a version of limited pluralism in decision-making, especially since each of the 'segments', or 'circles of power' links into sections of the society, which makes it easier to pre-empt discontent (and, from the regime's point of view, to co-opt). But in key areas such as economic policy and political reform, it would appear that output has suffered, contradictory strands of policy have stymied each other, and little concerted, in-depth and trans-sectoral reform has been effected.

Intra-family disagreement and competition have been an element in this. As long as King Fahd remained the notional head of state, this situation was perpetuated, as Crown Prince Abdullah and his 'circle' proved unable fully to stamp their authority on the policy process and the 'vision' for the kingdom. While there can be little doubt that this will improve with his accession, it remains to be seen how wholeheartedly the other senior princes will follow the traditional pattern and swing behind their half-brother at that point. Abdullah, moreover, while in good health, is nevertheless in his eighties, so that in the medium term a further succession looms—probably to Prince Sultan. Hence the fundamental direction of policy will remain in doubt for some years—unless Abdullah can set in place a number of hard-to-reverse *faits accomplis*. For the sake of the regime's own long-term future, and for the sake of overall sustainable development in Saudi Arabia, that would seem to be important, but it is not at all clear whether the resistance built into the system as a whole (the segmented-clientelistic version of rentierism), powerful factions in the royal family, or even the likely limits to Abdullah's own reform-mindedness or acceptance of opposition voices, will allow this to happen. One needs to note also the absence of a natural pro-reform alliance among key parts of Saudi society: opposition exists, along with demands for reform, but this is not united nor does it yet stretch in any significant and organised fashion into those key middle-class and elite sectors of society that have proved necessary elements of a liberalising and democratising coalition elsewhere.

At the more radical end of the opposition spectrum it is notable that the violence of *Al-Qa'ida in the Arabian Peninsula* seems to have brought it up against the limits inherent in the Saudi 'cycle of contention' (of social movement theory), undermining its appeal with the wider population while attracting effective government counteraction. At the same time, however, more liberal trends in Islamist thinking and opposition appear at least for the time being to have come up against limits of their own, both because of regime unwillingness to countenance what was turning into a coalition of previously divided voices, and because of the tentative return to more purely Islamist agendas on the part of some within this Islamo-liberal movement.

This leaves a large body of Islamist- and economic-grievance-inspired discontent especially among the younger generation, spurred on by younger preachers who have parted ways with the pro-regime religious establishment and are harshly critical of the regime, but without the determination, clout or organisation to pose an imminent threat to the system. It also leaves a—much smaller—liberal elite who want to see greater transparency and a gradual political opening-up. The latter are not on the whole interested in fast, comprehensive democratisation for fear of the influence of radical Islamist activism. In between there remains the majority of the population, who may feel disgruntled and criticise aspects of royal family rule, but who remain otherwise unwilling to become politically active in pursuit of political change. In many cases this is reinforced by the clientelist links discussed in the chapter by Hertog—links that continue to be fostered in all sectors of society, including among members of the emerging new 'national bourgeoisie' discussed by Luciani. Especially when oil revenues are high, the regime can continue for some time to employ its time-honoured strategy of co-optation and clientelism combined with repression of more significant perceived threats. Indeed the Saudi state has been doing just what social movement theory predicts will be the most successful strategy in dealing with the various strands of 'contention': it has followed a combined strategy of repression + accommodation + facilitation.

Even so, the growing challenges already referred to, together with the continuing changes in the nature and composition of society and the demands of economic, technological and political globalisation, mean that adjustments at the social, economic and political levels will in the short-to-medium term become inevitable if the stability of the regime is to be assured. If such change is to come from within the royal family, it would seem that, after King Abdullah, the best prospects may lie in the next generation of princes—although opinion and interests among that generation are by no means undivided. When the shift to that generation is at last made, of course, the choices will be determined very much by the intra-family politics already in evidence, making the outcome unpredictable. Yet as Glosemeyer shows, the system has already begun tentatively to adapt. As she points out, after 9/11 and the attendant domestic but especially international challenges, the rulers 'for the first time found themselves in a situation where they needed the active cooperation of a variety of social groups' to help secure the Saudi polity and its reputation. This experience will probably inform future calculations, and the underlying dynamic is now unlikely to disappear for any great length of time.

Recent Reforms

The most immediately visible sign of reform has been the municipal elections of 2005. These came against a background of already expanded room for discussion both in the media and in the context of the 'National Dialogue' started by Crown Prince Abdullah, which had reached its fifth session by mid-2005 (when among other topics that of women driving was to be discussed). However constrained in its remit, and however limited the feed-through to society at large and to actual policy, the Dialogue was nevertheless an indication of a changing context and an awareness on the part of at least elements of the regime of a need for a different response (whether substantive or tactical). The very fact that a number of previously taboo issues could now at least be discussed, and that in the process previously 'illegitimate' voices such as those of Shi'a religious figures were given formally equal standing as discussion partners in a forum established publicly by the Crown Prince, was without question an important departure—even if conservative counter-pressure meant that the remit, participants and dissemination of the results of the Dialogue sessions became markedly restricted.

Another part of the background consisted of the earlier reforms in the shape of the Basic Law and the introduction of the Majlis al-Shura in the early 1990s—a Majlis that carved for itself an increasingly significant role even behind the curtain of secrecy that officially shrouded its work, especially through the workings of the specialised committees that were established in 2001.[5] Shortly before the com-

5 See Mohammad al-Muhanna, 'The Saudi Majlis ash-Shura: Domestic Functions and International Role' (PhD thesis, Institute of Middle Eastern & Islamic Studies,

pletion of the municipal elections in April 2005, the new Majlis was sworn in with an expanded membership of 150, and intimations that it was to be allowed, among other things, to scrutinise the budget. Its debates are now televised and increasingly watched. Moreover, Prince Mansour and Prince Sa'ud al-Faisal suggested that the Majlis would eventually be two-thirds elected.[6] Almost simultaneously, a major reform of the much-criticised judicial system was announced. Even if question marks inevitably hung over the time-scale and effectiveness of implementation, the comprehensive nature of the changes was striking: a Supreme Court was to be established (taking over the functions of the Supreme Council for the Judiciary), along with a network of appeal courts, commercial courts and labour courts.[7]

But it was the municipal elections, for half of the nearly 12,000 seats of the country's 178 municipal councils, that drew the most attention internationally among media and policy-makers. Originally announced for 2004, they took place in three regional rounds between 10 February and 21 April 2005. The remaining half of the seats were to be appointed; the councils deal not with 'political' issues but only with local services and planning matters; women were barred from either standing or voting, albeit for 'logistical' and not legal reasons; and no group campaigns, platforms or manifestos were allowed—let alone political parties. Moreover, and contrary to the ubiquitous assertion of almost all commentary on the elections, these were not in fact the kingdom's first-ever. When first conquering the Hijaz, Abd al-Aziz Al Sa'ud had taken account of local sensitivities by establishing an elected Majlis ash-Shura for the region in addition to five municipal councils for the main towns;[8]

Durham University, 2005). This is also the only study to provide comprehensive detail on the nature, extent, and effect of the work of the Committees, and to survey systematically Majlis members' views on their own powers.

6 Strikingly also, a debate was held on Saudi TV in early April on the merits of elections for the Council (even if both invited speakers advocated gradualism, thus mirroring the majority view among members). *Saudi Gazette*, 13 April 2005; *Arab News*, 13 April 2005; SPA dispatch 13 April 2005; Economist Intelligence Unit, *Saudi Arabia Report* May 2005, pp. 12–16; for the views of Council members themselves see also Al-Muhanna, 'The Saudi Majlis ash-Shura.'

7 Economist Intelligence Unit, *Saudi Arabia Report* May 2005, pp. 12–16.

8 Al-Muhanna, 'The Saudi Majlis ash-Shura', chapter 4; and Abdulaziz Al Fahad, 'Ornamental Constitutionalism: The Saudi Basic Law of Governance', paper for

and in the 1950s under King Sa'ud local elections were begun, only for the experiment to be shelved when King Faisal came to power.[9]

Even so, from the perspective of the post-1960s era the 2005 elections were a significant development, both in themselves, and for the way in which they evolved, including the atmosphere that developed around them. The three rounds[10] produced a similar pattern:

(1) fairly low voter registration, varying between a quarter and one-third of the possible electorate—whether due to unfamiliarity, uncertainty about relevance and purpose, or cycnicism;
(2) high turn-out among those registered, at 70-75% in the first two rounds and well over 50% in the third;
(3) vigorous competition for the seats, with for instance in the first round over 1,800 candidates fighting for 127 seats. There were hard-fought and sometimes expensive campaigns by individual candidates (the only campaigning officially allowed), complemented by mobile phone message campaigning for slates of moderate Islamist candidates by anonymous senders, claiming that they were supported by religious scholars (they became known as the 'golden lists'). Because this was banned under the election rules, complaints were lodged with the Grievances and Complaints Committee and widely discussed in the local media, but as the sources could not be traced, the complaints could not be upheld.
(4) In many places those moderate Islamist candidates swept the board, not least because—as was recognised in Saudi media commentary afterwards—they had been the better organised.
(5) There was a clear sectarian tinge to the results in those areas where minorities feature, particularly in the Eastern Province. Thus Qatif and Ihsa returned almost exclusively Shi'a members,

---

the Sixth Mediterranean Social and political Research Meeting, Montecatini, 16–20 March 2005, Workshop 13; to be published as a chapter in a forthcoming book: Giacomo Luciani & Abdulhadi Khalaf (eds.), *Constitutional Reforms and Political Participation in the Gulf.*

[9] Robert Vitalis, *America's Kingdom* (pre-publication version, 2005, posted on http://cas.uchicago.edu/workshops/cpolit/papers/vitalis.doc).

[10] On 10 February in Riyadh and the surrounding region, on 3 March in the Eastern province, Najran, Al Baha, Jizan and Asir, and on 21 April in the Hijaz and Tabuk.

whereas Dammam elected Islamist Sunnis. This, like the text messaging campaign, showed that, even though group platforms and campaigning had been banned, the election process did in fact feature clear evidence of group politics.

(6) Even so, it was also striking that the essence of the campaigning was very much on real local issues of practical importance to the daily lives of local residents, and not on broader philosophical or ideological questions.[11]

In sum, while this was by no means a democratic breakthrough, the elections both illustrated and stimulated interest in participatory politics and in the wider issues and questions associated with it. Much will depend on how the councils and elected members are seen to perform over their term in office, but it is conceivable that this will become not merely an incremental institutional move but add to the patterns of discussion and behaviour in society that may become increasingly hard to ignore or reverse.[12] In combination with the expansion of numbers and powers of the Majlis al-Shura, the mooted introduction of elections for this body, the expected expansion of voting rights for women (an expectation further strengthened and discussed in the Saudi media after the Kuwaiti parliament passed a law in May 2005 granting women the vote), this may indicate that further reform is indeed a likelihood. It will continue to be very gradual at best and controlled by the Al-Sa'ud, while by contrast a concerted and determined social alliance for democratisation is

[11] *Saudi Gazette*, 13 & 22 April 2005; *Arab News*, 13–29 April 2005; SPA dispatch 13 April 2005; Economist Intelligence Unit, *Saudi Arabia Report* May 2005, pp. 12–16; 'Third Round balloting Marks End of Landmark Elections', on *Saudi–US Relations*, 23 April 2005 (www.saudi-us-relations.org/newsletter2005/saudi-relations-interest-04-23.html) (plus the links offered there); and *Gulf News*, 24 April 2005, 'Citizens debate Islamists' win in municipal elections.'

[12] Such a pattern has been recognised in comparative literature on political development and liberalisation/democratisation. For the Middle East and North Africa, see e.g. Dale Eickelman, 'Foreword', in Augustus Norton (ed.), *Civil Society in the Middle East*, Vol. II (Leiden: Brill, 1996), p. xiii (commenting on the effect of the 'process of elections' in Morocco); Anoushiravan Ehteshami, 'Power Sharing and Elections in the Middle East', in Sven Behrendt & Christian Hanelt (eds.), *Bound to Co-operate: Europe and the Middle East* (Gütersloh: Bertelsmann Foundation, 2000), pp. 359–375; and Abdo Baaklini et al, *Legislative Politics in the Arab World* (Boulder: Lynne Rienner, 1999).

unlikely to crystallise for many years. But, together with the growing challenges enumerated above and the changing structure of Saudi society, these signs of change do seem to point in the direction of medium-term change to the Saudi polity—fairly smooth if a coherent reform-minded leadership emerges soon, rather more unsettled if that condition remains absent.

Towards liberalised autocracy or beyond?

It has been plausibly suggested that monarchies may be the type of Middle Eastern regime best prepared—and most likely—to effect such reforms.[13] This argument suggests that a non-ideologically buttressed monarch has less to fear from reform than a president in a one-party republic tied to a particular ideological platform. As Lucas has noted, in monarchies such as the small GCC states, tolerance or mobilisation of social pluralism is 'dramatically different' from the nationalist mobilisation used by most republican regimes in the Arab world. Indeed, such monarchies have often allowed or even reinforced social pluralism all along, hence opening up does not necessarily mean fundamental discontinuity.[14] If anything, such monarchies may be particularly well-placed to use a measure of political liberalisation as a survival strategy: it may not only take the sting out of immediate pressures, but may in effect serve as a 'divide-and-rule' tactic, wherby the opposition or its various strands become 'submerged' in a more diverse number of social groups now given access to a limited form of political participation. The various groups and representatives may both acquire a stake in the system and continue separately to seek the ear and favour of the monarch, who remains the ultimate arbiter and source of authority.

[13] Key contributions to this argument have been made by Lisa Anderson, e.g. in 'Dynasts and nationalists: why Middle Eastern monarchies survive', in Joseph Kostiner (ed.), *Middle Eastern Monarchies* (Boulder: Lynne Rienner, 2000), pp. 53–69. See also the review articles by Gerd Nonneman, 'Rentiers and Autocrats, Monarchs and Democrats, State and Society', in *International Affairs*, Vol. 77 (2001), no. 1, pp. 141–162); and Russell Lucas, 'Monarchical Authoritarianism: Survival and Political Liberalization in a Middle Eastern Regime Type', in *International Journal of Middle Eastern Studies*, Vol. 36 (2004), pp. 103–119.

[14] Russell Lucas, 'Monarchical Authoritarianism.'

Thus reform and liberalisation do not equate to democratisation—nor do they necessarily lead to it. The constraints referred to above mirror factors that elsewhere, and especially across the Middle East, have been recognised as obstructing moves beyond the limits of 'liberalising' or 'modernising autocracy', or 'political decompression': i.e. moving beyond the stage where reform and liberalisation are in essence no more than a tool used by the regime to maintain ultimate control.[15] Three central and intimately interrelated factors are: evolving variants of rentierism (intertwined in the Saudi case with segmented clientelism and more generally with corporatist features); the limited and particular character of civil society with its own divisions, not least between an arguably illiberal majority and a liberal minority (even if both want a greater say and greater transparency); and a middle class lacking a united political purpose. It is especially in such an environment that regimes may use liberalisation to co-opt and/or divide actual and potential opposition forces most successfully, without intending to cede their position as the ultimate source of authority. Brumberg has argued that the longer such 'liberalised autocracy' is practised, the harder it may be to move to real democratisation; as he puts it, 'The very success of liberalized autocracy can become a trap for even the most well-intentioned leader.'[16]

Can Saudi Arabia—or other 'modernising autocracies'—escape this trap? Brumberg has classified the Kingdom as a 'full' or 'total' rather than a 'partial' autocracy, and therefore not yet even at the 'liberalising' stage.[17] The evidence of this book—not least in the chapter

[15] The term 'political decompression' was introduced by Hinnebusch for the case of Syrian instances of liberalisation but given wider relevance (Raymond Hinnebusch, 'calculated Decompression as a Substitute for Democratisation', in R. Brynen et al (eds.), *Political Liberalization & Democratization in the Arab World* , Vol. 2 (Boulder: Lynne Rienner,1998), pp. 223–240. Bernard Lewis refers to 'modernizing autocracies' ('A Historical Overview', in Larry Diamond et al. (eds.), *Islam and Democracy in the Middle East* (Baltimore: Johns Hopkins University Press, 2003), pp. 208–219); 'liberalized autocracy' is the term used by Daniel Brumberg in 'The Trap of Liberalized Autocracy' in Diamond et al., *Islam and Democracy*, pp. 35–47, and 'Liberalization versus Democracy: Understanding Arab Political Reform' (Washington: Carnegie Endowment, May 2003 [Working Papers, Middle East Series, no, 37]).

[16] Brumberg, 'Liberalization versus Democracy,' p. 12.

[17] Brumberg, 'The Trap of Liberalized Autocracy.'

by Glosemeyer—shows that, even if the system remains undoubtedly autocratic and includes repression among its tools, such a judgement must be challenged. Some of the features associated with 'partial autocracies' have been present to a certain extent in Saudi Arabia for some time, and certainly the reforms that have been tentatively introduced since the 1990s make it seem appropriate to place the country in that category—albeit still at the lower end of the spectrum. While it seems likely that Saudi Arabia will move further in the direction of liberalisation, it is, for the reasons indicated, unlikely that it will move beyond the confines of 'liberalised autocracy' for at least a generation.

Even so, there are both generic and specific reasons for thinking that the Saudi polity need not *necessarily* remain trapped there. The generic reasons are that, just as happened in Europe in transitions from absolutism, and in the more recent Latin American transitions from autocracy, limited moves made by ruling elites as a tactic of 'decompression' can, in combination with growing pressures from below, lead such trends to slip beyond the control of what these elites originally intended, especially when alliances develop between key social groups and elements within the regime.[18] In some sense this may already have begun to happen in Kuwait, and it may be in its initial stages in Bahrain. It is true that, just as in various European precedents over past centuries, there may be setbacks when the regime attempts to reverse the tide. This indeed has been the pattern rightly identified, and feared for the future, by Brumberg. But that may not be a sustainable strategy in the long run, if those earlier precedents are anything to go by. (Also, of course, they tell us once again that the dynamics producing real democratisation may only bear fruit in the much longer term.)

In the case of Saudi Arabia the fundamental *status quo* may ultimately not be sustainable against the changes and challenges that the

[18] See Adam Przeworski, *Democracy ad the Market: Political and Economic reforms in eastern Europe and Latin America* (Cambridge: Cambridge University Press, 1991); Gerd Nonneman, 'Patterns of Political Liberalization', in Nonneman (ed.), *Political and Economic Liberalization* (Boulder: Lynne Rienner, 1996), pp. 45–62; and N. Hamilton & E. Kim, 'Economic and political liberalization in South Korea and Mexico', *Third World Quarterly*, vol. 14 (1993), no. 1, pp. 109–136.

system will increasingly face. Social, economic and technological change will over the long term change the 'distribution of power resources.'[19] The growth of a more independent bourgeoisie will be only one element in this. Practices and institutions that are being gradually established may take on a life of their own: there has been some evidence of this with the judiciary in Egypt, the parliament in Kuwait, and indeed the cautious drive towards a greater role in decision-making from within the Majlis al-Shura in Saudi Arabia.[20] It is also conceivable that a key factor in other processes of democratisation—namely allies for further reform emerging within the ruling elite—becomes a reality in the kingdom. Saudi Arabia will not go the way of those Eastern European regimes that collapsed dramatically amid a fiscal and legitimacy crisis: material and legitimacy resources remain more abundant, so a sudden overall change of the system is highly unlikely. Hence the outlook for change must be divided in two stages.

Further reform towards liberalised autocracy is likely in the short-to-medium term. It is impossible to predict whether the Saudi polity will remain locked in that stage for the foreseeable future, with all the inevitable dysfunctionality this would bring in the longer term. Quite possibly the continued segmentation and clientelism that characterise the country's political economy, together with the limitations of Saudi civil society, differentiate the Saudi case from a considerable number of comparable cases where democratisation did take hold. Additionally, some of the factors that have been suggested as making the smaller Gulf states candidates for eventual democratisation of sorts (including their very smallness, and the absence of a formal legitimising ideology) do not apply to Saudi Arabia. Even so, the possibility that this polity, much more complex in its dynamics than usually recognised, and subject to continuing change in its domestic and external environments, might eventually escape the 'trap' of liberalised autocracy also cannot be dismissed. *If* that happens, it will come as the result of a very gradual process, driven and signalled as much by

[19] T. Vanhanen & R. Kimber, 'Predicting and Explaining Democratization in Eastern Europe', in G. Pridham (T. Vanhanen (eds.), *Democratization in Eastern Europe* (London: Routledge, 1994), pp. 63–96.

[20] See also Baaklini et al, *Legislative Politics in the Arab World.*

the incremental expansion of the grip of representative institutions on day-to-day and technical decision-making, and of the habit-forming effect of even limited exercises in political participation and discussion, as by grand political departures.[21]

[21] One particularly interesting development has been the stance of the Shura Council on matters of taxation: in the words of one acute Saudi observer, the pattern of the Council's decisions shows it 'has taken a decision in principle not to agree to any imposition of taxes or higher fees unless they get a say over expenditure' (personal communication, March 2005): about as literal a reflection of the old 'no taxation without representation' maxim as it is possible to get.

A
Ali
Ango

INDEX